Gender and Journalism

Gender and Journalism

An Intersectional Approach

MARY ANGELA BOCK

ROWMAN & LITTLEFIELD
Lanham • Boulder • New York • London

Published by Rowman & Littlefield
An imprint of The Rowman & Littlefield Publishing Group, Inc.
4501 Forbes Boulevard, Suite 200, Lanham, Maryland 20706
www.rowman.com

86-90 Paul Street, London EC2A 4NE

British Library Cataloguing in Publication Information Available

Library of Congress Cataloging-in-Publication Data

Names: Bock, Mary Angela, author.
Title: Gender and journalism : an intersectional approach / Mary Angela Bock.
Description: Lanham : Rowman & Littlefield, 2023. | Includes bibliographical references and index.
Identifiers: LCCN 2023020828 (print) | LCCN 2023020829 (ebook) | ISBN 9781538159453 (cloth) | ISBN 9781538159460 (paperback) | ISBN 9781538159477 (ebook)
Subjects: LCSH: Journalism—Objectivity—United States. | Sex role. | Feminist theory.
Classification: LCC PN4888.O25 B63 2023 (print) | LCC PN4888.O25 (ebook) | DDC 302.230973—dc23/eng/20230802
LC record available at https://lccn.loc.gov/2023020828
LC ebook record available at https://lccn.loc.gov/2023020829

In memory of
Klaus Krippendorff
and
Rosalie Mary Bock

Contents

Detailed Contents

Preface

This textbook is designed to help you understand how one dimension of our humanity—gender—has affected people in journalism, the stories they tell, and what it means for the news audience. Much of this book centers on the United States, but it also presents accounts from the rest of the world and considers the political, economic, and cultural aspects of gender and journalism broadly. This textbook takes an intersectional approach and covers the experiences of people of color across the full gender spectrum, though the concerns of women are central.

This book is based on a course I've taught since 2013. To be honest, I was surprised to receive this course assignment, as I had never conducted gender-related research. I'm a visual scholar, and while I studied representation generally, I had not delved very deeply into feminist theory. Once I started, however, I came to enjoy the subject matter and worked to enhance its materials every semester, adding units on masculinity, queer studies, and intersectionality. More importantly, I came to love watching my students learn the role of gender in their own lives and careers. Educators know the joy that comes when students have an "aha!" moment, and this course is filled with them. Second-wave feminists sometimes called these incidents "lightbulb" moments, and they are the reason this course so often follows students way past graduation.

The book covers three interrelated subjects: the gendered experiences of individuals in journalism, gender's relationship with society, and the way news coverage frames gender in society. In presenting this material, I make three arguments:

1. Change occurs from the work of individuals.
2. Language shapes social systems.
3. The current structures of hierarchy and oppression involve multiple dimensions of human experience.

I endeavor to humanize members of media institutions and highlight the real lives of individuals who have worked as writers, journalists, activists, and media producers. The media are often written about as a giant, single entity, but they are actually a group of many different types of organizations staffed by individuals, every one of whom lives in a world where gender is a primary marker of identity and social standing and interacts with other people in that system. In this way, this textbook also serves as a media literacy course, demonstrating that even though media are often conceptualized as an autonomous unified entity—something "out there" we can criticize—the media really are us. Understanding the way gender affects media offers insight to the way it affects everyday life.

Unlike most diversity and media textbooks, this one prioritizes gender while acknowledging and describing its intersectional relationships with other dimensions of our humanity. It also places heavy emphasis on American journalism while contextualizing news media amid the larger media landscape. The course is designed to provide students with a grounding in history and a theoretical tool kit to enrich their futures, whether they take on a media career or simply wish to be more thoughtful media consumers. The book focuses on the stories of many individuals, not to encourage name memorization, but to personalize the accounts of journalism's treatment of those within its profession and the gendered patterns of news coverage. Many people of color, nonbinary individuals, and representatives of historically marginalized groups have advanced the cause of equality within their newsrooms and through their storytelling.

This is why the book takes an intersectional approach. It is impossible to detach a person's gender identity from their race, ethnicity, and class, as these and other markers make a difference in the way we navigate the world and are treated by it. I avoid writing about the gender rights movement in monolithic ways. Where appropriate, I highlight the ways that women of color have been marginalized by news, within both journalism and society at large. I also call attention to the way homophobia and transphobia have affected journalists and the communities they cover.

The book is designed as a semester-long course. Each chapter includes a preview to guide your reading, a list of key words, some suggestions for self-reflection, short biographies of key individuals, and excerpts from original key works. You'll find a glossary at the end of the book of important vocabulary.

Throughout the book, I rely primarily on the *Associated Press Stylebook* for guidance regarding the terms of diversity.[1] One of the principles for writing about diverse groups is to always be as specific as possible for the sake of respect and accuracy, so I minimize the use of *people of color*, and in accordance with the AP's policy, I avoid acronyms like *POC* and *BIPOC*. I capitalize *Black* because that community has historically been marginalized, but I lowercase *white* to stay clear of white supremacist culture and its nomenclature. Labels for Spanish-speaking communities are not uniform, as the term *Latinx* is not universally accepted and does not apply to all Spanish-speaking people.[2] *Hispanic* is similarly imperfect, for it addresses language and culture but not race. And while the term is no longer in favor, the civil rights movement for Spanish-speaking people in the United States in the 1960s and '70s called itself the Chicano movement. Where appropriate, I also rely on the *Elements of Indigenous Style* when writing about Native Americans and Indigenous people.[3]

The book uses the word *women* to describe anyone who identifies as a woman and *man* to describe anyone who identifies as such. Certain sections covering the trans community and biological functions, such as breast-/chest-feeding and menstruation, use more precise terminology as appropriate. In accordance with AP style, I use *LGBTQ+* to describe people who do not identify as heterosexual or cisgender, an acronym intended to honor a wide range of diversity. Also, per GLAAD and the AP, I occasionally use the word *queer* where respectfully appropriate. Readers will find nearly all these terms in the pages that follow, as I endeavor to use the most accurate and respectful language according to context. The language of identity has always been malleable but is currently evolving very quickly, so there's always a possibility that by the time you read this, some terminology may have already shifted.

My thanks and gratitude go to the women who first hired me as a teenage reporter in Douglas County, Colorado, and to the men and women who mentored me as a young journalist and in my second career as an academic. I'm grateful, always, to my husband and daughters, who let me complain about the writing process during its tedious times. Thanks go to the undergraduate students who helped me hunt for the images in this book, Michael Hernandez and Aruna Muthupillai. I also am grateful to the anonymous reviewers, who made excellent suggestions for improving this book, and to Natalie Mandziuk for her support and guidance throughout the project. She brought this book to life. My heartfelt thanks to my dear friend Amy Brenholts, the exceptional TV videographer who literally gave me the space to write this book. This book also gives me a chance to honor to my mother, Rosalie Mary Bock, who gave me a daily, gentle push every day while I wrote it, but passed away before it was printed. Thank you, Mom.

This text is intended to honor every woman who has been told to smile more, every LGBTQ+ reporter who had to hide their identity to stay on TV, every Black woman who was told she could not wear her hair the way she wished, and every photographer who's been groped on assignment. This book is also for, but not in honor of, the radio announcer who told me I could have a good career in the business if I stopped acting like such an uppity woman. It's for the deputy who leered gleefully at the opportunity to pat me down at a courthouse security checkpoint. It's for the manager who suggested that I dye my hair blond, the other manager who complained about the size of a coworker's derriere, and yet another manager who hit me in the head with a law book for daring to talk back to him. My list of indignities is mild compared to what others have endured in the form of discrimination, harassment, tokenism, assault, and even rape.

I am proud to call myself a journalist, and I have dedicated my life to serving the public with truthful and thoughtful coverage, and so my heart hurts and has hurt for a long time to know how cruel the profession can be and has been to the marginalized people it covers and considers colleagues. It is my sincere hope that students who work with this book will be inspired to learn more and answer journalism's call to defend the democratic voice of all humanity.

We cannot change what we do not acknowledge.

CHAPTER 1

Gender, Society, and Media

This chapter presents concepts and vocabulary that will be useful throughout the rest of the book. You will be able to apply these concepts to your own media examples and your future careers.

Key Concepts: Stereotypes, Gender as Social Construction, Framing, Intersectionality

A national journalist is fired after she tweeted in protest of a colleague's sexist joke.[1]

A *New York Times* reporter who produced an in-depth account of white supremacy's long-standing influence on American politics is denied a tenure-track job at the prominent journalism school she once attended.[2]

Teachers in Florida hide away photos of their spouses for fear of being fired when the state's "Don't Say Gay" went into effect.[3]

Gender is at the heart of each of these news stories and likely plays a role in many of the headlines you read today. Gender affects our lives, from our most intimate moments to our most public ones, yet it is only one dimension of our humanity. Race, ethnicity, age, ability, and other markers shape our identities and, in turn, the way we live, what we do, whom we love, and even how we are written about in news.

How do we come to learn our identity? It starts early, with our family. As we grow up, our parents, teachers, and friends give us a sense of who we are within a community, and for many of us, our gender identity is one of the earliest lessons. In Western culture, historically, it is treated as an immutable trait, and children are raised to dress, talk, and speak according to gendered expectations.

Today, when asked to introduce ourselves, we usually start with our name and a fact or two that is relevant to the situation: perhaps our level in school, where we live, or (if we're college students) what our major is. These days, we might also add our pronouns: *she/her, he/his,* or *they/them.* This is a historic shift in the way human beings interact in everyday life, as a person's gender has so long been assumed based on expectations regarding our physicality, clothing, and even our voice. Today, however, our gender identity is not always assumed, and during these introductions, we might be expected or invited to declare it. How did this enormous transformation in etiquette come about? Why are such small words—pronouns—so significant in our daily interactions with others? How do changes like this evolve?

This book is designed to give you the tools to answer these questions and others like them. Where do we get our ideas about what gender is and how it operates? Most of us learned quite a bit about gender roles very early in our lives, when the adults around us told us to behave like a "good girl" or "good boy." Sometimes the messages were direct: "Girls don't play with trucks!" "Boys don't cry!" Sometimes the messages were more subtle, as adults modeled gendered behavior in front us. We also learned from mediated messages: cartoons, commercials, movies, TV shows, books, magazines, greeting cards, video games, and websites. In the news, messages about gender are presented with the authority of objective reality. Considering that today we spend most of our waking hours with media, it is hard to understate its influence, including our ideas about gender. From words and images in media, we learn how to live in a social system in which gender is one of the most important markers of our humanity. What's more, those words and images can make a difference in the way we navigate that system.

This chapter covers a set of concepts about gender that will serve as a foundation for thinking about media, gender, and society. Our identities are multifaceted, with such dimensions as race, gender, sexual orientation, abilities, and ethnicity defining our place in the world. These dimensions overlap in ways that benefit some people and intensify challenges for others, a concept known as **intersectionality**. The way we think about ourselves and other people is rooted in language: the very words we use to describe and understand society. We become part of groups and learn other groups largely through representations and not direct interaction, so it makes sense to start with a concept that was coined around the same time that media became "mass" media in the early twentieth century: **stereotypes**.

Stereotypes

The term *stereotype* was popularized by journalist and media critic Walter Lippmann in his 1922 book *Public Opinion*. Lippmann was among the first public intellectuals to think deeply about the relationship between media and the mass audience. He is well known for using the phrase *pictures in our heads* to describe the way media portrayals supplant our firsthand experiences with the world. We see far more in media than we're able to observe directly, which, when it comes to human beings, enables stereotypes to develop. After all, we are less likely to stereotype our friends and relatives. If you were to read Lippmann's book today, its language might strike you as old-fashioned, archaic, and even (ironically) stereotypical according to today's standards. For example, he centers the perspective of white men—such as the "Harvard man" and "Yale man"—which was normal for the time. Nevertheless, the main points of his essay, now more than a century old, remain relevant.

One of Lippmann's more important observations is the way stereotypes regulate our thinking before we meet someone. In his words, "For the most part, we do not first see

Profile: Walter Lippmann, Journalist (1889–1974)

Walter Lippman.
Courtesy of Library of Congress, Prints and Photographs Division,
photograph by Harris and Ewing, LC-H25- 247207-T

Walter Lippmann was a journalist, writer, and political pundit in the early twentieth century. His book *Public Opinion*, published in 1922, has been held up as the founding book of not only modern journalism but also American media studies. A chapter from that book in which Lippmann popularizes the term *stereotypes* remains part of the foundational literature for researchers interested in the subject.

Lippmann started as a journalist while a student at Harvard. He was one of the original editors of the *New Republic* and wrote a syndicated column, *Today and Tomorrow*, for nearly twenty years. He was an informal advisor to several presidents, won the Pulitzer Prize twice for reporting on international affairs, and was awarded the Presidential Medal of Freedom in 1964. Some consider Lippmann's work to be elitist, as Lippmann was very concerned with the human tendency to "define first and then see." His call for the establishment of a system by which accurate information could be delivered to a democratic audience, however, seems prescient in the digital era's problematic mix of conventional, propagandistic, and overtly misleading news.

Source: Ronald Steel, *Walter Lippmann and the American Century* 1st Vintage Books ed. (Vintage Books, 1981).

and then define. We define first and then see."[4] He wrote that stereotype stamps itself on the evidence in the very act of securing the evidence. We'll notice people who match our stereotypical expectation but not notice those who do not (something known as **confirmation bias**).[5] We feel like we know something even before we've had a chance to check. This is especially oppressive for women and people of color because parts of their identities are embodied and visible, and it's easy to size up people simply on sight.

One helpful way to think about stereotypes is that they are a form of **heuristic** about people. A heuristic is a shortcut in our thinking, or a rule of thumb, that lets us quickly make decisions. Think about walking around a typical college campus. It's usually possible to determine who the students are—they are younger, probably carrying backpacks, and (these days) wearing comfortable clothing that works in the classroom or in the gym. Now imagine encountering someone who looks like me on campus: past middle age; wearing a dress, cardigan, and sensibly heeled shoes; and carrying a leather tote. My appearance screams "professor." These are heuristics: markers that help us navigate our social surroundings. We need these shortcuts to navigate the world. When we walk into a fast-food restaurant, we know who will take our order. At a nicer restaurant, the person carrying menus will usually show us to a table. Heuristics help us to identify people and size up situations. Imagine having to think through all possibilities for every decision you make during the day. You wouldn't make it past breakfast without using mental shortcuts.

Stereotypes, though, are more than shortcuts because they also represent judgments about other people. Stereotypes can trick us into thinking we know someone before we take time to get to know them. They usually imply a hierarchy and box people in without allowing them to disprove our negative expectations. If you identified me as a professor, then you're responding to a heuristic based on the visual cues. Based on that assessment, if you also decide that, as a professor, I must be boring, then that's a judgment, a stereotype that would interfere with your ability to get to know me. If I decided that every student I see around campus is shallow, lazy, and addicted to TikTok, then that would also be a stereotype.

Stereotypes are often connected to and necessary for systems of oppression.[6] It is easier to think that certain people belong in lower-wage jobs if we believe that's the best they can do. That is, if we believe that people with lower-wage jobs are not very smart, then we don't feel badly about a system that keeps them lower on the economic ladder. Gender stereotypes in our society are particularly problematic for a number of reasons, as they not only justify a hierarchal system but also are often treated as natural or determined by nature or biology.[7] The primary gender stereotypes label men as **agentic**, the sociological term for competent and independent, people who have the ability and drive to get things done. Women are stereotyped as warm and communal, the ones who support those getting things done. Categorizing people as agentic or communal was probably important in an evolutionary sense because survival depends on our ability to sense whether someone might hurt or help us. These stereotypes are complementary, too, as one stereotypical group builds the community while the other takes care of it.[8] Over time, the gendered dimensions of these stereotypes have come to feel natural, as women have been assigned childcare and homemaking roles, whereas men have been expected to go to war, build cities, and mow the lawn.

Why might some people object to this division of labor? After all, it does *seem* natural. Women do give birth, after all, so nurturing seems like an automatic extension of what they were built to do. Men usually have more upper-body strength, so why should they not be the builders and warriors? The problem for many individuals is that these roles do *not* feel natural or fair, and the historical record doesn't necessarily support the notion that these roles are biologically driven. Women have been Vikings, pirates, and warriors. Men have the capacity to be nurturing. In fact, men suffer psychological damage when they are denied warmth and connection because of the mistaken belief that these traits are beneath them. Claiming that these complementary stereotypes are natural ignores research that suggests that the assignment of roles came first and the stereotyped expectations grew from there.[9] Thinking of these stereotypes as benign and natural further hides the way that male traits are valued politically and economically while female traits are not. Scholars have traced patriarchal beliefs back thousands of years, noting the way childbirth affected tribal life and the way agricultural practices made women's ability to produce children valued above all else.[10] Women could be seen and treated as property, for they helped to populate communities, and, as property, they could be objectified for their sexual appearance. As civilizations grew, so did systems of hierarchy and control over women, and the ideologies behind such a system became ingrained and unquestioned. Sexist stereotypes simply feel natural.

So when media, including or especially news media, perpetuate gendered stereotypes in word and image, it is often hardly noticeable. Both men and women have been subjected to stereotypical representations in advertising, news stories, movies, and other media. Men have been stereotyped as unemotional, tough at work, and inept at home. News coverage of women running for office has highlighted their appearance or skills as mothers.[11] When women pushed for better roles in news organizations, they were stereotyped as overemotional and immature.[12] Feminists have pressured media to change, and much has changed, but men and women are still portrayed in ways that reflect the agentic/communal expectations.

When anyone, male or female, acts in ways that are contrary to stereotypical expectations, they are often socially punished. The mostly male mainstream press in the 1970s portrayed feminists as militant, angry man haters, and this stereotype stuck.[13] True, many women were angry, and many men felt threatened by this, but how is a person, once labeled as angry and militant, supposed to fight back? Any pushback only feeds that militant stereotype. Female politicians walk a fine line to appear strong but still feminine. Villainous women in entertainment, like children's animated movies, are often drawn in unattractive ways that defy feminine expectations. In movies and TV shows, female characters are often unhappy if they are single, no matter what other successes they have in life. The expectation that women should be nurturing and kind even extends to things like college course ratings. Research has found that students who believe their online (and unseen) professor is a woman will give her lower course ratings than those who believe their professor is male, even for the exact same online course, because women are not supposed to be high-achieving experts.[14]

Simply reminding a person about stereotypes can also increase their tendency to endorse a system of inequality, even if it's not in their best interest.[15] Merely being reminded of the (highly contested) stereotype that women are less adept mathematically has been shown to cause some young women to do more poorly on math tests.[16] Even when people believe themselves to be fair-minded, they resort to stereotypes in timed tests.[17] Psychologists have also found, however, that when motivated, people can learn to push back against stereotypes over time.[18] So while stereotypes are difficult to avoid, it is possible to learn new ways of thinking about other people. Lippmann suggests, "What matters is the character of the stereotypes and the gullibility with which we employ them." He asserts that when we remain open to our own intellectual fallibility, we "tend to know that they are only stereotypes, to hold them lightly, to modify them gladly. We tend, also, to realize more and more clearly when our ideas started, where they started, how they came to us, and why we accepted them."[19]

Gender and Sex

The belief that stereotypes are natural is one reason the pressure to conform to their expectations is so intense, but recent research suggests that they are not natural, and much of what makes us male or female is a matter of learned behavior. Scholars differentiate between sex and gender, emphasizing that gender is something we *do*.[20] Sex describes our biological characteristics, such as the existence of a penis or vulva. Gender describes the way we dress, walk, even speak. This was a revolutionary idea in the mid-1900s, though it is well accepted today. Philosopher Simone de Beauvoir introduces this idea in *The Second Sex* (1949), where she argues, "One is not born, but rather becomes, a woman."[21] More recently RuPaul, who hosts the popular show *RuPaul's Drag Race*, put a modern spin on this idea: "We're all born naked. The rest is just drag."[22]

RuPaul's point speaks to so much of what twentieth-century feminists and gender activists have tried to explain for years: the difference between our bodies and our identities. Sociologist Judith Lorber explored the mechanics of this process. She was one of the foundational theorists of what is called the "social construction of gender," noting that once we are assigned a gender at birth, we are dressed and treated accordingly, and

---

Excerpt: *The Second Sex*

One is not born, but rather becomes, a woman. No biological, psychological, or economic fate determines the figure that the human female presents in society; it is civilization as a whole that produces this creature, intermediate between male and eunuch, which is described as feminine. Only the intervention of someone else can establish an individual as an Other. In so far as he exists in and for himself, the child would hardly be able to think of himself as sexually differentiated. In girls as in boys the body is first of all the radiation of a subjectivity; the instrument that makes possible the comprehension of the world: it is through the eyes, the hands, that children apprehend the universe and not through the sexual parts.

Source: Simone de Beauvoir, *The Second Sex*, trans. H. M. Parshley, 1st American ed. (Vintage Books, 1974).

we learn how to fulfill our role, an idea extended later by philosopher Judith Butler. We learn how to be boys and girls, men and women. Our parents tell us how we are supposed to behave. Our grandparents buy us our baby clothes. We learn from the news, our social media feeds, and entertainment how men and women are expected to act. This is being challenged today, as more individuals reject gendered expectations and live as nonbinary, androgynous, or trans, but the gender binary and its gendered expectation remain powerful social forces.

Consequently, as Lorber puts it, for individuals, gender means sameness, while for society, gender means difference. That is, each person tends to follow the rules and fulfill our roles, often without thinking. We know that children are socialized extremely early to gendered roles. Babies are treated differently when they are known (or thought) to be male or female. Experiments using swaddled babies whose gender is invisible find that adults interact with the baby differently and even offer different toys to match the stereotypes attached to the label given to the baby. Even the congratulations cards sent to new parents are different in content and form (not just blue and pink) according to gender. Men learn that to be manly, they'd better not be emotional. Women learn it's OK to be emotional, but they'd better not be bossy. If we fail to do gender appropriately, we as individuals, not the institutional arrangements, may be called to account.

This leads to the second part of Lorber's observation: For society, gender means difference. There is and must be a clear difference between male and female. If men are strong, then women must be tender; if men are competent, then women must be dependent. "Night to His Day" is the poetic title Lorber uses for her chapter on the subject, and it's significant for the way language and art have so long represented gender as a natural binary, like the sun and moon, water and earth, order and chaos. Some cultures, in Thailand, India, and some Native American tribes, recognize multiple or third genders, but Western societies have had two and only two socially and legally recognized gender statuses. This is changing, as trans people continue to fight for rights and recognition, and some governments today do recognize identities beyond male and female. Binaries sort things or ideas into two categories, yes or no, this or that; and for many people, gender remains an either/or concept: One is either male or female, no in between. (Race has also been subject to binary regulation. The "one-drop" rule held that even if a person had only one distant Black relative, then they also would be classified as Black.)

Are there limits to the social construction of gender? The question of whether masculine and feminine traits can be ascribed to biology is unsettled. Books like *Men Are from Mars, Women Are from Venus* are popular because they speak to experiences that feel natural and real. Yet many scientific studies from the past that ascribed differences in things like brain size, vocational aptitude, or sexual inclination have been found to be flawed. Scientists living and working in a time when gender differences were accepted as natural, including Charles Darwin, were not accustomed to questioning stereotypes about gender or race. Consider also that people at the top of the hierarchy are motivated to defend their place in the world; it's more comforting to think that being on top is the natural order of things, something they rightfully deserve. While it is true that only a person with a uterus can give birth, the boundaries of what is biological and what is constructed are hotly contested today, and the issue is not likely to be settled soon.

Why might it be so important to use binary language for gender and to know who the men and women are? What purpose does binarism serve? Lorber and other gender theorists point out that it's been historically important to know a person's gender so we know what role they should take on. All societies tend to rely, at least to some extent, on assumed membership in groups to determine who is going to fill certain roles in society, and this division of labor might be based on class, caste, race, ethnicity, or gender. **Binary thinking** is essential to hierarchal systems, as a person must be in or out or they must win or lose. There is no in between because there must be a winner. As Lorber argues, gender not only determines how a person is expected to act but also where they are placed on the social hierarchy. Traditionally, men have taken leadership roles, while women have been expected to tend the home. The binary allows for people to be sorted out without having to consider their interests and needs as individuals.

The notion that gendered stereotypes are complementary and in balance collapses in the face of the reality of the historic hierarchy, in which men are able to participate fully in social decisions but women are not, a system known as patriarchy. The word *patriarchy* means *rule of law by the father*, but it has come to stand for a system built on the belief that men can and should hold power over women. Patriarchy is an ideology: that is, a set of largely unspoken and assumed values about society. It might be thought of as the world's oldest oppression. Patriarchal beliefs sustain a system that puts men in control of political, economic, and social realms. Major world religions, including Christianity and Islam, adhere to patriarchal beliefs. The tradition of the father being the head of the household, the belief that men are natural leaders, even the ritual of expecting the man to pay for dinner on a date—these unspoken rules grow from patriarchal assumptions. Patriarchy supports the expectation that men hold better jobs, make more money, take charge, and even manage the very system that keeps them on top. In this system, gay men are another subordinate group because they have been associated with femininity, as are transgender people, who disrupt the either/or binary. Journalism has upheld many of these suppositions over time, covering stories in ways that assume women want to be homemakers or treating LGBTQ+ people as abnormal.

Framing

Binary thinking is expressed in language, an integral part of the way gender has been constructed in society. How we talk about something shapes the way we think about things, and language itself is a human creation that evolves according to our needs. You've probably heard that Inuit people have a "hundred words" for snow, and while that example is overused and not perfectly accurate, it's true that people who live in the Arctic have and need more descriptors for something that affects their lives every day. The **Sapir-Whorf hypothesis**, also called the principle of linguistic relativity, suggests that language evolves according to social needs and also shapes our thoughts, that there's an interaction between what we think, what we say, and how we use language.[23] Consider, for example, research on the way people whose languages have gendered nouns describe a bridge. In German, *bridge* is feminine, and in Spanish, *bridge* is masculine; research has found that German speakers are more likely to use words like *elegant* or *pretty* to describe a bridge, while Spanish speakers choose adjectives associated with masculinity, such as *strong* or *sturdy*.[24]

A classic experiment with framing described possible responses to a pandemic to test the importance of language. In this famous experiment, some subjects were told that to imagine that the United States is preparing for the outbreak of an unusual disease that is expected to kill six hundred people. Half of the experiment's subjects are asked to choose between plan A, in which two hundred people will be saved, or plan B, in which there is a one-third probability that six hundred people will be saved and a two-thirds probability that no people will be saved. The other subjects in the experiment are faced with the same scenario, but with their plan A, four hundred people will die, and under their plan B, a one-third probability that nobody will die and a two-thirds probability that six hundred people will die. Note that the math is the same, but the words are different. The first condition uses the word *saved* to describe the responses, and the second condition uses the word *dies*. In the original experiment (and in subsequent iterations), people presented with the *saved* language are more likely to choose plan A, and people with the *dies* language choose plan B.[25]

The words we have at our disposal, the words we make, and the words we use, therefore, are incredibly important to the way we think about social phenomena. It follows, then, that the words used in media, particularly news media, which purport to present reality, also affect our thinking. Journalism scholars use the word ***framing*** to describe how news presents that reality. Journalists frame events when they choose which stories to cover; which facts to highlight; which photographs to make; and, of course, which words to use in their stories.[26] Framing is a central theoretical concept in media studies, one that has multiple facets. Even though journalists often have objectivity as a goal, the choices they make in the course of covering any story mean that some parts will be in the story, and others will be left out, hence, the metaphor of the picture or window frame. The choices a reporter or writer makes in framing force them to make judgments, even when they strive for objectivity. The most prominent definition of *framing* describes it as the process by which certain facts or ideas are shown and others are excluded *"in such a way as to promote a particular problem's definition, causal interpretation, moral evaluation and/or treatment recommendation for the item described. Typically frames diagnose, evaluate and prescribe."*[27] A news frame is not so much a matter of partisanship, pro or con, or positive or negative, but how a story's overall presentation points toward a particular ideology. For instance, a news researcher who observed the way journalists practiced their craft at multiple national news outlets in the 1970s identified shared values that frame the news, such as nostalgia for small towns, a belief in responsible capitalism, and the value of individualism.[28] (Chapter 6 discusses how these values overlap in many ways with masculine ideals.)

Framing often results from the way journalists collect facts and assemble information into stories. The objectivity norm compels reporters to give both sides to an issue while withholding their observations. This norm is so ingrained that some critics argue "both-sidesism" has undermined democracy when reporters give equal time to people who lie. News events are usually those that occur *outside* the norm, so when journalists frame stories through a lens of moderatism, people pushing for change (such as feminists and gay rights activists) are often framed as problematic and disruptive, a phenomenon researchers call the **protest paradigm**.[29] Even the methods journalists use to assemble facts into stories have come under fire from some media critics. Narratives, after all, rely on interesting characters and require some kind of conflict, which can interfere with providing helpful (and occasionally boring) information citizens need to participate in a democracy.[30] Recent research has also found that by emphasizing their role as storytellers, journalists may be turning off some members of the audience who equate *stories* with *falsehoods*.[31]

Framing is important for understanding journalism and gender because of the way media generally and news specifically have presented human rights activism. If protests are covered for their disruption, then their underlying purpose is forgotten. When gay rights activists demand respect for their humanity, the "moderation" frame implies there is another side. When women demanded rights in the workplace, their concerns were presented alongside women who preferred to stay home in the interest of strategic objectivity. The notion that equal pay was simply the right thing to do was framed as a side, not a moral principle.

Frames change over time, and this can be seen in the way journalists use words. Consider, for instance, the difference between *illegal immigrant* and *person who lives in the country without legal permission*. The Associated Press changed its stylebook in 2013 to discourage use of the former, as the phrase objectifies the person, while the latter, which is admittedly more wordy, separates the human from the action.[32] Simply changing the word choice makes a difference in the way individuals are represented. People-first language, such as *people with autism* instead of *autistic people*, can shift focus away from a challenge and onto the human being. To that end, many writers have started to use the phrase *enslaved people* instead of *slaves*. The word switch calls attention to the victims' humanity and reminds us that this was a condition imposed on them. Slavery is not a natural state.

Intersectionality

So far, this chapter has identified how stereotypes are naturalized and talked about according to such categories as race, ethnicity, gender, or ability, even though every human is a combination of such characteristics and these dimensions cannot be considered in discrete ways. Oppressions can overlap.[33] Kimberlé Crenshaw named this idea *intersectionality*. Crenshaw is a legal scholar, philosopher, and social activist who noticed that men's concerns were paramount in racial discrimination and white women's concerns were highlighted in sexism cases, further marginalizing Black women, who suffered from compounded discrimination.[34] She based her argument on legal cases in which Black women sued their employers for discrimination but lost, in some cases, because the employers did hire women (but just white women) or did hire Black people (but just Black men). Rather than treat Black women as doubly penalized, the

Profile: Kimberlé W. Crenshaw, Legal Philosopher (1959–)

Kimberlé Crenshaw.
Courtesy of the African American Policy Forum

Kimberlé W. Crenshaw is a leading civil rights advocate, lawyer, philosopher, and feminist theorist. She is the executive director of the African American Policy Forum and currently holds law professorships at Columbia University in New York and the University of California, Los Angeles. During her time as a student at Harvard, she was one of the founding theorists of critical race theory. She was born and raised in Ohio by parents who were both teachers and civil rights advocates who worked to desegregate the local swimming pool. Crenshaw was part of the legal team that represented Anita Hill in 1991 in her testimony during the Clarence Thomas Supreme Court confirmation hearings. In 1993, Crenshaw published a law review article titled "Mapping the Margins," which lays out the essentials of intersectionality.

Sources: Columbia Law School, "Kimberle W. Crenshaw," accessed July 18, 2021, https://www.law.columbia.edu/faculty/kimberle-w-crenshaw; Kimberlé Crenshaw, "Why Intersectionality Can't Wait," *Washington Post*, September 24, 2015, https://www.washingtonpost.com/news/in-theory/wp/2015/09/24/why-intersectionality-cant-wait/; Melissa Harris-Perry, "Where Are All the Black Feminists in Confirmation?" *Elle*, April 18, 2016, https://www.elle.com/culture/career-politics/news/a35699/hbo-confirmation-black-feminists/; Aamna Mohdin, "Kimberlé Crenshaw: The Woman Who Revolutionised Feminism—and Landed at the Heart of the Culture Wars," *Guardian*, November 12, 2020, http://www.theguardian.com/society/2020/nov/12/kimberle-crenshaw-the-woman-who-revolutionised-feminism-and-landed-at-the-heart-of-the-culture-wars.

courts in these cases treated race and gender as though they were separate theoretical concepts. In Crenshaw's words, "[T]he intersectional experience is greater than the sum of racism and sexism."[35]

Intersectionality helps to explain why media have tended to cover missing persons cases involving young, blond, white women but not those of Black, Brown, or Indigenous women, what the late broadcaster Gwen Ifill dubbed "missing white woman syndrome."[36] The 2021 coverage of Gabby Petito, for instance, overshadowed hundreds of missing persons cases that occurred in the weeks between her tragic disappearance and the discovery of her body. The attractive "damsel in distress" narrative captures the imagination of journalistic decision makers in part because women of color are stereotyped as tough and sexually mature, not innocent victims. Similarly, when the rapper R. Kelly was convicted of multiple counts of sex trafficking in New York in 2021 after evading legal sanctions for years, Crenshaw wrote an analysis for the *New York Times* "Opinion" section.[37] In her words, "Mr. Kelly's victims were hiding in plain sight throughout his long and destructive tour of abuse for the simple reason that people in the overlapping worlds of entertainment, law and media have been trained to see Black girls and women as dispensable."[38]

Intersectionality is a helpful concept for analyzing the way news represents the interests of people who are not white, cisgender, able-bodied, straight, and male. It points to schisms within such social equity movements as feminism, which has often advanced the interests of white, middle-class women to the detriment of Black women.[39] Researchers who study other forms of marginalization, such as disability or transness, have adopted intersectionality as a lens for examining how various demographic categories position individuals in society and, importantly, how power flows through these relationships.[40] Intersectionality also serves as a reminder to journalists and media creators to take care when discussing the interests of people in terms of demographic groups. Whose concerns are centered in a story or treated as legitimate and normal? Who is treated as an aberration, a troublemaker, or a special interest group? Every member of the news audience is an individual, but at the same time, every individual lives within multiple layers of identity. Even though this book focuses on gender, every chapter covers intersectional concerns. Both gender and race determined who could run a colonial printing press, for example, and it shaped priorities for managers who integrated newsrooms in the 1900s. Race, sexual orientation, transness, class, and ethnicity: These dimensions intersect in everyone, whether they write the news, read the news, or are covered in the news, as the pages ahead show.

Summary

This chapter introduces some key terms used throughout this book: *stereotyping*, *gendered performance*, and *intersectionality*. These concepts also play a role in today's conversations in the news about gender. You may have noticed also that individual people proposed and advanced these concepts; they did not fall from the sky. Thinking, caring people like Walter Lippmann, Judith Lorber, and Kimberlé Crenshaw attached words to the problems they saw. Words like *stereotyping* and *intersectionality* help advance conversations about social phenomena. Understanding how framing works and how representations of reality are constructions determined by which facts, images, or ideas are included makes it possible to imagine *other* frames. Language has a tremendous influence on the way we think about the world around us, and naming things is part of the way new ideas come to popular attention. Change only happens when a problem is identified; and for that, we need a shared vocabulary. This is especially important for understanding the role of news, entertainment, and social media in how we consider gender and the way it intersects with other markers of our identities. Media popularize concepts and bring these terms to our attention, and the way journalists use language makes a difference in how we understand reality. Finally, it's impossible to study only one dimension of human identity if we are to understand the way society works. Gender is but one marker of identity, but individuals are also always marked by such characteristics as race, sexual orientation, age, and ability. Advertising media may sort people out for demographic target marketing, but journalists are tasked with serving everyone for the larger, democratic good. Learning more about the lives of everyone in the audience and the challenges they face is essential to covering the news fully, completely, and fairly.

- **Reflection:** Think about the stereotypes assigned to people in your demographic. How does the stereotype match your reality? Who is served by negative stereotypes of people like you?
- **Reflection:** Think back to when you were very young. How did you learn to "do" gender? What kinds of messages did you receive about gender as a child? From your parents? Other family members? Media?
- **Reflection:** Some social critics have called such language changes as *people first* as political correctness or wokeness run amok, designed to prevent anyone from being offended. What do you think? What does *political correctness* mean to you?
- **Media Critique:** Have you noticed any stereotypes in the news and entertainment you consume? How was it constructed? What was its embedded judgment?

CHAPTER 2

Early American Journalism

Women were among the printers who produced newspapers in the American colonies and in historic Mexico. Yet while they were competent, they also struggled to operate their businesses in a society that expected men to be in charge. As literacy for white people spread in early America, so did the demand for print media. Early American magazines for middle- and upper-class white women provided opportunities for intellectual growth and taught women how they were supposed to behave.

Key Concepts: The Cult of True Womanhood, Public Sphere

Whether you've seen her on a billboard or through her social media accounts, you likely know of Malala Yousafzai. She is the youngest person to have ever won a Nobel Peace Prize, at the age of seventeen, after having been shot for her activism on behalf of girls' education in Pakistan.[1] Malala is part of a long line of women who have fought for the essential human right of an education.

Think back to the time you learned to read. It opens up a whole new world, right? Now imagine what life was like as education spread to everyday people, including white women, in the early years of the United States. Imagine also what life was like for enslaved people in the United States, who were forbidden to read and violently punished when they did. Literacy is a capability that constitutes a human right, and it is essential for self-governance.[2] Literacy is essential for participating in civic life, for journalists to write the news, and for citizens to read it. In a particularly cruel circular logic, women and people of color who were denied an education in the early years of the United States were also stereotyped as incapable of participating in democracy. Much of the news in this era was written by white men for white men. For women who could access education, literacy was a crucial factor in the earliest efforts for gender rights. As this chapter describes, educated women in North America used the power of language to raise their voices, often by publishing their own newspapers, in order to advocate for their own rights and those of others. Their efforts were uneven and often marked by conflicts over race as well as gender.

For centuries, literacy was only for royalty and church leaders, but Protestant forms of Christianity, to which many early American colonialists belonged, emphasized the importance of each person being able to read the Bible for themselves. During the 1700s, most women were not encouraged to go beyond reading Scripture, though some, like Mary Wollstonecraft in England and Abigail Adams in the American colonies, read far more widely and wrote, too. Again, keep in mind that enslaved people were not allowed to learn to read, and, generally, people of color were not granted the right to an education at this time. (Later in the United States, Native American and Hispanic children were often forced into schools that stripped them of their cultures and sometimes tore them away from their families, which, of course, further impeded civic engagement for people of color.)

Mary Wollstonecraft's essay "A Vindication on the Rights of Women" is remarkable for its relevance even today, as she calls attention to the need for women to be fully educated in order to participate in adult life. In the preface, she writes,

> I earnestly wish to point out in what true dignity and human happiness consists, I wish to persuade women to endeavor to acquire strength, both of mind and body, and to convince them that the soft phrases, susceptibility of heart, delicacy of sentiment and refinement of taste are almost synonymous with epithets of weakness, and that those beings who are only the object of pity and that kind of love, which has been termed its sister, will soon become objects of contempt.[3]

In other words, in limiting what women could read, learn, and do so they would remain ladylike, Wollstonecraft argues, society kept women childlike and dependent or, to repeat her words, the "object of pity." Treating a person like a child is called **infantilization**, and it has long been one of the ways women have been kept out of public life. A related concept in Hispanic cultures, **marianismo**, expects women to emulate the Virgin Mary of Catholicism by living subservient, pure lives and willingly enduring suffering.[4] By expecting little of them academically and professionally and by encouraging them to stay home and remain soft, nurturing beings, women were not expected to grow intellectually nor participate in democratic life. Infantilization often brings with it condescension, by which women who wish to do more are mocked or ignored.

A famous exchange between Abigail Adams and John Adams (who would become the second US president) during the colonial era exemplifies the way the language of infantilization kept women (and enslaved people) in their so-called place. Abigail Adams was not formally educated; she was often sick as a child, but her family was wealthy enough to have a library, and she was educated at home.[5] She was a prolific letter writer, and her correspondence with John, the Harvard lawyer she married in 1764, has provided historians with a rich source of information about their relationship, as well as the American Revolution. Abigail was interested in politics and opposed slavery. While her marriage to John is often described as one of devotion; it was hardly one of social equals. When John was working with other national leaders to write the Constitution, Abigail wrote to him and asked him to consider the rights of women.

Profile: Mary Wollstonecraft, Writer and Philosopher (1759–1797)

Mary Wollstonecraft.
Courtesy of Library of Congress, Prints and Photographs Division, LC-USZ62-64309

One of the earliest advocates of women's rights in the English-speaking world, Mary Wollstonecraft was born in England in 1759 to a farming family. She worked as a teacher, governess, translator, and eventually writer. She became part of a group of mostly male writers and thinkers supported by a London publisher who was concerned with politics and human rights. Her essay "A Vindication on the Rights of Women" (1792) argues that the educational system of England at the time was designed to keep women frivolous and childlike. Wollstonecraft continued to advocate for the equal rights of women until her death at the age of thirty-eight, only eleven days after the birth of her daughter, who went on to become a writer herself: Mary Shelley, the author of the classic Gothic novel *Frankenstein*. Wollstonecraft's efforts were largely unsuccessful during her lifetime, but her writing influenced the nascent suffrage movement in the United States and beyond.

Sources: Caroline Franklin, *Mary Wollstonecraft: A Literary Life*, Literary Lives series (Palgrave Macmillan, 2004); Elizabeth Robins Pennell, *Life of Mary Wollstonecraft* (Roberts Brothers, 1884), http://archive.org/details/lifeofmarywollst00pennrich.

Echoing the complaints of Wollstonecraft and other educated women of the time, Abigail beseeched him to give them rights and respect: "I desire you would Remember the Ladies, and [*sic*] be more generous and favourable [*sic*] to them than your ancestors. Do not put such unlimited power into the hands of the Husbands. Remember, all Men would be tyrants if they could."[6] He responded with humor and insisted that men were actually the oppressed group: "[I]n Practice you know We are the subjects. We have only the Name of Masters, and rather than give up this, which would completely subject Us to the Despotism of the Petticoat, I hope General Washington, and all our brave Heroes would fight."[7]

This exchange is significant. Abigail managed their household for many years while John practiced politics. She was educated and well informed about current events and crafted a solid argument for why women should be granted rights in the Constitution. (She also opposed slavery, but recall that the founders not only allowed slavery in the United States to continue, but they also *encoded* it with the Constitution's three-fifths compromise.) During this era, wives were essentially chattel, entirely controlled by their husbands. A man could beat his wife without legal or social sanction (though it might be frowned upon).[8] A woman's property rights were always superseded by her husband, father, or brothers.[9] And so, Abigail did not use the word *tyrant* loosely when she referenced husbands. For her husband to make a petticoat joke illustrates how infantilization undercuts arguments from oppressed people who wish for equality. His insistence that women were really the ones in charge draws from a stereotype that reverberates today, suggesting that women's sexuality, their wiles or beauty, was so irresistible as to render men powerless. This stereotype constitutes physical danger to women even today, as extremist misogynist groups use it as a justification for rape and abuse.

Colonial Women in Media

In spite of property laws that favored men, white women were active in the media during the colonial era. The first person to set up a printing press in New England was a woman, Elizabeth Harris Glover, who produced Bibles and almanacs with the help of male employees. (Hers was not the first printing press in North America, however. That distinction goes to a press established by Esteban Martín in Mexico City in 1534.[10]) Glover was able to run the business because her husband had died when the couple were sailing from England to the colonies. This was a common pattern that offered women opportunities only in connection to a male relative. Women who ran print shops usually inherited the business or worked through some other kind of arrangement with a man who could take over at any time. When Glover remarried, for instance, she gave up her printing business. Women in Mexico were similarly involved in the printing press during this time. Paula Benavides de Calderón, for example, took over a press after her husband died and was one of the era's most prolific book publishers in the 1640s. The preeminent poet and philosopher Sor Juana Inés de La Cruz, whose work advanced feminist ideals, wrote during this era. Her publications were some of the first from colonial Mexico to be exported and read in Europe.[11]

Owning a printing press in colonial America almost always meant producing some kind of newspaper, though the news of this time might seem unrecognizable to today's readers. Political opinion essays were usually mixed with announcements about cargo arrivals and other merchant information. Publishers like Benjamin Franklin would include information about phases of the moon, farming instructions, or other seasonal offerings. By the time of the American Revolution in 1776, at least seven women were publishing newspapers. One of them, Mary Katharine Goddard, was unusually successful. She is credited with publishing the first fully signed printing of the Declaration of Independence in her Baltimore newspaper. (The first printing was published without the names of all the signers, for their protection from the British forces.) Goddard became an important printer during the Revolutionary War because she was able to keep publishing the *Maryland Journal* despite material shortages and other interruptions. She even started her own paper mill. She served the colonies as postmaster of Baltimore for fourteen years, until she was replaced by a politically connected man. The presiding postmaster general suggested that the job required "more traveling . . . than a woman could undertake," despite that she'd already done that sort of traveling during a war. She appealed, even taking her case to the new president, George Washington, to no avail.[12] She went onto run a bookstore and lived with an enslaved woman named Belinda Starling, who inherited Goddard's property and was freed when Goddard died in 1816.[13]

Journalism students often learn about a key court case from the colonial era involving John Zenger, which established truth as a defense of libel. John Peter and Anna Catherine Zenger ran a newspaper, but in 1735, John was jailed and tried for criticizing a governor. In a major victory for the rights of a free press, the colonial court released him when his allegations were proven to be true, and truth as a defense for libel remains a central tenet of American law.[14] During his time in jail, Anna kept the newspaper going.[15]

As with other women at this time, Zenger's role relied on the permission of men to participate in the printing business. Keep in mind that at this time, enslaved people were not only unable to participate in the press, but they also were punished for even learning how to read.

The Cult of True Womanhood

The United States as a new entity expanded dramatically in the 1800s, and media developed to keep its people connected. As settlers headed west into territories inhabited by others, magazines and newspapers emerged to help people stay in touch with current events and trends across distances. Women's fashion magazines existed in England in the late 1700s and appeared in the United States in the early 1800s. These magazines (still out of reach for enslaved people, who were forbidden to read) were designed to please women without offending their husbands. So in addition to fashion news, they contained advice on how to be a good wife and mother; in other words, they advised readers on how to be good stereotypical women. In a classic feminist research project, Barbara Welter carefully analyzed these early American women's magazines, as well as church sermons and popular cookbooks, and found them to be a guide for what she dubbed the "**cult of true womanhood**."[16] Her research, which social scientists might call a **qualitative textual analysis**, underscores the importance of language to the way we think about social life. This type of research was one way early feminist scholars identified sexism in society and media, analyzing literature, movies, or magazine articles to identify the way stereotypes take shape.

Welter identifies four themes these magazines reinforce as essential for womanhood: piety, purity, submissiveness, and domesticity. She notes that the repetition of these four virtues in the media of the time creates an image women could strive for: "Put them all together and they spelled mother, daughter, sister, wife-woman. Without them, no matter whether there was fame, achievement or wealth, all was ashes. With them she was promised happiness and power."[17] Piety, or religious devotion, was foundational, for it served the other three. This passage from *The Ladies' Repository* by attorney Caleb Atwater illustrates this emphasis: "Religion is exactly what a woman needs, for it gives her that dignity that best suits her dependence."[18] A passage from an essay in the popular *Godey's Lady's Book* suggests that faith could support a woman's duty to be submissive: "To suffer and to be silent under suffering seems the great command she has to obey."[19]

These were not mere social expectations, for in some places a woman could be charged as a criminal for being a "scold." Some essay titles during this era describe what a "true" women should be:

- "Woman, Man's Best Friend"
- "Woman, the Greatest Social Benefit"
- "Woman, a Being to Come Home To"
- "The Wife: Source of Comfort and the Spring of Joy"[20]

Today's readers might think the authors were talking about a golden retriever. The ideals of true womanhood, or the cult of domesticity, tied women to the home.[21] According to this thinking, women belonged in the private sphere, while men belonged in the **public sphere**. The public sphere describes a literal or metaphorical place where democratic citizens can discuss the issues of the day.[22] It is a useful concept for thinking about where, when, and how democratic deliberation occurs, like the agora of ancient Greece or a meetinghouse in the early United States where citizens (in this case, white, landowning men) could debate the issues of the day.[23] Today, digital spaces might also be considered a type of public sphere.[24]

Historically, not everyone has been welcomed in these spaces. Researcher Catherine Squires suggests that marginalized people often create their own spheres to create community and advance social change.[25] She proposed three types: First, the **counterpublic** directly engages in debate with dominant society. When people protest for their rights or march for women's suffrage or Black Lives Matter, they are engaging in a counterpublic. Squires's second alternative sphere, a "**satellite**," is willfully separate, only occasionally engages with dominant society, and doesn't necessarily want inclusion. Finally, Squires suggests a third sphere, the **enclave**, where members of a marginalized community keep to themselves for safety. Enclaves hide from the dominant order

Godey's Lady's Book was a popular magazine that connected women across the expanding United States.

to avoid sanctions. Communicative spaces, whether actual and geographic or digital and metaphorical, are essential for groups to gather and express themselves, yet they can also be used to exclude people. The belief that women do not belong in the public sphere lives on, in so-called male preserves, like sports, the military, or video gaming.[26]

In early America, women and people of color were essentially shut out of the public sphere. Closeted gay men may well have participated in public deliberation, but they had to keep that part of their identities hidden, as any deviation from cisgender heterosexuality was both illegal and socially demonized across the Americas and Europe. Even white women who were literate were barred from discussing the issues of the day. They were infantilized, as Wollstonecraft describes, as though they were too delicate and childlike to handle democracy. If they weren't dismissed as children, then they were criticized as a scold. Anne Newport Royall, a travel writer and independent newspaper publisher, was tried in court as a scold for her political writing.[27]

Before you dismiss the cult of true womanhood as a thing of the past, take a look at how media address women today. What are the expectations of a true woman in the twenty-first century? What kinds of traits are celebrated in advertising, magazines, and social media? What do social influencers say is important for being a "good woman"? Is motherhood celebrated? Should married women defer to their husbands? Religious piety may no longer be an essential value of womanhood because fewer Americans regularly attend religious services today, but new beliefs have taken their place, such as strict nutrition and fitness regimens, especially for the sake of a healthy pregnancy.[28] As for discouraging women from speaking out, consider how the historic silencing of women reverberates today in the coverage of female politicians, women who are running for office, or women who lead corporations.

TEMPERANCE, ABOLITION, AND WOMEN'S RIGHTS

Much of the energy that drove early Americans to colonize and wage war for independence stemmed from religion. The original colonies in New England were divided according to various Christian denominations seeking separation from England.[29] Among the causes that united many Protestants at the time was temperance, or the battle against alcohol use. As cities grew, so did the problems associated with urbanization, such as alcoholism, addiction, and domestic violence. The temperance movement formalized in 1826 with the establishment of the American Temperance Society, which quickly grew to more than one million members pledging to abstain from alcohol.[30] The movement was energized by a growing middle class and the association of abstinence with white, masculine success. White men and women worked together in temperance efforts; indeed, women were welcomed, as femininity was associated with morality and domestic welfare. Amelia Bloomer, a temperance activist, started the *Lily* in 1849.[31] It was the first newspaper in the United States to be owned and operated by a woman, and it was originally devoted to "temperance and literature." In 1854, the *Lily* shifted focus to equality for women.[32] Bloomer wrote many of the articles, but other women involved in the temperance and early suffrage movements, such as Elizabeth Cady Stanton, Susan B. Anthony, and Jane Grey Swisshelm, contributed to the *Lily*.[33]

The Lily masthead.
Courtesy of Accessible Archives

One way early newspapers like *the Lily* succeeded in gaining support from women was by adopting the language of the "true womanhood" in order to eventually *subvert* it. That is, by situating temperance and abolition in religious terms, women could be permitted to engage in activism outside the home. As historian Martha Watson puts it, "*The Lily* helped its readers visualize themselves as reformers in a historical tradition of all great humanitarians. By presenting women with a moral precedent, transformed as a moral imperative to act as reformers, *The Lily* helped legitimize actions outside the domestic sphere."[34]

The religious motivations for temperance overlapped with concerns among Northern white women about slavery. During the constitutional convention—when John Adams mocked his wife for asking that women's rights be considered—the founders debated whether slavery should remain legal. Not only did it remain legal, but Southern states also were able to further benefit from the enslaved population. While the states denied enslaved people basic human rights, enslaved people counted as three-fifths of a person for census data. This means that those states gained greater congressional representation and thus legislative power to protect their exploitative economies. England banned slavery in 1807, but the nascent economy of the United States became more dependent on the free labor of enslaved people, especially for crops like cotton.[35] Yet many Americans, especially those who did not profit from slavery's economic benefits, were appalled by the institution's practice of separating families, torturing and maiming those who attempted to escape, systematically raping women for the sake of breeding more people to be enslaved, and just working people to death. The abolitionist movement grew as slavery grew, largely in connection with Northern Christian churches, which gave women the toehold they needed to fight for their own rights.

The cult of true womanhood and its emphasis on female piety remained highly influential during this era.[36] As more churches in the North called for the end of slavery and organized against it, however, women were able to become involved in the traditionally male public sphere. Because *churches* were involved in the movement, however, women (white women and a scant few freed Black women) could participate in the movement, and they did. They wrote essays, attended public meetings, and even delivered speeches.

Many abolitionists, male and female, were inspired by Harriett Beecher Stowe's best-selling novel, *Uncle Tom's Cabin*, a fictional account based on meticulous factual research that was the second-best-selling book of the century, exceeded only by the Bible.[37] Stowe was a deeply religious woman raised by a minister and the highly educated wife of a professor. Her novel started as a serial in a newspaper, the *National Era*, from 1851 to 1852, and the installments were turned into a book published in 1854.[38] Excoriated by critics in the South, Stowe published a book called *A Key to Uncle Tom's Cabin*, in which she defended her research, and the way she changed names but described real events to bring the story to life. For instance, while living in Ohio, Stowe and her husband helped a woman who was legally free escape slave hunters who crossed the border to reclaim "property" for Southern slaveholders. Experiences like this lent lifelike detail to her account of such an escape in the book. *Uncle Tom's Cabin* was an international success and was translated into more than twenty languages.[39] One drawback to the book is the way the stories of enslaved people were told by a Northern white woman with privilege. Given that enslaved people at the time were not able to read or write, however, the book made history, and when Stowe visited the White House, Abraham Lincoln is quoted as saying, "So this is the little lady who made this big war."[40] Stowe remained in public life and continued to write novels and journalistic articles for the *Atlantic Monthly* after the Civil War. She died in 1896.[41]

Excerpt: *Uncle Tom's Cabin*

In the course of the day, Tom was working near the mulatto woman who had been bought in the same lot with himself. She was evidently in a condition of great suffering, and Tom often heard her praying, as she wavered and trembled, and seemed about to fall down. Tom silently, as he came near to her, transferred several handfuls of cotton from his own sack to hers.

"O, don't, don't!" said the woman, looking surprised; "it'll get you into trouble."

Just then Sambo came up. He seemed to have a special spite against this woman; and, flourishing his whip, said, in brutal, guttural tones, "What dis yer, Luce, -foolin' a'?" and, with the word, kicking the woman with his heavy cowhide shoe, he struck Tom across the face with his whip.

Tom silently resumed his task; but the woman, before at the last point of exhaustion, fainted.

"I'll bring her to!" said the driver, with a brutal grin. "I'll give her something better than camphire!" and, taking a pin from his coat-sleeve, he buried it to the head in her flesh. The woman groaned, and half rose. "Get up, you beast, and work, will yer, or I'll show yet a trick more!"

The woman seemed stimulated, for a few moments, to an unnatural strength, and worked with desperate eagerness.

"See that you keep to dat ar," said the man, "or yer'll wish yer's dead to-night, I reckin!"

Source: Harriet Beecher Stowe, "Cassie," chap. 33 in *Uncle Tom's Cabin*, ed. Jean Fagan Yellin (Oxford University Press, 1998).

Women's Suffrage Takes Off

In 1848, the suffrage movement had attracted enough members to justify a gathering. Elizabeth Cady Stanton played a central role in organizing the convention in Seneca Falls, New York, which attracted about three hundred men and women, most of whom lived locally. Only women were allowed to attend during the first day. Abolition leader Frederick Douglass was among the men who attended the second day. Stanton was a longtime activist with the temperance and abolition movements. In fact, she and her husband attended an abolition conference in England in 1840 for their honeymoon, during which Elizabeth and Quaker activist Lucretia Mott were forced to sit with other women apart from the male delegates in a curtained-off room.[42] Like Mott, the other founding convenors were members of the Quaker Church, which was a major political force on behalf of abolition and human rights. At the start of the two-day conference, in ninety-degree heat, Stanton exhorted women to accept responsibility for their own lives and to "understand the height, the depth, the length, and the breadth of [their] own degradation."[43] The convention produced the Seneca Falls Declaration of Sentiments, the founding document of the American women's suffrage movement. In keeping with the strategy of using the traditional language to subvert oppression, the document borrows from the Declaration of Independence from the very start:

> When, in the course of human events, it becomes necessary for one portion of the family of man to assume among the people of the earth a position different from that which they have hitherto occupied, but one to which the law of nature and of nature's God entitle them, a decent respect to the opinions of mankind requires that they should declare the causes that impel them to such a course.[44]

The document declares the history of mankind to have practiced tyranny over women by denying them the right to vote, rendering married women "civilly dead," withholding her right to property, and denying her an education—among other grievances.[45] Not all the convenors were ready to grant women the right to vote, but eventually, the declaration was passed. Frederick Douglass was among those who spoke in favor of the declaration.

The Seneca Falls Declaration was not immediately embraced by the mainstream, and the women who participated were widely mocked and caricatured as unwomanly, desexed freaks. Mainstream news treated the subject as a scandal or a joke. An anonymous writer for the *Oneida Whig* asked, "Was there ever such a dreadful revolt?—They set aside the statute 'Wives, submit yourselves unto your husbands.' . . . This bolt is the most shocking and unnatural incident ever recorded in the history of womanity."[46] In keeping with the notion that women only have value in relationship to others, the *Philadelphia Public Ledger and Daily Transcript* responded, "A woman is nobody. A wife is everything. A pretty girl is equal to ten thousand men, and a mother is, next to God, all powerful. The ladies of Philadelphia, therefore, under the influence of the most serious 'sober second thoughts,' are resolved to maintain their rights as Wives, Belles, Virgins, and Mothers, and not as Women."[47]

Amelia Bloomer as illustrated in the *Lily*, September 1851, wearing the loose trousers for which she advocated for women.
Courtesy of Accessible Archives

Profile: Sojourner Truth, Abolitionist and Women's Rights Activist (1797–1883)

After years of brutal enslavement, Isabella Van Wagenen fled from her owners in New York State in 1823. As a child, she had been whipped bloody, leaving lifelong scars on her back. She was forced to marry a man and had five children, two of whom died. After running away, she worked as a domestic for twenty years and became involved in a number of different religious groups. In 1843, she gave abrupt notice to her employer that the "spirit" had inspired her to move on and set out with only twenty-five cents in her pocket to start life as a preacher. She adopted a new name, Sojourner Truth, and spent the next forty years in ministry and activism as an abolitionist and women's rights advocate. She is known for a powerful speech at a women's suffrage convention in Akron, Ohio, in 1851, but the phrase "Ain't I a woman?" is a mischaracterization of what she said and how. She did not speak in Southern Black vernacular, and according to a reprint of the speech from a witness, she did not use the phrase "Ain't I a woman?" Yet what she did say that day so moved the crowd that she was

I Sell the Shadow to Support the Substance.

SOJOURNER TRUTH.

Sojourner Truth.
Courtesy of Library of Congress, Prints and Photographs Division, LC-DIG-ppmsca-08978

able to write a book, *The Narrative of Sojourner Truth*. Because she was illiterate, her story of her years in slavery and struggles to help her children out of enslavement was crafted by a ghostwriter. After the Civil War, Sojourner Truth continued to work for social justice, taking on such causes as land reparations and integrating mass transit.

Sources: Olive Gilbert, *Narrative of Sojourner Truth* (Dover, 1997); Isabelle Kinnard Richman, *Sojourner Truth: Prophet of Social Justice* (Routledge, 2016), https://doi.org/10.4324/9780203081679; Sojourner Truth, *Narrative of Sojourner Truth* (Penguin, 1998).

The *Lily*'s Amelia Bloomer made waves when she suggested that women not only should vote but also should wear comfortable clothes. She invented an outfit with loose pants under a midlength skirt, and the *Lily* even offered free patterns for the outfit based on "Turkish pantaloons."[48] The very notion of wearing any kind of pants brought mockery to the movement, even though no one wore such an outfit to the convention.[49] Bloomer became known more for her fashion suggestion than her political work. *Bloomers* (pants) became an issue of their own, reflecting the patriarchal notion that women's attractiveness should be defined by men. Critics joked that men should be ready to start cooking and cleaning if women "wore the pants" and were granted the right to vote, a theme that recurred throughout the women's rights movement.

Constructing Community

The combined power of suffrage and abolitionism was a train that was hard to stop, and activists rallied to conventions across the Northern states. Sojourner Truth, a woman who fled slavery and became a preacher, was among those who fought for both, delivering her famous speech, "Ain't I a Woman," during a suffrage convention in 1851 in Akron, Ohio. In Mexico, Laureana Wright de Kleinhans was a prolific writer who advocated for women's rights to suffrage and education. She edited a journal, *Violets of Anahuac*, devoted to art, culture, and profiles of prominent Mexican women, and promoted the idea that women were intellectually equal to men. Similar to the way abolitionist women in the United States subverted true womanhood's language of piety to advocate for their own rights, Wright de Kleinhans was able to garner attention in the patriarchal culture of her time by adopting a very formal writing style usually known only to well-educated men.[50]

Another journalist who worked at the intersection of race and gender, Maria W. Stewart was married to a shipmaster and was part of Boston's Black middle class in the early 1800s. She wrote for the *Liberator* and framed her essays in biblical discourse, again turning that language of the cult of true womanhood into the language of freedom and emancipation. She eventually started a school near Baltimore. Mary Ann Shadd Cary was another feminist writer of this era. She was the first Black female newspaper publisher in Canada, a woman who was born free in Delaware but emigrated from the United States in 1851 to avoid being hunted under the Fugitive Slave Act. Shadd founded and edited the *Provincial Freeman*. Through her newspaper, she advocated for educational and voting rights for women and Black people and even set up her own integrated school in Windsor, Canada West.[51] When she publicly disagreed with abolitionists who supported segregation, a rival newspaper attacked her femininity: "Miss Shadd has said and written many things which we think will add nothing to her credit as a lady."[52]

The editors of these alternative newspapers rarely made money from their efforts, which often overlapped with activism and educational activities. Moreover, these newspapers, whether for women's rights or abolition, did more than share information; they created a sense of community.[53] Alternative presses did not adhere to modern journalistic ideas about objectivity; instead, they shared information with an express goal, such as the abolition of slavery or women's suffrage (or in some cases both). Some of these newspapers were managed by women. Communicating a cause was part of the work of organizing for it. As Susan B. Anthony, who joined with Stanton in the fight for women's suffrage after the Civil War, wrote, "Just as long as newspapers and magazines are controlled by men, every woman upon them must write articles, which are reflections of men's ideas. As long as that continues, women's ideas and deepest convictions will never go before the public."[54]

Both the abolition movement and women's suffrage relied on alternative public spheres for the advancement of their ideas, for safety within their groups, and for contending with and interacting with the larger public and advancement of people's rights. Recall that the public sphere can be thought of as a real and metaphorical space in which we discuss matters of public importance. The Greek agora, or market-place, is often held up as a perfect space where people could stand on a tree stump to give a speech about what they thought was important for the day in order to run a democracy.

Democracy depends on citizens' abilities to exchange information and ideas in a public sphere and have these kinds of discussions. But for groups in the minority, for oppressed groups, alternative public spheres are often all that is available to them. Marginalized groups need alternative public spheres because dominant groups have exclusionary rules for participating in public speech. In early America, women were considered domineering and unnatural if they tried to speak out and voice their concerns individually. During a time when women were simply not allowed to leave their homes or were considered unladylike if they entered the public square without their husbands, alternative newspapers provided a sense of community.

Reconstruction and Its Ruptures

The Civil War put the fight for gender rights on hold as it effectively ended slavery. The war and its aftermath also revealed intersectional fissures in the two causes. That is, some of the women working for women's suffrage fought against the rights of Black men. The *Revolution*, for instance, the newspaper run by Stanton and Susan B. Anthony, opposed the Fifteenth Amendment, which granted voting rights to only Black men. Stanton wrote, "If that word 'male' be inserted, it will take us a century at least to get it out."[55] Lucy Stone's newspaper, the *Women's Journal and Suffrage News*, also argued that the suffrage campaigns for women and for Black people should be separate. Of course, for Black women, the two campaigns were hardly separate.

Harriet Tubman, who is known for her work as an abolitionist and, of course, for helping people run away to freedom using the Underground Railroad, also worked for women's suffrage after the Civil War. The competition between Black men and white women for suffrage stoked deep resentments, prompting Frederick Douglass (who, remember, advocated for the Seneca Falls Declaration) to write,

[W]hen women, because they are women, are hunted down to the cities of New York and New Orleans; when they are dragged from their houses and hung upon lampposts; when their children are torn from their arms and their brains dashed out upon the pavement; when they are objects of insult and outrage at every turn; when they are in danger of having their homes burnt down over their heads; when their children are not allowed to enter schools; then they will have an urgency to obtain the ballot equal to our own.[56]

The Fifteenth Amendment did pass in 1870, giving formerly enslaved men the right to vote, and Southern states quickly sent a dramatic number of Black men to Congress. Women would wait another fifty years to be enfranchised. Even then, for marginalized people, the right to vote would be unevenly distributed, as this period saw the birth of the Ku Klux Klan and Jim Crow laws designed to keep people of color away from the ballot box.

Summary

The decades leading up to the Civil War and Reconstruction were a time of tremendous social upheaval that was often violent. An increasingly literate population took on temperance, abolition, and then women's rights in impassioned and occasionally violent tactics. The individuals who led the movement were mocked and shunned and faced physical danger. Alternative presses, run by antislavery and women's rights advocates, would advance the movement and help create a community for its participants. Writers subverted the language of the cult of true womanhood by insisting their Christian faith required them to publicly fight against slavery and liquor. Women in the abolition and temperance movement learned how to organize and speak publicly, skills they then used to defend their own rights. Fifty years passed between the Fifteenth Amendment and the Nineteenth, and the intersectional ruptures of that era continue today. Feelings of resentment and betrayal between white women, Black men, and other factions continued into the twentieth century and still haunt civil rights efforts.

- **Reflection:** How can humor be a form of oppression? Why might John Adams use humor instead of direct language to keep his wife "in her place"?
- **Reflection:** What similarities do the historic relationship between abolition and suffrage have with today's movements for gender- and race-based civil rights?
- **Media Critique:** How do today's media define *true womanhood* today? Are there similar messages for men?
- **Media Critique:** Where have you seen the infantilization of women in a movie, program, or advertisement? What form did it take?

CHAPTER 3

Media Industrialization and Women's Opportunities

This chapter covers the period after the Civil War until the Nineteenth Amendment was ratified in 1920. Women working for suffrage learned how to create media events, though they were often framed in news as deviants. News practices changed during this era in ways that are familiar to us today, presenting new types of opportunities for women in journalism.

Key Concepts: Mass Media, Protest Paradigm

The period after the Civil War up to the First World War ushered in a new industrial era for the United States, one that fostered the development of **mass media**. This changed both the way women could work in media and the way they consumed it. Steam-powered printing presses, railroads, special postal rates for newspapers and magazines—all these factors contributed to changes in the news industry. Publishers started to make money from advertising in addition to subscription and newsstand sales. This shifted their business model from delivering information directly to an audience to delivering an audience to advertisers.[1] Many small newspapers, including suffrage papers, continued to serve the interests of local communities and social groups, but others developed as parts of corporations and started using a factory model of production, with a division of labor. These mass-marketed newspapers appealed to a wider audience instead of political parties and came to be produced by larger, bureaucratic organizations instead of individuals.

The women's suffrage movement peaked in this era, as activists in Britain and the United States took to the streets in protest. Suffragists learned how to use visual symbols in their protests to garner media attention. They also suffered violence and arrests as they pushed for the vote. Intersectional fractures in the movement between white feminists and Black women reverberate today. Even when the Nineteenth Amendment was codified into the Constitution in 1920, it did not guarantee voting rights for all women in the United States, as Jim Crow laws and other institutional blocks disenfranchised many women of color.

Women's Newspapers and Women's News

After the Civil War, rivalries erupted between abolitionists and suffragists, for even though enslaved people had been freed, they were not granted civil rights. Only recently have historians contended in-depth with the racism of the suffrage movement for women in the United States. The American Equal Rights Association, founded in 1866, called for suffrage for all people, but Elizabeth Cady Stanton and Susan B. Anthony broke away, as women and Black men competed for voting rights. The *Women's Journal*, headed by Lucy Stone, accepted the idea that women would have to wait.[2] Stanton and Anthony, however, created their own organization, the National Woman Suffrage Association (NWSA), and Stanton, writing in the *Revolution*, stooped to invoking racist stereotypes, suggesting that white women in the South would be subjected to "fearful outrages on womanhood" should Black men get the vote first.[3] Much to the horror of some of their allies, Stanton and Anthony aligned with a racist groups in an attempt to defeat the Fifteenth Amendment.[4]

Debates over what suffrage could or should mean for a woman's femininity also raged among leaders and their associated publications. At its peak, the *Revolution*, published by Stanton and Anthony, had only three thousand subscribers, but it caught attention for articles on such controversial subjects as prostitution and sex education. It ran stories of women in nontraditional jobs, like sailors and farmers, and it could be considered the angriest of the suffrage press. Victoria Woodhull, the first woman to run for president, started her own paper, *Woodhull and Claflin's Weekly*, which advocated for suffrage and "free love," accepting of sex outside marriage.[5] However, Lucy Stone's *Women's Journal* focused solely on suffrage and was designed for middle-class women, offering a calm, reasonable, and responsible vision of voting women. These different voices of the movement showed that even suffragists considered

The Revolution.

"What, therefore, God hath joined together, let not man put asunder."

VOL. VI.—NO. 15.   NEW YORK, THURSDAY, OCTOBER 13, 1870.   WHOLE NO. 145.

Poetry.

AUTUMN WOODS.

Ere, in the northern gale,
The summer tresses of the trees are gone,
The woods of Autumn, all around our vale,
Have put their glory on.

The mountains that enfold,
In their wide sweep, the colored landscape round,
Seem groups of giant kings, in purple and gold,
That guard the enchanted ground.

Our Special Contributors.

THE SOCIAL EVIL IN ENGLAND AND AMERICA.

BY S. M. KING.

Two papers in THE REVOLUTION of August 11th I desire very much to offer a few comments upon. These are, the London letter by Emily Faithfull and an article entitled "The

corrupt French system of legislation came as an unexpected shock to many men even, and still there are in this country both men and women who can hardly believe that Englishmen *could* have passed a law so utterly cruel, unjust and unmanly as these Contagious Diseases Acts.

There are both wise and mature workers who are seeking to raise the position of women, by obtaining for them direct political influence, by opening a wider field for the employment of their time and talents, and by

Poetry is published on the front page of this edition of *The Revolution* from October 13, 1870, as many newspapers and magazines at the time included poems, literature, and essays, as well as news.
Courtesy of Accessible Archives

strong-minded women to be "repugnantly unfeminine," "arrogant," and "vulgar."[6] This theme—that women who want equality want to be like men, if not be men—will be seen again in the second wave of feminism. The cult of true womanhood does not merely associate women with passivity; it defines them that way, so it concludes that women who fight for equality cannot be women—they must be freaks.

Nevertheless, across North America, women persisted, publishing dozens of periodicals to push for a woman's right to vote. Not surprisingly, many of the women involved in the movement before and after the Civil War were involved in education. As more women became literate and engaged with the public sphere, they put their writing and speaking skills to work. Activist and writer Zitkala-Ša, also known as Gertrude Simmons, called attention to the oppressions of Indigenous people as a writer for the *Atlantic Monthly*. She went on to edit the *American Indian Magazine*, calling for reforms, including women's suffrage, and conducted an investigation into corruption and murder by politicians who plundered oil-rich tribal land in Oklahoma. The pamphlet she produced from this investigation led to federal policy reforms.[7]

Black women printed newspapers that combined their concerns for racial and gender rights. Mary Ann Shadd Cary, for instance, published the first abolitionist newspaper in Canada before the Civil War. After the war, she was the first woman to study law at Howard University. She continued to write and established one of the first organizations devoted to Black women's suffrage.[8] Mary Church Terrell, the first president of the National Association of Colored Women, started as a teacher, as did Mary McLeod Bethune, who organized Black voters, wrote for papers like the *Chicago Defender*, and started her own school for Black girls in 1904.[9] Jovita Idár, the Mexican American journalist and activist who advocated for civil rights and suffrage in the border communities of Texas, similarly worked as an educator. In California, Maria Guadalupe Angelina de Lopez worked to advance women's rights in the early 1900s as an educator and organizer. She was the first person to translate suffrage speeches into Spanish.[10]

The Rise of the "News Factory"

The Industrial Revolution moved jobs from agricultural areas into urban ones. Cities in the United States, like New York and Chicago, also grew dramatically during an unprecedented wave of immigration from Europe. Between 1870 and 1930, thirty million immigrants arrived in the United States, about half of them between 1900 and 1915.[11] Most of them settled in large cities, as the country shifted from farming to an industrial economy. Industrialization changed the way news was made, too, as newspapers became larger, more bureaucratic organizations with editors, reporters, and press operators. Child labor in the form of newsboys who sold papers on the street was also prevalent. Newspaper owners, like Joseph Pulitzer and William Randolph Hearst, engaged in extreme competition, giving rise to sensationalist news stories known as **yellow journalism**. Screaming headlines for stories about sex, crime, and war mongering filled pages and drew readers into exaggerated drama about the world around them.[12] To appeal to a broader audience, newspaper publishers changed the way their printed pages appeared, using fonts and blocks of text to guide readers, taking on the look and feel of today's publications. Publishers also created new sections for readers: for sports, business, and women. The decision to treat women as a special audience reaffirmed the gender stereotypes while creating opportunities, albeit often limited opportunities, for women in the newsroom.

Pulitzer's *New York Daily World* was one of the first papers to set aside a section for women on fashion and society that was actually written *by* women. Hearst soon followed with women's pages that included a romance column, and the Black press similarly developed women's pages. Publishers worked to appeal to women beyond these sections, with special promotions and emotional stories, usually written by women. These stories relied on female reporters, whether as "sob sisters," who wrote tear-jerking stories about social injustice and tragedies, or "stunt reporters," who would go on daring adventures or work undercover for investigations.[13] Annie Laurie, a sob sister who wrote for Hearst's newspapers, went undercover at a canning factory, spent time in Utah with polygamists, and interviewed a woman who ran a brothel.[14] Nellie Bly worked for Pulitzer. She wrote a series as she traveled around the world in seventy-two days and posed as a woman with mental illness in order to expose conditions in a New York asylum.[15] While the women's pages and female star-reporter jobs offered new opportunities for women in journalism, they were hardly equals in the newsroom. Only a few women could be stars for the front page, and once a paper had their girl reporter, there was no room for another, a practice known as **tokenism**. A token employee stands in for an entire demographic group, creating a false front of diversity. The stunt reporters were exceptional investigative reporters who often went undercover and used their femininity to get stories. Their work helped to sell newspapers but was dismissed as unprofessional scandal mongering when the profession tried to part ways with yellow journalism.[16]

Writing for the women's pages meant crafting stories about food, fashion, and family. The prestige beats, such as city hall, politics, business, and war, were reserved for men. One exception was Margaret Fuller, the first American women to serve as a foreign correspondent, who wrote for the *New York Tribune* in the 1840s during the Italian Wars for Independence. Fuller was already well known in literary circles when she started at the newspaper as a critic but soon moved to covering social problems. Her career was cut short when she drowned in a shipwreck during the voyage back to New York from Italy.[17]

Much like the women who ran presses in the colonies in connection with fathers and husbands, Miriam Folline Leslie took over *Frank Leslie's Illustrated Newspaper* after her husband died. Eliza Holbrook did the same thing, taking over the *New Orleans Picayune* in the 1860s. She is credited with making the paper profitable again and adding innovative content, such as cartoons, columns on household tips, popular science, and health care. She founded the Women's International Press Association in 1887.

Most women gained ground in news by writing for female readers. In 1890, the US Census reported that nearly nine hundred women worked in daily journalism. They made enough of an impact that a professional publication, the *Journalist*, devoted an entire issue in 1889 to notable female journalists. Women still faced

Excerpt: *Ten Days in a Madhouse*

[W]e heard someone yell, "Go out into the hall." One of the patients kindly explained that this was an invitation to supper. We late comers tried to keep together, so we entered the hall and stood at the door where all the women had crowded. How we shivered as we stood there! The windows were open and the draught went whizzing through the hall. The patients looked blue with cold, and the minutes stretched into a quarter of an hour. At last one of the nurses went forward and unlocked a door, through which we all crowded to a landing of the stairway. Here again came a long halt directly before an open window.

"How very imprudent for the attendants to keep these thinly clad women standing here in the cold," said Miss Neville.

I looked at the poor crazy captives shivering, and added, emphatically, "It's horribly brutal." While they stood there I thought I would not relish supper that night. They looked so lost and hopeless. Some were chattering nonsense to invisible persons, others were laughing or crying aimlessly, and one old, gray-haired woman was nudging me, and, with winks and sage noddings of the head and pitiful uplifting of the eyes and hands, was assuring me that I must not mind the poor creatures, as they were all mad. "Stop at the heater," was then ordered, "and get in line, two by two." "Mary, get a companion." "How many times must I tell you to keep in line?" "Stand still," and, as the orders were issued, a shove and a push were administered, and often a slap on the ears. After this third and final halt, we were marched into a long, narrow dining-room, where a rush was made for the table.

The table reached the length of the room and was uncovered and uninviting. Long benches without backs were put for the patients to sit on, and over these they had to crawl in order to face the table. Placed closed together all along the table were large dressing-bowls filled with a pinkish-looking stuff which the patients called tea. By each bowl was laid a piece of bread, cut thick and buttered. A small saucer containing five prunes accompanied the bread. One fat woman made a rush, and jerking up several saucers from those around her emptied their contents into her own saucer. Then while holding to her own bowl she lifted up another and drained its contents at one gulp. This she did to a second bowl in shorter time than it takes to tell it. Indeed, I was so amused at her successful grabbings that when I looked at my own share the woman opposite, without so much as by your leave, grabbed my bread and left me without any.

Source: Nellie Bly, "My First Supper," chap. 10 in *Ten Days in a Madhouse* (Ian L. Munro, 1877).

obstacles, as they were barred from the Washington Press Gallery in 1877, and editors bristled over having to provide them with escorts if they had to go home after dark. Women often signed their articles with only their initials or pseudonyms because editors balked at identifying any of their writers as female.[18]

Muckraking Women

Corporate excess and abuse also inspired important investigative reporting by writers who were maligned as **muckrakers** by President Theodore Roosevelt. Journalists at *Collier's* magazine investigated the deadly patent medicine industry in the United

Profile: Ida B. Wells, Journalist (1861–1931)

IDA B. WELLS.

Ida B. Wells.
Courtesy of Library of Congress, Prints and Photographs Division, LC-USZ62-107756

Ida B. Wells was an investigative data reporter before such a job description existed. She was a teacher, journalist, and activist who used hard data as ammunition for her cause. Wells was born into slavery. After the Civil War, she attended school, and by fourteen, she was teaching herself. She continued teaching while a student at Fisk University in Memphis. While living in Tennessee, Wells unsuccessfully sued a railroad company for forcing her to give up her seat and move to a "colored only" car. She started in journalism by writing articles criticizing the substandard educational system for Black children and eventually became part owner of the *Memphis Free Speech*. In 1892, after three of her friends were lynched by a mob in Memphis, Wells began an editorial campaign about this peculiarly American form of domestic terrorism. Her newspaper's office was ransacked and burned down, yet she continued to write, moving to New York and then to Chicago after marrying Ferdinand Barnett, a lawyer and newspaper editor. Wells-Barnett conducted painstakingly detailed research on lynching for her publications, *Southern Horrors* (1892) and *The Red Record* (1895), bringing hard data into public view. She was active in organizing local African American women in various causes, including women's suffrage. She participated in the meeting of the Niagara Movement in 1909, an effort that led to the establishment of the National Association for the Advancement of Colored People (NAACP). In 1913, she founded what may have been the first Black women's suffrage group, Chicago's Alpha Suffrage Club. That same year, when she was asked to march in a segregated part of a suffrage parade, she refused and joined her white colleagues in the Illinois delegation.

Source: Kristina DuRocher, *Ida B. Wells: Social Activist and Reformer* (Routledge, 2016); Jane Rhodes, "Woman Suffrage and the New Negro in the Black Public Sphere," in *Front Pages, Front Lines: Media and the Fight for Women's Suffrage*, ed. Linda Steiner, Carolyn Kitch, and Brooke Kroeger (University of Illinois Press, 2020), 98–114.

Excerpt: *The Red Record*

Delivered to the Mob by the Governor of the State

John Peterson, near Denmark, S.C., was suspected of rape, but escaped, went to Columbia, and placed himself under Gov. Tillman's protection, declaring he too could prove an alibi by white witnesses. A white reporter hearing his declaration volunteered to find these witnesses, and telegraphed the governor that he would be in Columbia with them on Monday. In the meantime the mob at Denmark, learning Peterson's whereabouts, went to the governor and demanded the prisoner. Gov. Tillman, who had during his canvass for reelection the year before, declared that he would lead a mob to lynch a Negro that assaulted a white woman, gave Peterson up to the mob. He was taken back to Denmark, and the white girl in the case as positively declared that he was not the man. But the verdict of the mob was that "the crime had been committed and somebody had to hang for it, and if he, Peterson, was not guilty of that he was of some other crime," and he was hung, and his body riddled with 1,000 bullets.

Source: Ida B. Wells-Barnett, "History of Some Cases of Rape," chap. 6 in *The Red Record: Tabulated Statistics and Alleged Causes of Lynching in the United States* (1895).

States, which allowed anyone to put a label on just about anything and call it medicine. These investigations are credited with inspiring Congress to pass the Pure Food and Drug Act of 1906.[19] Ida Tarbell was the sole woman among a team of investigative reporters for *McClure's* magazine, and she produced one of the most important exposés in American history. In 1902, she started publishing what she thought would be a three-part series about the illegal dealings of Standard Oil and its magnate, John D. Rockefeller, and ended up with a nineteen-part investigative series that bolstered the federal government's antitrust case against the company.[20]

Ida B. Wells did not work for a magazine but ran her own newspaper, which was burned down when she spoke out against lynching. She eventually published her investigations independently. Even though data journalism is a relatively new job category, Wells could be considered such an investigator for the way she meticulously mapped and detailed lynching incidents around the United States in her two publications, *The Red Record* and *Southern Horrors*.

News as Mass Media

As the business of journalism shifted dramatically in the early 1900s, so did the writing style for news stories. Journalism had long been a very personal and often political endeavor, with individuals who printed magazines or newspapers with their own points of view and without concern for nonpartisanship. Stories were often written in first person by writers who had witnessed events. Margaret Fuller, the first American woman to serve as a foreign correspondent, wrote in that flowery style in the 1840s during the Italian Wars for Independence. During an attack on Rome, she wrote, "But wounds and assaults only fire more and more the courage of her [Rome's] defenders. They feel the justice of their cause, and the peculiar iniquity of this aggression."[21]

Over time, journalism moved from this literary, ornate writing style to a simpler one, and technology had a hand in this change. The early telegraph system gradually connected cities and news agencies across the United States in real time and made the Associated Press and other wire services possible.[22] But the telegraph was not always reliable (not all that different than spotty mobile networks), and reporters learned to put the most important information first, what's known as the **inverted pyramid style**. The page designs of mass media papers were easier to read and were supported by stories written with clear, declarative writing and simple headlines.[23] Business demands also influenced news writing, as mass-marketed newspapers worked to attract as many readers as possible, not just those who were interested in a particular topic or cause. Additionally, journalists worked to establish their professionalism during this era and developed codes of ethics that standardized the kind of nonpartisan, fact-based reporting embraced by many journalists today.[24]

The shift from small, family-owned presses to industrialized news brought with it an increasing reliance on advertising. Rather than depend only on subscription or newsstand sales, a publisher could make money by selling ads, giving corporations access to their readers' attention.[25] This shift meant that publishers now served two sets of stakeholders: their readers and their advertisers. This, of course, can affect content decisions, depending on the goals of the publication. Also, as the United States industrialized, branding became an important tactic for corporate competition.[26] Previously, when people needed grain, they just went to a general store (probably the only store in town) and bought the oats that were available. In this new corporate era, however, it became possible to sell one particular company's oats, such as Quaker Oats, one of the first trademarked brands in America and one of the earliest media advertisers. As media grew and commercialized, branding became important not only for cereal, but also for social movements—like women's suffrage.

Votes for Women

With dramatic changes in the economy, population, and even the geography of the United States, the women's suffrage movement took on new urgency in the early 1900s. The next wave of leaders, like Alice Paul of the National Women's Party, brought fresh energy to the effort. Paul was roughed up and dragged by police while demonstrating both in England and the United States. She was known for a no-compromise approach to suffrage and developed innovative ways of influencing public opinion. In England and in the United States, Paul disrupted political events to demand votes for women and was repeatedly jailed and force-fed after participating in hunger strikes. She proved to be an effective media strategist and found ways to garner public sympathy, in part because she created a youthful, feminine image for the new woman, even as she proved to be an "iron-jawed angel."[27]

GAINING VISIBILITY

At the turn of the twentieth century, the American suffrage movement was in trouble. As Stanton's daughter writes in her memoir, "The suffrage movement was completely in a rut in New York State at the opening of the twentieth century. It bored its adherents and repelled its opponents." [28] News coverage of the suffrage movement in the early twentieth century was often negative. As the movement spread across the United States, antisuffrage organizations formed, many led by women.[29] Suffragists used a variety of tactics to garner public attention, such as pageants, posters, even cookbooks.[30] They did what they could to harness the attention of mass media using such displays, an early form of **visual activism**.[31] They also put their bodies on the line, marching, singing, and disrupting public meetings. These tactics attracted attention but not necessarily positive attention, as suffragists were framed as crazy, deviant, or bourgeois dilettantes who did not understand life's realities.

News coverage of the suffrage movement followed a pattern familiar to journalism researchers. The essential curriculum for journalism students includes a list of qualities that make for a newsworthy story: celebrity, proximity, importance, novelty. Stories out of the ordinary are news. Over time, the reverse became culturally understood: Events are seen as unusual for the very sake that they are in the news. This presents an opportunity and a problem for social justice activists. Doing unusual things, like holding a protest march, garners news attention.[32] That news attention, however, does not necessarily normalize the idea of suffrage. Indeed, it frames the women protesting as odd, agitating, or deviant. Researchers who have examined the way journalism stigmatizes dissent calls this the protest paradigm.[33] Protests are framed negatively, and any part of a protest that becomes violent or destructive is highlighted, even when the larger protest was peaceful. The news value of "unusualness" is one reason for the focus on disruption. Another reason protesters are often framed negatively is that journalists rely so heavily on official sources, such as police, politicians, and business leaders.[34] Though the public might consider the cause palatable, such as equal rights based on gender or race, the *protest* is covered as a problem.

Even when coverage was neutral or positive, it reflected stereotypes. In 1910, women from both the British and American movements put on a sold-out Suffrage Matinee in a New York theater. The event included speeches, poetry, and performances from suffrage activists, labor organizations, and a troupe of Māori women from New Zealand. Emmeline Pankhurst, an iconic suffrage leader from England, spoke about beatings, arrests, and force-feedings, yet it is not all that surprising that newspaper coverage of her speech skipped over the substance of her performance and instead devoted an entire paragraph to what she was wearing.[35]

Pankhurst's clothing that day was not out of the ordinary for a suffragist, as the movement had adopted a color scheme that helped brand it. In parades and demonstrations, suffragists wore white dresses and carried banners trimmed in green, purple, and gold. Just as they tried to upend the language of "true womanhood" during the abolition era, suffragists learned to work against stereotypes visually. As media historian Linda Lumsden put it, suffrage leader Alice Paul "wielded beauty as a political tool through public spectacle and aimed to prove women could be citizens without losing

ORIGIN AND DEVELOPMENT OF A SUFFRAGETTE.

At 15 a little Pet.

At 20 a little Coquette

At 40 not married yet!

At 50 A Suffragette.

VOTES FOR WOMEN

This antisuffrage postcard is notable for the way the woman is depicted as unattractive, implying a connection between being single, ugly, and aggressive and desiring the right to vote.
Courtesy of Palczewski Suffrage Postcard Archive, University of Northern Iowa, Cedar Falls

respectability and dignity."[36] White dresses were chosen for their symbolic connection to purity, and women in these costumes would carry torches like Lady Liberty. Postcards worked as the memes of the era, as suffragists and their opponents collected and traded cards with colorful images and political messages. There were even suffrage (and antisuffrage) valentines for declaring one's politics and love interest.[37]

Visibility is essential to a social movement, but it comes at a price. Just as Amelia Bloomer was mercilessly mocked as a freak for promoting "bifurcated trousers" for women, suffragists were often characterized in grotesque ways. Antisuffrage postcards depicted women's rights activists as brutes who terrorized men, often fat, stereotypically ugly, and occasionally beating their husbands with rolling pins.[38] This trope of women seeking equal rights as man haters unworthy of male attention lives on to this day. It combines several patriarchal tenets to emphasize that women are only valuable when they are attractive, worthy of impregnating, and docile.

In 1913, the National Women's Party organized an enormous march to coincide with the inauguration of President Woodrow Wilson. Organizers enlisted five thousand women for the parade. They stood on floats that depicted Bible scenes, the Red Cross, schools, and courtrooms. The displays used a feminine approach that risked trivializing the movement, but it worked: News organizations praised the parade for its visual splendor. The *Washington Post*, for example, described it as "Miles of Fluttering Femininity Present Entrancing Suffrage Appeal."[39] Violence, however, gave the parade the most headlines after hundreds of men attacked the women who were marching. Officers on horseback had to break up the melee. The news coverage of the attack and resulting congressional hearings brought more positive attention to women's rights than the parade alone.[40] Still, women did not win the vote in 1913, nor did they in 1917, when they started a vigil outside the White House. As the months went on, newspapers labeled the picketers as "crazy women," unwomanly," and "shocking."[41] Nevertheless, they persisted.

THE NINETEENTH AMENDMENT

The last few years of the suffrage movement were marked by more intense nonviolent demonstrations. After increasingly brutal harassment by police, the White House picketers were arrested in 1917 and demanded to be treated as political prisoners. In keeping with the protest paradigm, when one set of protesters was sentenced to three days in jail, a *New York Times* antisuffrage editorial took a swipe at the movement's hunger strikers with the headline "Militants Get 3 Days; Lack Time to Starve."[42] Yet years of nonviolent protest made a difference. Under Alice Paul's leadership, suffragists were able to frame their cause as the moral high ground, especially as the United States had joined World War I to defend democracy. As the suffragists' picket framed it, the United States could hardly claim to defend democracy if it was not truly democratic at home. Finally, in 1918, President Wilson relented, not because he cared about women's rights, but because he was concerned that his party could not win the next election. He encouraged his allies in Congress to approve the amendment and send it to the states.[43] The Nineteenth Amendment to the US Constitution, which reads simply, "The right of citizens of the United States to vote shall not be denied or abridged by the United States or by any State on account of sex. Congress shall have power to enforce this article by appropriate legislation," was finally ratified in 1920.[44]

While there was much to celebrate, the Nineteenth Amendment's ratification was only a partial victory, as millions of women of color continued to be denied the right to vote in many parts of the United States. Full voting rights for women took many more decades. Black Americans living under Jim Crow had the legal right but still faced practical, often violent barriers to voting. Black Americans did not win full

Profile: Jovita Idár, Teacher, Activist, and Journalist (1885–1946)

Jovita Idár was a teacher, activist, and journalist in the border town of Laredo, Texas, who fought for suffrage and the rights of Mexican Americans in the early twentieth century. Her father was a newspaper publisher, and she grew up learning about journalism and social justice. She went to school to become a teacher and taught briefly after earning her certificate in 1903, but she resigned in frustration over segregation and the poor treatment of Mexican American children. Mexican Americans endured violent discrimination, even lynching, during this era in Texas. The Texas Rangers patrolled border communities and killed Mexican American men without due process or consequence. Idár started working for her father's newspaper, *La Crónica*, and worked on behalf of social justice on multiple fronts. In 1911, she and her family organized the First Mexican Congress to unify Mexicans across the border. She founded the *La Liga Feminil Mexicaista* (the League of Mexican Women), which promoted education for Mexican American students, and she went to Mexico to assist people who were injured during the Mexican Revolution.

Jovita Idár.
Courtesy of the University of Texas, San Antonio, Special Collections

Idár is most famous, though, for what she did when she returned to Texas and worked as a writer for the *El Progreso* newspaper. She wrote an editorial criticizing President Woodrow Wilson's decision to send American troops to the border, which caught attention from the US Army and the Texas Rangers. When the Rangers arrived, Idár, who was twenty-nine years old at the time, stood in the door and denied them entrance. They backed down but only until the next morning, when they returned to destroy the building and arrest those inside. Idár returned to *La Crónica*, taking over its management when her father died while continuing to work as a hospital volunteer and educator. Idár understood the connection between literacy and power and was known for saying, "When you educate a woman, you educate a family."

Sources: Kerri Lee Alexander, "Jovita Idár (1885–1946)," National Women's History Museum, 2019, https://www.womenshistory.org/education-resources/biographies/jovita-idar; Gabriella González, "Jovita Idár: The Ideological Origins of a Transnational Advocate for La Raza," in *Texas Women: Their Histories, Their Lives*, ed. Elizabeth Hayes Turner, Stephanie Cole, and Rebecca Sharpless (University of Georgia Press, 2015), 225–48; Doug J. Swanson, *Cult of Glory: The Bold and Brutal History of the Texas Rangers* (Penguin, 2021).

suffrage until 1965 with the Voting Rights Act. Asian people in the United States were often denied property rights and access to citizenship, complicating their rights to vote. Mabel Lee, an Asian American suffragist and the first Chinese woman to receive a PhD from Columbia University, could not even apply for citizenship until the United States rescinded the Chinese Exclusion Act in 1948.[45] Along with Hispanic Americans, Asian Americans benefited when Congress amended the voting rights act in 1975 to include language access.[46] Similarly, Native American women were not covered by the Nineteenth Amendment, so they did not achieve true suffrage until 1962.

The pattern was similar around the world. In Britain, women over thirty won the right to vote in 1918, but it took another ten years for women aged twenty-one to be able to vote, in parallel with male voting rights. Even though the Mexican Constitution established "universal suffrage" after that country's revolution in 1917, the right was only universal for men. Women won suffrage gradually in Mexico, first at the local, then eventually national levels, when they were able to vote in the presidential election in 1958.[47] Canada similarly gave women the right to vote at the federal level in 1918, but their access to the ballot box varied at the local level, and certain ethnic and racial groups were explicitly denied the right to vote until Canada's federal Bill of Rights Act in 1960.[48]

Summary

History often seems so abstract and far away. The pictures are black and white. The list of dates makes social change seem like something that just happens over time. But reading the often heart-pounding stories of real women from the progressive era brings their efforts to life. To learn what it's like to be force-fed, to imagine Jovita Idár standing in a doorway against a band of armed men, and to consider that Ida B. Wells continued her antilynching investigations even after her newspaper was burned to the ground allow us to imagine ourselves in these moments. Students who want media careers can take inspiration from these individuals, who often blended the roles of teacher, journalist, and advocate as they applied their writing skills to a cause.

Suffrage newspapers helped to define the movement and provide women their own public sphere, albeit one marked by intersectional divisions. Women's rights advocates developed tactics for attracting public attention to their cause, though they were often met with disdain and mockery in news. Suffrage newspapers rapidly went out of business after the Nineteenth Amendment was ratified, but other media grew rapidly in the early twentieth century, offering some inroads for female journalists. Mass media industrialized and started target marketing to deliver consuming audiences for brands. Magazines and the "women's pages" in major newspapers were designed to attract female readers, though the content often perpetuated stereotypes and the cult of domesticity. In practical terms, the Nineteenth Amendment did not guarantee the right to vote for all American women, as people of color continued to face voter suppression. Women continued to fight for better roles in news through the Great Depression and into World War II, and their experience laid the foundation for what's known as feminism's second wave.

- **Reflection:** How far would you go to advocate for your right to vote? What physical risks would you be willing or able to take?
- **Reflection:** What kinds of stories could inspire you to commit to years of investigative reporting like Ida Tarbell or Ida B. Wells?
- **Media Critique:** How are protests for civil rights framed in media today?
- **Media Critique:** How have digital media changed the inverted pyramid and other newswriting conventions?

CHAPTER 4

The Second Wave and Civic Equality

Getting the vote turned out to be only the start of equality for women. The next phase, known as the second wave, started almost immediately after the Nineteenth Amendment was ratified in 1920 but was energized during the Second World War. While men were called to military service, women rallied to nontraditional jobs associated with the fictional icon Rosie the Riveter, often manufacturing airplanes and weapons. But the war created opportunities in other fields, including journalism. Many women found they liked working outside the home, even in physically demanding jobs in factories or shipyards. After the war, however, most women were sent back home to allow returning soldiers to have those jobs. This shift in labor practices fueled frustrations over inequality in the workplace and in civic life and set the foundation for the women's liberation movement.

Key Concepts: The Second Wave, Objectification

Freelance writer Martha Weinman Lear coined the term *second wave* in 1968 in the *New York Times* to describe the next generation of activists, who called for new ways of talking about and therefore thinking about women as citizens and workers.[1] Just as the abolitionists and early suffragists created advocacy publications to create community, so did activists for women's liberation. Media and the way women were represented in news and entertainment constituted an important battlefield in the push for equal rights in civic life. Such issues as equal pay, equal opportunity, and access to birth control, which took the stage during this era, continue to reverberate in global politics today. The way journalists framed (and continue to frame) these issues affected the public's support of women's rights. As with the suffrage movement decades earlier, the second wave was not unified, and it has often been whitewashed in historic accounts.[2] Intersectional rifts between white women and women of color, straight women and queer women, and evangelical and progressive women divided the movement then and now.

Roots of the Second Wave

Feminists started agitating for women's economic rights shortly after the Nineteenth Amendment was ratified. They introduced an early version of the Equal Rights Amendment in 1923 that faltered.[3] Despite having the right to vote, women in the 1950s were effectively second-class citizens. More than 28 million women were in the labor force at the time (nearly one-fifth of all adults), yet most of them earned far less than the median income for working adults.[4] Even when they graduated with college degrees and entered the workforce, they were usually paid less and given fewer opportunities for leadership or advancement. They could not apply for loans or hold their own credit cards. Women were not allowed to make decisions about birth control without their husband's consent. Women had little recourse if they were in violent marriages, and it was generally legal for a man to rape his wife.[5] It was legal to fire a woman who got pregnant, post job descriptions for male or female applicants only, and pay women less.

Dramatic political and economic shifts inspired social change around the world. The notion that women were people, three-dimensional *people*, who deserved economic and political equality took root globally. Simone de Beauvoir, now recognized not only as a feminist writer but also as a philosopher, published one of the world's most important books on gender equity: *The Second Sex*. First released in French in 1949, the book reached English-speaking audiences in 1953.[6] Her assertion that "One is not born, but rather becomes a woman" addresses the way women were socialized to a diminished role in society. De Beauvoir introduces the idea of women as an "other" in a male-dominated society, and she contextualizes how women have historically been valued as mothers and wives but not as individuals. *The Second Sex* provided a catalyst for feminist thought and remains one of the most important works of its kind (chapter 1 includes a short excerpt from the book).[7]

The Second Sex gave voice to women's unhappiness in the years after World War II. The popular impression of the 1950s is built on the fictions of advertising and entertainment television, centering a white women as a happy homemaker who vacuumed in a dress, cooked every meal, and doted on her family full time by purchasing all the right products. Of course, this was not the norm for everyone. Women of color, queer women, professional women, and happily single women are largely erased from these nostalgic marketing fantasies. Indeed, any woman who chafed under the expectations that they should be satisfied with a life of full-time domestic service to others is absent from these gauzy impressions of the era. Yet enough real women were unhappy in this patriarchal/consumerist role that psychologist Betty Friedan wrote a book about them: *The Feminine Mystique*, first published in 1963.[8] Friedan calls this quiet, simmering dissatisfaction the "problem that has no name." *The Feminine Mystique* was a best-seller that quickly sold one million copies.

The nameless problem Friedan identifies grew in part from the abrupt way women were laid off from their jobs in manufacturing after World War II. Called to service to build airplanes and weapons systems, thousands of women took on full-time, well-paid jobs during the war, and some of them enjoyed it. At the peak of the war effort, 40 percent of key aircraft construction jobs were held by women. For Black women who were able to take these jobs, Rosie-the-Riveter opportunities meant more than money: They were a chance to do more than serve as domestic workers for white women.[9] During the war, half the people working for small newspapers were women.[10] Thousands of women worked as news photographers in war zones, while men were drafted into military service.[11] They, like those who worked in the munitions factories, were summarily let go when the war ended so that the returning soldiers could have jobs—and traditional societal roles could resume. Approximately 16 million women entered the workforce during the war, and while many of them had said they would return home when peace resumed, many also changed their minds over time. A columnist for the *Ladies Home Journal* puts it this way: "There is no example, as far as I know, in which a class or group of people who have once succeeded in expanding the area of their lives is ever persuaded again to restrict it."[12]

Another factor in women's simmering dissatisfaction grew out of the increased educational level for women in the United States. While they were still outnumbered on college campuses by about two to one, college enrollments for both men and women increased by 49 percent in the 1950s and soared in the 1960s by 120 percent. Returning soldiers (for the most part, white men) were able to take advantage of the GI Bill, which granted them access to college educations, and postwar economic expansion plus the baby boom filled college campuses around the United States. Women did not necessarily attend college with a lifetime career in mind, as the so-called MRS degree was not entirely a joke, and many women did not expect to work for a living upon graduation, at least not for very long. While white people gained the most economically, college enrollments for nonwhite women also rose during this period. In 1950, 5.6 percent of nonwhite women completed at least one year of college. In 1960, that number rose to 8 percent, and by 1970, 12 percent of Black women in the United States completed at least a year of college.[13] (The US Census did not start collecting data on Latina women until 1970.)

Around the world, international discussions of human rights included the rights of women. In Japan, the YWCA included feminism in its postwar reconciliation efforts.[14] International activists, many of them labor activists, advocated on behalf of women before the war in places like Switzerland and Sweden with the Pan-American Union and the League of Nations and saw their work come to fruition with the establishment of the United Nations Commission on the Status of Women in 1946.[15] In the United States, these discussions centered around women in the workforce. So when John F. Kennedy was elected president in 1960, labor organizers seized the moment and pushed for the establishment of what became the President's Commission on the Status of Women (PCSW) in 1961. Eleanor Roosevelt, the former First Lady who had championed human rights with the United Nations, agreed to head the effort. The final report from the PCSW disappointed many advocates, as it merely recommended *voluntary* equal opportunity regulations only for employers who had federal contracts. Nevertheless, it inspired numerous commissions around the country at the state level and jump-started conversations about working women and marital rights.[16] The very fact that the *American Women* report legitimized women in the workplace rankled many commentators who thought women should be homemakers.[17] It also advanced the conversation about women's economic rights, paving the way for the Equal Pay

Act, signed by Kennedy in 1963, and soon thereafter the establishment of the National Organization for Women (NOW).[18]

The *American Women* report coincided with a national battle over civil rights for people of color. President Lyndon Johnson supported and signed civil rights measures first proposed by Kennedy, some of the most significant legislation ever in the US. Interestingly, women were also added to the landmark 1964 Civil Rights Act at the last minute. Representative Howard Smith of Virginia proposed adding the word *sex* to the list of protected categories in a move that some observers thought was an attempt to kill the entire bill only two hours before the vote.[19] He seemed to troll feminists during the floor debate, even joking about whether the government could balance the population to help "spinsters" find husbands.[20] Debate on the floor echoed themes from the suffrage movement, with jokes about henpecked husbands and warnings about drafting women to the military.[21] Historians have noted that Smith had worked seriously with women's rights advocates, so his amendment may have been proposed in good faith. Sincere or not, the Civil Rights Act did pass with protections for women, and Johnson signed into law one of the most sweeping policy changes in history, prohibiting discrimination based on race, color, religion, sex, or national origin.[22] The Civil Rights Act was followed by the Voting Rights Act a year later and the Fair Housing Act in 1968. Together, these laws compelled major shifts in policy in public and private life, though real change came more slowly and was far more complicated.

If women's rights were in the shadow of racial civil rights in the 1960s, then they took the spotlight after the Civil Rights Act was passed. In 1970, Gloria Steinem, by then an influential political writer, published a call to action in *New York* magazine titled "After Black Power, Women's Liberation," and in that same year, literary scholar Kate Millett published *Sexual Politics*. Based on her PhD dissertation, Millett's book examines how patriarchy is reflected in literature's depictions of sex.[23] Her idea that sex is imbued with power relations and that women are harmed by this subjugation was groundbreaking and shocking at the time.[24] Millett was featured as a cover in *Time* magazine, launching women's liberation into the mainstream.[25] The pressure for legal protections based specifically on gender was on.

EQUAL RIGHTS AMENDMENT

The text of the Equal Rights Amendment (ERA) seems simple enough: "Equality of rights under the law shall not be denied or abridged by the United States or by any state on account of sex."[26] The text is slightly different than one first proposed by former suffragists in 1923, which read, "Men and women shall have equal rights throughout the United States and every place subject to its jurisdiction. Congress shall have power to enforce this article by appropriate legislation."[27] The Great Depression and World War II interrupted the movement, but as the second wave gained momentum, so did enthusiasm for a federal law that would guarantee equality to women.

The version *still* under consideration today was first introduced in 1971. It passed both houses, and Congress set a deadline for the necessary ratifications from

Profile: Gloria Steinem, Writer and Activist (1934–)

Gloria Steinem.
Courtesy of Creative Commons, Jewish Women's Archive

Gloria Steinem is a feminist leader who started as a journalist. She graduated from the all-women's Smith College in 1956 and became famous after publishing an undercover story about what it was like to work as a bunny in the Playboy Club in 1963; the work was not nearly as glamorous as the Playboy empire made it out to be.

In the 1960s, Steinem helped to create *New York* magazine and worked as a political columnist there. She published her first overtly feminist essay, "After Black Power, Women's Liberation" in *New York*, which won the Penney-Missouri Journalism Award in 1970. Steinem soon became a full-time activist and helped establish the National Women's Political Caucus with Bella Abzug, Betty Friedan, and Shirley Chisholm in 1971. She took the lead in starting *Ms. Magazine*, which became the movement's flagship publication, covering issues that other publications often ignored or framed through a white male perspective. Steinem has garnered considerable criticism over the years, not only for her strong feminist views, but also for, in the eyes of critics, being too glamorous in her public life. Steinem was successfully treated after a breast cancer diagnosis in 1986. After years of criticizing the institution of marriage, she herself married David Bale, the father of actor Christian Bale, in 2000. Bale died only three years later of brain cancer. Steinem continues to advocate for women's equality and told *Ms. Magazine*, "The idea of retiring is as foreign to me as the idea of hunting."

Sources: Gary L. Anderson and Kathryn G. Herr, eds., "Steinem, Gloria (1934–)," in *Encyclopedia of Activism and Social Justice*, vol. 3 (Sage, 2007), 1334–35; Rachel Chang, "Inside Gloria Steinem's Month as an Undercover Playboy Bunny," Biography, March 23, 2020, https://www.biography.com/news/gloria-steinem-undercover-playboy-bunny; Joyce Duncan, ed., "Gloria Steinem (1934–)," in *Shapers of the Great Debate on Women's Rights: A Biographical Dictionary*, 9 (Greenwood Press, 2008), 131–34; Kate Hodges, "I Know a Woman: Gloria Steinem's Pathway as a Feminist Pioneer," *Ms. Magazine*, March 9, 2018, https://msmagazine.com/2018/03/09/know-woman-gloria-steinems-pathway-feminist-pioneer/.

thirty-eight states. The amendment had wide support and was quickly ratified by twenty-two states.[28] During the 1970s and '80s, opponents suggested that the ERA would harm children and families, but it continued to gain ratifications and seemed unstoppable, until the rise of an opponent who embodied traditional femininity and motherhood.[29] Conservative attorney Phyllis Schlafly waged war against the ERA on grounds that the law would harm stay-at-home mothers, enable same-sex marriage, and require women to be drafted into the military.[30] A mother to six children, she was a formidable opponent to feminist agitation. Schlafly lived in contradiction; she effectively created her own political organization yet started many meetings by declaring herself submissive to her husband with her trademark opener, "I want to thank my husband, Fred, for letting me come here."[31] She was funny and dressed according to traditional expectations, and she effectively framed the ERA and its supporters as radical, disruptive, and intolerant. She played on the fears of women who embraced traditional values and stoked their resentment against women who rejected those values. During a 1973 debate with Betty Friedan, Schlafly appeared well coifed and charming and argued that American women were the luckiest on earth. Then, with her trademark charm, she made things personal with Friedan, who had just been through a divorce: "You simply cannot legislate universal sympathy for the middle-aged woman. . . . *You*, Mrs. Friedan, are the unhappiest woman I have ever met." Friedan responded angrily, "You are a traitor to your sex, an Aunt Tom . . . and you are a witch. God, I'd like to burn you at the stake!"[32] The moment cemented the stereotype of feminists as angry, bitter, and lonely women, and while it hardly could be blamed for ERA's loss, it captured the essence of the conflict. Over time, some states rescinded their ratification votes, and even though the deadline was extended, the amendment was effectively defeated.

Some scholars argue that the ERA would not have made as dramatic a difference as its supporters had hoped. Support faltered after the 1973 Supreme Court ruling of *Roe v. Wade*, which confirmed women's constitutional rights to an abortion, dividing many women along religious lines (*Roe v. Wade* was overturned in 2022).[33] Opponents of the ERA suggested that other existing legislation, such as the Equal Pay Act, negated the need for a constitutional amendment. Even without a constitutional guarantee, women and queer people have enlisted the courts to help them join the military (even for combat roles), enable same-sex marriage, and achieve pay equity. Constitutional scholars still debate whether the ERA might cause harm to women by treating them exactly the same as men, by drafting them or denying them child support. Others have suggested that the Fourteenth Amendment does enough to guarantee fair treatment for all people.[34] In other words, some legal scholars argue, the impact of an Equal Rights Amendment would be complicated and probably not all that dramatic.

Even so, advocates continue to try to encode the ERA into law. The deadline set by Congress in the 1970s was not legally required, and in 2021, more than two hundred congressional representatives proposed eliminating the deadline.[35] Three states (Nevada, Illinois, and Virginia) ratified the ERA, bringing the tally back to the necessary thirty-eight, and now the battle over ratification is a matter of congressional action and interpretations from various court cases.[36]

News and the Second Wave

Opportunities for women in news grew during the latter part of the twentieth century, but newsroom leaders still tended to be white men, and the industry was largely homophobic. Women in news encountered discrimination and harassment and were often denied leadership roles. Without diverse perspectives in news organizations, coverage was marked by stereotypes and patriarchal thinking. The very practices of journalism, such as the beat system, sourcing, and narrative framing, also shaped coverage in ways that disadvantaged second-wave activists.

COVERING THE SECOND WAVE

Chapter 1 introduces the concept of framing as the *way* news presents reality. Media coverage of the second wave made a difference in the way it was understood. Infantilization, a concept introduced in chapter 2, is the way women have been traditionally framed as children in public discourse: sweet and acceptable when they know their place or as ungrateful brats when they dare to consider themselves equal to men. The protest paradigm, discussed in chapter 3, is the way social movements are treated as problematic deviants in news, and as with the suffrage movement, the second wave was framed as agitating the norm. Newsrooms at the time were dominated by white men, who chose what to cover and how to cover it. So-called women's libbers were caricatured as man haters. Conventional news coverage was constructed through the perspective of the men in charge of newsrooms, who often applied negative stereotypes to activists. News values, especially those that favored sensationalist headlines and conflict, often presented the women's movement in negative ways. Even work routines, such as reporter schedules, got in the way of fair and fully dimensional coverage. For instance, as Tuchman found in her study of big-city newspaper journalists, women's rights meetings often took place in the evenings in private homes, outside the typical reporter's beat in terms of time and location.[37]

When women were covered in media, they were often presented in stereotypical ways. Visual representations are particularly troublesome because images are more memorable and evoke more emotion than words do.[38] Female political leaders especially have been subjected to stereotypical depictions in political cartoons and in the way they're photographed. Women are also often **objectified**: that is, visually presented as *things* to be used to please others, usually straight men. Objectification is so much a part of patriarchal expectations that women often behave in ways to meet this expectation. In his wide-ranging art-criticism series and book *Ways of Seeing*, John Berger exposes how women have been objectified for millennia in art, represented as knowingly being seen by men. He found a pattern in the way women were portrayed in art over time, looking over their shoulders at an offstage viewer, not doing much other than posing for the pleasure of another: that is, a man.[39] Reflecting the stereotypes described in chapter 1, Berger notes that historic art tends to represent men as spectators.

Objectification took on even more significance in the mass media age. Advertising used images of women, often increasingly sexualized images of women, to sell products. During the second wave, *Ms. Magazine*'s "No Comment" page featured some of the worst: women posed as tables or other objects; jokes about domestic violence; sexually provocative images used to sell everything from cars to cigarettes to fast food.[40] Research using **quantitative content analysis**, which counts the incidents of certain types of coverage, has found that men and women are depicted in patterned ways in advertisements. Women are often posed to align with stereotypes, whether with a tilt of their heads, using their hands to touch another part of their bodies, or looking dreamily into the distance.[41] The beauty standard was decidedly white and valued very thin, blond women with narrow noses and straight hair. Feminists, however, were depicted as decidedly unsexy. Critics obsessed over women who didn't shave their armpits or wear makeup or who dressed for comfort instead of seduction. Journalists Lucianne Goldberg and Jeannie Sakol refer to women's rights activists as the "girls with the hairy armpits" in their book *Purr, Baby, Purr*, which encourages women to enjoy their traditional roles.[42] The end point of objectification is the expectation that women must please the eye of men in a very particular way—otherwise, what is their value?

The coverage of a protest of the Miss America Pageant in Atlantic City in 1968 exemplifies the way mainstream media framed feminists as disruptive, childish, and unattractive. Protesters convened on the Atlantic City Boardwalk to decry the pageant's objectification of women and the constraints of beauty expectations. In an act of visual activism, the women tossed cosmetics, bras, and similar objects into a burning trash can. *New York Post* reporter Lindsy Van Gelder equated bra burning with the draft-card burning of that era's antiwar protests, and the trope took hold, even though bra burning was rare and unrelated to the primary concerns of the feminist movement at that time: equal pay, workplace respect, and reproductive rights.[43] Popular humor columnist Art Buchwald was among those who turned the event into a joke.[44]

Bra burners became synonymous with *feminists*—a term that itself invited scorn. Women who attended the Atlantic City protest have since explained that the protest was not specifically about bras, and there's even some confusion about whether the trash can had a fire in it. Researcher

Women protesting what they called oppressive beauty standards during the 1968 Miss America Pageant in Atlantic City by tossing items, including lingerie, into a trash can.
Courtesy of Associated Press

Excerpt: "The Bra Burners"

I was flabbergasted last weekend to read that about 100 women had picketed the Miss America pageant in Atlantic City against "ludicrous beauty standards that had enslaved the American woman." Carrying signs deploring the "degrading, mindless boob-girlie system," the pickets also set up ashcans in which they threw girdles, lipstick, hair curlers, false eyelashes and wigs.

The final and most tragic part of the protest took place when several of the women publicly burned their brassieres.

As one who has always been on the side of protesters, I regret to say that I believe this demonstration in Atlantic City has gone too far. It is one thing to protest against a system or an institution, but it [sic] another to take the law into your own hands and burn your bra.

By demanding that women do away with all beauty aids, including false eyelashes, wigs, hair tints, girdles and the like, so they will be on an equal footing with men, these well-meaning but misled females were trying to destroy everything this country holds dear.

Source: Art Buchwald, "The Bra Burners," New York Post, September 12, 1968.

W. Joseph Campbell, whose book Getting It Wrong fact-checks historic news stories, located a journalist who witnessed the event and who stated for the record that there was indeed a fire in the trash can that day.[45] Campbell argues that nuance was lost once national commentators weighed in on women's rights, and the story provides a perfect illustration of the problems with second-wave coverage. Women are objectified for their breasts, so calling attention to bras (and the possibility of nipples showing through a shirt) was titillating for the news audience—a form of pre-internet click bait. The protest paradigm framed the women who participated in the protest as aberrant and deviant for setting a fire. The stereotype of the humorless suffragette appears here, too, because they criticized the Miss America contest, something male reporters and photojournalists frankly enjoyed covering. The event inspired tropes of shame (because breasts!) and mockery (these women are crazy!) and over time minimized the serious point the protesters had hoped to make about the constrictions of modern femininity.

Beyond Atlantic City, coverage of the women's movement in the 1970s was marked by condescension, dismissal, and even laughter as female leaders were caricatured much as the suffragists were at the start of the 1900s.[46] Men cast themselves as hapless victims of an ideological onslaught. News accounts framed the women's movement as aberrant and feminists as man haters. For example, Time magazine used a stylized, unsmiling portrait of Kate Millett in its cover story on feminism, even though she had specifically requested to not be featured as the face of the movement and had encouraged the magazine to use an image of multitudes of women for the cover.[47] Even the first line of the story sets up the women's movement as a problem: "These are the times that try men's souls, and they are likely to get much worse before they get better." It continues, "[T]he din is in earnest, echoing from the streets where pickets gather, the bars where women once were barred, and even connubial beds, where ideology can intrude at the unconscious drop of a male chauvinist epithet."[48] A few months later, Time published a story about Millett's bisexuality, a fact that would inspire yawns today but at the time discredited Millett. Just as during the suffrage movement, straight white men not only

Kate Millett was unhappy with the way she was portrayed on the August 1970 cover of *Time* magazine. She had suggested that the feminist movement would be better illustrated with an image that included many women.
Courtesy of *Time* Magazine

resisted the basic tenets of gender rights, but they also controlled how the movement was covered, whether with objectification, infantilization, or using a both-sides narrative that emphasized differences between activists.

Another impediment to fair coverage of the ERA and women's rights in mainstream news was the fact that the movement lacked a singular voice or central leadership. Without "officials" to quote, reporters were unable to rely on their usual news-gathering processes. Mainstream news reporters, who were predominantly male (and often sexist), were ill prepared to cover a movement organized outside their usual beats.[49] Women of color were largely invisible in coverage of second-wave feminism, as reporters tended to quote the mostly white leaders of such key national groups such as NOW. Feminist leaders pushed back against such stereotypical and dehumanizing coverage during the second wave. They criticized journalists who asked female political candidates about childcare or cookie recipes instead of focusing on campaign issues. Feminist publications decried the way women and their concerns were framed in news as trivial, illegitimate, even childish. Yet their concerns were drowned out in a media system controlled by straight white men. Even when they complained, their complaints were framed as man-hating whining.

THE CAT-FIGHT TROPE

Media researcher Susan Douglas applies the term *cat fight* to describe the way mainstream media covered (and still covers) gender rights activism.[50] This frame dominated during the effort to pass the Equal Rights Amendment and is particularly pernicious for the way it both dehumanizes and infantilizes women. It echoes the cult of true women for the way it sorts women into those who should be heard and those who should be silenced. Douglas argues that news coverage demonized feminists as abnormal, focused on divisions within the movement, and tended to ignore men's opposition to the ERA.[51] Narratives that use the cat-fight frame focused on individual leaders of the feminist movement, pitting them against one another in ways that proffered legitimacy to some and caricaturing others as grotesque—older or unattractive women who ought not take the public stage—as with *Time's* treatment of Millett. The young and attractive Gloria Steinem was compared with Betty Friedan, the founder of NOW, who was marginalized because of her age and appearance. A *New York Times Magazine* article suggests that Friedan would "happily have traded 30 points on the IQ scale for a modicum of good looks and popularity."[52] Any woman who did not fit expectations of attractiveness was fair game. Douglas notes that *Time* magazine used words and phrases like *Bellicose Abzug*, *rhinoceros*, and *sumo liberal* to describe Bella Abzug, concluding, "[I]f a woman wasn't attractive to men then she could not be a leader of women."[53] The cat-fight frame emphasized conflict, an element in news narratives generally but personalized in coverage of the ERA. Once the Eagle Forum's Phyllis Schlafly started her campaign, the battle over women's rights could be covered not as a social problem that affects everyone or a moral matter of human rights but as a nasty tiff between a few famous women that more serious citizens (i.e., men) could ignore.

Marginalized Waves

Second-wave feminism appeared in mainstream media as a largely straight, white, middle-class phenomenon, in part because of the way journalists tended to focus on such personalities as Betty Friedan, Gloria Steinem, and Phyllis Schlafly. Women of color often worked double duty on behalf of feminism and racial equality. As sociologist Benita Roth puts it, "[T]he second wave has to be understood as a *group* of feminisms," organized separately and often along racial ethnic lines.[54] Queer women were marginalized for their feared impact on feminism's image.[55] Sisterhood was not always recognized across race and sexuality and was largely ignored in mainstream news coverage. Alternative media gave voice to women on the margins, many of whom continue to wage battle with what's come to be known as white feminism.[56]

BLACK FEMINISTS

Black feminists were often inspired to organize along gendered lines because of discrimination within the civil rights movement. Black women did not always join white feminist organizations, on grounds that the white women's groups were often insensitive to the economic issues faced by Black women. Others sensed that members of the mainstream groups were personally racist, and still others sensed that their energies were better placed on behalf of Black people specifically—exemplifying the quandaries of intersectional oppression.[57] Two early Black feminist groups included the Black Women's Liberation Group (BWLG) and the Third World Women's Alliance (TWWA). Frances Beal, who was also a member of one of the most important Black civil rights organizations, the Student Non-Violent Coordinating Committee (SNCC), was one of the founders of the TWWA and published one of the founding documents of Black feminism in 1970, "Double Jeopardy: To Be Black and Female." She condemned the oppression *by* Black men that rendered a typical Black woman as the "slave of a slave" and the widespread nonconsensual sterilization of Black women, strict laws against abortion that were more likely to affect racial minorities, and the economic exploitation of Black women—topics often ignored by white feminist groups.[58] Unlike many white feminist groups, which often conceived of male chauvinism as *the* problem in need of repair, Black feminists organized on multiple fronts: race, gender, and *class*. Sexuality and the fight against heterosexism was not always articulated in these early efforts but became a more common inclusion of oppressions to be fought in the early '70s.[59]

One of the challenges for Black feminists came from within the civil rights movement itself. Black men were (and still are) stereotyped as absent or neglectful fathers, a notion that was popularized by the1965 Moynihan Report, a problematic sociological report that suggests Black people constitute a culturally inferior matriarchy. Assistant Secretary of Labor Daniel Patrick Moynihan, who worked in the Johnson administration but was not a social scientist, initiated the report to garner support for policies that would assist Black families economically.[60] The report suggests that Black families were poor because they were more likely to be led by women. Conservatives have interpreted this finding to mean that poverty is instilled in Black culture, while liberals believe it blames the victim and fails to account for other sociological factors, such as educational opportunities, wage discrimination, or inequality in the criminal justice system.[61] The report made an enormous impact in its time, one that had a gendered dimension, inspiring policy makers to argue that Black men—but not women—needed better economic opportunities. Many Black men pushed even harder to maintain the ideal of a traditional, patriarchal, nuclear family.[62]

CHICANA FEMINISTS

Chicana feminism grew out of the Chicano movement of the 1960s in recognition of the unique interests and oppressions faced by Latinas.[63] As noted in chapter 3, Chicana women were involved in the suffrage movement early in the 1900s. The Chicano movement gained power in the 1960s, as leaders like Cesar Chavez and Dolores Huerta organized on behalf of Hispanic communities, particularly laborers who worked in agriculture in California and the American Southwest. A group of students from California State University, Long Beach, helped organize on behalf of Chicana women and started publishing *Hijas de Cuauhtémoc* in 1971, giving voice and structure to their activism.[64] Organizers were angry that they were being sexually harassed by men within the Chicano movement and often were asked to cook or work as secretaries for the cause. The newspaper only published three issues but created helped to coalesce the cause.[65] That same year, more than five hundred women gathered in Houston for La Conferencia de Mujeres por la Raza, the first conference of its kind for Latina women, with workshops on issues common with mainstream feminism, such as economic and marital rights, but also on concerns specific to Hispanic women, such as the role of the Catholic Church in the oppression of women. The conference was plagued with organizational problems over housing and registration fees but nevertheless gave voice to Hispanic women, even though many of those attending did not consider themselves to be feminists.[66]

FEMINISM AND THE LGBTQ+ COMMUNITY

Queer people had started organizing for the sake of safety and support in the 1950s, but the gay rights movement was largely uncovered in mainstream media until the Stonewall riots in 1969. By then, lesbians had achieved visibility in the women's movement but were not necessarily welcomed. Betty Friedan famously called them the "lavender menace" in an interview with the *New York Times Magazine*, complaining that queer women complicated her organization's messaging.[67] Angry over being marginalized by women who should be allies, a group of lesbians took hold of the phrase and used it in protest, complete with matching lavender T-shirts, at the second Congress to Unite Women in 1970.[68] Some NOW members were overtly hostile to lesbians in the early '70s, but eventually the organization welcomed queer women and added the defense of lesbian parents' rights to its advocacy agenda.[69]

Profile: Dolores Huerta, Civil Rights Leader (1930-)

Dolores Huerta.
Courtesy of Creative Commons, US Department of
Labor

Dolores Huerta is a civil rights leader who has organized on behalf of Latino/a and Hispanic people for most of her life. Huerta was one of the leaders of the 1960s Chicano/a movement, working alongside Cesar Chavez to bring attention to the inhumane conditions endured by migrant workers. She was so committed to helping workers that some farm workers affectionally nicknamed her Dolores "Huelga"—the Spanish word for *strike*. Born in 1930 in New Mexico, she was inspired in her youth by her father's union organizing. She worked as a teacher after college but was inspired to organize for economic justice when she saw how many of her young students came to school hungry. She founded the Agricultural Workers Association in California to assist with voter-registration drives and improve conditions for poor neighborhoods. She eventually joined forces with Chavez, and together they founded the National Farm Workers Association. Sexism, including the chauvinism within the Chicano rights movement, compelled Huerta to advocate not only for the rights of Latino/a people but also for women in that community, an intersectional effort even before that word was coined. In 2012, President Barack Obama awarded her the Presidential Medal of Freedom, the highest civilian award in the United States. She is the mother of eleven children and remains politically active.

Source: Roger Bruns, ed., "Dolores Huerta," in *Icons of Latino America: Latino Contributions to American Culture*, vol. 1 (Greenwood Press, 2008), 261–83; Dolores Huerta Foundation, "Dolores Huerta," accessed July 18, 2021, https://doloreshuerta.org/doloreshuerta/.

As with the feminisms based in race and ethnicity, queer women's feminism operated both independently and in concert with mainstream feminism. For example, the Daughters of Bilitis, one of the early core organizations devoted to lesbian rights, started in 1955 in San Francisco. Its publication, the *Ladder*, was instrumental in shaping the language of the movement, giving queer women a common lexicon for their lives and their activism. As the second wave progressed, members of the Daughters of Bilitis were divided on how and whether to participate in mainstream feminist activism.[70] As lesbians started to politicize and form their own identity as a discrete entity, they developed more magazines, books, and art to articulate their interests. By 1975, more than fifty lesbian publications circulated, highlighting the specific concerns of the community while pushing back against popular stereotypes.[71] Mainstream media, however, continued to "demonize" lesbians, framing them as a problematic, unattractive, man-hating group that made feminism unpalatable to the public and bound to fail.[72]

Third-Wave, Postmodern Feminism

Third-wave feminism pushes back against some of the tenets of the liberal ideas from the 1970s. It challenges the domination of white women in the second wave and calls for feminism to more fully account for inequities based on race, class, and sexuality.[73] Writer and activist Rebecca Walker coined the term when she wrote to *Ms. Magazine* in 1992. Her letter responds to the confirmation hearings for would-be Supreme Court Justice Clarence Thomas, wherein one of his former employees at the US Equal Employment Opportunity Commission, Anita Hill, accused him of sexual harassment. Hill's testimony was remarkable for its detailed accounts of crude behavior and vulgar comments. The all-white and all-male judiciary committee pushed back with disbelief, and Hill's character was publicly maligned. The backlash, hate mail, and death threats followed her for years.[74] Hill's case angered many women, including Walker.[75] "I am the third wave," she declared in her rage-driven essay. "I intend to fight back. I have uncovered and unleashed more repressed anger than I thought possible. For the umpteenth time in my 22 years, I have been radicalized, politicized, shaken awake."[76]

With many legal and financial rights in place, third-wave feminists often challenge sexuality more generally. Third-wave feminism might overlap with postmodern feminism and question the notion of gender entirely, or it might advocate for girly culture. Second-wave feminists, for instance, rejected the constraints of uncomfortable lingerie, false eyelashes, and dyed hair as impositions intended to please men. But girly or femme culture argues that these marks of femininity have their own value and should be celebrated.[77]

Summary

Second-wave feminism in the 1970s represented a peak of activism that started decades earlier, in the years following World War II. Women's liberation was one of many strands of civil rights struggles that boiled over in the 1960s. The fight for gender rights took place both in media representations and within media organizations, as marginalized people fought for better representation in newsrooms. Second-wave feminism advanced the rights of women beyond the vote but fell short of achieving the constitutional right to equality in the United States. Coverage of feminism during the second wave often stressed rifts between women, using a cat-fight frame, or mocked women, accusing them of trying to be men.

Even though the ERA did not become law, women have continued to push for opportunities at work, school, and politics. The second wave was not only an American phenomenon: Women around the world have pushed for equal standing in civic life and have made progress. France, for instance, legalized contraception and abortion in 1975.[78] Japan established its national women's education center for the study of gender in 1978.[79] Protests and organized political action in India that started in the '70s led to a change in its rape laws in 1982.[80] Yet while gender rights have improved in many parts of the world, some have been lost in the wake of wars and revolution. Around the globe, women continue to struggle for essential human rights, such as access to an education; the right to own property; the right to choose how, whether, and when to marry; and the right to control their own reproductive health. The promises of the second wave have yet to be kept.

- **Reflection:** Have members of your family discussed feminism and its impact on their lives at home or work?
- **Media Critique:** Have you seen a woman represented in media in a nontraditional or feminist role? How would you describe the portrayal?
- **Media Critique:** Have you noticed the cat-fight frame in current news or entertainment? Why might that frame persist?

CHAPTER 5

Gender in Political News

This chapter describes how journalists have covered female and queer political leaders over time. Stereotypes remain central to the way women and queer politicians are represented. The chapter also introduces the rhetorical concept of the double binds, which frame female and queer candidates in such a way that they cannot win in public life.

Key Concepts: Double Binds, Reversibility

During the 2020 COVID-19 pandemic, New Zealand stood out for its response to the deadly virus. The island nation in the Pacific restricted travel; instituted lockdowns; and provided fast, widespread testing, leading to one of the world's lowest death rates for the pandemic.[1] Prime Minister Jacinda Ardern, age thirty-nine at the time, was highly praised for her management of New Zealand's response. She was one of several female world leaders who kept their county's death rate low during 2020, prompting the *New York Times* to ask, "Why Are Women-Led Nations Doing Better with Covid-19?"[2] Why indeed? And what to make of the fact that within the United States, this gendered effect disappeared state to state, as a governor's political party, not their gender, better predicted case and death rates.[3]

Was this because of the stereotype that women are more nurturing and caring? No. Public health experts theorized that a female executive signals a more diverse leadership team, which in turn makes room for multiple points of view for important decision making and reduces group think.[4] Yet while mixed groups have been found to be more effective and women have proven themselves as national leaders, men continue to dominate politics worldwide. Of the 193 UN member states, only 22 are led by women, only 13 have a cabinet with gender balance, and only 3 have balanced legislatures.[5] As of 2022, a record year for women in elected office, the United States has a female vice president, Kamala Harris, but has never had a female president, and the country does not have legislative equality. The US Senate had 24 women (out of 100), and women held 123 seats, about 28 percent, in the House of Representatives.[6] Nine states had female governors in 2022. More than a century after women were granted the right to vote, they remain marginalized in democratic life. Even though 2022 set records for American women in elective office, they have not achieved parity. Women of color, queer people, disabled people, and young people are marginalized even more. There were no Black women in the US Senate in 2022, though there were twenty-six in the House (roughly proportional to the US population). None of the nation's nine female governors in 2022 were Black, and only one was Latina.[7]

Underrepresentation in political life represents not only a lack of opportunity for female leaders but also a harm to the population at large. As the research explaining New Zealand's pandemic success shows, diverse groups make better decisions. It's not that women are nicer, warmer, or more nurturing, but having women in the room where decisions are made improves the process—and better represents the voting public. If this is the case, then why aren't there more women in charge? Why has the United States not elected a female president? The answer is complicated, as you would expect, and involves politics and media.

Running for Office

In 2016, Hillary Clinton lost the presidential election to Donald Trump in spite of winning the popular vote by a wide margin: 2.9 million.[8] The campaign was historic for many reasons, and its gendered dimensions went far beyond the fact that a woman was in the race. Donald Trump ran on patriarchal rhetoric and appealed to men and women who held a traditional view of America. Clinton's candidacy was complicated by the fact that she is a former First Lady, and political news coverage of her over time often evoked stereotypes, if not outright misogyny. Her 1996 speech to the United Nations World Conference on Women established her as a feminist leader.[9] Many other industrialized nations have had female executives: Great Britain was led by Margaret Thatcher, and Angela Merkel was the German prime minister, but Clinton's campaign was the closest the United States has come to having a female leader.

Clinton was not the first woman to run for president in the United States. That distinction goes to suffragist Victoria Woodhull, who asked Frederick Douglass to be her running mate.[10] Other women have made primary bids with major parties over time, including Republican Margaret Chase Smith, who in 1964 was the first woman to have her name put up for nomination at major party's convention. Shirley Chisholm, the first African American women to serve in Congress, was the first Black woman to wage a campaign on a major ticket in 1972. She lost the Democratic primary to George McGovern.[11]

Stereotypes play a role in the way voters assess candidates, presenting an uphill challenge for women running for office.[12] Recall that the primary gender stereotypes for men are that they are strong and capable, traits associated with leadership, while women are expected to be warm and nurturing. Research suggests that stereotypes are not the only thing voters consider and that partisanship might matter more, but stereotypes remain a factor, especially when any candidate, male or female, appears to contradict stereotypical expectations. It is not necessarily a disadvantage to be a woman running for public office, but it is difficult to run against sexist standards. Study after study has found that

Excerpt: "Women's Rights Are Human Rights"

United Nations Fourth World Conference on Women, 1996.

If there is one message that echoes forth from this conference, it is that human rights are women's rights—and women's rights are human rights. Let us not forget that among those rights are the right to speak freely—and the right to be heard. Women must enjoy the right to participate fully in the social and political lives of their countries if we want freedom and democracy to thrive and endure. Let me be clear. Freedom means the right of people to assemble, organize, and debate openly. It means respecting the views of those who may disagree with the views of their governments. It means not taking citizens away from their loved ones and jailing them, mistreating them, or denying them their freedom or dignity because of the peaceful expression of their ideas and opinions. Now it is time to act on behalf of women everywhere. If we take bold steps to better the lives of women, we will be taking bold steps to better the lives of children and families too. As long as discrimination and inequities remain so commonplace around the world—as long as girls and women are valued less, fed less, fed last, overworked, underpaid, not schooled and subjected to violence in and out of their homes—the potential of the human family to create a peaceful, prosperous world will not be realized.

Source: Hillary Clinton, "Women's Rights Are Human Rights" (Plenary Session, United Nations Fourth World Conference on Women, Beijing, China, September 5, 1996).

female politicians are covered for their personal, stereotypical traits, such as family and appearance, more than men.[13] To be taken seriously, female candidates must walk a very fine line between expectations that they act feminine while being strong leaders. Think about Kamala Harris having to say, "Mr. Vice President, I am speaking," instead of just shouting over him as a man would. Female politicians often face these no-win situations, or what political rhetorician Kathleen Hall Jamieson calls a **double bind**.[14]

Double binds describe the way that women are talked about and framed in media and in everyday conversation. They are binds because media are critical of women while offering no way for women to win. In news, these very specific types of frames punish women who wish to lead because they force them to stay within the bounds of the expected stereotypical behavior, which then prevents them from excelling as strong leaders. For instance, many women have heard the admonishment, "Don't be shrill." The word *shrill* is rarely ascribed to a male leader; only women who speak out are shrill because women are not supposed to angrily voice their opinions. The same goes for the way women are described as bossy, while men are thought to be strong managers. Double binds encourage women to remain subordinate and preside over the private sphere and not the public sphere.

Jamieson identifies five types of double binds that are used to label female leaders:

1. womb-brain
2. equal-different
3. silence-shame
4. young-old
5. femininity-competence[15]

The womb-brain double bind is the expectation that women cannot be good leaders and good mothers, as though running a company (or a country) makes it impossible to raise children. Women running for office are still questioned about whether they can raise their family while campaigning. Yet they are judged poorly if they are *not* mothers. Success in public life, it seems, requires female politicians not only to have families but also to have a very specific type of heterosexual, nuclear family and to talk about it. Men are simply assumed to be good fathers.[16]

The equal-different conundrum suggests that women want to be men or that men are going to have to be women if women achieve equality in the workplace. Recall the way Amelia Bloomer was mocked for simply suggesting women would be more comfortable in a knee-length skirt over trousers; the very idea of a woman wearing the pants in the family was scandalous. During the second wave, critics suggested that feminists wanted to *be* men, even replace them (it's true some lesbian organizations did argue that men were unnecessary for happiness). Stereotypes and images of women running for public office often depict them in mannish or unattractive ways, as if to illustrate their "unnatural" ambition.[17]

The silence-shame double bind is particularly difficult for women who have been sexually assaulted or for women who need to talk about things like domestic violence because if women are supposed to be quiet and obey the cult of true womanhood, then they shouldn't talk about the fact that they've even had sex, let alone been raped. This double bind makes it hard for women to come forward when they've been assaulted and criticizes them as being sluts for having been assaulted. The silence-shame double bind has deep roots in Western culture's religious traditions, which have frequently regulated women's sexuality.

The young-old double bind is particularly salient for women in TV news, as on-air journalists are expected to look young but are judged as naïve or unintelligent for their youthfulness. You can't possibly be a serious newscaster if you look girlish, but women in TV news lose their contracts when they start to look older. Men, though, are considered to be more authoritative with a touch of gray in their hair.[18] This also happens in politics and business, where women who look young are not taken seriously.

Relatedly, the fifth femininity-competence double bind suggests that women who are pretty are incapable. Alexandria Ocasio-Cortez, the Democratic representative from New York City, often referred to as AOC, has been subjected to both these binds by her critics. She's been slammed as a youthful upstart, obsessed with fashion, who cannot possibly know what she's doing, even though she has strong academic credentials and did so well in high school science that astronomers named an asteroid after her.[19] After the 2021 insurrection riot at the US Capitol, she also faced the silence-shame double bind for disclosing that, having experienced a sexual assault, her terror was intensified during the events of January 6.[20]

While double binds may be a matter of rhetoric, they have real consequences for women in public life. Throughout history, women who step out of their stereotypical expectations have faced social sanctions, violence, even murder. In colonial America, the silence-shame double bind was used to keep women in their place by calling any woman who spoke up about assault or abuse a witch. Women who reject constricting stereotypes have been called heretics, hysterics, or whores. These names specify a

Profile: Kathleen Hall Jamieson, Rhetorician (1946–)

Kathleen Hall Jamieson.
Photo by Kyle Cassidy. Courtesy of the University of Pennsylvania

Kathleen Hall Jamieson is a professor at the University of Pennsylvania's Annenberg School for Communication and director of the Annenberg Public Policy Center known primarily for her research on political rhetoric, with significant achievements in science communication and gendered rhetoric. She is a former dean of the Annenberg School and cofounded Fact-Check.org in 2003. Her 1995 book, *Beyond the Double Bind: Women and Leadership*, summarizes the catch-22 women in power face as they are represented in media. In 2020, Jamieson was awarded the National Academy of Sciences Public Welfare Medal, that group's most prestigious award, for her efforts to support the nonpartisan, factual public communication concerning complex scientific issues. She argues that women can resist oppression by repurposing language to dismiss these double binds, as they have done for centuries:

> A more inclusive view of the history of women shows them surmounting, sometimes one by one, a series of double binds whose roots are deeply embedded in the past. Women who unmasked one dilemma faced the next and challenged it, bumped into a third and pirouetted around it, confronted another, and denied it its power. In the process they enlarged the scope of science, changed laws, altered behaviors, and changed the political complexion of this country.

While she speaks here of the American context, the linguistic battle she describes is a significant force in the gender rights movement worldwide. Jamieson is not a journalist, but her rhetorical scholarship reveals the way language in news can advance social change. Naming a problem allows it to be solved; reframing a situation inspires a new perspective; reclaiming the right to speak demands visibility. These are examples of the way words, the ultimate journalistic tool, language, can advance the cause of human rights.

Sources: Annenberg School for Communication, "Kathleen Hall Jamieson, Ph.D.," University of Pennsylvania, accessed November 13, 2021, https://www.asc.upenn.edu/people/faculty/kathleen-hall-jamieson-phd; Kathleen Hall Jamieson, *Beyond the Double Bind: Women and Leadership* (Oxford University Press, 1995), 21.

nonrational genesis for female speech (i.e., a woman speaking out must not be rational); she's shrill and should be ignored or, worse, forcibly silenced.

Women who want to lead are punished rhetorically for not knowing "their place." As long as women are compliant, do their best to smile and to be pretty, and are willing and happy to be mothers, they can escape these double-bind criticisms. Running for office is a sure way to invoke the double binds, as female candidates are not smart enough if they're pretty. If they are stylish, then they are rumored to have slept their way to the top. If they are leaders of an organization, then they must be horrible mothers because they are somehow neglecting their children.

Political Reporting

Women gained a foothold into political reporting in the 1920s when the Associated Press decided it needed to modernize its approach to news. It hired several women to work in Washington, DC, and even though these four women were largely relegated to covering the wives of politicians and the social scene, they cultivated important sources (like First Lady Eleanor Roosevelt) and garnered significant exclusives. Still, they were in the slim minority: Only about 1 percent of journalists working for the AP during this era were women.[21] When Ruby Black, one of the first women to report from the White House, was interviewed on the radio about her career in 1931, she noted that sexism from other journalists was more of a problem than sexism from the politicians she covered: "It is years, usually, before a woman is admitted to the fraternity, years before other newspaper men give her tips and ask her for information in the way they trade with their male colleagues."[22]

The political beat, much like sports, was traditionally male territory, and women often struggled to break free of the home and lifestyle pages. They were denied membership in the National Press Club in Washington, DC, until the 1970s. This was not just about having lunch with male reporters: Press clubs offer access to newsmakers, and the National Press Club hosted presidents, kings, queens, prime ministers, members of Congress, and such social leaders as Martin Luther King.[23] Women had formed their own press clubs over time, but these could not replace the access provided by the National Press Club in the nation's capital, which had decided in 1948 to admit broadcast journalists and in 1955 to admit Black journalists. But as of 1970, it continued to restrict women to watching events from the balcony or briefly attending major events during luncheons before being escorted out.[24] The hostility against women was flagrant. When the National Press Club finally did vote to admit them as full members in 1971, the bartender was not joking when he served poured beers for the first four women and said he hoped they'd "choke on them." A member of the club opposed to the admission of women lamented that the club would no longer be a "quiet place to have a meal and a drink with your friends" and that the members "will be subjected to feminine chatter at all hours. . . . It is no reflection on the ladies to note that the female of the species is more talkative than the male. There ought to be one place left in the world where men wear the pants."[25] Women remained marginalized in the prestigious political pages well into the twenty-first century. According to

Profile: Helen Thomas, Journalist (1920–2013)

Helen Thomas was the unofficial ruler of the White House press corps for decades, having covered every president from John F. Kennedy to Barack Obama. Thomas was the seventh child of immigrants from Lebanon. She started her journalism career in Washington, first with a newspaper, then as wire service reporter in 1943, and she gradually worked her way up to the political beat. She covered Kennedy's presidential campaign, and when he won, she was assigned to cover him in the White House—the first woman in such a role. Thomas was known for putting in long hours and for asking blunt questions. President Barack Obama said, "She never failed to keep presidents—myself included—on their toes." She was the first woman elected to the White House Correspondents' Association and went on to become the first woman to serve as the group's president. She was the only female print reporter to accompany President Richard Nixon on his historic trip to China. Because of her long-standing tenure in the White House, Thomas had the privilege of the first question for briefings, and she was known for her signature closing, "Thank you, Mr. President."

Helen Thomas at work in Washington, DC.
Courtesy of Creative Commons, Library of Congress

Like many women in public life who defy stereotypes, Thomas was often mocked. Fox host Bill O'Reilly said in 2009 that she had a voiced that "cackled," prompting the Women's Media Center to demand an apology. President Nixon had publicly admonished her in 1973 for wearing slacks to a briefing. Two years later, Thomas was the first woman elected to the Gridiron Club, which until then had been a male-only enclave for Washington journalists. She was hired by the Hearst Company as a columnist and stayed in that role until her abrupt retirement in 2010, when she was recorded saying that Israel should get out of Palestine, a remark that some critics considered to be anti-Semitic. She later apologized for the remark, but her reputation for objectivity had come under attack. When she died in 2013 at the age of ninety-two, she was remembered by other journalists as a person who scooped them regularly. One colleague tweeted, "Pity the poor WH press aide who would try to tell Helen, 'You can't stand there.'"

Sources: "Helen Thomas," in *Encyclopedia of World Biography*, 2nd ed., vol. 19 (Gale, 2004), 381–84; Fox News, "Women's Group Calls O'Reilly Sexist and Ageist over Helen Thomas Joke," March 24, 2015, https://www.foxnews.com/transcript/womens-group-calls-oreilly-sexist-and-ageist-over-helen-thomas-joke; Carol Jenkins, "WMC Demands Apology from O'Reilly for Helen Thomas Insult," HuffPost, March 14, 2009, https://www.huffpost.com/entry/wmc-demands-apology-from_b_166069; David Stout, "50 Years of Tough Questions and 'Thank You, Mr. President,'" *New York Times*, July 20, 2013, https://www.nytimes.com/2013/07/21/business/media/helen-thomas-who-broke-down-barriers-as-white-house-reporter-is-dead-at-92.html; United Press International, "White House Lifts Ban on Women in Pants," *New York Times*, November 26, 1973, https://www.nytimes.com/1973/11/26/archives/white-house-lifts-ban-on-women-in-pants.html.

the Women's Media Center (WMC), they made up about a third of the American political press as of 2017, though a significant number of women were elevated to key roles in network TV after the 2020 election, in part the result of years of pressure and perhaps because of a heightened awareness of gender in politics in the wake of the Donald Trump presidency.[26]

Visual Stereotypes

Visual media are particularly powerful for perpetuating gendered stereotypes. The human brain processes images differently than words; the messages we receive from images are more memorable and emotionally powerful than what we understand from language. Repeated use of a stereotype embeds it into the culture around us.[27] News images, powerful for the way they capture visual reality, can be used in ways that perpetuate stereotypes or reverse them. Cartoons and caricatures, which are expected to be satirical, can also be used to cultivate stereotypes. Political cartoons are especially problematic because they can be used for propagandistic purposes while their creators can also claim, with a disingenuous wink, that they were "just kidding."[28] Political caricatures always exaggerate some aspect of a person's appearance, such as Nixon's prominent nose or FDR's square jaw. But caricatures of women in politics often draw from negative stereotypes. Remember the way early suffragists were depicted as stupid, ugly, or shameful for neglecting their homes.[29] Even before she ran for president, Hillary Clinton was the subject of cartoons that masculinized her or represented her as a nagging shrew.[30] By the time she did run for president, she was photoshopped into monstrous half-male/half-female characters or as objects—like a nutcracker.[31] Indeed, an actual Hillary nutcracker was manufactured and sold in 2016, as were blow-up dolls of Sarah Palin, whose beauty-pageant looks inspired brainless Barbie caricatures (illustrating, quite clearly, the brain-beauty double bind).[32] In 2017, British Prime Minister Theresa May and Scottish National Party Leader Nicola Sturgeon were featured on the cover of the *Daily Mail* with the headline, "Never Mind Brexit, Who Won Legs-it!" next to a photo that featured their legs.[33]

This 2017 front page of the *Daily Mail* exemplifies how female politicians have often been sexualized in news coverage.
Courtesy of the *Daily Mail*

Clearly looks matter for all politicians, whether they are male or female.

Taller men tend to win elections, and men who are unattractive are judged poorly.[34] People who are conventionally attractive are also usually assumed to be competent, which is known as the **halo effect**.[35] Research has found that attractive candidates are seen as more politically competent and persuasive.[36] Gender complicates this effect, though, particularly when it comes to voting decisions. In one experiment, subjects were asked to rate candidates for office according to attractiveness and competence. As expected, attractiveness was associated with competence. But when asked whether they would vote for a candidate, attractiveness did *not* make a difference when the candidate was female and the (potential) voter was male. The men in the study were biased against female candidates generally, while the women in the study did not differentiate their assessments based on gender.[37] A more recent study found that age also makes a difference for women, as well, with study subjects assessing women more negatively than men as they get older.[38] Race, of course, makes a difference, too, because conventional beauty standards have traditionally skewed toward whiteness; even within the Black community, "colorism" discriminates against women who are very dark or who have natural hair or broader noses.[39]

GENDER IN POLITICAL RHETORIC

Gender plays a role in politics beyond individual candidates and leaders. Researchers who study the way language is used note that conservativism uses heavily patriarchal language and even takes the role of a "stern father" in the public's imagination, while progressives are seen as more caring and, therefore, feminine.[40] In the United States, women are more likely than men to vote for the Democratic Party, a phenomenon known as the gender gap. More recently, however, researchers argue that the gap is due not so much to a voter's gender as to their attitudes about the role of women in society. Men vote Democratic, too, after all, and women vote Republican, so political scientists suggest that the important gap is a matter of social values.[41] This argument underscores the long-standing feminist premise that feminism opposes not men but patriarchy. President Donald Trump's use of masculine language is a key factor in his popularity with social conservatives, who embrace the image of a strong protector, even if that machismo comes with a dose of misogyny. What matters, in this political sense, is that a leader embodies strength.[42]

FLIPPING THE SCRIPT

In 2013, the *New York Times* obituary of an acclaimed rocket scientist who'd been recognized by Barack Obama started,

> She made a mean beef stroganoff, followed her husband from job to job and took eight years off from work to raise three children. "The world's best mom," her son Matthew said.

> But Yvonne Brill, who died on Wednesday at 88 in Princeton, N.J., was
> also a brilliant rocket scientist who in the early 1970s invented a propulsion
> system to keep communications satellites from slipping out of their orbits.[43]

Public outcry over the sexism of this lead was strong enough that the *Times* edited
out the stroganoff reference in the online version of the obituary. The public editor
addressed the matter in a column, concluding, "The emphasis on her domesticity—
and, more important, the obituary's overall framing as a story about gender—had the
effect of undervaluing what really landed Mrs. Brill on the *Times* obituaries page: her
groundbreaking scientific work."[44] The public editor's assessment is noteworthy not
only for its critique of a colleague but also for its incorporation of the key concept of
framing. By choosing to emphasize facts about Brill's role as a wife and mother, the
lead sentence perpetuates the notion that there's something unusual about a female
scientist. While the obituary writer professed to admire Brill, that didn't stop him
from centralizing her gender.

How might journalists do better? Here are key concepts anyone writing for the
public ought to consider. First, reporting fairly about diverse communities is a form
of accuracy. Second, fair representations (and their opposite, stereotypes) make a difference in how the audience understands social groups. Reporters might adopt ethics
that allow for adjustments in their approach in response to individual human needs,
as opposed to a one-size-fits-all reporting style.[45] Finally, there's the "flip test," or
the principle of **reversibility**, which can sometimes reveal sexism in a dramatic, even
humorous way. Imagine, for a moment, an obituary for a male rocket scientist mention-
ing—anywhere, no less the lead sentence—his cooking. It's hard to imagine, of course,
and that's the point. The principle of reversibility is what makes the "Man Who Has It
All" account on social media so funny. When "Man Who Has It All" posts, "Dad with a
career? Beat stress by snacking on raw veggies, staying hydrated, teaming up with other
Dads and dressing for your face shape!" it's funny because it addresses men in the same
way women have been addressed by media for decades and reveals how mothers have so
long been expected to cheerfully do chores and neglect their own needs.

It's not funny at all, though, for female political candidates who are asked about
their childcare arrangements while male candidates are not, or for queer candidates who
are covered primarily through a gender frame that emphasizes their sexuality. Though
there is evidence of some recent improvement, studies of news content have repeatedly
found that coverage fixates on the women's clothing and bodies.[46] The WMC, an organization devoted to fighting sexism in news and entertainment, has developed a guide
for gender neutral writing. As the WMC guide puts it, "To ensure gender-fairness, ask
yourself: Would I write the same thing in the same way about a person of the other sex?
Would I mind if this were said of me?"[47] Reporters should not ask sexist questions, and
they should avoid terms that call attention to gender and demean women, terms that
are rarely, if ever, applied to men, such as *shrill* or *high-strung*.

The *Associated Press Stylebook*, the gold standard for journalists around the world,
also provides guidance on how to write inclusively. As illustration of the way language
changes over time to reflect society, the AP constantly updates its stylebook. In terms of
gender, the AP dictates that people over the age of eighteen who identify as female are

Saturday is YOUR day. Why not ask your wife to babysit so you can get on with the laundry in peace?

@manwhohasitall

This Facebook post by the "Man Who Has It All" from November 4, 2016, illustrates the way the account parodies gendered advice in media.
Public domain

not girls but women. People who are married have husbands or wives, whether they are straight or gay. According to AP style, a person's pronouns are the pronouns they use, not "preferred," and deadnames (the name a person had prior to transition) should be used as rarely as possible, only when essential for clarity.[48] The introduction to this book explains the AP's basics regarding terms for racial and ethnic groups, which encourages journalists to be as specific as possible while showing respect for a person's preference. *Black* is capitalized, and *Latino*, *Latina*, and *Latinx* are all acceptable when correct. It's possible, for instance, to be Hispanic but not Latinx. The media criticism organization Fairness and Accuracy in Reporting (FAIR) offers advice for covering criminal justice in ways that avoid stereotypes. For instance, FAIR discourages reporters from parroting police jargon and instead encourages them to use more common language. The word *juvenile*, for instance, is largely a criminal justice term, not one used in everyday life. Considering the racial stereotypes that hypersexualize, criminalize, and "adultify" Black and Brown people, reporters might well remember to write about all people eleven and under as children and use the word *teenager* when appropriate.[49]

Summary

Women in leadership have traditionally been written about stereotypically and have been judged unfairly according to double binds. Women running for office are criticized for being too pushy as well as too weak, too pretty and not pretty enough. While decades of pressure from women's rights organizations have won some improvement, news coverage still is more likely to mention a woman's appearance more than a man's or to describe her parenting status. The language of politics itself is often gendered, and voter preferences seem to reflect conservative or progressive values regarding feminism. Reporters are encouraged to use gender-neutral language and treat all candidates fairly. Reversibility, or the mental trick of flipping genders in a story, headline, or question, can help media producers to test whether their writing is sexist.

- **Reflection:** How do you work differently with male and female leaders? Do you have a preference? What role might your own socialization and media habits play in the way you perceive women in power?
- **Media Critique:** As you read the news, do any stories stand out to you as good candidates for the "flip test"? Is political coverage of female politicians getting better?
- **Media Critique:** Take a look at the political cartoons that depict female leaders. How is gender reflected—if at all—in the caricatures?

CHAPTER 6

Masculinity and Media

It's impossible to understand gender-equity issues faced by women and the queer community without a close look at men and what society expects from them. This chapter introduces students to masculinity studies and the way news reflects and extends the social hierarchy known as patriarchy.

Key Concepts: Color-Blind Racism, Hegemony, Episodic Framing

One of the most famous paintings of Louis XIV, king of France from 1643 to 1715, shows him wearing a fur cape, tights, and heels, all of which would be considered feminine today. Yet Louis XIV was a powerful ruler who kept the nation united and had at least six mistresses.[1] His life—and the painting—illustrate how cultural ideas about gender may come and go but the association of masculinity with power has remained far more stable. Chapter 1 introduces the idea of complementary stereotypes and the way men are expected to be competent and in charge. Recall that while these complementary stereotypes represent a balanced system, they also tend to justify a hierarchy in which male characteristics are valued over female ones. The resulting system of beliefs, known as patriarchy, holds not only that men are on the top of that hierarchy but also that this is the natural order of things.

Hegemonic Masculinity

Patriarchal ideology has been the norm in most of the world for centuries, though its cultural manifestations have varied over time. The fashion sense of Louis XIV is but one example. Men in colonial America wore wigs and heels, too. Men in Scotland have traditionally worn kilts—skirts, really. At the start of the twentieth century, boys were welcomed with pink, not blue, clothing, and prior to that, mothers were warned against putting pants on their sons too early.[2] Today's fashion is complicated, yet mainstream clothing offerings continue to use color as a gender marker, with more items in neutrals, grays, and tans for men and pinks, lavenders, and floral prints for women. In 2017, when Target announced its stores would no longer have aisles labeled for "boys" and "girls" toys, some outraged customers threatened a boycott.[3] The markers of gender may change, but the need to make distinctions endures. In 2021, four people died from gender-reveal party stunts.[4] A 2017 fire in Arizona that burned 47,000 acres was blamed on fireworks from a gender-reveal party.[5] Though some parents are moving toward gender-neutral child-rearing, the impulse to celebrate difference is as strong as ever.

A concept known as **hegemonic masculinity** helps explain this cultural impulse. It's based on the more general concept of **hegemony**, the "historically combined forms of political domination and ideological leadership within a class society," or, more plainly, the way our belief system is enmeshed with the social hierarchy.[6] Italian philosopher Antonio Gramsci developed the concept to explain why people often work against their own interests in favor of a dominant group. He argues that it's because people are influenced by cultural messages of "common sense" that are controlled by those in power.[7] In the 1980s, Australian scholar R. W. Connell applied the concept to gender, using the term *hegemonic masculinity* to describe the "most honored way of being a man."[8] Hegemonic masculinity, then, is how patriarchy is enacted in a social system and enforced because of the ideological belief that it is common sense or natural. A hegemonic system reproduces itself because it is deeply embedded in everyday thinking, whether it involves the colors appropriate for children's clothing, who should pay for a date, or who should lead a country. Because complementary stereotypes seem so natural, the system that puts men above women sustains itself.

Masculinity is also marked by binary, or either-or, thinking. One researcher calls this "Lombardi-ism" for the way it echoes the rhetoric of Vince Lombardi, the football coach who preached the existential importance of *winning*.[9] Binary thinking (first introduced in chapter 1) sees the world as black or white, good or bad. People win or lose; they either have it, or they don't; they are male or female. Anyone who sees shades of gray is mistaken at best or, more likely, a loser. The 2016 presidential campaign was a classic lesson in hypermasculine, binary rhetoric, as President Donald Trump used the language of dominance and autonomy to great effect with voters who saw him as a patriot who broke the rules of a "woke" media.[10]

Theodore Roosevelt, the US president at the turn of the last century, made a point of embracing the positive qualities of hegemonic masculinity in his political rhetoric and was successful in doing so.[11] Roosevelt was a progressive who supported women's suffrage. Even though he coined the term *muckraker* in criticism of negativity in the press, he was generally successful in his dealings with the press, in part for how he cultivated his masculine image.[12] He loved to box and hunt big game and volunteered to fight in the Spanish-American War with a cavalry regiment later nicknamed the Rough Riders. His memoir about the war helped to shape his image as a virile reformer.[13] He shared his ideals about masculinity in a letter for the first *Boy Scouts Handbook*, which concludes, "Mind, eye, muscle, all must be trained so that the boy can master himself, and thereby learn to master his fate."[14] Roosevelt's version of masculinity encouraged respect for women while emphasizing gender differences. His support of

Profile: Vince Lombardi, Football Coach (1913–1970)

Vince Lombardi was one of the most famous sports figures of the twentieth century. He rose to fame as professional football itself took over the national stage. He was an assistant coach at West Point Military Academy before working his way up the ranks to become head coach of the Green Bay Packers. Lombardi turned their record around and led them to two back-to-back Super Bowl victories, in 1967 and 1968. He was a bit of a media darling, quick with one-liners flavored with militarism and self-help. Lombardi is often credited with saying, "Winning isn't everything; it's the only thing," a statement that speaks to the binarism of toxic masculinity. Indeed, scholars use the word *Lombardiism* to describe the winner-takes-all mentality. It's true—he did say these words—but over time he also tried to put it into a larger context and to disassociate himself from critics who accused him of letting the ends justify the means.

Lombardi left the Packers in 1969 to lead Washington, DC's football team, and he died of cancer a year later. His son wrote a book on leadership in tribute to his father and includes this quote, hoping to set the record straight on Vince Lombardi's sense of grace, strength, and decency:

Vince Lombardi. This sculpture of Lombardi stands outside the Green Bay Packers' Lambeau Field in Green Bay, Wisconsin, memorializing the team's much-revered coach. Courtesy of Creative Commons, Jim Bowen

> Being part of a football team is no different than being a part of any other organization—an army, political party. The objective is to win, to beat the other guy. You think that is hard or cruel—I don't think it is. I do think it is a reality of life that men are competitive, and the more competitive the business, the more competitive the men. They know the rules, and they know the objective, and they get in the game period and the objective is to win—fairly, squarely, decently, by the rules, but to win.

Sources: Vince Lombardi Jr., *What It Takes to Be Number #1: Vince Lombardi on Leadership* (McGraw-Hill, 2001), 229; David Maraniss, *When Pride Still Mattered: A Life of Vince Lombardi* (Simon and Schuster, 1999).

women's suffrage retained his belief about gender roles, arguing that women ought to be able to vote in order to be better wives and mothers.[15]

Many of the characteristics of Roosevelt's ideal man overlap with the elements of hegemonic masculinity identified by cultural scholar Nick Trujillo. Trujillo studied how sportswriters covered baseball player Nolan Ryan, who had a long and very successful career as a pitcher and was considered a living legend. Using a method similar to the one used by Judith Welter to study historic women's magazines, Trujillo carefully examined the sports pages and identified five elements that comprise hegemonic masculinity: athletic prowess, capitalistic success, fatherhood, frontiersmanship, and domination over women.[16] Trujillo describes the way physical force and control is part of the idealized man or what it means to be masculine, as a "true man" is strong and is in charge. A "true man" is also successful in his job; a good father; proficient in sports; and able to conquer nature by hunting, fishing, or building a campfire. In the rhetoric of hegemonic masculinity, a "true man" is also straight and not only wants to have sex with women but also dominates them, overcoming any objections they may have with his personal power.

Think about how this language, of what makes a "true man," complements the language Welter found for "true womanhood." Men are expected to dominate, while women are supposed to submit; it's "natural"—so natural that this way of thinking is hardly noticeable, the very essence of hegemony. Subsequent scholarship on gendered language in news has similarly found the way masculine language often frames issues like policing and climate change.[17] Hypermasculine rhetoric is also reflective of national populism, or the belief that a country should dominate over nature and other people and that only certain kinds of people (i.e., white and male) are worthy citizens.[18]

These ideas are hegemonic because they are so ingrained in our culture to the point where we stop questioning them. What's interesting about the dimensions Trujillo identifies and about hegemonic masculinity generally is that these qualities of masculinity are thought to be something inherent in a man. Men are thought to come by these characteristics naturally simply by being born male.

Excerpt: "The Man in the Arena"

It is not the critic who counts; not the man who points out how the strong man stumbles, or where the doer of deeds could have done them better. The credit belongs to the man who is actually in the arena, whose face is marred by dust and sweat and blood; who strives valiantly; who errs, who comes short again and again, because there is no effort without error and shortcoming; but who does actually strive to do the deeds; who knows great enthusiasms, the great devotions; who spends himself in a worthy cause; who at the best knows in the end the triumph of high achievement, and who at the worst, if he fails, at least fails while daring greatly, so that his place shall never be with those cold and timid souls who neither know victory nor defeat.

Source: Theodore Roosevelt, "Address at the Sorbonne in Paris, France: 'Citizenship in a Republic,'" American Presidency Project, April 23, 1910, https://www.presidency.ucsb.edu/documents/address-the-sorbonne-paris-france-citizenship-republic.

Masculinity and Violence

Violence makes domination possible. Violence or its threat might be hidden behind polite behavior, but it is omnipresent in a patriarchal society. Masculinity is so deeply connected to violence that it's hard to disentangle. Today's media often glorify violence, even in stories that appear to condemn it, presenting it in ways that offer the viewer a safe peek at the lives of "real men."[19] Superhero movies save the world with violence. Gangster movies, crime dramas, zombie shows, and war epics all depict violence, often very graphicly. Video games often require players to use violence to win, and many sports, such as rugby or football, are won by violence, even with (or in spite of) rules intended to promote safety. The violence embedded in patriarchal rhetoric fuels gun culture, as a gun can be seen as a form of fatherly protection and a means of self-reliance.[20] The intertwining of masculinity with societal violence supports rape culture (covered in greater depth in chapter 7), and the belief that it is natural for men to control women perpetuates the cycle of domestic violence.

You might ask, "Aren't women ever violent? Can men be the victims of domestic violence? Don't women enjoy gun culture?" Absolutely. In fact, some female politicians, such as Sarah Palin, who ran for vice president in 2008, and Lauren Boebert (Republican US representative from Colorado) have benefited from aligning themselves with gun culture.[21] Yet women are far more likely to be victims of violence than perpetrators. Women constitute 16 percent of the people charged with any sort of violent crime, including murder, assault, and robbery.[22] According to the US Department of Justice, the victims of murder vary by gender: Men are more likely to kill strangers, and women are more likely to kill their family members. Overall, however, men convicted of murder outnumber women by more than ten to one.[23] Women are about four times as likely to be victims of domestic violence, and approximately three women die at the hands of an intimate partner every day.[24] That's an astounding number that bears a closer look: In the United States, a woman dies of intimate-partner violence about every eight hours.

News about domestic violence, however, tends not to treat this as a societal problem but instead covers a small subsection of domestic violence murders as discrete events. Covering news stories one by one without a look at the bigger picture is known as **episodic framing**.[25] Episodic frames contrast with issue frames, or **thematic frames**, for their focus on individual actions instead of larger social forces.[26] Crime news is especially important for local news, which covers such events as aberrations, unusual happenings that affect one family or victim. The cause of an intimate partner murder is blamed on individual circumstances: a wedding where a woman thought she had escaped a violent ex, sisters who asked for the locks to be changed on their apartment to keep a violent father away, or a tumultuous relationship.[27] Episodic framing is problematic because it presents events as disconnected. Storms, forest fires, and floods that might be blamed on climate change, for example, are often covered as natural disasters, often with inadequate contextualization regarding the larger factors at work.[28]

Recall that hegemony is the way groups in power exercise social and cultural leadership in order to maintain political and economic control and the way outgroups go along, becoming complicit in their own subordination. As long as people believe that the system is normal and generally fair—and natural—they will work within that system. Individuals will acquiesce without violence or force. If something goes wrong, then it must be because they did something wrong, not because the system is wrong. Hegemonic patriarchy, which assumes that men can and should control women, is so invisible that it disappears. Because patriarchy is so widely considered to be part of the natural order of things, its impact on social life fades into the background.

The Gabby Petito case provides a helpful example of how patriarchal assumptions permeate public life and the way episodic framing hides larger social forces. Petito was a social media influencer who traveled with her boyfriend and posted stories from the road. In 2021, she went missing, and the case attracted national attention. Prior to her disappearance, Petito and her boyfriend were stopped by police when witnesses observed the pair fighting. Video of Petito tearfully telling police the disagreement was her fault filled the airwaves during the search, which eventually ended with the discovery of her body more than a month later.[29] Weeks later, her boyfriend was found dead of an apparent self-inflicted gunshot to the head in Florida. Not only was the Petito case framed as a unique episode of domestic violence, but also video of the police response to a sobbing girl asking them to not blame her boyfriend reflects a patriarchal blind spot by police. They were apparently swayed by Petito's emotion and her boyfriend's claims that she suffered mental health issues but not by the evidence that an assault had occurred. Instead of investigating domestic violence, their decision allowed it to escalate.[30]

The fact that the case made national news also inspired critics to point out that this was yet another case of "missing white woman" syndrome, which prioritizes pretty, white, female victims while ignoring hundreds of other cases of missing women.[31] "Missing white woman" syndrome is an intersectional phenomenon that results from racist assumptions that some women are more valuable than others, in combination with the sexist trope of a damsel in distress in need of the community's support. Petito absolutely did need protection and likely would have received it had officers followed protocol. Instead, they ignored well-known facts about domestic violence in order to give a tearful young woman a break. She ended up dead, and the national media seized on a story of a (white) social media star's tragedy. By covering the case with an episodic frame, most news organizations managed to elide much larger social problems: domestic violence *and* the hidden plague of nonwhite women who go missing and are murdered every day without media attention.

Patriarchy's Price

Men benefit from patriarchy and its racist, homophobic forms and have for centuries. Men have more power and money than women, they constitute the majority of elected officials, and white men are more likely to be promoted into leadership positions. Yet their place on the social hierarchy, upheld by hegemonic masculinity's rules that men must control and hide their emotions, control others through violence, and always be in charge, comes at a price. Neither men nor women are able to enjoy their full humanity in a patriarchal system. The zero-sum thinking associated with

Mitt Romney was roundly criticized by political opinion writers for riding a jet ski driven by his wife while on vacation, on the grounds that the image emasculated him during his campaign for president in 2012.
Courtesy of Associated Press

masculinity is harmful for individuals and society at large. In public life, men are criticized for acting in any way that is considered feminine, as when Mitt Romney, who was running for president in 2012, sat on a jet ski behind the operator, his wife.[32] After the photo was published, pundits pounced on its symbolism. A *Wall Street Journal* columnist called it a potential "catastrophe" for Romney's campaign.[33] *Newsweek* ran a full story the following month suggesting Romney had a "serious wimp problem."[34]

Toxic masculinity is a form of manliness that is dangerous to the self or others, such as domestic violence, rape, or emotional repression. Gender scholars prefer not to use the term, however, because of the way it has been misunderstood as a foil to positive forms of stereotypical masculinity. That is, presenting courage, protectiveness, or strength as healthy *masculine* traits interferes with the notion that women can *also* be courageous, protective, and strong. Patriarchy is the *belief* that men are superior and should control women. Feminist activists say this ideology, rather than any particular group of people, is the problem, and therefore *hegemonic masculinity* is a more accurate term for the way stereotypical beliefs affect society. The term *toxic masculinity* has also been criticized (and misinterpreted) by those who oppose gender rights and claim that the term is antimale, an argument popularized during the suffrage movement that continues to circulate today. Former Fox commentator Tucker Carlson, for example, created a documentary called *The End of Men* in 2022, which claims in one of its trailers, "One of the biggest stories of our lifetimes is the total collapse of testosterone levels in American men."[35] Ultraconservative congressional representative Josh Hawley wrote

Profile: Phil Donahue, Media Personality (1935–)

Phil Donahue.
Courtesy of PhotoFest

Phil Donahue changed daytime television in the 1980s with a new kind of talk show for a female audience, one that treated them as thinking human beings. Donahue started as a TV announcer straight out of college and eventually became a talk show host. Eventually, the *Phil Donahue Show* was syndicated to two hundred stations around the United States. Daytime television had traditionally been produced for a female audience under the assumption that women were the people at home who could watch TV in the afternoons. The choices included serial dramas, or soap operas, named for their advertisers, and talk shows about celebrities or household tips. He called himself a "fainthearted feminist" and broke the mold with a show that covered political topics, including birth control and divorce. He was known for controversy, once wearing a skirt for a show about cross-dressers and airing tape of an actual birth during an interview with an obstetrician. Women in the audience were able to ask questions of the guests.

Donahue quit in 1996, the same year he won a Lifetime Achievement Emmy. The ratings for his show had been falling, and he faced new competition from shows that were more sensational. Donahue's intelligent and humanistic approach to his guests, as well as his penchant for controversy, had forever changed the talk show format. In 1992, he told a *Washington Post* interviewer he'd like his epitaph to read, "Here lies Phil. Occasionally he went too far."

Sources: Patricia Bauer, "Phil Donahue," Britannica, December 17, 2022, https://www .britannica.com/biography/Phil-Donahue; Phil Donahue, *Donahue, My Own Story* (Simon and Schuster, 1979); Simi Horwitz, "Evolution of the Talk Show: In the Beginning, There Was Phil," *Washington Post*, November 15, 1992; Dan D. Nimmo and Chevelle Newsome, *Political Commentators in the United States in the 20th Century: A Bio-Critical Sourcebook* (Greenwood, 1997).

a book in 2023 similarly decrying what he believes is a decline in masculine virtues and claiming, "A free society that despises manhood will not remain free."[36] His concerns are not new: The Boy Scouts of America were founded during the suffrage movement on fears that feminism would weaken young men.[37]

Gender rights activists counter that *patriarchy* is the problem, not men. That is, the problem is not a group of people but the belief that men are and should be superior to women and all the social and cultural structures built to support this belief. Therefore, they argue that it's possible for anyone to be feminist, including men, by opposing an ideology that harms all people. Some men did openly become allies in the 1970s, but like women in the movement, they were often mocked. The zero-sum thinking associated with hegemonic masculinity framed feminism as the battle of the sexes, which belittled feminism's allies and its issues.

Men's Rights

It is impossible to tug at one end of the social fabric and not expect movement on the other side. While many men support women's rights and some call themselves feminists, others established their own men's rights groups in opposition to what they saw as reverse discrimination at work or unfair family law practices that favored mothers.[38] A different strand of men's activism, called the mythopoetic men's movement, held retreats and group events to offer an emotionally supportive space for masculine activity, inspired by the psychological theories of Carl Jung.[39] Poet Robert Bly was a key figure in the movement, and his 1990 book *Iron John*, which uses fiction to interpret men's lives, was a best-seller.[40]

Another men's rights figure, Jordan Peterson, uses the internet to advance his ideas about men's rights and masculinity. He created a series of popular YouTube videos that attack feminism and the gay rights movement as harmful to Western civilization. Peterson uses essentialist ideas: that is, he argues that masculine and feminine traits are innate, not learned, as feminist scholars have proposed. Peterson believes that feminists and gay rights activists have undermined the good qualities of masculinity. In an interview with the *New York Times*, he argues that ancient myths that represent chaos as feminine reflect natural conditions and contends, "The people who hold that our culture is an oppressive patriarchy, they don't want to admit that the current hierarchy might be predicated on competence."[41]

MEN UNDER PRESSURE

There are reasons to be concerned about men in American society today. Across the world, girls do better in school overall, especially with writing, spelling, and language skills.[42] Women earn the majority of undergraduate and graduate degrees.[43] Boys have long outperformed girls in math, but girls are catching up and tend to get better grades in math classes.[44] Boys are more likely to be diagnosed with ADHD and similar disorders, and they are more likely to drop out of high school.[45] Some observers blame the schools, suggesting that boys are overpunished for simply being boyish, moving around, and being loud.[46] Girls are socialized to sit still and be quiet, behaviors that are valued more in school, and because these skills are more valued in the workforce today, women seem to have the upper hand in what it takes to be successful.[47] Among young adults (aged eighteen to twenty-nine), far more men (68 percent) report being single than women (34 percent).[48]

Another factor might be that boys are socialized to appear strong, nonchalant, and unworried about academic achievement.[49] This "cool factor" means that even when boys want to do well in school, they don't want to show it, and if they start to get poorer grades, then they are compelled to pretend they don't care. If doing well in school becomes associated with girls, then the binary beliefs associated with hegemonic masculinity will drive boys away, as nothing in the patriarchal system is more socially harmful than appearing to be feminine. If a man is supposed to always be in control, then he cannot be seen to struggle, and he most certainly cannot ask for help. The challenges continue past childhood. Michael Kimmel, who spent time with four hundred young men from all walks of life as he researched his book *Guyland*, found that modern men go through an extended form of adolescence, encouraged by today's social and economic conditions to put off living like an adult.[50]

The twenty-first-century job market has hit traditionally masculine employment hard, even before the COVID-19 pandemic damaged the global economy. Manufacturing jobs that require physical strength are disappearing in the United States, and service jobs, which require the sort of communication skills women excel in, are up. This is not to say men cannot do service jobs; of course, they can, and many do. For example, male enrollment in nursing schools is up.[51] Even so, the stigma of women's work discourages many men from entering professions like nursing, and men's participation in the workplace has decreased. A presidential report in 2016 found that millions of American men had left the labor force; that is, they were not disabled but stopped looking for work.[52] The trend is international and tied to opioid use, depression, and failed marriages.[53] Men may receive confusing signals from women about their expectations and heterosexual relationships. Some men report getting mixed messages about the need to meet traditional standards of masculinity but also be tender, caring, and vulnerable. How is one to be aggressive but vulnerable simultaneously? In response to these combined pressures, some men are escaping online; they are more likely to become addicted to video games.[54] Research suggests that young men who are underemployed (i.e., not working at the level of one's potential) are playing video games instead of pursuing more hours on the job.[55]

Many men in the United States are suffering from depression. Before the pandemic, men who were unemployed often used pain medication more than women.[56] Yet women are still more likely to be *diagnosed* with depression.[57] Suicide is a leading cause of death for men, and they are more than three times as likely as women to kill themselves, often with a gun.[58] Why might this be? Again, it gets back to the association of masculinity with aggression and control. If a man is not supposed to ask for help, if a man is supposed to know what to do, and if a man is supposed to be aggressive, then he cannot ask for help when he is sad or struggling. The pain becomes so intense that it's no wonder suicide is the second-highest cause of death for men aged twenty-two to forty, behind accidental injury. It's the eighth-leading cause of death overall for all men.[59]

Intersectional Misandry

Race complicates the challenges of hegemonic masculinity. **Misandry**, or a bias against men, is heightened in combination with race. Stereotypes about nonwhite men take myriad forms, but all place them lower on the social hierarchy. Queer men, trans men, and nonbinary people are similarly associated with femininity and are thus not "real" men, according to this way of thinking.[60] Asian men have been stereotyped as a "model minority" in academic and professional success but simultaneously as sexually inadequate.[61] Hispanic men have been stereotyped as lazy, unintelligent, and criminal. Black men are similarly stereotyped as criminal, lazy, and hypersexual, even animalistic. These stereotypes are not something from the past. In 2008, *Vogue* magazine featured basketball star LeBron James and actress Gisele Bündchen in a pose evocative of King Kong, the monster gorilla.[62] While Black boys and men are more likely to suffer from depression, they are less likely to seek care.[63]

Only recently, as more police use-of-force incidents have been caught on video, more people have seen (literally) that the US criminal justice system is racially unequal.[64] Black men are far more likely to be imprisoned than any other racial or gender group. There are 18 million Black men in the United States, and in 2013, more than 500,000 were in prison, with another 200,000 in jails awaiting trial. In 2010, 33 percent of all Black male high school dropouts between the ages of twenty and thirty-nine were in prison, compared with only 13 percent of their white peers. The criminalizing stereotype of Black and Hispanic men also has had deadly consequences. Black people are two and a half times more likely than white people to be killed by police.

Having a father in prison creates problems for their children, such as behavior problems and delinquency, especially among boys. By 2000, more than one million Black children had a father in jail or in prison. Roughly half of those fathers were living in the same household as their kids when they were locked up. Additionally, the incarceration of Black men in the United States far outpaces that of other countries; the United States puts more people in prison generally than any other country in the world. It represents just 5 percent of the world's people but 25 percent of its imprisoned population.

News stories about the US prison system are less common than those about crimes and trials. Prisons are usually far away from cities and closed to news cameras, which constrains coverage. Even when national organizations cover incarceration stories about poor conditions or racial inequity, they are usually not met with much public sympathy, in part because of stereotypes about inmates and an overall belief that the criminal justice system is fair.[65] This belief in a fair system fosters **color-blind racism**, which blames a person's difficulties on the individual and ignores structural inequalities. Color-blind racism assumes that everyone is equal in the United States, and just bringing up racial inequality is itself racist.[66]

Many stereotypes about Black men reach all the way back to the 1966 report by Patrick Moynihan, a sociologist who suggested that there was a crisis regarding fatherhood in Black families. Moynihan argued that unemployment among Black men created a pathology that led to fatherless households, holding tightly to the gendered idea that a good dad is a good provider. While Moynihan's report is complex and was intended to persuade leaders to improve employment opportunities for Black men, press coverage seized on the notion that the structure of Black families was the cause of poverty and perpetuated the stereotype of absent Black fathers.[67] Today, while it is true Black men do live apart from their children at higher rates than other demographic groups, the reasons are complex. Disproportionate incarceration plays a role, as does employment, which is, of course, affected by incarceration.[68] Families are changing in the United States: Many more children grow up without a father living at home across all demographic groups. In 2017, the CDC found that in two-parent homes, Black fathers are slightly *more* likely than white fathers to have dinner with their children and to take them to daily activities, which is just one measure of parenting but, in this case, a measure that pushes against stereotypes that persist because of the Moynihan report.[69]

Summary

In *The Will to Change*, scholar and critic bell hooks wrote that the crisis facing men is not the crisis of masculinity but one of *patriarchal* masculinity.[70] Until this distinction is clear, men will continue to fear that any critique of patriarchy represents a threat. As long as men are defined *by* the hierarchy, that their very existence is a matter of being financially successful, violent, and controlling women, a rejection of patriarchy is an attack on their personhood.

This belief in a social hierarchy—that men must establish themselves above others and embody the traits of hegemonic masculinity, like aggression, violence, the oppression of women, the domination of other people, and the domination of nature—is harmful to *all* people, including the people on top, who are forced to hide behind this mask of a masculinity that doesn't fit everyone. Some women are aggressive. Some men are vulnerable. Some women know how to build a cabin, knock down a tree, and set up a campfire, while some men are not natural frontiersmen.

News frames have historically held up patriarchal norms, whether by accepting hegemonic masculinity as natural or by using binary frames in coverage. Episodic frames that present crimes as unique, out-of-the-ordinary incidents instead of reflections of larger systems of inequality tend to hide the role of patriarchy in society. Journalists would benefit from a deeper understanding of the roots of violence in their communities. News will always cover the events of the day, but the relationship of many contemporary social ills to hegemonic masculinity and its binary philosophy are hard to deny: from mass shootings to domestic violence, even to the destruction of the environment for the sake of economic gain. Until media contend more deeply with the larger process or system frames of these stories, there can be no systematic response.

- **Reflection:** What traits do you associate with masculinity, and which of those do you find appealing? What has influenced your ideas of what is manly? How closely do they reflect stereotypical expectations?
- **Reflection:** Are there aspects of hegemonic masculinity that you believe ought to stay in place? How might women's expectations perpetuate hegemonic masculinity?
- **Media Critique:** When you read news about domestic violence or other crime, do the stories reflect episodic frames? Is masculine-driven violence ever mentioned as a cause of crime or domestic terrorism?

CHAPTER 7

Rape Culture and Pornography

This chapter presents current controversies regarding pornography and explains how rape culture perpetuates social inequality. Journalism has a significant role in the way sexual assault is perceived and understood, and news organizations are continually debating the best way to approach the topic. Note: This material may be troubling for some readers.

Key Concepts: Pornography, Rape Culture, Stigma

What do you do to avoid sexual assault? In the past, when I have posed this question to my classes, the women and queer students have lists of measures they take to stay safe, while the cisgender straight men have had little to say. Interestingly, that is changing, and even those cisgender straight men have started to worry about sexual assault. These precautions are not irrational: Sexual assault is a serious problem on college campuses and beyond. News coverage of sexual assault often uses the episodic frame, focusing on individual crimes but not the larger cultural force behind those crimes: that is, the patriarchal belief that men have the right to control women. Relatedly, pornography, especially in the digital age, cannot be shown to have caused any particular sexual assault, but it often perpetuates misogyny.

Rape Prevalence

Rape is a crime marked not only by physical violence but also with the shame and **stigma** of forced intimacy. Stigma is a form of embarrassment that can prevent people from reporting a rape or openly discussing any other problem that is considered shameful. People who are raped experience physical and emotional trauma, from the crime itself and often from what happens subsequently: submitting their bodies to further investigation; questioning by law enforcement; and, in one out of seven cases, pregnancy.[1] Consequently, rape is widely underreported, as its survivors often choose to avoid additional, seemingly pointless trauma.

Statistics about sexual assault are complicated, and headlines often throw out numbers without adequate context. Sexual assault includes any sort of unwanted sexual contact, such as forced kissing, groping, or obscenely pushing against a person on the bus. Researchers consider any forced or unwanted penetration to be rape, whether or not the people who are involved know one another or are in a relationship. *Sexual coercion* is unwanted penetration after a person has been coerced in a nonphysical way, *unwanted sexual contact* is nonpenetrative touching, and *non-contact unwanted sexual experiences* include things like flashing or forcing a person to display their own body. These are the definitions used in the National Intimate Partner and Sexual Violence Survey, which reported that one in four women say they've been raped or experienced an attempted rape. Men are victimized, too: In the same study, one in twenty-six men reported being assaulted in their lifetime (a majority of those cases involved male perpetrators), and one in nine told researchers they'd been forced to penetrate someone in their lifetime. Contrary to stereotypes of strangers in dark alleys, most victims of sexual assault know their perpetrators.[2]

The risks are highest for young women, and those risks are rising. The Centers for Disease Control reports that as of 2021, nearly 15 percent of teen girls said they had been forced to have sex, which experts believe is connected to record levels of depression.[3] College students are vulnerable, as well, as women aged eighteen to twenty-four are the most likely to be assaulted. Those on campus are especially vulnerable during their first semesters in school.[4] A recent report on college students counts incidents of "nonconsensual sexual contact involving physical force or inability to consent or stop what was happening" and finds that 25 percent of female undergraduates experienced this kind of contact, but only 20 percent of those students reported the incident to police. The incidence was almost as high (22 percent) for trans and queer students in the study, and nearly 7 percent of male undergraduates had been sexually assaulted.[5]

Title IX, a federal law that guarantees all students an education without discrimination, has compelled many universities and colleges to combat sexual assault on campus. Victim advocates are often critical of campus responses because accused perpetrators may remain enrolled during an investigation. Current federal guidelines require campuses to include trans students in their protective efforts, and accusers can no longer be required to meet with the alleged perpetrators during investigations.[6] Under the updated federal Clery Act, universities are required to issue annual reports about crimes on their campuses, including stalking, intimidation, dating violence, domestic violence, and sexual assault. The act was named for Jeanne Clery, a Lehigh University student who was raped and murdered in 1986. Her parents had not known that thirty-eight violent crimes had been reported on Lehigh's campus over three years prior to their daughter enrolling. They lobbied tirelessly for the reporting requirement, first approved in 1990 and updated several times, most recently in 2013.[7]

The case of Columbia student Emma Sulkowicz, who accused a fellow student of rape, illustrates the challenges for university administrators dealing with campus sexual assault. Sulkowicz carried a fifty-pound mattress around campus, to classes, and even to her 2015 graduation to protest the fact that the man she accused of raping her was still on campus as an active student. She received academic credit for the performance project, "Carrying the Weight," and made public appearances to talk about campus

Emma Sulkowicz carries her fifty-pound mattress to the Columbia University graduation ceremony in 2015.
Courtesy of Creative Commons, Adam Sherman

sexual assault while the university investigated her claims.[8] The case became much more complicated when the man she accused, Paul Nungesser, disclosed friendly social media messages he'd shared with Sulkowicz after the assault.[9] Nungesser maintained that the sex had been consensual. Nungesser sued Columbia for harming his reputation, and the university eventually settled with him for an undisclosed sum.[10]

Rape Culture

Rape culture is a term that originated with second-wave feminism to describe a social system in which rape is "both prevalent and considered the norm."[11] The assumption that rape is a natural part of everyday life and could happen at any time reflects social attitudes about the status of women, queer people, and children, as they are the most likely to be affected and are the ones expected to prevent their own victimization. In rape culture, sexual assault is something to be expected, like the flu, and its roots in patriarchal ideology are not questioned. Rape culture fosters an atmosphere that controls women because assault is so pervasive and can happen at any time, so the responsibility to avoid it is shifted to victims. To avoid being assaulted, don't drink, don't stay out late, and don't walk alone.

The notion that women and young people ought to be able to live their lives freely, wear what they want, and travel where they wish is *not* assumed in rape culture—quite the opposite. Fear, as feminist critic Andrea Dworkin points out, controls women in patriarchal culture: "By the time we are women, fear is as familiar to us as air. It is our element. We live in it, we inhale it, we exhale it, and most of the time we do not even notice it."[12] Fear of rape compels women to turn down jobs that require working in an office alone or walking at night. Fear of being called a slut or a whore prevents them from reporting assaults. Rape culture is the violent enforcement of patriarchy, and fear upholds the gender hierarchy.

Rape and Public Policy

Rape is a crime that controls the way women, children, and queer people are able to live their lives, and, for that reason, it is political. The roots of American antirape activism are intersectional and can be pinned to 1866, when a group of Black women testified to Congress about enduring gang rape by a white mob during a riot in Memphis.[13] Black women continue to be more at risk of rape, in contrast to the lingering stereotypes of hypersexual Black men victimizing white women, as identified by Ida B. Wells. More than a century later, in the 1970s, rape was one of the most important touch points of second-wave feminism. Journalist Susan Brownmiller published *Against Our Will: Men, Women, and Rape* in 1975, a book that changed how rape is framed in public conversation. Once thought of as a crime of passion and lust, Brownmiller's book explained why rape is a violent act of *power*.[14]

Armed with this new language to describe sexual assault, second-wave feminists fought to improve the way police investigate rape, the way courts adjudicate it, and the way health-care institutions treat it. Women held discussion groups to bring the issue into the open. They established crisis hotlines and fought for laws to protect women against rape by their own husbands because in many states, it was legal for a man to force his wife to have sex. The issue caught national attention in 1978, when a man in Oregon was criminally charged with raping his wife, "Laura X." He was eventually acquitted, but Laura X went on to establish the National Clearinghouse on Marital and Date Rape in California. Gradually, individual states passed laws to eliminate marriage as an exemption to rape charges, and by 1993, all fifty states prohibited spousal rape. Laura X led efforts to combat marital rape internationally, as well, and in 1995, every nation represented at the United Nations Women's Conference voted in support of a resolution declaring that women had the right to refuse sex to their husbands. Even so, many states continue to prosecute marital rape differently, often treating it as a lesser crime than other forms of sexual assault.[15]

Second-wave feminists also advocated for improvements in the way rape victims are treated, giving way to the establishment of rape crisis centers. Hospitals were encouraged to provide female caregivers to assist women who'd been raped and to not force victims to report cases to police. Before the 1970s, nurses might throw away a woman's clothes and help her clean up without gathering any physical evidence. Police often questioned victims with the assumption that they were somehow responsible for an attack.[16] Many officers still believe that women make false accusations of rape far more frequently than research suggests they do. (Studies estimate

Profile: Andrea Dworkin, Writer and Activist (1946–2005)

Andrea Dworkin was an activist and feminist who focused on the way pornography contributes to the oppression of women. In her autobiography, *Heartbreak*, Dworkin describes being punished in the sixth grade for refusing to sing "Silent Night" at school because she was Jewish, a moment that inspired a lifetime of social justice activism. Dworkin started writing about politics as an undergraduate when she became involved in protests of the Vietnam War. In the 1980s, she testified before Congress about the harms of pornography, noting, "When your rape is entertainment, your worthlessness is absolute. You have reached the nadir of social worthlessness." She worked with an attorney to draft a law that would allow victims of sexual assault to sue pornographers if specific material could be tied to their cases. The law was adopted by several cities but later declared unconstitutional. Dworkin was a lesbian who was often mocked for her appearance and caricatured as a sexless man hater. She never backed down from her essential argument that entertainment that degrades women supports a system that keeps women under control.

Sources: Andrea Dworkin, *Heartbreak: The Political Memoir of a Feminist Militant* (Basic Books, 2002); Andrea Dworkin, "Rights Issue for Women," *University of Michigan Journal of Law Reform 55* 21, nos. 1–2 (1988): 58; Editors of Encyclopaedia Britannica, "Andrea Dworkin: American Activist and Author," Britannica, updated April 5, 2023, https://www.britannica.com/biography/Andrea-Dworkin.

that only 3 to 7 percent of rape accusations are fraudulent.[17]) Today, women are no longer forced to provide evidence that they fought back against their attackers. Crisis centers provide resources and choices about what to do after an assault. Rape kits, developed in 1979 in Chicago, are officially credited to a police laboratory scientist, but evidence suggests the idea for such kits came from a woman who volunteered at a teen crisis center.[18]

Just because investigators had kits, however, did not mean rapes were investigated. Many were simply shelved and forgotten, as Detroit's first Black female prosecutor Kym Worthy discovered in 2009. More than 11,000 rape kits, spanning more than a decade, had never been tested. Once prosecutors started using the kits to track down attackers, more than two hundred men were convicted, some of whom were serial rapists.[19] As DNA testing has become more accurate, the backlog is becoming even more tragic. In Virginia, a woman's rape kit went untested for five years while she waited for her case to be investigated. When her kit was finally tested, it turned out her rapist was already serving time for other assaults and was subsequently sentenced to life in prison. Smith's case inspired Congress to combat the backlog with federal funding for cities and states.[20] A national organization for sexual assault victims founded by actor Mariska Hargitay (one of the stars of *Law and Order: SVU*) now tracks efforts to test rape kits nationally and lobbies states and cities to test the kits.[21] Since the Debbie Smith Act was first passed in 2004, hundreds of thousands of tests have been matched with DNA in the FBI's database, assisting with investigations, but many testing labs remain overwhelmed and unable to keep up.[22]

Rape in Media

Rape culture is perpetuated in large part by how we talk and write about sexual assault. Consider, for instance, how Thomas Jefferson's relationship with enslaved woman Sally Hemings has been normalized, even romanticized, in vernacular history. Hemings is estimated to have been fourteen when Jefferson took her to France; by the time she was sixteen, scholars believe she was pregnant by him, and Jefferson was in his forties.[23] Early history diminished or romanticized her story, but the reality is that she was enslaved; she literally belonged to Jefferson, like a horse, his house, or a wagon. Hemings had no choice in her situation. Was there affection? How can that be measured? Coerced sex is rape. For historians to have cast her as a mistress in a romance with Jefferson reflects the male perspective and erases Hemings's point of view.[24] Not until Black studies historians worked to frame the facts to include Hemings's perspective was her victimization understood—at least by those who would read these new interpretations. The erasure of Hemings's humanity in early accounts is a historic illustration of intersectionality and its overlapping oppressions. Hemings was enslaved because she was Black, and she was Jefferson's sex partner because she was a woman.

The Hemings story is just one example of the way media have romanticized rape, portraying it from a male perspective. The classic movie *Gone with the Wind* presents a rape scene that leaves Scarlett O'Hara smiling and peaceful the next morning.[25] If anything, rape has only become more prevalent in entertainment media. In the popular HBO series *Game of Thrones*, nearly every female character is raped, with brutal graphicness, as part of the story. The glut of rape scenes on television has sparked debate not only about *whether* to include rape in movies and TV (because, after all, it is prevalent) but *how*.[26] The Rape, Abuse, and Incest National Network (RAINN) occasionally advises shows on how to portray rape in a way that supports real-life survivors.[27] Writer Jada Yuan, in response to the show *Orange Is the New Black*, offers up this prescription for how to determine if a portrayal of rape is adequately sensitive: "Is the victim's point of view shown? Does the scene have a purpose for existing for character, rather than plot, advancement? Is the emotional aftermath explored?"[28]

Rape culture can also be perpetuated in news. Recall the way language and word choice can change how an audience interprets a story. A 2018 research project analyzes how often news articles in particular cities used words that diminish the severity of rape or connote victim blaming. It finds that some newspapers perpetuate rape culture more than others. Even more striking, the analysis finds a link between language that perpetuates rape culture and the incidence of rape in the newspaper's city. The study also suggests that in cities where the newspapers use more rape-culture language, police are less likely to make arrests in rape cases. The researchers note that they did not necessarily find a *causal* relationship, but at the very least, they conclude that the language used in news, which likely reflects community norms, could predict the incidence of sexual assault.[29]

Profile: Geneva Overholser, Journalist (1948–)

Geneva Overholser is a journalism consultant and advisor based in New York City. She was the editor of the *Des Moines Register* from 1988 to 1995. In 1991, the paper won a Pulitzer Gold Medal for Public Service for its series on Nancy Ziegenmeyer, a rape survivor who agreed to be identified by the newspaper. During her time with the *Register*, Overholser was recognized as editor of the year by the National Press Foundation and named the "Best in the Business" by *American Journalism Review*.

Overholser later joined the faculty at the University of Missouri School of Journalism and served as director of the USC Annenberg School of Journalism from 2008 to 2013. She was a member of the Pulitzer Prize board for nine years, with one as chair. She published *On Behalf of Journalism: A Manifesto for Change* with the Annenberg Public Policy Center in 2006. Overholser has served as a member of the editorial board for the *New York Times*, the ombudsman for the *Washington Post*, a member

Geneva Overholser.
Courtesy of David Westphal, used with permission

of the editorial board of the *New York Times*, and a reporter for the *Colorado Springs Sun*. Overholser continues to advocate against the secrecy of rape. She resigned from her columnist position with the Poynter Institute when the organization edited out a rape survivor's name from a column on the subject. "An awful lot of cruelty surrounds the crime of rape," Overholser writes in a 2003 essay. "Cruelty feeds on ignorance. And I have yet to see ignorance effectively addressed by secrecy."

Sources: Geneva Overholser, "Geneva Overholser Bio," May 19, 2014, https://genevaoverhoser.com/about-3/geneva-overholser-bio/; Nat Ives, "Online Columnist Quits, Citing Excessive Editing," *New York Times*, September 20, 2004, https://www.nytimes.com/2004/09/20/business/media/online-columnist-quits-citing-excessive-editing.html; Geneva Overholser, "Name the Accuser and the Accused," Poynter, July 23, 2003, https://www.poynter.org/reporting-editing/2003/name-the-accuser-and-the-accused/.

STIGMA AND ANONYMITY

What is the best way to cover rape in news? Most news organizations protect victims by keeping their names out of coverage. Some journalists, however, believe this only perpetuates the shame and stigma of rape culture. In 1990, the *Des Moines Register* published an extraordinary series of stories based on the experience of a woman who'd been raped and was willing to be named in the paper. Nancy Ziegenmeyer was sexually assaulted by a stranger who forced his way into her car. After months of frustration

---

Excerpt: "It Couldn't Happen to Me: One Woman's Story"

She wanted to go home.

Nancy Ziegenmeyer, rape victim, wanted just to get out of that place and go home. But she was lost in an unfamiliar city.

The clock on the car's dashboard read approximately 7:35. Only half an hour had passed.

She began to drive, turning here and there, until she recognized Mercy Hospital Medical Center, where her children had been for doctors' appointments. She parked her car in the lot and ran into the emergency room—not for medical attention, but just to be safe from a world that suddenly had turned on her.

Once inside, she became hysterical.

"I've just been raped," she cried. A nurse whisked her away from a waiting room of shocked, nameless faces. Within minutes, hospital workers called Polk County Victim Services, and sexual assault counselor Dee Ann Wolfe was on her way.

Source: Jane Schorer, "It Couldn't Happen to Me: One Woman's Story," *Des Moines Register*, February 25, 1990.

---

with the legal system, she contacted the *Register*. She agreed to tell her story, to be named, and even to be photographed for the series. She had been inspired by an editorial written months earlier by then editor-in-chief Geneva Overholser, who wrote that the journalistic practice of keeping victims' names secret cultivated shame. "Rape is an American shame," concludes Overholser's editorial. "As long as rape is deemed unspeakable and is therefore not fully and honestly spoken of the public outrage will be muted as well."[30] Ziegenmeyer's story made national news. She wrote a book about her experience and went on to advocate for other victims.[31] The *Register* won a Pulitzer Prize for the series.[32] Yet the idea Overholser floated more than thirty years ago fell away. Most news organizations continue to name those arrested and protect the names of victims out of deference to their trauma.

THE *ROLLING STONE* STORY

One of the tenets of rape advocacy is that women ought to be believed when they make assault accusations and that false accusations are rare. This stance runs counter to the journalistic ethos of skepticism. This, in combination with what reviewers found to be too much deference to an alleged victim, led to a reportorial disaster at *Rolling Stone* magazine in 2014. The story, "A Rape on Campus," describes a gang rape reported by an anonymous accuser, "Jackie," as illustration of the larger problems of sexual assault on college campuses. The story implies that the University of Virginia was more concerned with its public image than in investigating the attack.[33] Fallout from the article was swift and severe, as the university, the fraternity named in the story, and three men from the fraternity sued for libel, eventually costing *Rolling Stone* millions of dollars in court settlements.[34] To restore its reputation, the magazine commissioned an investigation of its editorial processes with Columbia University. Findings from the investigation faulted the magazine's use of anonymity and lack of attention to detail. *Rolling Stone*'s editors published the painfully critical findings with a public apology to "our readers and to all of those who were damaged by our story and the ensuing fallout, including members of the Phi Kappa Psi fraternity and UVA administrators and students."[35] The report's conclusions were harsh:

> *Rolling Stone*'s repudiation of the main narrative in "A Rape on Campus" is a story of journalistic failure that was avoidable. The failure encompassed reporting, editing, editorial supervision, and fact-checking. The magazine set aside or rationalized as unnecessary essential practices of reporting that, if pursued, would likely have led the magazine's editors to reconsider publishing Jackie's narrative so prominently, if at all.[36]

Rolling Stone promised change to its editorial processes, survived the fallout from the incident, and remains a culturally relevant magazine that continues to do investigative journalism. Unfortunately, what also remains is the fact that rape continues on college campuses. The details of the *Rolling Stone* story fell apart under scrutiny, but rape is still a threat to female students on campus.

Pornography: Sexy, Sexist, or Violent?

What is pornography, exactly? The late Justice Potter Stewart famously wrote, "I know it when I see it," in his judgment on a case that questioned the difference between what is sexually explicit and what is legally "obscene."[37] Medical books can be explicit, but they are not necessarily pornography. One useful definition of pornography is "sexually explicit media that are primarily intended to sexually arouse the consumer. Such media include magazines, the Internet, and films."[38] Nearly all men report having used porn for sexual arousal at some point in their lives, and many women use it, too.[39] Porn is often distinguished from erotica, which also depicts sexual scenes in a graphic way but is considered to be more artistic and less degrading, involving partners who are equal.[40] Erotica celebrates, while porn dehumanizes, prompting radical feminist scholar Robert Jensen to call pornography "propaganda" for patriarchy. In his words, "Power is eroticized" in porn.[41]

Child pornography is criminalized, but adult pornography is protected by the First Amendment.[42] Interestingly, adult porn has united traditional conservatives and some feminists in its opposition. Religious conservatives condemn porn on moral grounds, while radical feminists, like the late Andrea Dworkin, consider pornography to be a key component of rape culture.[43] The morality frame is common in news coverage of porn, pitting religious groups against sex-positive feminists, many LGBTQ+ activists, and groups that support a separation of church and state.[44] Porn is also commonly framed in news as a matter of free speech and not human rights, as advocated by Dworkin during the 1986 congressional hearings.[45] In many ways, the free-speech frame is understandable, as US journalists operate under the protection of the First Amendment. Prominent attorney Alan Dershowitz, who wrote a column about legal issues, uses this frame and characterizes Dworkin as the leader of a "pack" of women who "demanded that American citizens be denied personal choice in what they read, watch, and hear."[46] Men historically dominated newsroom management, which also may have influenced news coverage of porn over time, though research on porn coverage tends to focus on framing, not journalistic practice.

Porn has not been found to directly cause men to rape; many men use porn and do not assault women. It is being researched as a risk factor for sexual aggression, especially for young men, who are more likely to develop unrealistic expectations about sex from porn.[47] For heterosexual couples, porn use can be invigorating when viewed together, but intimacy can decrease when individuals use it alone and often.[48]

The internet has changed porn, and vice versa. The pornography industry pioneered secure credit card transactions online.[49] Social media have made DIY porn easier to create and share. Traditional porn movies had plots and costumes and scripts, but today's market also includes what's called Gonzo porn, which presents sex acts without a "fourth wall" to narratively separate the viewer from a story.[50] DIY porn and sites like OnlyFans, which thrived during the pandemic, make it possible for people to make money displaying their bodies without dealing with a production company.[51] Traditional porn companies like *Playboy* have lost revenue as DIY porn has flooded the internet. In fact, in 2015, *Playboy* announced it was getting out of the business of printing images of naked women: Why bother, when such images can be so easily viewed online?

As for sales figures for the industry overall, researchers have had a very hard time pinning them down because so much of the industry is illicit and underground. One estimate is that people spend $3,000 a minute on porn worldwide, but that's impossible to prove. Download figures are more concrete, such as the 78 billion downloads reported in 2014 by Pornhub, one of the leading internet porn sites.[52]

The pure glut of porn online today, along with its many niche products involving multiple participants, sadism, and even animals, has alarmed many observers. It has become increasingly violent, portraying the domination over and even the torture and killing of women, thereby perpetuating the belief that men can and should control women. Psychologists worry that contemporary porn creates unrealistic ideas about sex.[53] Medical researchers worldwide report a dramatic increase in erectile disfunction, even among young men, and point to the steady diet of internet porn as the likely cause.[54] Even without causing medical problems, cultural observers are alarmed at the amount of cruel misogyny in today's porn.

INTERSECTIONALITY IN PORN

This ideology of pornography is intersectional, too, as porn so often portrays the objectification and consumption of the bodies of women of color by white men. Porn that depicts Black men having sex with white women is one of the more popular genres, stereotyping Black men as insatiable and animalistic.[55] Black women's bodies have historically been objectified for consumption by men, and representations of nude Black women are common in media, perpetuating stereotypes of Black women as hypersexual Jezebels or animalistic.[56] In porn, they are more likely to be victims of sexual aggression.

Activists say gay and lesbian porn lends visibility and normalizes queer sex.[57] As with straight porn, images of men having sex with one another date back to the invention of photography. Historically, lesbian pornography was more likely to appear in written form than photographs. Lesbian sex is often part of heterosexual pornography, too, for the pleasure of male viewers. Lesbian porn has been criticized by some feminists as being just as exploitative as its straight counterpart, while other advocates argue that as with any other normalizing representation, lesbian pornography celebrates the very existence of queer people.[58]

IS PORN ADDICTIVE?

Online porn is especially alluring because of what researchers call the "triple A engine": affordable, accessible, and anonymous.[59] Is it possible to become addicted to it? In a clinical sense, no; at least, psychologists have yet to categorize it as a formal addiction. While the *Diagnostic and Statistical Manual of Mental Disorders* (*DSM*) does not recognize such a diagnosis, viewing porn can become compulsive, and people might seek treatment for what's called hypersexual disorder.[60]

Both men and women consume pornography, though at different rates. Nearly all men have viewed it at one time in their lives, and men tend to view it more often than women. Survey results vary, but an estimated 9 to 16 percent of women and 27 to 40 percent of men ages eighteen to thirty-nine use pornography in an average week.[61] Research has found that heavy use of porn by men is associated with less relationship satisfaction, though a number of factors, such as a partner's acceptance of porn and whether a man watches porn alone, complicates the findings.[62]

REVENGE PORN

Imagine breaking up with an abusive boyfriend, only to log online and find that they have posted nude photos of you to a website that lets users share images and comment on them. That's what happened to Rebekah Wells, who created a website to end what is now also called cyberrape.[63] **Revenge porn**, defined as "sexually explicit images that are publicly shared online, without the consent of the pictured individual," is a form of harassment made possible by the internet.[64] According to a 2016 research report, one in twenty-five internet users has been subjected to the posting of sexual photos, and while men have been victims of revenge porn, it happens most often to young women.[65] Many of the photos shared online started as selfies or shared intimate moments within a relationship, but then one party decides to share the images with friends; the public; or, devastatingly, porn sites. These sexually explicit posts are motivated by a person's desire for revenge against the victim or as a means of harassment, typically after an intimate relationship has ended.[66] Most states in the United States have instituted laws against posting intimate photos without a person's consent, yet the number of victims of revenge porn continues to rise.[67]

SEX WORKERS VERSUS PROSTITUTES

Should a person have the right to have sex with others for money? Is sex work something that should be decriminalized and accepted? Many human rights advocates argue that prostitution should not be criminalized when it involves two consenting adults and that the real problem is coerced sex work, or human trafficking. Research around the world has found that when prostitution is illegal, sex workers face more violence from clients and police, and victims are less able receive help. Trans people are also disproportionately harmed by the criminalization of sex work.[68] Advocates suggest that decriminalization treats sex workers as adults, whereas vice laws infantilize them.

Human trafficking, though, is not a victimless crime but one that forces people into slavery, often sexual slavery. The US State Department reports that nearly 25 million people are trafficked worldwide. Women and children are especially vulnerable, especially if they are poor, unhoused, or victims of intimate partner violence.[69] The shift in the public conversation, from prostitution to human trafficking, is another example of how word choice can affect the way we think about an issue.

Porn and Sex Work in Media

Entertainment media, such as movies and TV shows, have long romanticized prostitution and sex work. Think of the number of times a crime show depicts male detectives meeting in strip clubs. Movies like *Pretty Woman* and *Breakfast at Tiffany's* romanticize sex work and gloss over its risks. In news, prostitution and pornography are often covered through the lens of the criminal justice system or public safety. Sex always sells, and news organizations walk a fine line when they cover stories about sex in order to stay on the serious policy side of a publicly very alluring subject. TV news organizations have been criticized for crossing that very line with salacious, bikini-laden coverage of alleged problematic behavior by college students on spring break.[70]

Prostitution has historically been covered in news through a patriarchal lens. The people who are involved, whether consenting, professional sex workers or trafficked victims, are often absent from stories, featuring instead the (often male) perspectives of police and law enforcement.[71] Police occasionally invite news crews along for stings of prostitution businesses or roundups of customers, which can make local headlines but do not address actual safety issues. Some publications have also struggled with how and whether to allow sex workers to advertise their services, again contending with the question of whether prostitution itself is harmful or whether consenting adults have the right to enjoy sex, even when money is exchanged.[72]

Summary

Rape, prostitution, and pornography are often covered in news through the lens of stereotypes. Women are stereotyped as liars when they report rape; prostitutes have long been stereotyped as streetwise fallen women; and anyone who speaks out against porn has historically been labeled as a prude. Digital media have worsened the social harm from sexual violence. Rapes can be recorded on camera and distributed to further humiliate a victim, and pornography is more easily distributed than ever. Digital media might offer some havens for sex workers but also present new ways to create harm, such as revenge porn.

Covering these deeply intimate issues is difficult in news, where simple headlines travel better than intricate ones and event-driven frames predominate. What protections for rape victims are appropriate? How can reporters use language to reduce stigma and stereotyping? How can a person's First Amendment rights to make and to view porn be balanced with a person's right to feel safe? Finally, how can news organizations avoid salacious coverage of about sex? Even the most thoughtful, sober story can be undone with a click-bait headline or exploitative photo. Gender rights advocates have pressured journalists to change how they cover stories about sex, but the digital media environment presents new challenges without quick and easy answers.

- **Reflection:** What do you think about the controversy regarding whether to name rape accusers? If you were in charge of a news organization, what would your policy be?
- **Reflection:** Think back to your first encounter with erotic imagery. Most likely you saw something online, not printed in a magazine. How might online pornography make a difference in its social impact?
- **Media Critique:** Find a story about a sexual assault in your local news publication. Are there references to drinking or partying that might lead one to blame the victim? Is there language about the accused suspect's accomplishments and education, which might elevate their reputation? What difference might this language make?

CHAPTER 8

Sexuality and Media

This chapter opens with a short review of the way queer and trans people have been oppressed historically and then describes the events that led up to the Stonewall uprising and beyond. News organizations have been historically homophobic, which affected how the public understood the AIDS crisis in the United States. While much has changed in the twenty-first century, queer and trans people continue to face marginalization, discrimination, and even violence today.

Key Concepts: Doxing, Gender Dysphoria, Outing, Reclamation

In 2022, the state of Florida instituted what was nicknamed the "Don't Say Gay" bill, which restricts what teachers can say about sexuality in elementary school classrooms. Supporters wanted to prevent children from being exposed to the idea that same-sex attraction is normal. Teachers worried about whether to display photos of their same-sex spouses or post rainbow stickers in their classroom.[1] The notion that children need to be protected from messages about sexuality frustrated the LGBTQ+ community because children get messages about sexuality all the time from movies, cartoons, and books—messages that being straight and being married is the only way to be normal. History tells us that that is simply not true.

During the second wave of feminism, scholars made a distinction between a person's biological attributes and gender, those cultural attributes that we learn how to perform. A third dimension of our sexuality is orientation: Who do you love? For centuries in most parts of the world, the only people who could publicly proclaim love for one another were those in a traditional heterosexual pairing of a cisgender woman and a cisgender man. Queer relationships existed, of course, but they were largely hidden, as they carried significant social stigma. News organizations have always included queer people, too, but, again, the social stigma kept them closeted. Things are much different today, thanks to the work of dedicated individuals who risked their jobs, their social standings, and their personal safety to fight for their own dignity and the humanity of others. Language, whether the way naming something can grant it visibility or reclaiming a slur can shift the power structure, has played a significant role in the way media have represented queer people over time.

The three dimensions of our sexual identity—body, gender, and orientation—are not all that clear-cut and exist more on a continuum than as the culturally popular binary. People might have an androgynous identity and be attracted only to women. A person might be born intersex, with anatomy that is not typically male or female.[2] A person can be born with a woman's body but feel uncomfortable with the assignation of female, identify more strongly with men, live as a trans man, and have bisexual love interests. The complexity of our sexuality is reflected in how various acronyms have developed and are debated for representing individuals who are not straight or cis. Language and culture evolve together, as reflected in the continuing updates to the *Associated Press Stylebook*, which serves as the primary guide for this textbook.[3]

The use of a rainbow flag for the LGBTQ+ movement is apt not only for its representation of the many ways our sexuality might be expressed but also for the way colors mix, have different intensities, and work together. In combination with the striped chevron for trans rights, these symbolic banners are visual reminders of how gendered identities intersect with other dimensions of our humanity. As actor Daniel Levy's character David Rose put it in the TV show *Schitt's Creek*, "I like the wine and not the label."[4]

Of course, our sexuality is just one part of our identity. Our sense of self has many facets. We're students, sons, daughters, uncles, sisters, workers, parents, and professors, and that's just the start of a very long list. We have cultural identities based on ethnicity and race. We have social identities. And all of these can shift and change over time, including, researchers say, our sexuality. First-wave feminism was about getting the vote for women, and second-wave feminism fought for equal rights in civic life. Among other things, third-wave feminism asks, "What does it mean to have gender at all? Is it related in any way to our biology? Is all of it a performance? And what happens when our bodies do not match up to our identities?"

Queer History

Same-sex attraction and nonbinary-gendered expression has forever been part of the human experience. What's changed over time is where and how it has been accepted, encouraged, or condemned. It was considered perfectly normal to have a same-sex love in ancient Greece, and there are many renditions of such relationships in art from that era. Anthropologists have identified at least one hundred different tribes that accepted individuals who represented "two spirits."[5] Most forms of Christianity have not traditionally accepted homosexuality, however, at least in part for the fact that it might involve sex for pleasure only, not for the purpose of procreation. Heresy and sodomy (gay sex) were treated similarly as the church spread through Europe, with often violent oppression of queer people, who were hanged, drowned, or burned alive for their sins. During the Renaissance, an estimated 16,000 people were tried for sodomy, and 400 were executed.[6]

Remember that patriarchy is the belief in male superiority. Same-sex attraction, or homosexuality, challenges that belief system because that male dominance over women is not expressed through such relationships. The challenge to patriarchal expectations about relationships and their sexual expression is often enforced through violence. Consider some of the premises of hegemonic masculinity: that a man should not be sensitive, that violence is the province of patriarchy, and that only certain kinds of sex are OK or sanctioned for a man to truly be manly. Sex between men contradicts this ideology, placing gay men lower on the social hierarchy and stigmatizing them for engaging in sexual acts associated with women. If men are supposed to be the penetrators, not the penetrated, then in this way of thinking, gay men are seen as feminine and therefore subordinate.

Lesbianism also confronts heteronormativity and patriarchy, although in different ways. Lesbians have often been stereotyped negatively as not really women because they might reject stereotypically feminine ways of dressing and grooming, and they engage in nonprocreative sex. If piety, purity, domesticity, and submissiveness are the ideals within the cult of true womanhood, then lesbians break every rule. By engaging in sex not intended to make children, they are "impure," irreligious, and most certainly not domestic. Rejecting sex with men is hardly submissive, and doing so has often been met with rape and violence. So while women have always loved and lived together, they usually had to do so in secret to avoid condemnation.

Queer individuals were killed for their sexuality in Europe well into the 1800s; the last known execution was in England in 1835 for two men who were convicted of what was then called buggery, or gay sex.[7] In Germany, a little over thirty years later, the conversation started to change, at least a bit. In 1867, Carl Heinrich Ulrichs, sometimes referred to as the world's first gay man, bravely appeared before a council of jurists in Germany to call for gay people to be granted civil rights. He was shouted down but not before he declared that there was a group of citizens "exposed to an undeserved legal persecution for no other reason than that mysteriously disposing creating nature has planted in them a sexual nature that is the opposite of that which is in general usual."[8] Over time, Ulrichs wrote a series of essays and pamphlets in opposition to Germany's antigay laws and started what historians believe to be the world's first magazine for gay men. He was widely mocked in media, and his writings were often confiscated by police.[9] Today, Ulrichs's pioneering efforts are considered the starting point for gay rights.[10]

One of the most famous gay people of the 1800s was Oscar Wilde, a playwright and poet of the Victorian era who wrote such classics as *The Importance of Being Earnest* and *The Portrait of Dorian Gray*. Wilde was a major celebrity but could not live openly as a gay man. In 1895, he was put on trial for gross indecency on the grounds that he had a same-sex relationship. After serving time in prison, he moved to France and died there a few years later without ever returning to England.[11] His flamboyant clothing and his acerbic wit gave visibility to his sexuality, but this also imprinted a "dandy" stereotype for gay men that extended well into the 1900s.[12]

Same-sex attraction was and is widely considered a sin in many religious groups. In the United States, sodomy laws prohibited gay sex until 2003, when the Supreme Court struck down such a law in Texas. In the case of *Lawrence v. Texas*, Justice

Anthony M. Kennedy, writing for the majority in the 6–3 decision, said that gay people are "entitled to respect for their private lives," adding that the "state cannot demean their existence or control their destiny by making their private sexual conduct a crime."[13] Coverage of the decision varied by state, as newspaper stories in states with laws prohibiting gay sex were more likely to take on a negative tone.[14] Gay rights activists were frustrated by coverage that included comments from conservative leaders suggesting that legalizing gay sex was a slippery slope to legalizing sex with animals and incest.[15]

US ACTIVISM

Early civil rights efforts on behalf of queer people in the United States started in 1924, when a veteran of the First World War, Henry Gerber, established the first gay rights group in the United States, the Society for Human Rights in Chicago. Its newsletter, *Friendship and Freedom*, was the first recorded gay rights publication in the United States. When the Chicago police found out about *Friendship and Freedom*, they destroyed as many copies as they could get their hands on, so very few printed editions of the magazine exist today. Gerber was charged with violating the Comstock Act, a federal law that prohibited the distribution of contraception or obscene materials. He lost everything as a result of this trial but continued to publish under a pseudonym on behalf of LGBTQ+ rights until he died in 1972.[16]

A bartender puts his hand over drinks served to members of the Mattachine Society upon finding out that they are gay, providing evidence the group needed to file a discrimination lawsuit.
Courtesy of Getty Images

The earliest group to organize publicly for gay men's rights was the Mattachine Society, established in the 1950s with chapters in several cities, including New York and San Francisco.[17] Remember: To be out of the closet at this time was extremely risky. Gay sex was considered a manifestation of mental illness and was criminalized. People lost jobs, were rejected by their families, and were violently attacked by police, so consider the courage it took in 1966 for members of the Mattachine Society in New York to stage what they playfully called a "sip-in." The protest, staged for the sake of media coverage, was planned to challenge the city's law against serving gay people in bars. (The city would shut down bars if they served gay people because of a belief that they were unruly and would create problems.) As a media event, the protest hit a snag when a reporter from the *New York Times* arrived at a tavern first, tipping off management, who shut down the bar before the group arrived. Members of the Mattachine Society simply moved to another bar, ordered drinks, and then announced that they were gay. The bartender put his hand over a drink to deny the men service—giving the group the evidence necessary to file a discrimination lawsuit, which they eventually won.[18]

THE BREAKING POINT: STONEWALL

Chapter 2 introduces the concept of enclaves, where marginalized groups can meet or communicate safely outside the mainstream. Underground publications for gay men and lesbians offered metaphorical spaces, but gay nightclubs offered a physical space where people could feel at home and be themselves. The Stonewall Inn in New York City was one such place. Queer people came to Stonewall to dance, drink, date, and enjoy some social safety, except for when police came to raid the place. On those nights, police conducted genital checks to enforce a city law that required individuals to wear at least three items of clothing appropriate to their physical traits. So a person wearing women's clothes whom police suspected was not biologically female could be forced to display their anatomy to an officer.

On June 28, 1969, patrons at Stonewall had had enough. Witnesses say police were rough with a couple of the women under arrest, and a crowd gathered. Some onlookers started throwing things at police, first coins, then rocks and bottles, and the Stonewall riot ensued. The incident inspired the formation of the Gay Liberation Front and other groups to organize for their civil rights.[19] News coverage of Stonewall varied according to geography. New York newspapers recognized the event's significance, while outlets in other parts of the country did not run stories until much later, when it was clear the riot was a watershed moment for LGBTQ+ rights. The New York media may have understood Stonewall's significance, but it did not mean that stories were written respectfully. The headline on the first story from the *New York Daily News* read, "Homo Nest Raided, Queen Bees Are Stinging Mad." Slurs like *fags* and *nellies* appeared in news coverage, and words like *squealed* and *falsetto* were used when quoting Stonewall patrons.[20] It would be years before news portrayed the community with respect, but Stonewall inspired many people in the LGBTQ+ community to start demanding it.

PSYCHIATRY AND ACCEPTANCE

The gay rights movement enjoyed a significant victory in 1973, when the American Psychiatric Association's board of directors removed homosexuality from its official list of mental illnesses in the *Diagnostic and Statistical Manual of Mental Disorders* (*DSM*). Until then, gay and lesbian people were considered to be mentally ill. If they loved a person of the same sex, then their feelings were dismissed as insane. They were subject to lobotomies and electric-shock conversion therapy in ill-conceived attempts to convert their orientation.[21] In 2015, President Obama called for a ban on conversion therapy after a transgender teen committed suicide. The practice remains legal in many parts of the United States.[22]

While queer people have gained acceptance and legal protections in many spaces, they still encounter discrimination in the United States. A 2020 Supreme Court ruling established the rights of LGBTQ+ people in the workplace, but Congress has not passed the Equality Act, which would extend protections for housing, education, and health care.[23] Policies affecting people in the military can change according to presidential politics. For example, President Bill Clinton, in order to open the military to LBGTQ+ people, instituted a policy called "Don't Ask, Don't Tell" in 1993, which allowed LGBTQ+ people to join (or remain) in the military as long as they did not discuss their sexuality.[24] The Human Rights Campaign and other advocates pushed against what was still a form of discrimination (after all, straight people were allowed to talk about their love life), and LGBTQ+ people were granted full rights in the military in 2011 under President Barack Obama.[25] When Donald Trump became president, he ordered transgender people to be banned from the military, a policy that was scrapped a couple of months after Joe Biden became president.[26]

LGBTQ+ News Coverage

Given the historic lack of open representation in newsrooms, it's no surprise that coverage of the LGBTQ+ community was unsophisticated and often insensitive. Journalists were largely ignorant of the challenges faced by queer people, and, therefore, so was the news audience. News about the gay and lesbian rights was covered in stigmatizing and stereotypical ways. Chapter 3 discusses the protest paradigm, which is how news marginalizes protests and covers them as deviant, with little emphasis on the underlying the issues. This was common in the way news covered Pride parades and LGBTQ+ protests.[27] Visual coverage also tended to focus on the most outlandish or shocking images possible.

The perpetuation of the belief that queer people were immoral deviants who didn't matter had tragic consequences. For example, the New Orleans Upstairs Lounge fire in 1973 killed thirty-two people, many of them trapped in the flames. Until the Pulse Nightclub shooting in Orlando in 2016, it was the deadliest crime against queer people in American history. The event made national headlines, but even though there were surviving witnesses, no one was ever arrested. Some of the dead were buried in an unmarked grave. The Upstairs Lounge was known as a gay club, and the police and public simply

Profile: Audre Lorde, Poet (1934–1992)

Audre Lorde was a poet whose work gave artful voice to gender rights and intersectional ideas. Lorde was born in New York to immigrant parents and started writing poetry as a girl. Confident in her own abilities, she wrote a poem about romance that was rejected by a teacher, but she sold it to *Seventeen* magazine. "Words would get me high," she once recalled. After high school, Lorde worked in a factory and as a nurse's aide but eventually left the United States to study at the National University of Mexico. She found inspiration in the region's culture and returned to New York empowered to give voice to her life and experience.

Because she was a lesbian, Lorde surprised her friends when she married a man in 1962 and had two children. During this time, her poetry started gaining recognition, and Lorde's writing career took off. She went on to work as an English professor at the John Jay College of Criminal Justice and Hunter College. She was granted the Walt Whitman Citation of Merit in 1991

Audre Lorde.
Courtesy of Alamy

and was appointed as the poet laureate of New York State from 1991 to 1992. Her descriptions of lesbian lovemaking broke barriers, and her writing on motherhood crossed borders at a time when LGBTQ+ people were not thought of as parents. Lorde's work is accessible, political, and linguistically graceful. Her essay "There Is No Hierarchy of Oppressions" is an intersectional rallying cry for all marginalized groups to unite in opposition to injustice. Through her teaching, speaking, and writing, Lorde used her voice and encouraged others to raise theirs, a theme well summarized in the final line of one of her most famous poems, *A Litany for Survival*: "So it is better to speak / remembering / we were never meant to survive."

Sources: Academy of American Poets, "Audre Lorde," accessed January 24, 2023, https://poets.org/poet/audre-lorde; Judith C. Kohl, "Audre Lorde: Overview," in *Gay and Lesbian Biography*, ed. Michael J. Tyrkus and Michael Bronski (St. James Press, 1997); Audre Lorde, "A Litany for Survival," in *The Collected Poems of Audre Lorde* (W. W. Norton, 1978).

didn't care enough to pursue justice.[28] Nearly fifty years later, in 2022, New Orleans leaders acknowledged the city's indifference and voted to honor the victims.[29]

ALTERNATIVE NEWS

While the mainstream press ignored or vilified the queer community, alternative publications devoted to gay and lesbian rights helped to galvanize the movement. Recall that Ulrichs's historic activism included the publication of pamphlets and that Henry Gerber used his magazine, *Friendship and Freedom*, to educate, advocate, and organize. Alternative press publications helped to establish community while reporting on the movement. These early magazines had a very small circulation because of the stigma associated with being queer, and people were prosecuted for merely owning such materials. In the 1950s, a postmaster in California refused to deliver issues of *One*, published by the Mattachine Society. The case went to the Supreme Court, which delivered an important victory for free speech and gay rights when it ruled in 1958 that writing about same-sex affairs was not legally obscene.[30]

Freed from the threat of prosecution for obscenity or immorality, lesbian and gay people were able to publish many more magazines and newspapers with varied perspectives. Some, like the *Mattachine Review*, were more conservative. Lesbian publications included magazines that called for separatism from mainstream feminism and others that encouraged women to abandon men completely. One publication, *The Ladder*, was intended to help the public understand and accept lesbianism.[31] Some publications, such as the *Philadelphia Gay News*, were devoted to local activism. One magazine pushed through to the mainstream for the way it focused on news and leveraged advertising. The *Advocate* stood out with an editorial style that boldly supported Gay Pride. It used photos of seminude men on the cover to boost newsstand sales, and it helped to shape the image of queer people as a valuable consumer group.[32] Today, the *Advocate* is the longest-running gay rights magazine in the United States and has a reputation as the movement's publication of record.[33]

OUTING AND PRIVACY

If a public leader calls for laws against gay marriage but is a closeted gay man, does the public have the right to know? On one side is an individual's private sexual life, and on the other is the public interest in their political activity. Consider the case of Lee Liberace, who used only his last name on the stage. He set the bar for flamboyance before Elton John or David Bowie entered the scene, performing in sequined suits, capes, and furs and playing piano with his fingers adorned with gaudy diamond rings. He kept his sexuality secret, however, knowing that in the 1950s, coming out would kill his career. He would tell the gossip magazines he was engaged, then not, and say he was waiting for the perfect girl. When a gossip magazine, *Confidential*, published details about Liberace's sexuality, he sued for libel. He swore under oath that he was straight and won a settlement. He did so again with another publication, the *Daily Mirror*. His legal defense was that his feathers and feminine act was just that—a show business act—and his lie succeeded.[34] Liberace remained closeted even in death. He died of AIDS in 1987, but his death certificate read that he passed away from heart disease.[35]

By 1990, the LGBTQ+ rights movement had gained strength, numbers, and a public voice, and some journalists decided to change the rules. That year, a magazine called *OutWeek* published a story revealing that Malcom Forbes, who'd recently died, was gay. His sexuality had been an open secret among members of the gay community in New York, who surmised that Forbes dated Elizabeth Taylor as a cover.[36] The

Forbes story was the first **outing** of a celebrity, and more, including stories about living people, would follow. Outing was extremely controversial. One side argued that sexuality should be private, especially because of the social stigma and shame imposed on queer people. The man who approved the original Forbes story, Gabriel Rotello, defended the practice as necessary for change:

> We said it was hypocritical for journalists to routinely disclose the private lives of straight celebrities in ways those celebrities disliked or considered damaging while routinely covering up all mention of gay celebrities' lives. We argued that if homosexuality is a healthy facet of the human condition, the media have to stop treating it as the only unmentionable in journalism's inky sea of candor.[37]

Those who were outed responded with anger and sometimes denied the stories, but fears that the truth would destroy their careers eroded over time. As controversial as it was at the time, outing accomplished what it set out to do: normalize queer people. The reporter who wrote the original Forbes article, Michael Signorile, put it this way: "If anything, the goal behind outing is to show just how many gay people there are among the most visible people in our society so that when someone outs the milkman or the spinster everyone will say 'So what?'"[38]

Concerns over privacy remain. It may seem fair to out celebrities or politicians who publicly criticize queer people, but what about people who aren't famous? Whose sexuality is relevant to the public? What other matters about a person's life, such as their address or phone number, should be private? **Doxing**, the practice of publishing a person's address or other documentation, is a more recent controversial practice that became common in the internet age.[39] Professional reporters work with such information all the time—after all, they need home addresses and phone numbers to do their jobs—but journalistic ethics regulate how and when that information is *published*.[40] Like outing, the ethics of publishing a person's personal information depends on the public's legitimate interest. Doxing contrasts with outing because it usually uses information in publicly available documents, such as marriage licenses or birth certificates, and is not related to a person's sexuality. Doxing has become weaponized online, however, and can be used to harass or intimidate individuals, including journalists.[41]

Covering AIDS

The gay and lesbian press covered the AIDS crisis when mainstream news downplayed the disease. AIDS was covered as a "gay disease" for people who chose a "risky lifestyle": that is, people who did not matter. In spite of years of activism for LGBTQ+ acceptance, even members of the medical community stigmatized gay sex, which translated into indifference to the disease. Framing AIDS as something that could be prevented with "behavior change" instead of medical research implied that those with the illness somehow deserved their fate.[42] Note, for instance, how the disease is framed in 1981 in the first story about AIDS to appear in the *New York Times*: emphasizing its association with gay men.

Excerpt: "Rare Cancer Seen in 41 Homosexuals"

Doctors in New York and California have diagnosed among homosexual men 41 cases of a rare and often rapidly fatal form of cancer. Eight of the victims died less than 24 months after the diagnosis was made.

The cause of the outbreak is unknown, and there is as yet no evidence of contagion. But the doctors who have made the diagnoses, mostly in New York City and the San Francisco Bay area, are alerting other physicians who treat large numbers of homosexual men to the problem in an effort to help identify more cases and to reduce the delay in offering chemotherapy treatment.

The sudden appearance of the cancer, called Kaposi's sarcoma, has prompted a medical investigation that experts say could have as much scientific as public health importance because of what it may teach about determining the causes of more common types of cancer.

Source: Lawrence K. Altman, "Rare Cancer Seen in 41 Homosexuals," *New York Times*, July 3, 1981, https://www.nytimes.com/1981/07/03/us/rare-cancer-seen-in-41-homosexuals.html.

Randy Shilts, a reporter for the *San Francisco Chronicle*, was one of the first to write about AIDS. His book, *And the Band Played On*, describes the indifference of health officials, government leaders, and news organizations as thousands of gay men died.[43] The AIDS crisis inspired a new wave of LGBTQ+ activism and the

These are some of the panels from 2012 AIDS Quilt Project. Different panels were displayed each day for two weeks to commemorate the project's twenty-fifth anniversary. Panels continue to be added to the original AIDS Quilt every year, and it is now too large for the Washington, DC, Mall.
Courtesy of Creative Commons, Elvert Barnes

Profile: Randy Shilts, Journalist (1951–1994)

Randy Shilts.
Courtesy of Scott Sommerdorf, San Francisco Chronicle, Polaris

Randy Shilts was the first openly gay journalist to work for a major newspaper. He was raised in a conservative household and came out to his parents at the age of twenty while attending college in Oregon. Upon graduating with his journalism degree, he became the Northwest correspondent for the *Advocate*. He soon moved to San Francisco, first to work for the *Advocate*, and then as a freelance reporter covering the LGBTQ+ community for print and television. His first book, *The Mayor of Castro Street*, chronicles the life of Harvey Milk. Milk, who was assassinated in 1978, was an openly gay politician whose election to the San Francisco City Council marked a significant moment for the gay rights movement.

Shilts was one of the first reporters to sound the alarm about AIDS, and his second (of three) books, *And the Band Played On: Politics, People, and the AIDS Epidemic*, is a detailed account of the epidemic's spread in the early 1980s. The title comes from the apocryphal story about the orchestra continuing to play while the *Titanic* sank, a metaphor for Shilts's portrayal of the way health experts, the government, and news organizations ignored the crisis as thousands died. Shilts was vilified by some gay leaders for pointing out the role of anonymous sex and bath houses for the spread of AIDS.

Shilts's third and final book, *Conduct Unbecoming*, was equally impactful for how it carefully documents the way the US military selectively enforced its ban on LGBTQ+ people. The book exposes the military's hypocrisy, but Shilts was denounced by some gay leaders because he refused to name names and "out" his closeted sources. Same-sex marriage was not legal at the time, but in 1993, Shilts and his boyfriend, Barry Barbieri, commemorated their relationship with a commitment ceremony. Shilts died of AIDS a year later.

Sources: Joseph M. Eagan, "Randy Shilts: Overview," in *Gay and Lesbian Biography*, ed. Michael J. Tyrkus and Michael Bronski (St. James Press, 1997); William Grimes, "Randy Shilts, Author, Dies at 42; One of First to Write about AIDS," *New York Times*, February 18, 1994, https://www.nytimes.com/1994/02/18/obituaries/randy-shilts-author-dies-at-42-one-of-first-to-write-about-aids.html; Randy Shilts, *And the Band Played On: Politics, People, and the AIDS Epidemic* (St. James Press, 1987).

establishment of ACT-UP, whose members fought for funding and attention to the disease. The media framing of AIDS shifted when a young man with hemophilia, Ryan White, got the disease from a blood transfusion. He had to fight to be allowed to attend school because officials thought he would put other students at risk, and he was bullied by other students.[44] White's story went national, and he became the "innocent" face of AIDS. While White and his family supported the LGBTQ+ community and they themselves were not homophobic, the frequent use of the word *innocent* shifted the news frame of AIDS—it was finally covered as a disease anyone could get.[45] White died in 1990, one month shy of his high school graduation and just a few months before Congress passed the Ryan White Act, in 1990, which assists low-income patients and helps to pay for lifesaving treatment.

In addition to demanding a better public health response to AIDS, activists wanted to call attention both to the humanity of those who were sick and to the sheer numbers of people who were dying. The AIDS Quilt Project, an extraordinary form of visual activism, accomplished both goals. Supporters were invited to make fabric panels in honor of a person who died from AIDS. The first display of these panels took place on the National Mall in Washington, DC, in 1987 and included 1,920 panels, covering a space larger than a football field.[46] The drama of the display could not be ignored. Still, it took the death of a young, presumably straight white boy for many Americans to grasp the tragedy of this disease.

RECLAIMING LANGUAGE

This book describes how word choice can frame an issue or idea and how language can be used to name a problem. Language can also be used to hurt. Insulting words are a form of social control; they mark certain people as unworthy of respect and belonging. One way to resist the insults is to reclaim the slur. This is not a matter of taking back a word, as marginalized groups aren't the sources of their own slurs. Instead, **reclamation** is the process of taking *control* of the word to eliminate the pain associated with it.[47] To reclaim a slur is a form of resistance, and one of the clearest examples is the word *queer*. Once a nasty thing to say against a gay or lesbian person, the word has now been reclaimed by a marginalized community in dramatic fashion. In the 1980s, a group of activists called Queer Nation started to use the word in a confrontational way, giving rise to the protest slogan "We're here, we're queer, get over it!"[48] Today the word is part of the mainstream, an umbrella term for people who are not cisgender or straight.[49] Universities offer classes in queer studies, academic groups conduct queer research, and media organizations like NPR use the term regularly. Of course, some older individuals who were targeted by the term in a pejorative way still might not be entirely comfortable with it.[50]

Simply using a word can change public perception. In 2015, Obama was the first president to use the words *lesbian, bisexual,* and *transgender* in a State of the Union speech, lending visibility and legitimacy to the community.[51] The framing of gay marriage as *marriage* rather than merely some kind of civil partnership made a difference in the civil discourse. Framing a relationship as a civil union doesn't carry the same connotation, the same legitimacy, or the same normalcy as straight marriage. Activists fought for the exact same kind of marriage that heterosexuals had long enjoyed, which comes with financial rights, healthcare rights, and other privileges. In 2015, when penning the ruling that confirmed the legality of gay marriage, Justice Anthony Kennedy wrote, "No union is more profound than marriage, for it embodies the highest ideals of love, fidelity, devotion, sacrifice and family."[52] Same-sex marriage is now far more widely accepted and normalized in news and in entertainment media, though some observers worry that this perpetuates the idea that monogamous marriage is and should remain the norm for all people, straight or gay. Discussions about polyamory, pansexuality, asexuality, and other ways of existing and living in relationships are just starting to enter the mainstream.

Today, LGBTQ+ Pride is part of corporate culture. One of the forces that elevated the movement, in fact, was the recognition by corporations that gay and lesbian people were a distinct consumer market worth targeting. Advertisers sought couples without children who were more likely to spend significant money on travel, home decor, and clothing.[53] Some cities and other resort operators now offer special events for LGBTQ+ people.[54] During June, which is Pride Month, stores and commercials are filled with so many multicolored packages that critics warn against rainbow-washing: that is, empty marketing that exploits Pride by corporations that don't necessarily support LGBTQ+ rights.[55]

Mainstream news organizations generally cover the LGBTQ+ community with more respect today. Resources from GLAAD and other advocacy groups offer support for journalists to better cover the LGBTQ+ community. The *GLAAD Media Guide* is now in its eleventh edition and offers help with LGBTQ+ terms. It offers advice for inclusive language and respectful coverage, as well as suggestions for covering such current topics as conversion therapy and monkeypox.[56] The *Associated Press Stylebook* also offers guidance for fair coverage. Since 2013, for instance, the AP has directed reporters to use the words *wife* or *husband* regardless of whether a couple is gay or straight and to use *spouse* or *partner* when sources request those titles. In the past, reporters might use a phrase like *gay spouse* or *life partner* to describe a husband or wife in a same-sex marriage, but the Associated Press decision gives linguistic sameness to all marriages.[57] In 2017, the AP approved the use of the singular *they* in news, even though that usage has been part of the English language for centuries.[58]

The AP also cautions that reporters should not assume a person's gender identity based on their first name, and they warn, "Don't refer to *preferred* or *chosen* pronouns. Instead, the pronouns they use, whose pronouns are, who uses the pronouns, etc."[59] Should reporters always ask a source their pronouns? There may be rare instances when asking about their pronouns might confuse a source or derail your interview, but the more often this practice is part of asking for the spelling of someone's name, the faster this courtesy will be normalized.

Trans Rights

Not all trans people have **gender dysphoria**, but it can be part of a person's decision to choose to live according to a different sexual identity. Gender dysphoria is when a person feels like their external body does not match their internal identity.[60] Don't confuse it with dysmorphia, which is a general dissatisfaction with one's body and is often associated with eating disorders. The word *transgender* is an "adjective to describe people whose gender identity differs from the sex they were assigned at birth." It is not acceptable to use the term as a noun or to refer to a person as "a trans."[61]

Trans individuals fought for greater visibility and essential rights in the twenty-first century. Most Americans learn about trans issues by way of celebrities like Caitlyn Jenner. Perhaps the most famous trans person anywhere, Jenner announced her transition with a cover story in *Vanity Fair* and a splashy video that showcases her feminine beauty.[62] *Vanity Fair*'s coverage of Jenner's coming-out story helped to educate the public about trans issues, but it also neglected the economic and personal struggles of the typical trans person.

The person who most dramatically introduced the idea of trans rights to the public is Renée Richards, whose chosen first name means *reborn* in French. She was forced into the public eye when she wanted to play tennis on a women's circuit and had to sue for that right.[63] Today's audience is likely more acquainted with actress Laverne Cox, who starred in *Orange Is the New Black*. Cox has advocated for trans acceptance in her work and public life. She made national news in 2014 in an interview with Katie Couric, who pressed for information about her genitals. Cox responded by shifting attention to the problems faced by trans people at large: "The preoccupation with transition and surgery objectifies trans people, and then we don't get to really deal with the real lived experiences."[64] In a follow-up interview, Couric discussed her own "learning curve" about the trans community, saying, "I think I made a mistake."[65]

CHALLENGES FOR TRANS PEOPLE

While Jenner's story may have educated the public about what it's like to live as a trans woman, most trans people do not have her resources or support. Trans people are at greater risk for violence, discrimination, and poverty than members of the cis community. In 2021, more than fifty people in the United States were killed because they were trans. Worldwide, the killings totaled 375 trans people.[66] According to a survey by the National Transgender Center for Equality (NTCE), nearly a third of trans people live in poverty, double the national average for the entire population. A third of trans people have experienced homelessness at some point in their lives, and 8 percent of those surveyed had been kicked out of their family homes for being trans. More than half had been harassed in school, and 17 percent had left school because of pervasive harassment and assaults.

Trans people are routinely refused medical care and fired from their jobs. They also attempt suicide at nine times the national average. For trans people of color, the risk of violence is even higher. According to the same survey, trans people of color are more likely to receive mistreatment in health care and three times more likely than cis people to live in poverty.[67] A report about high school students from the CDC found that 1.8 percent of teens consider themselves to be trans, putting them at much greater risk for violence, harassment, and sexual assault.[68] Most trans people feel that they cannot go to the police for help. The NTCE has found that a majority of trans people have been harassed or abused by police and that most departments lack clear policies for the fair treatment of trans people. Few departments, for instance, have policies that respect a person's current name, so police departments might release information about a crime victim using their deadname.[69]

Bathroom laws and concerns about gender-segregated bathrooms have been part of the debate about gender rights since the Equal Rights Amendment was first proposed in 1971, but transgender visibility renewed and inflamed these controversies. Transphobia is often presented as concern for children or religious freedom. Antibullying programs are sometimes criticized by religious groups on the grounds that by protecting LGBTQ+ youth, schools promote immorality.[70] Parents and politicians are often in conflict about when and how a young person should undergo gender-affirming treatment.[71] Though the US State Department announced in 2021 that it would start allowing individuals to use *X* as a gender designation, many trans people cannot change their gender on government identification cards to match the lives they live.[72]

Media coverage of transgender people has made some progress, but advocates remain concerned for the way some issues are framed. For example, a 2018 *Atlantic Monthly* cover story about trans people who regret transitioning as teenagers was denounced by critics as sensationalist.[73] The person whose face is used on the cover was surprised to find his likeness there with a headline that misgenders him and mischaracterizes his situation.[74] Other people who participated in the story were disappointed for how it focuses so heavily on the fraction of people who regret their transition without adequate coverage of those who believe it saved their lives.[75]

The fact that journalists are discussing how to best frame transgender issues might be cause for some optimism. Trans advocates welcomed the AP's decision in 2017 to allow the singular *they* for people who use that pronoun.[76] The Associated Press came out with even more details for trans coverage in 2023—including reminders to avoid binary references and to identify people by the name they use publicly: that is, to avoid deadnames unless they are somehow essential to a story.[77] To be trans is no longer newsworthy by itself, as it was when Renée Richards came out in the seventies.

If gender is socially constructed, then why might someone need surgery to live comfortably and authentically? Trans activists counter that cis people undergo gender-affirming surgery all the time, with breast and buttocks implants, tummy tucks, and even penile

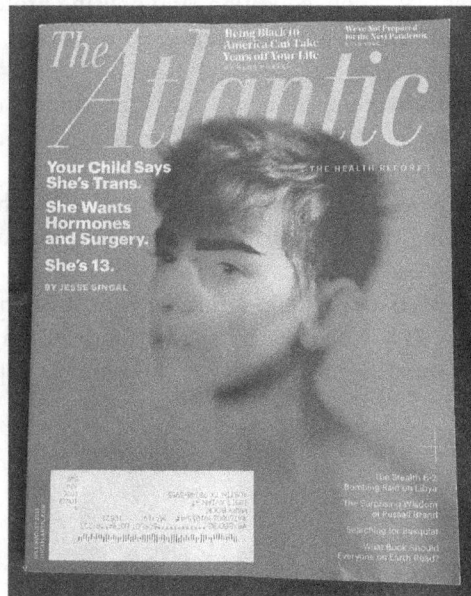

The 2018 cover of the *Atlantic Monthly* misgenders the teen whose face it features.
Courtesy of *Atlantic Monthly*

enlargements. Some feminists, such as J. K. Rowling, reject the idea that trans women ought to be treated as women generally; these feminists have been labeled as transexclusionary radical feminists, or **TERFs**.[78] Rowling was strongly criticized for tweeting about trans women in 2020 and pushed back against critics, writing, "[O]ne of the objectives of denying the importance of sex is to erode what some seem to see as the cruelest segregationist idea of women having their own biological realities. Or just as threatening, unifying realities that make them a cohesive political class."[79] Rowling's position has cost her fans. Even Daniel Radcliffe and Emma Watson pushed back against Rowling's statements. These actors and many others stood firm in saying that women are women and trans women are women.[80] The Associated Press advises journalists to avoid using the politically charged term TERF unless it is needed for a compelling reason, and to be "specific about a person's or group's objections."[81]

Summary

For centuries, queer people were unable to live open, honest lives without fear of losing their social statuses, their jobs, and even their lives. Activists in the twentieth century started pushing for respect and acceptance, and they succeeded on multiple fronts. Gay marriage now has a constitutional protection, and it is no longer a career killer for journalists to be out of the closet. Entertainment media and many news organizations have improved the way they represent the LGBTQ+ community, but stereotypes and sensationalism at the expense of real human beings persist. Queer people lack consistent legal, job, education, and housing protections, and trans people remain marginalized in ways that can keep them in poverty and in physical danger.

- **Reflection:** How much do you conform to masculine or feminine representations in media? Is there something you do or enjoy that's not expected of someone with your gender identity?
- **Media Critique:** Think about the TV shows and movies you watched while growing up. Do you recall any representations of same-sex relationships? What were those representations like?
- **Media Critique:** Consider how Caitlin Jenner was portrayed in *Vanity Fair* in 2015. How might her story and the way it was framed affect the public's understanding of the average trans person's experience?

CHAPTER 9

Newsroom Diversity

Race, ethnicity, and sexuality affect the struggle for gender rights generally and within journalism. Women of color, gay men, lesbians, trans people, and many other individuals have been marginalized in society, in news, and often even within the organizations that purport to support democracy.

Key Concepts: Kerner Commission, Sexual Harassment

While women have been part of journalism throughout history, the field only accepted them relatively late in the twentieth century. Gay people have also always been part of journalism but have only recently been able to be open about their sexuality with colleagues and the news audience. On the plus side: There are more women in newsrooms and in more roles than ever. The bad news is that women are not proportionately represented in leadership positions. As of 2022, an international survey by the Reuters Institute of 240 news organizations (representing twelve markets across five continents) found that only about one in five of those newsrooms were led by women.[1] In eleven of the twelve markets studied, the majority of top editors were men. Even in places where women outnumber men on the staff, men tend to be in charge of a newsroom. Whether straight, lesbian, or trans, women have made significant progress, yet true parity remains elusive.

Chapters 2 and 3 describe how women worked as writers, editors, and even publishers of their own papers in early America. Yet while such women existed, they were a tiny minority and often were shut out from larger news organizations. The number of women in news grew from only 4 percent in 1890 to 37 percent by 1960, and it was legal to pay them less. In 1957, the average newspaper pay for men was $76.96 per week, compared with $66.00 for women. Universities with journalism programs, such as the University of Missouri and Columbia University, admitted women early in the twentieth century, though female professors were scarce.[2] By the time of the second wave, more women than ever were working in print and broadcast news, and

Nina Totenberg.
Courtesy of Creative Commons, Kenneth C. Zirkel

some achieved star status as anchors and reporters; but for the most part, women were second-class citizens who were paid less, had little editorial power, and endured harassment from sources and coworkers. In some instances, they were still treated as tokens, as in the days of the female stunt reporters. In a 2014 interview, radio reporter Nina Totenberg recalled what it was like to so often be the only woman in the room:

> I was thinking of leaving NPR, . . . and I had lunch with a guy I knew well and liked and respected. He was bureau chief at a major newspaper chain. And I would lay odds that he doesn't remember this because he would be ashamed to remember this. So I said I was thinking of leaving NPR, and he said, "But you know we already have our woman."[3]

A Tolerated Presence

As the American newspaper business grew in the 1900s, women continued to work their way into journalism. They were still considered unusual "girl reporters," assessed as much for the way they dressed as how they wrote. Most worked on beats far from the front page, usually for the "women's section." Those who did manage to put their

Profile: Katharine Graham, Newspaper Publisher
(1917–2001)

Katharine Graham ran the *Washington Post* from 1963 until 1979, steering the newspaper through some of the most dramatic stories of the time, such as the Vietnam War and Watergate. Women in the newsroom were rare at the time and even more rare in leadership roles, and Graham felt unprepared to take over the role after her husband had committed suicide. Columnist Walter Lippman (see chapter 1) was among the journalists who helped Graham adjust to the job. Graham made the decision in 1971 to publish the Pentagon papers, which detail the way the American government withheld key information from the public about the war in Vietnam. She supported Bob Woodward and Carl Bernstein as they investigated the Watergate break-in in the face of vitriolic attacks from President Richard Nixon's allies. Her support for women's liberation grew gradually. The *Washington Post* owned *Newsweek*

Katharine Graham.
Courtesy of Creative Commons

magazine, so when the "Good Girls" rebelled at the magazine with their 1970 discrimination lawsuit, Graham was caught in the middle and asked her colleagues, "Which side am I supposed to be on?" In 1972, when the Gridiron Club, a historically segregated group for political and media decision makers, invited her to their annual dinner, she declined.

Even after her son took over as publisher of the *Post* in 1979, Graham stayed on as CEO. She is referenced but never seen in *All the President's Men*, the movie about Watergate, and she is depicted by Meryl Streep in *The Post*, a movie about the Pentagon papers. A TV drama called *Lou Grant* includes a character named Mrs. Pynchon, who was partly inspired by Graham. Graham was a dedicated journalist and a savvy business leader. She was the first woman to lead a *Fortune* 500 company and was successful in that role, as the *Post*'s stock continually rose during her tenure. In her Pulitzer Prize–winning autobiography, written at the age of seventy-nine, she writes, "[W]e operated under the philosophy—which I have espoused and practiced from the time I took over the company . . . that journalistic excellence and profitability go hand in hand."

Sources: Susan Baer, "Shy Debutante Became Giant in U.S. Journalism," *Baltimore Sun*, July 18, 2001, https://www.baltimoresun.com/bal-te.graham18jul18-story.html; Katharine Graham, *Personal History* (Knopf Doubleday, 2011), 425, 620; Caroline Hallemann, "The True Story of Katharine Graham and the *Post*," *Town and Country*, February 27, 2018, https://www.townandcountrymag.com/society/a15857333/katharine-graham-true-story-the-post/; John J. O'Connor, "TV: CBS Presents 'Lou Grant,'" *New York Times*, September 20, 1977, https://www.nytimes.com/1977/09/20/archives/tv-cbs-presents-lou-grant-comedic-spinoff-moves-asner-from.html.

bylines on political or international stories were often treated as tokens, hired to represent their demographic groups. Tokenism is a form of window dressing, as it grants only superficial accommodations to members of a group.[4] That is, a person is hired more for the sake of appearance, not true inclusion. In these situations, LGBTQ+ journalists and women, especially women of color, have been accused of lacking the objectivity necessary to cover stories about race and gender. Some women learned to act like men in order to succeed, drinking, smoking, and swearing their way into a boys' club that only tolerated them as long as they knew their place.

The success of Agness "Agee" Underwood in the 1940s exemplifies this balancing act. Underwood started at the *Los Angeles Times* as a crime reporter and fought her way into crime scenes, even when police thought her too delicate. She eventually became the country's first female city editor, with the *Los Angeles Evening Herald and Express*. Her unique success might be attributed, at least in part, to the way she combined masculine traits (strength and competitiveness) with feminine ones (warmth and nurturing). Later in life, in keeping with the masculine perspective that helped her succeed, Underwood criticized second-wave feminists, attributing her success solely to her own hard work.[5]

Newspapers' women's sections, where most female journalists worked at this time, presented women with opportunities and obstacles. Women were able to get jobs, but those jobs, covering the four *F*s—food, fashion, furnishings, and family—were off the front-page politics and crime beats. During the second wave, newspaper leaders felt pressure to rebrand these sections, not necessarily for the sake of gender equality, but because it would be good for business. Even with new, less sexist titles, the sections continued to publish material associated with feminine stereotypes instead of political issues of concern to women, such as childcare, sexual harassment, and birth control. Rebranding these sections was its own form of tokenism, as most newspapers simply changed the names but not the content of these sections, achieving exactly the opposite of what female writers were advocating.[6]

Integrating the Newsroom

After a series of riots in the 1960s, the **Kerner Commission**, appointed by President Lyndon B. Johnson, cast part of the blame for racial discontent on the fact that media did not represent the interests of Black Americans. The famous report used the nomenclature of the time to note, "By failing to portray the Negro as a matter of routine and in the context of the total society, the news media have, we believe, contributed to the black-white schism in this country."[7] Even in the face of this extraordinary indictment by the government, American news editors balked at the notion that they should hire more journalists of color. They complained that there were no qualified candidates and that such edicts interfered with press freedom. It took until 1978 for the American Society of News Editors (ASNE) to commit to at least keeping count of the number of minorities working in newsrooms. A similar commitment to monitor gender hiring took place twenty years later.[8]

RECRUITING WOMEN

Leaders of the ASNE started talking about racial integration in the 1950s, but many were openly hostile to proposals to advance more women in the profession. While openly racist comments were gradually moving to the back rooms for the sake of public politeness, there was no such deference to women. Articles in the organization's newsletter, the *Bulletin*, were as likely to portray female reporters as "pretty young things" as they were to profile the few newsrooms with female editors. Discussions in the *Bulletin* about the "woman problem" were overtly sexist, as when one editor wrote, "We think our troubles with women stem from the fact that they are always in one of four stages: premenstrual, menstrual, post-menstrual or pregnant. . . . Dispositions vary from charming to snarling." Another was quoted in the same professional publication: "Where there are women, there are problems."[9]

As the second wave crested, so did women's dissatisfaction with their second-class status in news. At *Newsweek*, for instance, female employees were relegated to fact-checking stories written by male correspondents, they were paid less, and they were blocked from any sort of promotion. In spite of having the same educational background and skills as the male writers, they could not publish an article with their own bylines. Ironically, the magazine was owned by the same company as the *Washington Post*, which at that time was led by a woman, Katharine Graham. In 1970, a group of female fact checkers from *Newsweek* filed a discrimination suit against the magazine on the same day the magazine published a cover story about feminism. Lynn Povich was one of those women, and her book about the event, *The Good Girls Revolt*, was the subject of a TV show by the same name in 2016. They won that case and inspired women at other publications to file similar lawsuits.[10]

Women also had to fight simply to report the news. During the second wave, female journalists protested at events they were not allowed to cover, such as the annual Gridiron Dinner, a social gathering for journalists and prominent politicians in Washington.[11] They were finally admitted to what was headlined as the "newsmen's dinner" in 1975.[12] The National Press Club (NPC) did not admit women as members and only allowed women to observe events from a gallery. This was no small problem, as the NPC hosted some of the most important newsmakers in history, including heads of state. When Soviet Premier Nikita Khrushchev was scheduled there in 1959, he refused to appear unless women were admitted, and the club made an exception, allowing a small number of women on the main floor and—significantly—giving the leader of the Women's National Press Club, Helen Thomas, a seat at the head table. Not until 1971, however, did the male members of the NPC vote to admit women and grant them access to the bar and card room. Even then, their presence was not entirely welcomed. The club bartender told the first women he served that he hoped they'd "choke" on their beers—and he wasn't joking. But for some men, the move was a joke. A male columnist from the *Daily Oklahoman* wrote a column titled "Women in the Bar? A Sobering Thought." His take is typical of male writers at the time, dismissing women's demands for equality as something irritating if not amusing, even as he voted yes on the measure: "Carried away with their sudden spirit of sexual equality, my colleagues voted to allow the new distaff members admittance to what since ancient

An unidentified woman walks past the bar entrance at the National Press Club. Women were not allowed on the floor of the Press Club until 1971.
Courtesy of the National Press Club

times has been called the men's bar. . . . And the women's lib rules were even applied to the pool room." He concludes, "Perhaps it will be for the good of the club, but the place will never be the same."[13]

INTERSECTIONAL CHALLENGES

More women than ever are involved in journalism now, though they remain marginalized from management positions. According to the Women's Media Center's 2021 report, women comprised 41 percent of the media landscape overall. They were 39 percent of the workforce for newspapers, 45 percent of the internet, and 36 percent of the wire service. Most evening news broadcasters and hosts were men. At only 15 percent, women were the most outnumbered on the sports beat.[14] The people in charge still tend to be men worldwide. An Oxford University study in 2022 found that only 22 percent of top editors for major outlets were women.[15] The shrinking of the overall journalism job market is especially bad news for women and minorities because newest hires tend to be the first to be let go during economic downturns.

Some research suggests that women may also face a credibility gap with male news consumers, but this effect is complicated by topic and format. A study using male, female, and neutral bylines for the same story, for instance, found no difference in the way readers judged a reporter's credibility.[16] More recently, studies of blog posts found that male authors were considered more credible, but experiments involving Twitter found female journalists more credible.[17] When writing about stereotypical male issues, such as sports or politics, research finds a pronounced negative effect on women's credibility.[18] Attractiveness makes a difference too: Viewers rate female sports journalists more credible if they are good looking.[19]

Within news organizations, racial disparity continues: The *New York Times*, long considered the flagship of American liberalism, was sued for racial discrimination in 2016.[20] And despite its youthful reputation, online news is not immune. According to an ASNE survey of online news organizations in 2013, of sixty-eight organizations, forty-three (63 percent) had *zero* minority staffers.[21] The numbers were slightly better in the 2018 survey. Traditional newspaper organizations reported that 22.6 percent of their employees were a racial minority; for online news organizations, the increased to just 25.6 percent.[22] Keep in mind that about 40 percent of the US population is nonwhite, so these numbers do not reflect parity.[23] An overwhelming lack of diversity within an organization is likely to present incomplete and tone-deaf coverage, one reason some critics suggest mainstream news in the United States is undergoing catastrophic financial failure.[24]

Even when newsrooms integrate, the new hires do not always feel part of a team. Some women adopt masculine habits to fit in, as historians suggest Agee Underwood did. If they are decisive and confident, however, they run the risk of being labeled a bitch and, therefore, someone who can be dismissed, a classic double bind. Jill Abramson, who led the *New York Times* for just under three years, recalls being criticized as a tyrant, though her behavior was not as aggressive as men who held leadership jobs there. For instance, after an argument with Abramson, (male) Managing Editor Dean Baquet punched a wall and stormed out of the newsroom. He later apologized for throwing a "tantrum." Yet Baquet remained popular with *Times* journalists, and insiders spoke of Abramson as the one who was "difficult to work with."[25]

Research suggests that women also tend to think the sexism they encounter is isolated rather than part of a larger social system.[26] Black and Hispanic journalists experience tokenism, and Hispanic journalists find themselves being asked to act as translators for mundane assignments.[27] Integration efforts failed and continue to fail when a person of color is expected to report only on their racial or ethnic communities.[28] Journalists who feel their individual perspectives are discounted become dissatisfied and leave, perpetuating a negative cycle for newsrooms.[29]

SEXUAL HARASSMENT

A common and persistent stereotype about female journalists often promoted in entertainment media is that they are willing to have sex with their sources.[30] While it is not commonplace, it does happen. In the 1970s, a reporter for the *New York Times* had an affair with a prominent Philadelphia politician (whom she eventually married). She was fired for this breach of professionalism.[31] More significant is the degree to which women experience **sexual harassment** on the job. In fact, for many years it has been an accepted, *even expected*, part of the job.[32] Defined as "unwanted verbal or physical behavior that is sexual in nature," sexual harassment has two categories according to US law: One creates a hostile work environment, such as bullying, dirty jokes, and unwanted touching. The other type of sexual harassment is called quid pro quo, in which a person is pressured for sex in return for favors in the workplace. Sexual harassment is more prevalent in male-dominated spaces and enforces patriarchal norms. That is, it reinforces stereotypes. It's associated with decreased job satisfaction and increased turnover. Sexual harassment is racialized, as women of color are at greater risk, having historically been stereotyped as hypersexual.[33] Women often blame themselves for "letting" it happen, and they are often blamed for "asking for it" with how they act or dress.[34]

Sexual harassment made national headlines in 2017 with a resurgence of #MeToo. The #MeToo movement originated with the phrase coined in 2006 by Tarana Burke, an organizer and youth worker who was inspired by stories from girls she counseled.[35] Years later, when actress Alyssa Milano used the hashtag on Twitter in 2017, she ignited a firestorm, as women shared their stories of abuse, harassment, and bullying.[36] Thousands of women and men shared their deeply personal stories on Twitter.

The overwhelming number of #MeToo messages lent support to women who decided to come forward publicly and name their accusers. Actress Ashley Judd publicly named Harvey Weinstein in an article with the *New York Times*.[37] With the media floodgates open, accusations poured in, and cases started going to court. Six men accused actor Kevin Spacey of assault; he was fired from *House of Cards* on Netflix and sued for millions.[38] The list got longer and longer, as musicians, business owners, and entertainers were accused, investigated, and sometimes criminally prosecuted.[39] Burke's organization continues to promote healing in response to sexual violence. Inspired by #MeToo, a group of women in Hollywood established another project in 2018, Time's Up, which focuses on workplace harassment.[40]

As journalists covered the #MeToo movement, they also were compelled to tell their own stories of sexual harassment on the job. In 2017, Moira Donegan, a former assistant editor at the *New Republic*, started an anonymous online page titled Shitty Media Men that listed seventy names of alleged harassers, with accusations ranging from lecherous comments to assault. Donegan eventually took down the page, but it continued to circulate and eventually led to some men losing their jobs.[41] A global poll by the International Women's Media Foundation found that 46 percent of the respondents had been harassed in the office or in the field. Part of the problem is that interviews and meetings for news gathering are often private. An international business writer, Shaheen Pasha, wrote of male sources, powerful executives, who would shake her hand, refuse to let go, then pull her in close to chat. More than one of her sources would grant her a business interview during the day, then send lewd, flirty texts at night.[42] Travel writer Martha Mukaiwa explains that she kept quiet about harassment, knowing it would brand her a troublemaker and limit her opportunities: "Intuition tells me that if I talk about the porter grabbing me in my hotel room, pushing me backwards and forcing a hot, wet, soul-destroying kiss, I'll be some kind of nuisance."[43] Radio journalist Nina Totenberg ate one-handed at a White House dinner when a federal official put his hand on her thigh. Rather than make a scene during the event, she chose instead to just hold his hand to keep it from moving any further.[44] A Columbian journalist who was kidnapped and raped by three men while trying to cover a story continues to work as a reporter; she's been able to help other women combat sexual violence by going public with her case.[45]

Seemingly no institution has escaped accusations. In 2022, a woman sued the international publisher of *Bild*, a German tabloid, for pressuring her into a sexual relationship when she started as a trainee. The man in question denied the allegations and vowed to fight them in court.[46] CBS network officials were sued by women for sexual harassment in 2018, not long after host Charlie Rose was fired. Matt Lauer of NBC lost his job, and harassment lawsuits ended the career of Roger Ailes and Bill O'Reilly at Fox News.[47] Student journalists report being harassed within their newsrooms and by sources, and discouragingly, their complaints are often minimized by their universities. Many journalism educators now believe that their programs should include discussions of harassment to prepare students and that school newsrooms should be better prepared to respond to harassment cases.[48]

QUEER VISIBILITIES

While there is no doubt that queer and trans individuals have been part of journalism for as long as there has been journalism, they were largely invisible. Coming out as LGBTQ+ could destroy a person's career for much of history, and, indeed, individuals could be criminally prosecuted for it (see chapter 8). The Association of LGBTQ+ Journalists was established in 1990 in San Francisco by Roy Aarons, an editor with the *Oakland Tribune*. Aarons had come out to his family and some colleagues over the years, but it was not until 1990, when he shared the results of a survey of gay and lesbian journalists to the American Society of Newspaper Editors, that he announced, "I, as an editor and gay man, am proud of ASNE for having done this study."[49]

The ASNE survey was a turning point for queer people in news organizations. A majority of those surveyed had not come out to their coworkers. They also critiqued the way their organizations covered LGBTQ+ issues as largely mediocre. The industry responded. Ten years later, the survey was conducted again, this time including broadcast journalists. By then, more than 90 percent of the journalists surveyed had come out to their colleagues, but only about one in four considered their newsroom to be a welcoming environment.[50] A subsequent study surveyed newspaper editors and found that editors thought their media institutions were doing a better job covering the issues than the queer journalists who were surveyed for ASNE believed. Gay and lesbian journalists even differed on word choices, for instance, on whether using the phrase *people with AIDs* (instead of *AIDS sufferers*) was an acceptable or prejudiced term.[51]

Profile: Steve Rothaus, Journalist (1958-)

Steve Rothaus.
Courtesy of Cristian Lazzari, used with permission

Steve Rothaus is a Florida journalist who helped bring LGBTQ+ coverage to mainstream journalism. He worked for thirty-three years at the *Miami Herald* and covered LGBTQ+ issues for twenty-one of those years, advancing a beat that had not previously existed. When he started, he wrote a column in the *Herald*'s features section that had his picture next to it to personalize the coverage. "We wanted people to know that I was a real person so they would feel more comfortable having their name in the paper, knowing that they were talking to someone who was in the paper and who also was gay," he told the *Columbia Journalism Review*. Later, his articles were incorporated into the rest of the newspaper, just like all other news. He also advised colleagues at the paper on how to write respectfully about LGBTQ+ issues at a time when there were no style guides to help.

Rothaus served on the board for the NLGJA: The Association of LGBTQ+ Journalists for five years, and in 2003, he founded the organization's Newsroom Outreach Project for professional and student journalists. As part of that program, Rothaus traveled the United States to discuss newsroom workplace issues and how to cover LGBTQ+ stories with respect and sensitivity. Also, he was part of two *Miami Herald* teams that won Pulitzer Prizes, and he coproduced an Emmy Award–winning documentary, *The Day It Snowed in Miami: A Chronology of the LGBT-Rights Movement*, in 2014. His work has been recognized by GLAAD, Equality Florida, SAVE LGBTQ, and the National LGBTQ Task Force. In 2019, Rothaus was named to the NLGJA Hall of Fame, the same year he took a buyout from the *Herald*. He continues to write as a freelance journalist.

Sources: Susannah Nesmith, "How the *Miami Herald*'s Steve Rothaus Became an LGBT Pioneer in Mainstream Journalism," *Columbia Journalism Review*, April 6, 2016, https://www.cjr.org/united_states_project/miami_herald_steve_rothaus_lgbt_coverage.php; NLGJA: The Association LGBTQ+ Journalists, "Steve Rothaus," accessed February 7, 2023, https://www.nlgja.org/blog/2019/08/steve-rothaus/; Jason Parsley, "Steve Rothaus Takes Buyout from *Miami Herald*," *South Florida Gay News*, February 27, 2019, https://southfloridagaynews.com/Local/steve-rothaus-takes-buyout-from-miami-herald.html; Steve Rothaus, communication with the author, February 8, 2023.

JOURNALISM AND PARENTING

Parenting remains difficult for journalists worldwide because of the job's odd hours and frequent travel demands. The United States does not have nationally mandated family leave, so it is up to each newsroom to determine policies. Small news organizations often have no policy at all. Mid-size to large news organizations are more likely to offer parental leave of more than six weeks for men and women, though sometimes these require women to burn up their sick leave or classify their leave as a disability.[52] When surveyed about gender in the newsroom in Australia, one woman told a researcher, "The company values people who can give unlimited time to their job, which working mothers cannot do."[53]

But replacing an employee who must leave a company with inadequate benefits is expensive and time consuming. The cost and effort of hiring new staff helped one group of women at the *New York Times* to convince the institution to offer better parental benefits. When organizations do offer parental leave, family advocates say it's important for men to actually take that time to reduce the perceived disadvantage of leave taking by women.[54] Journalism is especially difficult for breastfeeding parents because even when they might have space to nurse a baby or pump milk in a newsroom, it can be next to impossible in the field.[55]

DIVERSITY AND NEWS COVERAGE

News organizations historically have perpetuated stereotypes of women, queer and trans people, and people of color by treating their concerns as unusual or deviant. Journalism's coverage of street crime and an overreliance on police narratives are just part of the reason Black men have been stereotyped as criminals in the news. Journalism claims to be objective, so how does this happen? Chapter 6 introduces one explanation, color-blind racism, or the belief that the system is fair and that an individual's suffering is the result of their own shortcomings. The way journalism practices objectivity can cultivate color-blind racism. Episodic frames tend to focus on individual failures or achievements. To be objective about race promotes the use of nonracial language, which can hide the facts about structural inequality.[56]

Because newsrooms have historically been mostly white and male, notions of objectivity have overlapped with their perspective. Researchers know that newsrooms that are mostly white and male tend to neglect the interests of minorities in their communities.[57] The late Dori Maynard, former president of the Robert C. Maynard Institute for Journalism Education, argued that covering all members of a community, representing its full diversity, fulfills the journalistic ideal of accuracy.[58] If portions of a community are never represented or always are represented stereotypically, then the news is simply not accurate.

Researchers have found that diverse newsrooms produced a better product because they rely on more sources from different walks of life.[59] Journalists of color tend to cover stories about their communities that would otherwise be overlooked, which, while important, can be demeaning.[60] Affirming the Kerner Commission's findings, research has found that diverse newsrooms do a better job of breaking down stereotypes and racism.[61] They better identify the problems faced by minority citizens in a community.[62]

White men still tend to dominate the sourcing for news. The Global Media Monitoring Project reported that 25 percent of the world's news includes female sources. The number was slightly higher for news from North America at 30 percent.[63] The BBC started its 50/50 Project in 2018. Within a year, most units in the network had achieved gender parity, and even departments like politics, business, and sports had found ways to include more female broadcasters, experts, and sources.[64] Women's advocacy groups have created sites to promote female sources. For instance, Women Also Know Stuff promotes the work of female political scientists.[65] The Women's Media Center has a site called SheSource to similarly promote women as potential expert sources.[66] Source audits can help newsrooms learn who is quoted in their work and how to improve. A public broadcasting organization in San Francisco, for example, did such an audit and found that while they quoted Black sources at a rate proportionately *higher* than the Black population, the organization quoted Asian Americans only about 10 percent of the time, much lower than the proportion of Asian Americans in the Bay Area, at 28 percent. Not surprisingly, men were included in stories more often than women, especially as sources from academia, government, and business.[67]

Today's Challenges and Opportunities

There are more media outlets than ever competing for attention, yet this fragmentation comes at a price because the audience is similarly divided. Digital media also make it possible for anyone to serve as a journalist, whether reporting on something directly as a citizen witness or merely commenting on a news item. Even with these dramatic changes in the public sphere, the old problems of discrimination, sexual harassment, and stereotyping persist. Decades after the Kerner Commission report, thousands of people took to the streets to protest the police murder of George Floyd, a moment many observers called a "reckoning" on race in the United States. Yet as of 2022, most coverage continues to focus on the disruptive nature of protests rather than the substance of the complaints.[68] Mostly white newsrooms continue to portray Black and Brown people as poor and criminal, perpetuating stereotypes and advancing the interests of the wealthy and white.[69]

After the 2016 election in the United States, some news organizations established gender beats. Metropolitan papers in Boston and Salt Lake City have assigned reporters to the specialty, along with small start-up organizations and digital natives like Buzzfeed.[70] The gender beat not only is about women's issues but also covers stories about the LGBTQ+ community, workplace harassment, and masculinity. Many news organizations established these projects in the wake of the #MeToo movement and the highly gendered presidential campaign of 2016. The *Washington Post* started a section titled after the historic suffrage publication, the *Lily*, and has a columnist who writes on gender issues, Monica Hesse. The *New York Times* established a digital team devoted to gender; a newsletter titled *In Her Words*, focusing on women's issues globally; and a feature called "The Working Woman's Handbook."[71]

The efforts have already changed course. The *Times*' newsletter is no longer offered, and the *Lily* at the *Washington Post* has been incorporated into a new page on gender and identity.[72] The 19th, a nonprofit online news organization that started in 2020, continues to publish gender-oriented news. Research interviews with gender beat reporters find that they tend to take an intersectional approach and are conflicted about their assignment. As one reporter put it, women's issues "should be everyone's issues," but because they're not, the beat is necessary.[73]

Summary

Women have worked in newsrooms for centuries, but they have not necessarily had leadership power in those newsrooms. People of color have also been underrepresented, and when they are present in a newsroom, they often have been assigned stories that reflect stereotypical views about their identities. Queer people have always worked as journalists, but not until recently have they been able to be open about their sexuality.

Research has found that having a more diverse newsroom improves the news. Even so, women and people of color continue to face challenges in news organizations. Mothers in particular often find it very difficult to remain in the profession. Audience studies suggest that some readers and viewers still rate female journalists as less credible. Journalists who are not white, male, and straight have had to defend their own perspectives because, historically, the idea of objectivity has been defined by those who are white, male, and straight. Questions about objectivity in a democracy demand consideration of perspective. Whose objectivity should count? In the twenty-first century, under pressure from new technologies and a shifting social system, journalists are experimenting with new approaches, styles, and beats. It is becoming more and more clear that while facts can be objective, people have a perspective, and fairness to all means including as many of those perspectives as possible.

- **Reflection:** How would you ethically manage your various identities in a media role? How should journalists consider their various identities in covering news?
- **Reflection:** Does it matter to you who tells a news story? Who is most credible to you?
- **Media Critique:** As you read the news, look to see whether the people affected by a proposal or controversy are represented in the story. Does the story rely only on the perspective of government leaders or public officials? How might the story change with additional voices?

CHAPTER 10

Gender and Broadcasting

Women in broadcasting face the extra challenges that come with physical performance in news. This chapter starts by describing the way girls and women participated in early radio, whether as amateur radio operators or by working at the country's earliest radio stations. As radio became a profitable business, women were usually pushed to the sidelines, a trend that repeats itself in other media quarters. On television, women are far more visible on the air today but have not achieved parity in management. Women of color continue to face challenges in TV because of colorism and white standards of beauty. While queer broadcast journalists remained closeted through much of the 1900s, they are more likely to come out today and receive support from their employers.

Key Concepts: Colorism, Consumer Culture

One of the plainest markers of gender is the body, and bodies that are not clearly white, straight, and male are easily noticed. Media that represent the body, both by voice for radio and by voice and image for TV, complicate inclusion in news for people who are female, queer, or nonwhite. These performance-based media deliver news as presented by real human beings who are judged not only for their journalistic abilities but also their appearance. Broadcasting also has been historically a very profitable business in which journalists have worked as writers, producers, editors, and news managers. Whether in front of the camera or behind the scenes, gender has played a role in the way people have contributed to this powerful form of news.

Radio

Radio was the first form of mass communication in the United States that could unite people in time. Never before could so many experience the same content simultaneously. This had an enormous impact on the United States, both in terms of media consumption and in advertising and its cultivation of consumer culture. It also, of course, created opportunities for female journalists to enter this new form of communication.

Women had already been involved in electronic communication as telegraph operators, and women were often hired for keyboarding work, under the stereotypical belief that their smaller hands were better suited for it.[1] Recall from chapter 3 that the period after the Civil War was a time of dramatic geographic, economic, and population growth in the United States. The telegraph united the country with information and was integral to the development of the Associated Press.[2] Journalists could post stories from a small town in the Midwest to be printed in a big city newspaper on the coast within minutes. This cooperative news model not only united the country with information, but it also influenced the way news was written. The style of newswriting familiar to us today arose from a combination of technological advances and changes in media economics—the way news organizations operated as commercial entities.[3]

The country was not united in real time, however, until the growth of the broadcasting industry. Radio was invented in the late 1800s and quickly became useful for the military during World War I. It took time for entrepreneurs to figure out how radio could be turned into a business, so it started as a hobby for people who liked to make homemade kits and communicate with one another. Boys were encouraged to participate in amateur radio clubs, where they built radio sets and learned about the electronic engineering that goes into creating a radio. In these early years, women and girls participated in ham radio, but, for the most part, they were not encouraged nearly as much, and few of them obtained radio licenses.[4] Only four years after it was established in 1914, the American Radio Relay League (ARRL) started a merit badge for the Boy Scouts, and Scouts now use radio to communicate with each other worldwide.[5] (It took ninety-eight years for the ARRL to start a similar badge for Girl Scouts in 2016.[6])

In Australia, Florence Violet Mackenzie was one of the exceptions to the predominance of men in the radio world. Mackenzie became that country's first female electric engineer and started a signal corps for women, which is like the military's version of a communication corps.[7] The first woman in the United States to receive a radio license from the Federal Communication Commission was Gladys Kathleen Parkin at the age of fifteen. A 1916 issue of the *Electrical Experimenter* welcomes her this way:

> Just because a man, Signor Guglielmo Marconi by name, invented commercial wireless telegraphy does not mean for a moment that the fair sex cannot master its mysteries. To prove that the girls and women of the country are rapidly awakening to the fact that radio operating is a worth-while accomplishment, both vocationally and intellectually, we have the pleasure of presenting herewith a number of photographs showing the Radio activities of our fairer sex.[8]

Once business leaders realized that radio could be used for advertising, the US government developed a system to regulate the electromagnetic spectrum, which is really a physical resource, much like land or water. Soon, small stations were established around the country, many of them family owned and many with women working as technicians; managers; performers; and, in some cases, owners.

Gladys Kathleen Parkin as she appeared in the *Electrical Experimenter* in 1916. The original caption read, "Allow us to present Miss Kathleen Parkin, Expert Radio Operator at Fifteen Years of Age. She has made her own apparatus."
Public domain

By the 1920s, radio carried all kinds of entertainment; children's stories; music hours; women's programing; and, of course, news. As radio became more profitable and its business corporatized, women were pushed into the same sort of stereotypical roles as in the newspaper industry. Women were able to work as performers if they read children's stories or hosted shows about food, fashion, and family. Radio networks grew and reached a much larger audience, with shows not just sponsored by but also produced in concert with advertisers. Soap operas, or serial dramas that aired in the afternoons for a female audience, were so nicknamed because they were sponsored by companies that sold household cleaning products. Betty Crocker, the fictional character who is still used to sell cake mix, moved from print ads to the radio, with a show hosted by an actress who would share home tips, cooking tips, and recipes.[9]

Radio united Americans in the 1930s and '40s as the country endured first the Great Depression and then the Second World War. Media histories often mention the way President Franklin Delano Roosevelt used radio to deliver his fireside chats to reassure the public during the war, but his wife also harnessed the medium effectively. Eleanor Roosevelt took to the airwaves to discuss her own projects, such as the Universal Declaration of Human Rights. As entertainers, women were popular on the air. Gracie Burns, for example, performed with her husband, George, in a comedy act they carried over from vaudeville. Their act was extraordinarily successful, with George playing the serious husband, while Gracie hid her cleverness with a childlike voice and a dizzy-dame demeanor.[10]

Women had a harder time breaking into radio news. Their voices were still considered unlistenable for serious topics and not authoritative. An editorial in *Variety* magazine suggested, "[W]omen announcers are without voice lure on the air. Difficult to handle and most are general nuisances."[11] Some stations sponsored surveys to find out whether the audience enjoyed listening to women, and many responses were critical of women's voices. To make matters worse, some of the earliest microphones and transmitters really did make it hard to listen to higher tones and made women's voices sound shrill. These older microphones were fabulous for capturing the mellow tones of male performers like Bing Crosby, but they were unable to capture higher, softer voices with much accuracy.[12]

The preference for male voices as authoritative was rooted in stereotypes, as was another belief: that radio *leadership* was better suited for men because it required an interest in math and science. As radio became a stronger commercial business in the 1930s, it wanted to target advertising to specific audiences. This, in combination with the economic pressures of the Great Depression, cut opportunities for women. They were pushed out of jobs in management or news broadcasting into daytime shows designed for female listeners. Much as they were in newspapers, women in radio's golden age were relegated to hosting homemaking shows or reading children's stories at night. There were exceptions. WHER in Memphis was one of the first of several stations to adopt an all-woman format, in 1955. Sam Phillips of Sun Records radio fame opened the station, and his wife, Becky, was one of its first DJs. This radio station, which worked as a segregated all-women's format, was in operation until 1973.[13]

The growth of radio and then TV advanced what scholars call **consumer culture**, which is the way branded products construct social meaning.[14] Think of the reasons you chose what you wore today or what meaning you attach to a particular type of car. Recall from chapter 3 that advertising's support of mass media inspired the development of brands. Consumer culture cultivates our shared sense that what we buy contributes to our social identities. With TV added to the mix of radio, magazines, and newspapers, advertisers started to divide consumers up into target markets and supported media that allowed them to reach those targets. Radio had already targeted women in the afternoons with soap operas and shows about housework, but the mass media explosion of the midcentury set off a process of dividing the audience into smaller pieces. The youth market, for instance, was able to coalesce in the 1950s and '60s because of the postwar baby boom, economic growth, and global stability. How to reach teens? By developing radio stations not for everyone but specifically for young people—with rock and roll.[15] While target marketing by itself is an important way for advertisers to reach the right customers, the consumer culture it creates can also perpetuate stereotypes about those customers. This is significant for the way women were so often targeted with ads that depicted them as homemakers who could be made happy with the right stove or vacuum cleaner. The unstated message of this kind of advertising is that buying the right brands can make a woman a good wife and mother—and that there's something wrong with the woman who doesn't care about housework.

Opportunities for Black Americans were very sparse in the twentieth century in radio, but as with newspapers, some business pioneers made a difference. The first Black-owned radio station, WERD, was established in Atlanta in 1949. Some Black women also achieved prominence as DJs during this time. Chatty Hattie Leeper was one of a handful of Black female DJs in the 1940s and '50s. In 1989, she was inducted in the Black Radio Hall of Fame. After she finished her radio career, she went on to become a college professor. She told an interviewer,

> There were mixed emotions there, me being the only female, there were some die-hard men there that thought, well, you know, "Females should be home having babies or in the kitchen cooking. This is not an industry for females." And they tried to do little things to discourage me. Some of them, you know, they'd pull my hair. They would take my bows off, you know, 'cause I was 16. They'd say, "My God, you know, get your education, because this is no place for you."[16]

The first Spanish-language radio station in the United States was established in San Antonio, Texas, in 1946. KCUR developed its own radio theater using local talent. Prior to this first station, brokers bought time at Anglo stations for Spanish-language programming, spreading across California, New York, Texas, and Arizona. Hispanic entrepreneurs had to appeal to the Supreme Court for access to the airwaves, which ruled that there was a public need for diverse programming. Spanish-language radio grew in importance in the 1960s, as advertisers recognized a new market. The 1970s saw the development of several Spanish-language radio networks.[17] Opportunities for women in Spanish-language radio reflected the industry generally and were, therefore, limited. Yet some women did push through, among them Gilda Mirós from Puerto Rico, who worked for a number of radio stations in New York and eventually moved to Miami, where she ran a show that was broadcast from coast to coast.

Television News

TV's development was interrupted by World War II, very much like radio's development had been interrupted by World War I. But the biggest sale of sets came in 1947, a couple of years after World War II ended, when it was announced that baseball's World Series would be aired live on television. During this era, most television programming was live, just as it was on radio, and even the entertainment shows were much like vaudeville shows, just with a live camera in front. Television took off very

Profile: Gilda Mirós, Actor (1938–)

Gilda Mirós.
Courtesy of Spanish Language Broadcasting Collection, Archives
Center, National Museum of American History, Smithsonian
Institution, used with permission

Gilda Mirós is the stage name of Carmen Gilda Santiago Rodríguez, a radio icon whose career as a performer, multimedia producer, and writer continues today on New York Public Access Television. Born in Puerto Rico and raised in the Bronx, Mirós started as an actress performing in TV shows and movies in Mexico, Puerto Rico, and the United States. She went on to work with numerous radio and television stations in New York and Miami and hosted the first live national daily radio show to run simultaneously in New York, Los Angeles, and Miami. Her radio programs have been transmitted across Latin America and Spain. She's produced and narrated documentaries, and she's written several books, including children's books. In 2018, she produced an online documentary called *Seniors Say #MeToo*, chronicling the experiences of older women with sexual harassment. Recently the Puerto Rican Studies Department at Hunter College and the City University of New York posted her oral history and created the Gilda Mirós file in their archives, which is available to the public. At age seventy-seven, she told an interviewer she still enjoys producing media: "If I were born again, I would like to be a historian and communicator." Her contributions to American culture have been commemorated in the collections of the Smithsonian's National Museum of American History. Mirós remains active in media production. She produced a recording of interpretations of iconic female poets from Latin America for release in 2023 and currently produces *Latin Icons Past and Present* for All Access Cable TV in New York.

Sources: Roberto J. Bustamante, "The Other Face of the Talent of Gilda Mirós," *Ahora News*, October 16, 2015, https://ahoranews.net/la-otra-cara-del-talento-de-gilda-miros; Gilda Mirós, communication with the author, January 26, 2023; Performing Arts Legacy Project, "Gilda Mirós," accessed September 17, 2022, https://performingartslegacy.org/miros; *Seniors Say #Metoo! Documentary Part One*, dir. Gilda Miros (2018), https://www.youtube.com/watch?v=ZpF0kwHb8Xc.

quickly, and in 1950, 92 percent of Americans had a TV set. From 1949 to 1959, more than 63 million TV sets were sold.

Famed media scholar Marshall McLuhan is known for saying, "The medium is the message." A less famous observation but one that is perhaps more apt for the digital age is "A new medium is never an addition to an old one, nor does it leave the old one in peace. It never ceases to oppress the older media until it finds new shapes and positions for them."[18] In other words, when new technologies come along, we tend to use them in ways we already know, and the evolution of TV news illustrates this well. Early TV news was basically a radio commentator being filmed with a camera: a man behind a desk with a microphone. The short, fifteen-minute newscasts were originally styled after the newsreel films shown in movie theaters. It took years for TV news to take on the format we know today, one that starts with the hard news, before weather and sports, musical interludes, and a lot of attention-grabbing previews between stories. As television news evolved, women pushed for stronger roles on and off the air. Martha Rountree created *Meet the Press*, and reporters like Nancy Dickerson, Cokie Roberts, and Diane Sawyer blazed trails for other women. Advances behind the scenes were slow, as most TV networks and stations were dominated by white male managers for decades. This is changing, however, and today many more news directors and station managers across the United States are female.[19]

Women in broadcast news worked in front of the camera and behind it, but, again, opportunities were limited. Nancy Dickerson was one of the pioneers in this area, eventually becoming the associate producer of *Face the Nation*. In 1960, CBS made her its first female correspondent.[20] Many other women became household names on network TV in spite of tokenism, which often limited their opportunities, and the long-enduring stereotype that women were not serious enough to deliver the news. As one female anchor puts it, "Gravitas is sexist code for 'should be a man.'"[21] The first woman to sit on a national anchor desk was Barbara Walters, who shared the role with Harry Reasoner on ABC News. Reasoner, who opposed the Equal Rights Amendment and considered himself to be a benign chauvinist, publicly welcomed Walters but privately was unhappy about it. She was the highest-paid woman in broadcasting at the time, and she had less hard-news experience than most network anchors. The coanchored show lasted about two years with lackluster ratings, but Walters went on to become one of broadcasting's most famous interviewers.[22]

Today, women are anchors and reporters on network and local news. They also risk their lives along with their male colleagues in wartime coverage while contending with sexism from viewers, colleagues, and sources. For example, Christiane Amanpour made her name by covering the Afghan War and the Iran-Iraq War. In the Middle East, some governments require women, including journalists, to wear headscarves or dress in particular ways. Amanpour complied with these foreign governments' rules while on their soil, but in 2022, she refused to wear a headscarf in New York City for an interview with Iranian president Ebrahim Raisi, who responded by cancelling. Amanpour remains unapologetic about her decision to exercise her rights while in the United States.[23]

Another network TV reporter, Lara Logan, was the victim of a violent sexual assault in 2011 while covering protests in Cairo's Tahir Square for the CBS program

60 Minutes. She went back to work after recovering from the assault, but years later, she sued *New York Magazine* for publishing a 2014 article by Joe Hagan ("Benghazi and the Bombshell: Is Lara Logan Too Toxic to Return to *60 Minutes*?") that downplayed the incident as a mere groping and questioned whether Logan used her sexuality to advance her career.[24] While Logan claimed that the article impugned her journalistic integrity and damaged her professional reputation, the lawsuit was dismissed in court.[25] Logan left CBS in 2018 and became active with conservative media.[26]

TV News and Appearance

The headline of the Logan story captures the way women in TV news have been objectified over time. As described in chapter 4, objectification is when a person is viewed as a *thing* to please others—usually straight men. While it's true that TV news is a performative medium and so a journalist's appearance makes a difference, stereotypical expectations mean female TV presenters are scrutinized more than their male colleagues. Many women on network news are former beauty pageant winners.[27] Unlike their male colleagues, women are expected to be pretty but not too pretty—a classic double bind. After all, if a woman is pretty, then she can't be smart. But if she's not hot, then she has no job. Women are judged differently than men by their colleagues and audiences, and they are held to unrealistic expectations, usually within white standards of beauty. They report being scrutinized more about their appearance than their skills, like writing, reporting, fact-checking, producing, and vocal performance.[28] All that matters, it seems, is whether they look good.

Networks are also concerned about whether TV anchors are well-liked by the audience. For women, likeability is directly linked to attractiveness. Hiring women for their looks feeds stereotypical expectations that undermine the credibility of all women.[29] Patriarchy compels women to please the male gaze, so they feel obligated to look attractive. This is especially true for women who work for conservative networks, like Gretchen Carlson, formerly of Fox News. She was not allowed to wear slacks on the set like her male colleagues. As part of the job, she had to wear skirts and show off her legs, along with using her actual journalistic writing and interview skills.[30] Years later, Carlson would share much more about the sexism she endured at Fox in a lawsuit that targeted her former boss, Roger Ailes. The network settled for $20 million and gave her an unprecedented apology.[31]

In study after study, through surveys and interviews, women in TV news have reported that they are judged harshly for their appearance.[32] One woman fought back in the 1980s. Christine Craft sued her station after they demoted her on the grounds that she was "too old, too ugly and not deferential to men." She won her lawsuit and went on to practice law.[33] Her case seems not to have made a difference for today's women in TV news, though, as so many women still maintain the slim, white, blond look. Even their clothing today is more feminine than it was in the '80s, when it was appropriate to wear long sleeves and suit jackets.[34] Women who work as solo video journalists are expected to maintain this look and usually wear a pencil skirt or form-fitting dress and heels. The physical demands of operating a video camera are also

Excerpt: Gretchen Carlson's Lawsuit

20. On those occasions when he spoke directly with Carlson, Ailes injected sexual and/or sexist comments and innuendo into their conversations by, among other things:

   a. Claiming that Carlson saw everything as if it "only rains on women" and admonishing her to stop worrying about being treated equally and getting "offended so God damn easy about everything."
   b. Describing Carlson as a "man hater" and a "killer" who tried to "show up the boys" on Fox & Friends.
   c. Ogling Carlson in his office and asking her to turn around so he could view her posterior.
   d. Commenting that certain outfits enhanced Carlson's figure and urging her to wear them every day.
   e. Commenting repeatedly about Carlson's legs.
   f. Lamenting that marriage was "boring," "hard" and "not much fun."
   g. Wondering aloud how anyone could be married to Carlson, while making sexual advances by various means, including by stating that if he could choose one person to be stranded with on a desert island, she would be that person.
   h. Stating "I'm sure you [Carlson] can do sweet nothings when you want to."
   i. Asking Carlson how she felt about him, followed by: "Do you understand what I'm saying to you?"
   j. Boasting to other attendees (at an event where Carlson walked over to greet him) that he always stays seated when a woman walks over to him so she has to "bend over" to say hello.
   k. Embarrassing Ms. Carlson by stating to others in her presence that he had "slept" with three former Miss Americas but not with her.
   l. Telling Carlson that she was "sexy," but "too much hard work."

21. In September 2015, Carlson again sought to bring to an end the retaliatory and discriminatory treatment she had endured by asking to meet with Ailes.

22. During that meeting in Ailes' office on September 16, 2015, Ailes stated to Carlson: "I think you and I should have had a sexual relationship a long time ago and then you'd be good and better and I'd be good and better," adding that "sometimes problems are easier to solve" that way.

23. Prior to and during that meeting, Ailes had made it clear to Carlson that he had the power to make anything happen for her if she listened to him and "underst[ood]" what he was saying.

24. Carlson refused to engage in a sexual relationship or participate in sexual banter with Ailes so Ailes retaliated.

Source: Gretchen Carlson v. Roger Ailes (Superior Court of New Jersey Law Division, Bergen County, July 2016).

discounted for women. Research on multimedia journalists (MMJs) who shoot, write, and edit alone, found that women carry at least one extra bag with a change of shoes along with their usual makeup and hair tools. Male MMJs might take their suit jacket off while shooting, but otherwise, the outfit they're expected to wear is appropriate for shooting video.[35]

Hair is particularly important for a TV journalist's appearance. A 1986 study included an anchor who lost out on a job because her hair was not the color station management wanted. Another woman got a job and created a bit of a stir when she later dyed her hair a different color. "The station switchboard lit up," she told the interviewer; it was a local news story of its own. In that same study, a male anchor offered his attractiveness standard as "Would I want to look at that face for half an hour?" without acknowledging that what people want to look at for a half-hour is very different when they're watching a man compared with a woman.[36] White women tend to wear their hair with the same cut: shoulder length or slightly longer, straight and smooth. Slate once called TV news an "Aryan sisterhood for female journalists" because the attractiveness standards were so white and so blond.[37] A 2018 study that examined local TV station publicity photos found that 49 percent of the women had blond hair, far above that color's natural occurrence.[38]

AGING ON TV

What Slate doesn't mention is that this cookie-cutter look is not only white and blond; it is also young. A detailed content analysis of publicity photos found that while male anchors in the United States represent a wide age range, most women appear to be in their twenties. Not a single woman appeared to be in her fifties. None had gray hair. Male anchors in the sample occasionally did have gray hair, and some were even a little overweight.[39] Not surprisingly, the expectation of youthfulness has compelled some women to get Botox or plastic surgery.[40] The project only used the pictures as evidence, so the study could not explain why women might leave in their thirties: whether they are pushed out or leave for personal reasons.

WHITE BEAUTY STANDARDS

Black women are more visible in TV news today though not in all roles and still not in proportion to the population. About one in four TV journalists is a person of color (male or female), even though Black, Latinx, Asian, and Native American people comprise nearly 40 percent of the US population.[41] Asian American and Pacific Islander journalists are underrepresented on air.[42] Latinas are particularly underrepresented in TV news, comprising only about 6 percent of broadcast journalists (roughly the same as Latino men).[43]

While some Black women have prominent roles in national news, they are less represented among the most scientific (and therefore stereotypically male) job in TV news: meteorology.[44] Though all women in TV news are judged for their looks, Black women are subjected to even more scrutiny, especially for the way they wear their hair. Historically, Black women in TV news were pressured, formally or informally, to straighten their hair. The norm is so entrenched that a study has found that some young Black women would prefer to not even pursue on-air reporting as a career.[45] More recently, Black women in TV news have made a point of wearing their hair with a natural curl or in braids.[46] This represents a change from a 2018 study sample that had no Black women with natural hair on the air in broadcast TV. That same analysis noted that most of the Black men in the sample seemed to avoid the styling issue altogether by shaving their heads.

The whiteness standard goes beyond hair, however. That same study measured just how white and how dark TV news journalists appear. Borrowing a scale used by skin care specialists, researchers found that while the number of Black people in the sample was roughly proportionate to the American population, an insignificant number of them were very dark.[47] The finding reflects a form of discrimination known as **colorism**, in which the darkest members of a racial group are marginalized. Novelist Alice Walker is credited with coining the word. Darker skin is statistically associated with inferior education, lower salaries, fewer job prospects, and longer prison terms.[48] Even when Black people are considered attractive enough to appear on TV news, they are subjected to preferences for lightness. Colorism is a global problem, especially for women. In India and Nigeria, for instance, colorism is part of the social hierarchy and helps to sell billions of dollars' worth of skin-lightening products.[49]

QUEERNESS AND BROADCASTING

Sexual orientation is not visible for people who dress and act according to binary expectations. As with other professions, coming out was risky to a broadcast journalist's career throughout the 1900s. Thomas Elbert Roberts, who was a network anchor, made news in 2006 when he announced at a convention that he was gay. Anderson Cooper came out as gay in 2012 and is open about his sexuality, as is lesbian Rachel Maddow. In 2017, the *Advocate* named Cooper and Maddow the top two most influential queer people in media.[50] Trans broadcasters are making inroads into the industry, too. Eden Lane, a freelance video journalist in Denver, is the first person known to be trans and work for a TV news organization.[51] And in 2015, *Inside Edition* hired a trans journalist, Zoey Tur, a former helicopter pilot whose claim to fame came from live coverage of the O. J. Simpson freeway chase.[52]

Representation on and off Camera

What difference does it make who delivers the news? Recall from chapter 9 that diverse newsrooms better cover their communities. TV news representation takes things a step further, though, because it is a visual medium. Visual media "teach" the audience who matters and who does not, who is attractive and who is not. No one can argue against the fact that TV is a visual medium and that attractiveness matters, but the expectations for women border on obsession. TV news anchors might be the most prominent professional women children grow up seeing, yet they are still subject to the patriarchal expectation that they please the male gaze. Just as importantly, the standard of beauty in TV news remains very white, perpetuating a sense that only one type of beauty is

Rachel Maddow, Broadcast Journalist (1973-)

Rachel Maddow.
Courtesy of PhotoFest

When Rachel Maddow took over the top anchoring position at MSNBC in 2008, she doubled the audience in a matter of days. Only thirty-five at the time, she blended her journalistic talent with social media skills to build a successful following for the *Rachel Maddow Show*.

Maddow was only seven when she started reading the newspaper, and she showed her concern for social issues as a teenager when she volunteered at an AIDS clinic. She studied public policy at Stanford University and started working for the AIDS activist group ACT UP after graduation. She was recognized with a Rhodes scholarship and pursued a PhD in political science from Oxford University in England. Maddow worked in radio before starting as a liberal pundit on cable TV. MSNBC hired her as a political analyst in early 2008, only to give her the major anchoring role months later.

A self-described "mannish policy-wonk," Maddow is known for her ability to explain complicated issues and for her unique, unfussy appearance. She was the first openly lesbian on network TV, and in a controversial interview in 2011, she suggested that LGBTQ+ broadcasters had a responsibility to come out. Maddow has won two Emmy Awards, a prestigious Dupont Award (for TV and online reporting), the Walter Cronkite Faith and Freedom Award, and a GLAAD Award for outstanding journalism. In 2022, she announced she would take a break from nightly newscasts, hosting one night a week for MSNBC, so she could work on other projects, including a book and a podcast. She is married and shares two homes with her wife, one in New York and the other in Massachusetts.

Sources: Biography, "Rachel Maddow," updated May 20, 2020, https://www.biography.com/movies-tv/rachel-maddow; Hadley Freeman, "Rachel Maddow: 'I'm Definitely Not an Autocutie,'" *Guardian*, April 25, 2011, https://www.theguardian.com/media/2011/apr/25/rachel-maddow-us-news-anchor; IMDb, "Rachel Maddow," accessed February 11, 2023, http://www.imdb.com/name/nm1882629/awards/; Mark Joyella, "Rachel Maddow Returns to MSNBC, Will Transition to Anchoring One Night a Week," *Forbes*, April 11, 2022, https://www.forbes.com/sites/markjoyella/2022/04/11/rachel-maddow-returns-to-msnbc-will-transition-to-anchoring-one-night-a-week/; Lisa Rogak, *Rachel Maddow: A Biography* (St. Martin's, 2020); Brian Stelter, "Rachel Maddow, a Web-Savvy Cable Host," *New York Times*, October 21, 2008, https://archive.nytimes.com/mediadecoder.blogs.nytimes.com/2008/10/21/rachel-maddow-a-web-savvy-cable-host/.

valued. Viewers cannot help but see who is on TV, so they are bound to learn the lessons of who matters and who does not.

While they face more pressure about their looks than men, on-air female journalists have achieved parity; in fact, they represent just more than half of American local TV journalists. This is important for the sake of representation and for reaching a diverse public, yet most TV reporters and anchors are not the people who make newsroom decisions. When it comes to those jobs, women remain outnumbered. Among all TV stations, 73 percent of general managers are men. The overwhelming majority of general managers, 90 percent, are white. In 2022, slightly more than 40 percent of news directors, the leaders who make the most day-to-day news decisions, are female, a record high. People of color are underrepresented in TV management, as only 17.5 percent are news directors. Radio is a largely white, with only about 18 percent of its workforce representing people of color. Major-market radio news directors and general managers are overwhelmingly white, at 90 percent. About a fourth of radio news directors are female.[53] Underscoring the importance of managers to newsroom diversity, a recent study that correlated the number of people of color on TV with the race of their leaders found that nonwhite bosses tended to lead more integrated news operations.[54]

Summary

In many ways, the experience of female journalists in broadcasting has been similar to that of their colleagues in newspapers, with widespread discrimination, marginalization, and sexual harassment. Because broadcast journalists are simultaneously performers, they are subjected to an additional layer of stereotypical expectations and critique. In radio, women were often pushed to jobs associated with homemaker stereotypes. In TV, women face the double bind of being attractive but not too attractive. Black women continue to push back against white beauty standards, especially with their hair. To become visible, queer people have had to discuss their sexuality openly, and today it is no longer a career killer. Women have made gains in broadcast management, but few organizations have achieved parity in the corner offices.

- **Reflection:** How important is it to see someone who looks like you in roles of authority and power?
- **Reflection:** What does the pattern of TV news teach young people about who is important, who is beautiful, and what is truly desired in terms of attractiveness in our society?
- **Media Critique:** Watch a local newscast and pay attention to what the presenters are wearing. Do their clothes accentuate or hide their bodies? What might this reflect about gendered expectations and stereotypes?

CHAPTER 11

Gender and Visual Journalism

Women have been involved with photography for as long as the craft has existed. Their experience in photo*journalism*, however, has been filled with challenges. Recent research on sexual harassment in the field finds that because female photojournalists are especially visible and must work with their bodies, they are highly susceptible to harassment and even assault. Although most photojournalism majors are women, the field remains dominated by men.

Key Concepts: Representation, Embodiment

No doubt you've seen the image—it's one of the most famous photographs ever created—the result of a chance meeting between two women. The portrait of a weary Florence Thompson with her children was created by Dorothea Lange, a documentary photographer working for the federal government to record the plight of migrant farm workers. The resulting photograph, *Migrant Mother*, became and remains an iconic symbol of the Great Depression.[1] While millions of people know her image, few people know that Florence Thompson was not happy about being the face of the Depression's downtrodden, nor that Lange, who was a documentary photographer, not a photojournalist, may have staged the scene by asking people to move within the tent. Lange didn't take notes that day, as was her usual practice, and Thompson's family disputes Lange's claim that the family had sold their tires to buy food.[2]

The story of *Migrant Mother* encapsulates many of the issues still facing visual journalists. Photojournalists, documentary photographers, and editorial photographers follow ethical standards that vary according to their specialization. Concerns about the power relationships between photographers and their subjects remain relevant, especially when those subjects are poor, in crisis, or members of marginalized groups. Lange was one of only two women working for the US Farm Services Administration during the Great Depression; she was hired by the government to garner support for the Roosevelt administration's policy proposals. If not for today's widespread acceptance of the New Deal's necessity, this project could easily be categorized as propaganda.

In a portrait widely known as *Migrant Mother*, Florence Owens Thompson sits with her children in Nipomo, California. She was photographed in 1936 by Dorothea Lange, who was working for the Farm Services Administration.
Courtesy of Library of Congress, Dorothea Lange, Farm Services Administration

What is true about a photograph? What kinds of control should anyone have over the use of their likeness? What responsibilities do photographers have when they record images of human suffering? Visual journalists and documentarians face all the ethical demands that writers do and more because images are so emotionally powerful, memorable, and dependent on context. In the digital age, images are easily manipulated, which means that the ethical standards of photojournalism are more important than ever.

Women face additional challenges beyond the ethics of documentary and visual journalism. (Here, as in rest of this book, references to women include all people who identify as women.) Working with a camera involves the body in ways that writing does not. Visual journalists cannot phone it in. They must always be on location to cover stories and witness events. They must work to gain access to events and news sources, which involves physical labor, if not outright danger in some instances, such as covering war or civil unrest.

When women haven't been passed over for challenging assignments, they've proven that they can work under the same demanding conditions as men. They also face danger from their male colleagues. Women in the field report widespread sexual harassment in the form of verbal comments, unwanted touching, and even assault. Today, while the industry has made progress, female visual journalists still have to fight for the best assignments and are paid less than their male colleagues.

Photography's Invention

Women have been part of photography since it was invented. In the early 1800s, Constance Fox Talbot worked with her husband as he developed a negative-based form of photography, and she was one of the first women to ever make a calotype, an early kind of photograph. Henry Fox Talbot introduced his process the same year Louis Daguerre introduced the daguerreotype in 1839, and these early systems for capturing images were considered hobbies. This meant that in the late 1800s, middle- and upper-class white women with money could enjoy photography in the same way they might enjoy painting or gardening. Female photographers of the Victorian Era tended to turn their cameras to scenes considered appropriate for women: children, flowers, or the traditional still-life tableau. Many of the photography clubs during this time were open to men and women, though, again, this was primarily a pursuit for white people who had time and money.[3]

Several decades passed between the invention of photography and the onset of photojournalism. Photos could not be published in newspapers or magazines until the invention of the half-tone process, so while photographers *were* able to travel in wagons with glass-plate cameras to capture the aftermath of war's battles, these could not be called news images.[4] Not until cameras became smaller and more portable could photographers cover news events, and in spite of the stigma against their working in public, a few women did venture into photojournalism.

Jessie Tarbox was one of them. Considered the first published female photojournalist, starting with a newspaper in Buffalo, New York, Tarbox was known for her unorthodox ways of breaking norms. She dressed according to contemporary expectations, with a skirt and bustle, but that did not prevent her from climbing ladders or even riding hot air balloons to get the shot she wanted.[5] England's first female photojournalist, Christina Broom, made history photographing soldiers training to fight during World War I, as well as other events, such as suffragist marches in London. Broom learned photography in her forties out of necessity, hoping to earn money to support her family by making postcards. During the war, she was named the official photographer to the prestigious Household Division of the British Army.[6]

Coincidentally, photography and the suffrage movement developed together, and the work of another pioneering woman from this era, Frances Benjamin Johnston, reflects that spirit.[7] In her famous self-portrait, she is smoking a cigarette, holding a

With this self-portrait, Frances Benjamin Johnston rebels against the norms of her time for feminine behavior.
Courtesy of Library of Congress, Frances Benjamin Johnston

stein of beer, and showing off her ankle—a scandalous move at the time. Johnston, who worked in the same circles as Tarbox, was known for her straightforward, unemotional portrayals of working people, including Black and Native American women.[8]

COVERING WAR

Because it involves humanity's extremes, war is the ultimate photojournalistic subject, so much so that its coverage has shaped the very ethos of what it means to be a photojournalist. Photographers ventured to battlefields early after the camera's invention. Technology at the time was limited and could not capture the sort of immediacy today's audience might expect. Bulky cameras and glass plates limited photographers to making either grand portraits of soldiers posing in front of their tents or images of the bodies left behind.

By the time of the Spanish-American War (1898), cameras were smaller and lighter, and the stereotype of a war photographer as a swashbuckling adventurer took root. This macho ethos was epitomized by Jimmy Hare. Hare's reputation as a daring risk taker started when he hid in the brush to capture the first news photograph of the Wright brothers testing their airplane. He reportedly became so used to getting burned by flash powder that he learned to work through the injuries. He covered five global conflicts, including the Spanish-American War, inspiring his employer to brag, "Wherever there is an army in the field . . . there, too, is a man from *Collier's*."[9]

This image of the brave war photographer as the ultimate professional became even more entrenched with the career of Robert Capa. He is credited with capturing the moment a Loyalist soldier was shot and killed in Spain, inspiring the *Picture Post* to declare him the "Greatest War Photographer in the World" in 1938—even before he stood on Normandy Beach to capture images from D-Day.[10] This elevation of war photography as the profession's ultimate form cultivates hypermasculine ideals. The ethos reveres bravery, risk taking, and physical strength. The Capa myth is deeply woven into photojournalistic education, and these hypermasculine norms are part of the field's indoctrination.[11] If journalism generally has historically been a male-dominated profession, then *photo*journalism is that profession on steroids.

This has not prevented women from covering war. The first female war photographer to be killed in action was Gerda Taro, Capa's partner. They covered the Spanish Civil War together until Taro was killed by a tank in 1937.[12] During the Second World War, when men were drafted to the battlefield, news organizations hired women. About 10,000 women took jobs as professional photographers during the conflict, though not all of them were in news. The war also opened opportunities for Black women with the establishment of the Women's Army Corps.[13] Margaret Bourke White, one of *Life* magazine's stars, was among the women who covered the war. She made an effort to maintain a feminine image while in the field. Among her assignments was the liberation of the Buchenwald Nazi Death Camp. Later she told an interviewer she needed to remain emotionally detached to cover this and other horrors of war: "I have to work with a veil over my mind. . . . I believe that many correspondents worked in the same self-imposed stupor. One has to, or it is impossible

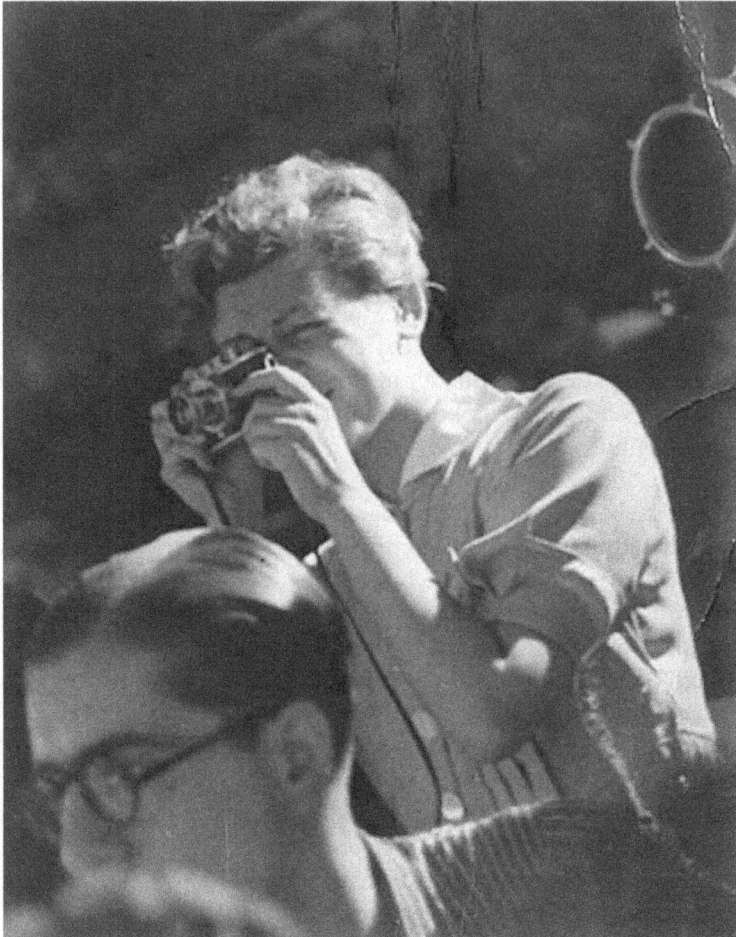

Gerda Taro using what appears to be a Leica, one of the cameras that revolutionized spot news photography. One of the earliest female war photographers, she was Robert Capa's partner. She died when she was run over by a tank during the Spanish Civil War.
Public domain

to stand it." Years later, she wrote, "Even though I did not realize how soon people would disbelieve or forget, I had a deep conviction that an atrocity like this demanded to be recorded."[14]

Even though the Second World War presented opportunities for female photojournalists, they often faced significant disadvantages. They were not allowed to be near the fighting, they had limited freedom to travel, and they were often cut out of security briefings.[15] In war zones and at home, women endured sexism, harassment in the field, even sabotage. One female photographer opted to process her photos in a hotel bathroom when she realized that men were scratching her negatives and adding improper chemicals to her developer.[16] At the end of the war, many women were laid off, but they had proven themselves and established their right to opportunities in the profession.

OPPORTUNITIES AND CHALLENGES

The end of World War II also marked the establishment of the National Press Photographers Association (NPPA), devoted to advancing and supporting professional photojournalists. The NPPA's creation was significant for the way it established a code of ethics, bringing legitimacy to a field marked by occasional tabloid-style excess. All the people who established the original organization were male, and the profession remained mostly white and male for years to come.[17]

In the 1970s, pressured by the Kerner Commission report (introduced in chapter 9) and second-wave feminism, news organizations made more of an effort to hire female visual journalists. The *New York Times* hired several women during this time, including Ruby Washington, the paper's first Black female photographer, who went on to become the first woman to manage the photo department.[18] The prestigious Magnum Photos Agency took on women for the first time in 1979.[19] Women like Dickey Chapelle were able to prove their worth during the Vietnam War, many with help from the Associated Press chief photographer who worked out of Saigon and made a point of helping diversify the staff.[20] Chapelle died in Vietnam, the first American female war photographer to die on the job.[21] She was honored by the Marines with a temporary monument at the site of her death.[22]

More women work as photojournalists today, but they remain outnumbered in the profession—even though they are the majority of the *students* in photojournalism

---

Excerpt: *What's a Woman Doing Here?*

In this excerpt from her autobiography, Dickey Chapelle recalls what it was like just get to the war zone during the Algerian Civil War in the 1950s.

I had reached the area by being passed like a package through a working underground that, as Abdel Kadar [a rebel leader] had told me, spanned borders halfway around the world. I had been moved by plane, car, truck, horse, mule and on foot. My escorts, changing almost every day, had been Algerian sympathizers in Europe, and Algerian refugees, couriers and infantrymen in North Africa. I had traveled blindfolded in a borrowed dress as a German tourist, and as a veiled and berobed Arab woman. I had been quartered in Arab homes and stables and ammunition dumps in half a dozen Moroccan towns, in the tribal tents of Berber herdsman and finally in the rock caves of the Ksour foothills three days walking from the border between Morocco and Algeria.

One of the caves, supplied with two blankets and a bed of alfalfa, had been my home for ten days. Other nearby caves on a cliff comprised the battalion command post, the base from which the rebels almost every night sortied out to halt any vehicle by mining the roads or by ambush. The battalion, like the Arab tribesmen, did not miss the roads, for they had no vehicles of their own. The roadside wrecks I'd seen were of French army trucks and armored cars. The rebel unit called itself the Scorpion Battalion (after its home among sun-warmed rocks) and had just been decorated by the FLN for blowing up the French rail line from nearby Colomb Bechar to Oran regularly three times a week.

Sources: Dickey Chapelle, *What's A Woman Doing Here? A Reporter's Report on Herself* (William Morrow, 1962), 222.

Profile: Ruby Washington, Photojournalist (1952–2018)

Ruby Washington. *New York Times* **photojournalist Washington collecting caption information while on assignment.**
Courtesy of Alamy

Ruby Washington was the first Black woman to work as a staff photographer for the *New York Times*. One of twelve children, she grew up on a farm in Georgia and started working with a camera early. In the 1970s, she was hired by the *New York Times* and started in the lab, helping develop photos, before she was promoted to photojournalist. At the time, her promotion ruffled feathers, and years later, her colleagues remembered that Washington's response to harassment and negativity was merely silence. In the field, she was known for staying cool under pressure, even saving a writer-colleague from a beating during a riot by pulling him into a car and escaping the violence.

One of her most famous photos was taken over then secretary of state Colin Powell's shoulder after he'd made a speech to the United Nations supporting the US invasion of Iraq. Washington had a long lens and was well positioned to document the note itself, which praised Powell for his speech. Writing about the image upon her retirement in 2014, Washington describes the process behind many of the world's best news images: "You wait and watch and hope to get lucky. Then you have to be ready." Washington died in 2018.

Sources: David Gonzalez, "Ruby Washington: A Quiet Trailblazer in Photojournalism," *New York Times*, September 15, 2018, https://www.nytimes.com/2018/09/15/lens/ruby-washington -a-quiet-trailblazer-in-photojournalism.html; Ruby Washington, "Ready and Waiting for the Moment to Unfold," *New York Times*, December 22, 2014, https://archive.nytimes.com/lens .blogs.nytimes.com/2014/12/22/ready-and-waiting-for-the-moment-to-unfold/.

programs.[23] A World Press Photography survey found that internationally, 85 percent of photojournalists are men. In the United States, that proportion is about the same. Women Photograph, a nonprofit dedicated to elevating women and nonbinary visual journalists, monitors credit lines and has found about 17 percent of front-page photos are made by women.[24] Female photographers in North America earn less than men, with very few women in the top range. Women around the world report that they are passed over for the best assignments and have less control over their work.[25]

Spurred by this evidence of persistent inequality, professional and arts organizations have initiated efforts to improve conditions for women. For example, the NPPA code of ethics now includes an admonition against harassment.[26] The NPPA also hosts an annual conference for women, and Women Photograph works to promote women's work with its research. Foto Feminas similarly works to elevate the work of women working in Latin America and the Caribbean.[27] These efforts face an uphill battle, however, given the unique characteristics of the job.[28]

PHOTOGRAPHY AND EMBODIMENT

War zones are not the only spaces that pose risk to photojournalists. One truism of photojournalism is that it is a physical job that engages the body; it is **embodied**. Scholars believe this embodiment may be one reason photojournalists are often overlooked within newsrooms. They are seen as blue-collar workers who use their muscles, in contrast with white-collar writers who work with their minds. This is changing, as more newsrooms demand visual skills from everyone, but the notion that pictures are easy and words are hard has historically affected the way journalists collaborate. Photojournalists complain that they are often left out of the planning process for big stories.[29] Gendered stereotypes place an additional burden on women, who find themselves constantly having to prove themselves. Fear of harassment and abuse affects their ability to simply do their job. Within the profession, women report that they continue to be treated in stereotypical ways—as women, not professionals.[30]

Embodiment means that photojournalists face physical risks in many situations. They cannot do their job without being present on the scene. During the COVID-19 pandemic, many reporters worked from home. Photojournalists cannot do that, and the NPPA held online meetings to share strategies for keeping its members healthy.[31] The job can also require strength, stamina, and agility to carry cameras around a sporting event, a protest, or a war zone. People with cameras are automatically visible and therefore vulnerable in violent situations. Linda Tirado was covering the George Floyd protests in Minneapolis in the summer of 2020 and lost an eye when struck by a rubber bullet fired by police. She sued, and the city settled with her for $600,000. Officers maintained that they had not intentionally fired at her face as she'd alleged.[32]

Sports, politics, and even rock concerts have historically been covered mostly by men. Internationally, more than 92 percent of sports photojournalists are men.[33] Women who want to photograph sports find themselves especially unwelcome. A study of women who cover football found that their work is impeded by stereotypical beliefs that women don't understand sports, they're not strong enough to work the sidelines, and they can't handle the technology. Women in the study reported that they'd been denied field access even when they had their credentials. If they traveled with the team, they might not have a place to change into work-appropriate clothes, while the male photojournalists were simply allowed to use the players' locker room. One woman was so worried about seeming overemotional that even when she injured her leg badly on the job and needed emergency care, she didn't want to cry out.[34]

Female concert photographers have similar stories of bullying and harassment. In interviews with photographers, one researcher found that *both* men and women used patriarchal language when talking about what happens in the pit. Their language reflects the overarching power of patriarchy, as they noted the impact of physicality on this very crowded, stressful work. One woman referred to herself as a "mom" the men didn't want invading the pit. Another referred to a female photographer who got jostled as a "girl." Beyond the language, women in the study also reported instances of overt harassment. "I've had male photographers hit on me or come to me and touch me, pushing up against me in a sexual way," one subject said, noting that the men in question thought "they could get away with it."[35]

PHOTOGRAPHY AND HARASSMENT

The nature of the job means that women in photojournalism are vulnerable to sexual harassment. Its embodiment means that people must interact physically, sometimes very closely. Photojournalists don't work in a newsroom, where there may be other people around to provide social support. For freelancers especially, an editor is often the one and only person they talk to, the contact who can provide material support and security. Add the Capa ethos, which celebrates machismo and daring, and conditions are ripe for a culture of harassment and abuse.

Based on interviews with female photojournalists aged twenty-two to eighty-two, researcher Rachel Somerstein has found that the sexual harassment of female photojournalists is pervasive and global. Every one of the women in one study shared stories of sexual harassment. The form it took ranged from innuendo to outright sexual assault. The women she interviewed tended to see the harassment as their individual problem, not a systemic one, reflecting the sort of victim blaming endemic to rape culture. Somerstein's subjects were afraid to ask for help. "If I complain, then they will always send the guys out to be with the firefighters," one told her, adding, "Fire assignments are important."[36]

Somerstein's subjects underscored the extra vulnerability of nonwhite women. Because they are stereotyped as "the help" or as sexually lascivious, they are more likely to be harassed or attacked on the job. Finally, women are more likely to be freelancers as a result of the shrinking market for journalism jobs. This means that they are even more vulnerable because they are supposed to keep clients happy if they are to get repeat business.

One of the more prominent #MeToo cases in photography came out of the fashion industry, which has a history of imbalanced relationships between male photographers and female models. In 2017, fashion photographer Terry Richardson lost

Profile: Melina Mara, Photojournalist (1962–)

Melina Mara. Mara rests on the floor during the 2017 NPPA Women in Visual Journalism Conference in Austin, Texas. Photojournalism is a physically demanding job that often entails standing for hours, sitting on the floor, and running while on assignment.
Photo by Mary Angela Bock

Melina Mara is an award-winning photojournalist who covers Capitol Hill for the *Washington Post*. As a child, she was inspired by her father, a photographer for CBS News. Her first job out of college was as a kindergarten teacher, and she pursued photography as a hobby. An Associated Press photographer noticed her work and encouraged her to work for the New Jersey Bureau, and she took on photojournalism as her career. She returned to graduate school at the esteemed University of Missouri School of Journalism and went on to work for newspapers and magazines around the country, including the *Southeast Missourian*, the *Oregonian*, and the *Seattle Post Intelligencer*. She says that while she received excellent mentoring from many men in her early career, she also faced sexual harassment, even from some of her closest colleagues. It did not deter her from the career, though.

While in Seattle in 2003, inspired by the number of women elected to the Senate and with two female senators from Washington, she pitched a story about female politicians to her editors. That project, "Changing the Face of Power: Women in the US Senate," became an exhibit hosted by the Smithsonian Institution and later a book. Mara was hired as the national political photojournalist at the *Washington Post* in 2004 and continues to cover stories on Capitol Hill, in the White House, and on the campaign trail.

Sources: Melina Mara, communication with the author, May 11, 2022; "Melina Mara," *Washington Post*, accessed September 18, 2022, https://www.washingtonpost.com/people/melina -mara/; Melina Mara et al., *Changing the Face of Power: Women in the US Senate* (University of Texas Press, 2005).

a number of high-level magazine contracts based on multiple allegations of sexual improprieties with models—activity once so taken for granted in the field that he openly told an interviewer, "It's not who you know, it's who you blow."[37] Eventually changing attitudes brought about by the #MeToo and Time's Up movements convinced leading magazines to break their relationships with Richardson.[38]

The news industry also has its own open secrets. A *New York Times* photo editor left his job in 2021 after years of complaints by staff and freelance photographers of verbal and emotional abuse. David Furst, who oversaw work that garnered Pulitzers and other international prizes, was accused of bullying everyone, male and female, and of discriminating against women. In one case, he reportedly denied assignments to a war photographer because she'd had a baby.[39] How can such behavior go on for years? Recall from chapter 6 that men are socialized to be controlling and to win. They are expected to be violent, so bullying is accepted, especially, as with Furst, when they have a winner's reputation.

Visual Representation

Visual journalism lets the audience see the world without having to leave home. It brings images of the day's horrors and joys straight to our smartphones. The camera's technological perfection makes it easy to forget that images are *constructed*. They are crafted, chosen, and produced for the audience through complex organizational systems. Who is portrayed and how? Who appears to be important? Who appears to be a problem? **Representation** is the production of meaning through language, discourse, and image. It shapes our understanding of the world and each other.[40] Representations seem to be real, but they are not. Visual culture shapes what we know and think about society, and it is in no way neutral. Images are more emotionally powerful, memorable, and dependent on context than words. A visual stereotype can make a stronger, longer impact than a verbal one.[41] What this means for the field of photojournalism is that everything we know about newsroom diversity is especially important for visual journalism. What we see depends greatly on who holds the camera, where they work, and where they point the lens.

Visual journalists must also be mindful of how and whether to engage with public activism. Politicians and activists often put on media events specifically for the sake of camera coverage. A **media event** is designed to attract press coverage. Critic Daniel Boorstin used the term *pseudo-events* for events that wouldn't even happen if not for press coverage.[42] Think of the times gender rights activists have used visual communication to make a point, whether by the suffragists wearing all white for their parades or AIDS activists spreading quilts across the Washington Mall. Some spectacles attract attention and can influence public opinion, but some events may not represent a genuine group effort. Advertisers, corporations, or political operatives often try to attract attention with self-serving gimmicks.

Visual journalists must also consider how to cover protests in which incidents of violence or property damage might occur. While a broken window or burning car is exciting to look at, coverage that centers such a visual frame can distort the message of an otherwise peaceful demonstration.[43] Visual journalists, therefore, have ethical concerns that are unique to the image. They must always walk a careful line, covering events as they happen without being used by skillful public relations managers and working to present a complete picture, literally and metaphorically, of the day's events.

One of the philosophical puzzles about photography is that it presents us with visual truth; the camera delivers an accurate record of the light waves before it, but at the same time, photography always presents a particular point of view, as the camera must be pointed *at* something. Most news photos are also edited, cropped, captioned, and contextualized in a report. And so, just as with the written word, visual journalism inspires questions about just what objectivity is and how news practice can best represent the world.

Visual professionals generally choose one of two perspectives. Documentary producers, whether they work with stills or film, embrace and defend a point of view. For example, Dorothea Lange, whose image opens this chapter, made images specifically in support the government's effort to assist migrant workers.[44] Documentary photographers are truthful, but not necessarily in ways that are distant or nonpartisan. One of the attributes that sets Lange's work apart was her willingness to spend time in camps; inserting herself professionally into the lives of rural and working-class people allowed her to also better contend with the lives of women with families.[45] Photojournalists who adhere to NPPA's code of ethics, though, avoid taking a position.[46] They are expected to keep some emotional distance as they record events visually. Yet because their work is tangible, concrete, and embodied, their work still involves representational choices.

Some critics ask whether there is such a thing as a woman's eye in photography.[47] Does identifying as female mean a person's pictures are different? There's no evidence that women have a different photographic *style*, but there may be a difference in what they choose to focus on—where they point their camera. That is, they may choose to take different angles on a story, metaphorically and visually. For instance, one of the most important images made about Central American gang violence by internationally acclaimed photographer Donna DeCesare is not a street scene of fighting but a little girl holding a bird. DeCesare's decision to focus on the families affected by gang warfare in turn changes our perspective on the issue.[48] Similarly, Danielle Villasana's book *A Light Inside* portrays trans life in Peru to highlight the courage and resilience of trans people as they struggle for acceptance and safety in the course of their daily life.[49]

What does this mean for women in the field? Chapter 9 describes the challenges faced by women and minorities when newsrooms started to integrate. They were expected to represent their group but also to take on the perspective of the (mostly white and straight) men around them. Given the many choices a photographer must make in the field, such as angle of view, composition, or distance, can we say that visual journalism is objective in the traditional sense? Cameras may accurately record the light waves around them, but once that happens, an image is captioned, shared, and contextualized in language. Is it possible that women might have distinct visual perspectives? Some women in visual journalism believe their femininity has helped them gain access to people and to stories, though it is hard to know how much of this stems from social stereotypes.[50] The answer seems not in clicking a camera's shutter but in how they position the lens. To live in a woman's body is to experience the world in a particular way. Just as women and minority writers might focus on topics in their own way, photographers who are not white and male will navigate the world and document it differently. Their work is no less truthful, and it broadens the viewer's perspective.

Summary

More women than men are enrolled in photojournalism programs in the United States, yet they remain marginalized at the highest levels of the profession. The Capa myth that idolizes war photography imbues the field with an extra layer of masculinity. The embodied nature of the job brings with it additional forms of discrimination, as female photojournalists are pushed, groped, and physically assaulted while trying to do their jobs. Women remain outnumbered in the profession, but recent efforts are underway worldwide to offer more support. Diversity of perspectives remains an important goal for fair representation of the world and its events.

- **Reflection:** Is it possible that women have a different photographic eye? What do we know about stereotypes and gender socialization that might make a difference?
- **Reflection:** Photojournalism is a job that requires people to be physically present on location. What difference might that make for queer and trans photographers?
- **Media Critique:** As you read and watch news, look for photo credits or cutlines for the images you see. How often do you see a female name in a photo credit?

CHAPTER 12

Gender in Digital Spaces

When and how did the internet change from a place that women helped to create into an unwelcoming den of trolls? This chapter looks at women's roles in the development of the early internet and today's tech empires and the challenges they face online, especially when they work as journalists. Even though women were part of the very invention of computers and the internet, the online environment has become hostile in many ways.

Key Concepts: Gamergate, Incel

Years ago, Julia Carrie Wong enjoyed being online, but that changed in 2019. A technology reporter based in San Francisco, Wong had to take a leave of absence in the wake of vicious online harassment. Abusers posted racist comments about her Asian and Jewish heritage. They wrote about where she lives. They threatened her with rape and murder. She took time off when the panic attacks started, and while her employer, *Guardian*, was supportive, Wong was dismayed that she'd reached the point that she could not do her job.[1] That may well have been the harasser's intent.

The harassment of female-identifying journalists around the world has become so serious that the United Nations issued a report in 2022 decrying what has become a form of censorship.[2] (Here and throughout the book, *female* and *women* refer to anyone who identifies as such.) Female journalists are mocked and threatened in frightening ways. Abusers look up and post the addresses of women's homes, a practice known as doxing. Fueled by misogynistic networks, the posts can come in torrents. Newsrooms have only recently started to formulate systems to support women who are attacked in this way, and the harassment is considered by many to be just part of the job. How did this become so commonplace? Why female journalists? There is no single answer. The culture of the internet, patriarchy, and contemporary politics helped to create this perfect storm, and there's no easy way out.

Internet Culture and Gender

Women were very much part of the internet's beginnings. In fact, coding was largely a female job because it was tedious and involved keyboards. Women were considered natural for the job.[3] Just as with radio, though, once computing became profitable, it became male territory. Today, some men consider the digital realm to be a male enclave where women are unwelcome. Misogyny pervades many corners of the internet and has become so vicious that women and their supporters have had to create defense systems. Social media, while often cruel, has also proven to help women through hashtag activism and other digital organizing.

WOMEN AND CODING

Women were among the people who invented computing. In fact, Augusta Ada Lovelace is often credited with writing the world's first computer code in the 1800s. She was friends with Charles Babbage, who invented a mechanical calculation machine, and Lovelace figured out how to give it instructions.[4] In the twentieth century, mathematician Alan Turing served the British military during World War II by developing a mechanical computer that could break a code used by the Germans. Turing was honored as an Officer of the Most Excellent Order of the British Empire (OBE) for helping the Allies win. After the war, his work contributed to the development of today's digital computers. A gay man, Turing was prosecuted for "gross indecency" in 1952 and forced to endure hormonal treatment, also known as "chemical castration." He was found dead two years later of an apparent suicide. Turing's treatment by the British government became cause for regret as time went by. Prime Minister Gordon Brown issued an apology in 2009, and Queen Elizabeth II issued a rare royal pardon for Turing in 2013.[5]

In the mid-twentieth century, computers were no longer purely for the military and had spread to the business world. Here, women were integral to their use, so much so that *Cosmopolitan* magazine even ran a feature on the 20,000 so-called "computer girls" with lucrative programming jobs. Famed software developer Grace Hopper told the magazine, "Women are naturals at computer programming."[6] Women did much of the computational work for NASA during the space race; indeed, their job title was "computer." There was a severe shortage of people who could do this work in the 1960s, and NASA was willing to hire people without college degrees, which meant that some women could apply.[7]

So what happened? When did the stereotypical computer hack become a white, male, bespectacled nerd? As chapter 10 shows with the radio business, when an activity professionalizes, it tends to exclude women. Also, as computers got larger (the early ones took up entire rooms), they needed down time, and programming needed to be done at night, when women were forbidden to enter corporate buildings because of safety concerns. As the machines became more important to business processes, large corporations started to require math degrees for programmers, even though evidence suggested that advanced math was not required for the work. Computing had roots

A sculpture of Alan Turing memorializes his work for the codebreakers at their World War II headquarters in Bletchley Park, England.
Courtesy of Creative Commons, Jon Callas

in the military, which used aptitude tests that tended to marginalize women, and these exams took a tenacious hold on corporations like IBM. These aptitude tests and psychological profiles suggested that the ideal programmer was not just a man but an independent, antisocial man at that.[8]

Today, the computer industry and media associated with tech is dominated by men. Women make up 47 percent of the US workforce but only 25 percent of computing roles. Women earned only one in five computer science degrees in 2016. Even when women do get computer jobs after graduation, they are more likely to leave early. According to the Pew Research Center, half the women in tech experienced

Profile: Grace Hopper, Computer Scientist and Navy Rear Admiral (1906–1992)

Grace Brewster Murray Hopper was a pioneering computer coder who made it possible to use words to program a computer instead of abstract characters and numbers. She had an MA and PhD in mathematics from Yale when she joined the Navy after Pearl Harbor was bombed. Hopper is sometimes credited with being the first to use the word *bug* to describe a glitch in software, but the term *debugging* had already been in use by programmers for years. She *was* on a Navy team that discovered an actual moth in a computer in 1947 and disrupted its operation, which perhaps is how the legend started.

Hopper was involved with some of the most important computer innovations of the twentieth century. In 1953, she developed the first compiler able to translate mathematical code into something a machine could read. This led to Hopper's eventual invention of programs that could

Grace Murray Hopper.
Courtesy of Creative Commons, US Navy

use English words. Her work made computers accessible to people without engineering experience, helping spread computing into the business world and beyond. "I kept calling for more user-friendly languages," she told an interviewer in 1980. "Most of the stuff we get from academicians, computer science people, is in no way adapted to people."

Sources: Computer History Museum, "Hopper, Grace, Oral History," December 11, 1980, http://www.computerhistory.org/collections/catalog/102702026; *Computerworld* Staff, "Moth in the Machine: Debugging the Origins of 'Bug,'" *Computerworld*, September 3, 2011, https://www.computerworld.com/article/2515435/moth-in-the-machine--debugging-the-origins-of--bug-.html; Office of the President, "Biography of Grace Murray Hopper," Yale University, February 10, 2017, https://president.yale.edu/biography-grace-murray-hopper; Kathleen Broome Williams, *Grace Hopper: Admiral of the Cyber Sea*, Library of Naval Biography (Naval Institute Press, 2004).

gender discrimination, a number that went up to 78 percent for women working in male-dominated workspaces. Another 36 percent said sexual harassment was a problem in their workplace.[9] The number of *Forbes'* female CEOs for tech startups in 2022 was higher than the year before, with eight—out of one hundred.[10] For the female journalists who cover the tech industry, harassment is rampant. A 2015 survey found that 62 percent had experienced sexist abuse, 20 percent had disguised their gender in a publication to avoid abuse, and 39 percent said fear of abuse changed their work practices.[11]

Gaming and Gender

Gaming is also hostile to women, whether they play or cover the industry as journalists, even though there are more female gamers than many people expect. The stereotype of a gamer is a teenage boy playing for hours in his basement. It's true that video games are very popular among teenage boys. But gamers come in all ages and genders. Americans spent more than $60 billion on video games in 2021.[12]

They may be outnumbered, but millions of women play video games. A majority of young men (72 percent) often or sometimes play video games, compared with 49 percent of women ages eighteen to twenty-nine. Among all adults, 43 percent own a gaming console.[13] Even seniors play video games. The American Association of Retired Persons (AARP) reports that 44 percent of its members (people fifty and older) play video games.[14] Queer people play, too, and in fact there is an entire library of games devoted to the LGBTQ+ community.[15] Men are more likely than women to call themselves gamers. Most Americans, including a majority of female gamers, believe that most video game players are men. The shooting and military games associated with the male gamer stereotype are not as popular with women as puzzle, strategy, and adventure games.[16]

Gendered Spaces

Women who play online games often face a hostile environment, particularly when they play better than men do. A 2015 study found that men who are of lower skill were more positive toward men and more negative toward women. Interestingly, the study also found that higher-skilled men were more positive to female players.[17] A 2021 poll found that online gaming is highly hostile to female and LGBTQ+ players, and of those who reported harassment, 72 percent said it was misogynistic. A third were harassed for their sexual orientation. Not all that surprisingly, the aggressive and avatar-driven massively multiplayer online role-playing games (MMORPGs) were the most toxic. The report found that because there is no moderation to improve the online gaming environment, misogynistic hostility is becoming normalized.[18]

What is it about gamer identity and this particular space that causes such hostility to women? For one thing, it is anonymous, so nastiness is not prohibited or punished with any regularity. Another dimension is the notion that computing is a male space, much like sports (or, once upon a time, news), where women "do not belong," except to please the male gaze. Female avatars are often highly sexualized, with outsized breasts and tight or barely there clothing. Male avatars usually have big muscles and wear more practical clothes.[19] Avatars, or playable characters, who are clearly queer or nonbinary are rare.[20]

Finally, the games themselves have a hypermasculine dimension; they offer zero-sum logic. Recall from chapter 6 that in zero-sum thinking, someone must win, and someone must lose—there is no gray area. Considering that many of the more popular games involve violence and warfare, it becomes a little clearer why gaming is so hostile to women. These competitions have a clear winner and loser, and the themes are associated with masculinity, so women don't belong unless they're decorative.

Profile: Adrienne Shaw, Game Researcher (1983–)

Adrienne Shaw, a professor at Temple University in Philadelphia, studies queer gaming culture. A longtime gamer herself, she studies the way queer gamers are often invisible yet comprise a significant and influential part of online culture. She founded the LGBTQ Video Game Archive, a publicly available online archive that catalogues LGBTQ+ representation in video games, and she managed to resurrect the oldest known example of an LGBTQ+ video game, C. M. Ralph's *Caper in the Castro*, released in 1989. In 2014, she was among the writers and scholars targeted for harassment by Gamergate. Trolls called her a "social justice warrior." Gamergate chatter suggested that because Shaw had a federal research grant, her work was a government conspiracy. Shaw and one of her colleagues later put the incident into perspective by noting that #Gamergate is recognition of the importance of gaming culture and its scholarship.

Sources: Shira Chess and Adrienne Shaw, "A Conspiracy of Fishes, or, How We Learned to Stop Worrying about #GamerGate and Embrace Hegemonic Masculinity," *Journal of Broadcasting and Electronic Media* 59, no. 1 (January 2, 2015): 208–20, https://doi.org/10.1080/08838151.2014.999917; Jordan Pearson, "You Can Now Play the First LGBTQ Computer Game, for the First Time," Vice, December 20, 2017, https://www.vice.com/en/article/ne4nzz/play-the-first-lgbtq-computer-game-for-the-first-time-caper-in-the-castro. See also *Adrienne Shaw* (blog), accessed May 17, 2023, https://adrienneshaw.com.

GAMERGATE

Gaming's misogyny has created a hostile environment for female journalists who cover the gaming industry and tech more generally. In 2014, an online accusation (later disproved) that a journalist acted unethically in her game reviews snowballed into a situation that almost became violent. In the episode, known as Gamergate, male gamer identity came under threat from women who entered this enclave, like game critic Zoe Quinn. It started when an ex-boyfriend wrote a long online post accusing Quinn of cheating on him and exchanging sex for good game reviews. Kotaku, the website where she worked, investigated this claim and exonerated her, yet Gamergate, under the guise of promoting "journalistic ethics," continued to grow.[21] Writer Milo Yiannapolis, who at the time worked for Breitbart, helped fuel hatred against female gamers. Female gaming writers and critics, he declared, were an "army of sociopathic feminist programmers and campaigners abetted by the achingly politically correct American tech bloggers who are terrorizing the entire community."[22]

The trolling and misogyny inspired by Gamergate went well beyond mean tweets and escalated to threats of physical violence. One woman had to go into hiding after being doxed. Another woman, Anita Sarkeesian, had to cancel a public appearance because of violent threats.[23] She and Quinn had to leave their homes after their addresses were published online. Gamergate illustrates just how strongly the identity of male gaming is associated with a particular kind of masculinity and that gaming is considered by these participants as a hypermasculine space where women are not welcome. Sarkeesian has since established an organization devoted to helping people under attack from these sorts of pile-ons. The Feminist Frequency offers a hotline for reporting abuse and seeking help. One of the surprises the hotline produced: Many

Profile: Anita Sarkeesian, Media Critic (1983-)

Anita Sarkeesian speaking at the Game Developers Choice Awards, where she won the Ambassador Award in 2014.
Courtesy of Creative Commons, Game Developers Choice Awards

Anita Sarkeesian is a media critic who founded Feminist Frequency, a web-based educational nonprofit that critiques pop culture's representations of women. In 2012, Sarkeesian was targeted by a hate campaign that attacked women who were criticizing homophobia and misogyny in video games. That campaign escalated to rape and death threats, including one in 2014 that warned of the "deadliest school shooting in American history" and prompted her to cancel an appearance at the University of Utah. Sarkeesian appeared before the United Nations in 2015 to address global online harassment of women and girls, and she has spoken at various media, fan, and technology conferences. She was named one of *Time*'s one hundred most influential people in the world, and she received the 2014 Game Developers Choice Ambassador Award and an honorary award from the National Academy of Video Game Trade Reviewers in 2013. In 2020, the Feminist Frequency launched the Games and Online Harassment Hotline to provide support for gamers targeted by abuse.

Sources: Erin Alberty, "Anita Sarkeesian Explains Why She Canceled USU Lecture," *Salt Lake Tribune*, October 16, 2014, https://archive.sltrib.com/article.php?id=58528113&itype=CMSID; Feminist Frequency, accessed November 14, 2021, https://feministfrequency.com/; Allegra Frank, "Anita Sarkeesian, Zoe Quinn and More Take Aim at Cyber Harassment against Women," Polygon, September 25, 2015, https://www.polygon.com/2015/9/25/9399169/united-nations-women-cyber-violence-anita-sarkeesian-zoe-quinn.

people reporting harassment were abused not by strangers but by people they know and compete with online, such as coworkers and colleagues, an indication of how gaming is so much a part of everyday life.[24] Hotline calls come from people bullied by classmates or engaged in fights with roommates or conflicts with colleagues.

Online Harassment and Journalism

The online harassment of female journalists has spread far beyond Gamergate and is so pervasive that many women have come to expect it. The misogyny is nonpartisan and not just a characteristic of social conservatives. For example, during the 2016 Democratic primary, a group of self-proclaimed Bernie Bros (fans of the highly progressive candidate Bernie Sanders) sent threatening messages to the women covering the race, with such messages as this tweet from Daniel Kohn to veteran NPR reporter Tamara Keith: "Good job lying about the primary you dumb c*nt."[25]

The harassment of female journalists strikes at a perpetual double bind for women, who have long been expected to be professionally tough as they compete with male colleagues. Even those working to combat the problem worry that framing online harassment as misogyny risks suggesting that women are somehow weak or helpless.[26] Studies find repeatedly that women are expected to tough it out and are enculturated to expect negative comments as part of the job.[27] Freelancers have it especially hard, as they don't have any social support from newsroom colleagues.[28]

The problem is so pervasive that the United Nations has become involved. The harassment of female journalists affects their health, well-being, and ability to have a civic voice. The United Nations Educational, Scientific, and Cultural Organization (UNESCO) interviewed more than seven hundred women journalists in 125 countries. The UNESCO study found that 73 percent of the respondents said they had experienced online violence. A fourth of them had been threatened physically, and 18 percent were threatened with sexual violence. These are not mere words. One out of five of the women in the UNESCO survey said they'd been attacked or abused offline in connection with the harassment they'd experienced. Online harassment follows a pattern. Women are more likely to be harassed after writing about gender issues, and the attacks often seem to be associated with orchestrated disinformation campaigns.[29] Democracy itself is threatened by the extent of the abuse. Research also suggests that as much as they *want* to shake off the harassment, some journalists prefer to avoid certain topics after particularly violent threats.[30]

While journalists of both genders are targeted with online negativity, the abuse women receive is unique for the way it includes threats of rape, dismemberment, and murder.[31] The messages can be disturbingly graphic. When men are harassed, their intelligence is often insulted, and they are less likely to be threatened with graphic sexual violence. A crowdsourced study by Amnesty International found that a female politician or journalist is targeted with an abusive tweet every thirty seconds. The study also found that Black women were far more likely to be targeted with abuse that includes threats of violence or rape, along with racial slurs.[32]

An international study that preceded UNESCO's found nearly all the women interviewed had been harassed online and that the abuse was exacerbated when women reported on traditionally male issues or gender rights. Their male colleagues also get harassed but not in a sexual way. Women are expected to engage with their audience online, but engagement only intensifies the abuse.[33] Journalists also often use their personal social media accounts to gather news and may be targeted there instead of through a newsroom account, and they still need protection in these spaces.[34]

Critics charge that news organizations and social media companies do too little to help. Journalists who are harassed are usually disappointed by the response of their newsrooms and often feel abandoned by management. Suggestions for protections include content moderation (having someone keep an eye on the comment section) and managers taking legal action against violators. The Committee to Protect Journalists (CPJ) found that while most journalists feel less safe, less than half had received any training in how to protect themselves from harassment and abuse.[35] More recently, the Center for Countering Digital Hate found that the social media site Instagram failed to assist the targets of misogynistic, racist, even anti-Semitic abuse nine times out of ten.[36]

More organizations are stepping up. Trollbusters, one of the earliest antiabuse organizations, was established by Michelle Ferrier after she was targeted online with misogynistic and racist abuse. Trollbusters offers information, helps root out troll nests, and will flood a victim's feed with positive and affirming messages when necessary.[37] CPJ offers support and advice specific to the countries where reporters work. India, for instance, has seen some particularly pernicious campaigns against female journalists.[38] The International Women's Media Fund established a program in 2022 that provides newsrooms with guidance for assisting reporters, including a template that organizations can use to establish a policy for when staff should report abuse and what management will do about it.[39]

Bodies in Cyberspace

Covering internet culture requires journalists to understand how it compares and contrasts with offline life. The online environment, known as cyberspace, is largely nonphysical but can have very real implications for offline life. For instance, the anonymity of cyberspace is freeing, but as the abuse crisis shows, it can also be toxic. An online incident during a game in the internet's earliest days shows that just because people are not physically present, they are still at risk for trauma. The "rape in cyberspace" incident (see excerpt) unsettled the people who gathered in a text-only online community called LambdaMoo, a game that today would seem primitive. When one member started describing violent sexual assaults against other named players, the community tried to solve the "crime," changing the game's social system and showing the world that online reality can feel very violent.[40] Julian Dibbell's story about the incident in the *Village Voice* was one of the first mainstream accounts of the way the online world overlaps with real life.

CYBER BODIES, REAL EXPERIENCE

The physical freedom and anonymity of the web is potentially liberating. In the early days of the internet, many observers were optimistic about how the web would free people to be themselves in ways they never could before. If we leave our bodies behind, the logic went, then we could be rid of sexism, racism, and heteronormativity.[41]

Excerpt: "A Rape in Cyberspace"

These particulars, as I said, are unambiguous. But they are far from simple, for the simple reason that every set of facts in virtual reality (or VR, as the locals abbreviate it) is shadowed by a second, complicating set: the "real-life" facts. And while a certain tension invariably buzzes in the gap between the hard, prosaic RL facts and their more fluid, dreamy VR counterparts, the dissonance in the Bungle case is striking. No hideous clowns or trickster spirits appear in the RL version of the incident, no voodoo dolls or wizard guns, indeed no rape at all as any RL court of law has yet defined it. The actors in the drama were university students for the most part, and they sat rather undramatically before computer screens the entire time, their only actions a spidery flitting of fingers across standard QWERTY keyboards. No bodies touched. Whatever physical interaction occurred consisted of a mingling of electronic signals sent from sites spread out between New York City and Sydney, Australia. Those signals met in LambdaMOO, certainly, just as the hideous clown and the living room party did, but what was LambdaMOO after all? Not an enchanted mansion or anything of the sort—just a middlingly complex database, maintained for experimental purposes inside a Xerox Corporation research computer in Palo Alto and open to public access via the Internet.

Source: Julian Dibbell, "A Rape in Cyberspace: How an Evil Clown, a Haitian Trickster Spirit, Two Wizards, and a Cast of Dozens Turned a Database into a Society," *Village Voice*, December 23, 1993.

Anonymity offered a chance to provide reviews and critique in ways that could never happen before. But even in these earliest days, individuals who were not white, cis, straight males saw the darker side of the online environment.[42] It is possible to pass as another race or gender online. Both men and women gender-swap in games but for different reasons. Women will play as a man to avoid harassment, while men will play as a woman to build extrafeminine avatars or receive gifts within the game.[43]

INCELS

Cyberspace has also been described as an echo chamber, in which like-minded people can reinforce one another's beliefs. This can create pathological spaces on the internet where individuals can radicalize one another. **Incel** groups are an example. *Incel* is a term borrowed from the phrase *involuntarily celibate*, coined in 1997 by a woman (ironically) who started a website to discuss her feelings of loneliness and sexual deprivation. Over time and across several online sites, such as 4chan and Reddit, the incel community has become more misogynistic and extremist; in fact, Reddit banned the incel subreddit account in 2017 for repeatedly violating the site's rule against inciting violence.[44]

Incels believe that women are superficial and have created a world in which a person's value rests entirely on physical appearance, creating a social hierarchy that puts most men at a disadvantage. Incels are able to see themselves not as losers in the dating game but as victims—who, in some instances, believe rape and misogynistic violence is therefore justified. Self-described incel Elliot Rodger went on a shooting rampage in

2014, killing six people before shooting himself. He left behind a 133-page manifesto in which he complained, "All I ever wanted was to love a woman."

Rodgers was the first person to cite incel philosophy as reason to murder, but there have been others since, and law enforcement now considers incels to be a violent extremist group, a form of domestic terrorism.[45] In 2022, the US Secret Service and Office of Homeland Security issued a report on the threat of incel behavior as potential "targeted violence."[46] These hypermasculine spaces have turned into a jumping-off point for another pathology that overlaps with extreme misogyny: white supremacy. Alt-right extremist groups are using the internet to recruit even tween boys. Fascist sites offer secrecy, anonymity, and a sense of being part of something special or grownup. They lend hate groups an edge in recruiting young men into their ideology.[47]

HASHTAG ACTIVISM

Not all the news about women online is negative. Marginalized communities are able to use social media to help one another. In Latin America, women use WhatsApp and other social media to organize and protect one another from gendered violence. *Autodefensas feministas* provide security for women through online collectives that combat domestic violence and work to hold abusers accountable.[48] Black Twitter, an informal network within Twitter, is a source of support and activism for people of color.[49] And it was a hashtag, #MeToo, that brought light to the incredible pervasiveness of workplace sexual harassment. Hashtag activism works by connecting like-minded people for emotional support and help in solving real problems.[50] Twitter was such a significant platform for organizing that when billionaire Elon Musk bought it in 2022 and changed its policies, activists around the world expressed concern for the future of digital activism.[51]

Summary

Women helped develop the digital world, but today they are not welcome in many parts of it. While incivility affects everyone on the internet, people who identify as female are targeted with extreme misogynistic abuse, sometimes the result of coordinated campaigns. Female journalists are especially vulnerable, as their work is public, and they are expected to engage with the public. Gamergate was a watershed event for women and LGBTQ+ people online. The episode highlights sexism in the gaming industry and reveals the extent of misogynistic harassment. Representations of LGBTQ+ people are rare in gaming, and storylines are often homophobic. Some women who have been harassed have organized efforts to help victims of online abuse. Advocacy organizations are working to advise newsrooms on how to better protect female journalists in order to maintain press freedom. Today's media professionals need to be acquainted with internet culture in order to cover contemporary society.

- **Reflection:** What does it mean to be in a safe or a welcoming space? How do digital media complicate our sense of being in a particular space?
- **Reflection:** How might online harassment be regulated in a society that values free speech? When does it cross a line into something that is harmful to society?
- **Media Critique:** Have you ever seen mean tweets directed at a journalist? What did you notice about the apparent identities of the people involved?

CHAPTER 13

The Personal and Political in News

Bodies make the news, and women's bodies are especially scrutinized in ways that generate controversy. This chapter describes the gendered news stories of everyday life and the way the human body has been represented in media. Whether in news, entertainment, or social platforms, these representations tend to reflect and sustain oppressive systems. Men are portrayed in ways that cultivate the unwavering belief that they must be strong, active, and sometimes violent. LGBTQ+ and trans people have been portrayed in ways that perpetuate stereotypes. Nonbinary or trans people are often subjected to criticism and harassment when they do not appear to comport to the gender binary. The patriarchal belief that women's bodies must be controlled and monitored is at the heart of many news stories, from birth control policies to prom dress guidelines. An overarching expectation that women exist to have babies and be beautiful is evident in the way women's bodies are scrutinized and regulated in contemporary society.

Key Concepts: Bechdel Test, False Equivalence, Mental Load, Symbolic Annihilation

In 2022, women in two countries protested rules about wearing the hijab, a headscarf worn by many Muslim women. In Iran, women risked their lives to protest rules that *required* them to cover their heads after a woman died in custody when she was arrested for violating the country's strict religious dress codes.[1] In France, Muslim women pushed back against French law that *forbade* them to wear the hijab.[2] Critics joked that these seeming oppositional positions were evidence that women are irrational. The protests were completely sensible if one considers that the issue was not really about the veil. The target for these protests was the patriarchal belief that the government had the right to tell women what to wear.

Patriarchy, the ideology that places men at the top of the social hierarchy, is a system that requires women to please the male gaze. (Here and throughout the book, *women* refers to all people who identify as female.) Recall the concept of objectification as described in chapter 4. Art critic John Berger's famous phrase, "Men act, women appear," exemplifies the way women are not only objectified in traditional art but also that they know their role and take it on.[3] Women and female-identifying people are often subjected to scrutiny for how they appear, and they are expected to conform to rules, sometimes overt and sometimes unspoken, that maintain this power relationship.

Women's bodies, therefore, become problems that must be regulated. By calling attention to bodily fluids or characteristics, including menstruation, lactation, child-birth, breasts, or female genitalia, misogynistic rhetoric frames women as odd, gross, chaotic, or messy. A girl's bare shoulder in school becomes a problem if boys might find it sexy; a woman's armpit hair is offensive. Women are criticized for being too fat, too thin, too sexy, and too frumpy. Oh, but women should always be themselves. There's no winning. Women's bodies are subjected to the same sorts of double binds (see chapter 5) Kathleen Hall Jamieson found in the rhetoric about female leaders.

This chapter reviews the various ways the bodies of girls and women are monitored, whether it's how Black women wear their hair, what high school girls wear to prom, or where mothers are able to comfortably breast feed. The way news organizations frame these controversies might perpetuate patriarchal norms, as when stories are framed with the assumption that it's perfectly normal to regulate an individual's appearance. These assumptions perpetuate objectification, which treats women not as living, breathing, thinking equals but as decorations for a man's world. In visual media, women have faced challenges because of the often unstated but very strong assumption that they exist to be visually appealing: It is their job to look pretty and to smile. Messages about what it means to be a true woman sustain a hierarchy that marginalizes women; people of color; LGBTQ+ people; and anyone who is not a white, straight, cisgender male.

Symbolic Annihilation

The bra-burning stereotype, like that of the loud-mouthed, rolling pin–wielding suffragist, shows how powerful representation can be in perpetuating public attitudes. Media have historically played a role in perpetuating heteronormativity, sexism, and racism through their representations. Communication researcher George Gerbner coined the term **symbolic annihilation** to describe the way twentieth-century media, particularly TV entertainment, center the stories and interests of some people (straight, cisgender, white men) while marginalizing others.[4] Sociologist Gaye Tuchman and her colleagues apply the concept to the way women are represented in media, and identify three ways media denigrated strong, capable women in entertainment: (1) omission, (2) trivialization, and (3) condemnation (shaming).[5] Omission is simply the historic absence of female leaders in TV entertainment. Trivialization is the way stories that include a female leader might portray her as unfeminine, ugly, loud, or even evil. The narrative trope of condemnation might portray a female leader as flawed, someone who rose to the top by having sex with the boss or finds herself in charge but single and depressed. Media analysts have also identified the symbolic annihilation of other groups, such as queer, Indigenous, even unhoused people.[6]

Profile: Alison Bechdel, Cartoonist (1960-)

Alison Bechdel is an American cartoonist who originated a simple test by which films could be measured for gender representation. She prefers to call it the Bechdel-Wallace Test to honor the friend who inspired it. Bechdel created the comic strip, *Dykes to Watch Out For*, and wrote a graphic memoir *Fun Home*, which was adapted into a Tony Award–winning musical. *Dykes to Watch Out For* started as a single-panel comic that first appeared in a feminist newspaper and was gradually picked up by other publications. The strip ran for twenty-five years in various forms. Bechdel draws illustrations for magazines and websites and is known for her autobiographical comics and plays. The success of *Dykes to Watch Out For* allowed her to start drawing full time in 1990. Bechdel was named a Mellon Residential Fellow at the University of Chicago in 2012 and a MacArthur Genius in 2014 and was appointed poet laureate in Vermont in 2017.

Sources: Alison Flood, "Cartoonist Alison Bechdel 'in Shock' after Winning $625,000 'Genius' Grant," *Guardian*, September 17, 2014, https://www.theguardian.com/books/2014/sep/17/alison-bechdel-wins-macarthur-foundation-grant; Brent Hallenbeck, "Alison Bechdel Named Vermont Cartoonist Laureate," *Burlington Free Press*, March 28, 2017, https://www.burlingtonfreepress.com/story/entertainment/2017/03/28/alison-bechdel-vermont-cartoonist-laureate/99737676/; MacArthur Foundation, "Alison Bechdel," September 17, 2014, https://www.macfound.org/fellows/class-of-2014/alison-bechdel; Michael Ray, "Alison Bechdel: American Cartoonist and Graphic Novelist," Britannica, accessed September 30, 2022, https://www.britannica.com/biography/Alison-Bechdel.

The **Bechdel Test**, which measures sexism in entertainment, is a pop culture response to symbolic annihilation. It asks three simple questions about a story: First, does it have at least two women characters? Second, do they talk to each other? Third, do they talk about something other than a man? Based on a comic panel by Alison Bechdel titled "The Rule," the test has become part of everyday language; it's even in the dictionary.[7]

Policing Women's Biology

In spite of efforts by feminist advocates, the notion that women's bodies exist to be regulated by others is not fading away. The assumption that society has a stake in a woman's reproductive system—and the associated belief that women are naturally maternal—is one of the factors behind the debate about whether women should have the legal right to abortion, birth control, or sex education. For decades, polls have indicated that a majority of Americans support legal abortion with reasonable regulation, but news coverage has historically used both-sides equivalence, framing the debate to make it seem like the public is divided 50–50.[8] The labels used for the two sides, *pro-life* and *pro-choice*, favor antiabortion activists because the binary opposite of their label would be *pro-death*, and *pro-choice* clouds the notion of liberty supported by abortion rights activists.[9] The Supreme Court's 2022 decision that put abortion laws back into control of the states disrupted the health care of many women.[10] Antiabortion activists, energized by the *Dobbs* decision, have turned their attention to additional ways to regulate women's reproductive decisions.[11]

The abortion debate may be the most extreme form of regulation for female bodies, but such scrutiny spans a wide spectrum, and media coverage often uses patriarchal or stereotypical frames in coverage. Sex, even when presented clinically, with concern for women's health, can always be counted on to attract an audience.

PARENTHOOD

Teen pregnancy attracts public outcry by focusing on the responsibility of young mothers and rarely on the fact that many teens become pregnant by adult men.[12] Teenage pregnancy *is* a problem, of course, because children born to teen mothers on average start out with many economic and educational disadvantages, but it's not a *growing* problem, as the popularity of reality shows like *Sixteen and Pregnant* and *Teen Mom* might imply.[13] The rates have been going *down* in most states for many years and hit a record low in 2020.[14]

Breasts and breastfeeding are often in the headlines, as well. Breast cancer, as deadly as it is, does not kill as many women as heart disease, yet the former is more likely to be the subject of a TV news series.[15] Breastfeeding presents a physical double bind for many mothers, who are pressured to be the best moms they can be, with slogans like "Breast is best," and yet they are condemned for breastfeeding in public. Much of the furor can be explained by the logic of objectification. If women exist to please the male gaze, then baring a nipple to feed a baby can be condemned. In news, the word *nipple* rarely appears except in stories about cancer or Hollywood wardrobe mishaps; it's often not even in stories about public breastfeeding controversies, though it is clearly the offending body part.[16]

MENSTRUATION

In 2015, then presidential candidate Donald Trump criticized Fox News anchor Megyn Kelly for how she questioned him during a presidential debate: "She gets out and she starts asking me all sorts of ridiculous questions. You could see there was blood coming out of her eyes, blood coming out of her wherever. In my opinion, she was off base."[17] Trump's use of the phrase *blood coming out of her wherever* was widely interpreted as an insulting reference to menstruation, though Trump insisted later that he was talking about her nose. The incident served as a reminder of the lingering ignorance and stigma that surrounds menstruation and marginalizes women.

Menstruation is part of life for women and trans men, a topic that remains largely taboo in polite company. Boyfriends and husbands are often celebrated if they feel comfortable picking up a box of tampons while on errands. Menstruation is an economic fact of life, too, as menstrual products in many states continue to be taxed as luxuries. In South Carolina, for instance, ballet slippers and adult incontinence products are tax exempt but not pads or tampons. The Period Project, a nonprofit that works to increase access to menstrual products, pressures states to drop such taxes and make products freely available in schools.[18]

Awareness is spreading globally. In 2020, Scotland became the first country to legislatively combat this issue by making menstrual products free in public facilities nationwide. The Scottish government set up a universal system so that anyone in need of period products can get them for free. Schools, colleges, and universities will also be required to make free menstrual products available in restrooms. Local authorities and education providers will be responsible for ensuring free products are made available.[19] Upon the law's enactment, one of the members of the Scottish Parliament sent out the punny tweet, "About bloody time."[20]

Menstruation is a particular source of stress for people in prison. As of 2017, the federal prison system was required to provide menstrual protection to inmates for free, but many other state prisons and local jails still deny prisoners these essentials. According to the Period Project, incarcerated people in American prisons have been forced to show used pads to male guards or grant sexual favors in exchange for supplies. Doing without means risking embarrassment, stained clothes, and health. This is no small issue, as three-fourths of incarcerated women and trans men in the United States are of menstruating age.[21]

Simply talking about menstruation in media can reduce the stigma. Activists use social media accounts to post images of bedsheets or pants with bloodstains to normalize what is an everyday fact of life for menstruating women.[22] Such posts are a

---

Excerpt: "If Men Could Menstruate"

So what would happen if suddenly, magically, men could menstruate and women could not?

Clearly, menstruation would become an enviable, boast-worthy, masculine event:

Men would brag about how long and how much.

Young boys would talk about it as the envied beginning of manhood. Gifts, religious ceremonies, family dinners, and stag parties would mark the day.

To prevent monthly work loss among the powerful, Congress would fund a National Institute of Dysmenorrhea. Doctors would research little about heart attacks, from which men were hormonally protected, but everything about cramps.

Sanitary supplies would be federally funded and free. . . .

Generals, right-wing politicians, and religious fundamentalists would cite menstruation ("*men*-struation") as proof that only men could serve God and country in combat ("You have to give blood to take blood"), occupy high political office ("Can women be properly fierce without a monthly cycle governed by the planet Mars?"), be priests, ministers, God Himself ("He gave this blood for our sins"), or rabbis ("Without a monthly purge of impurities, women are unclean"). . . .

Street guys would invent slang ("He's a three-pad man") and "give fives" on the corner with some exchange like, "Man you lookin' *good!*"

"Yeah, man, I'm on the rag!"

Sources: Gloria Steinem, "If Men Could Menstruate," *Ms. Magazine*, October 1978; Gloria Steinem, "If Men Could Menstruate," in *Outrageous Acts and Everyday Rebellions*, 3rd ed., 2nd Picador ed. (Picador, Henry Holt, 2019), 337–40.

visual form of reclamation, which, as explained in chapter 8, is to make use of a word others use as an insult in order to remove its power. In 2015, Kiran Gandhi ran the London Marathon without a tampon, even though her period had started the night before. She'd decided she wanted to be comfortable and not hide the blood. She wrote about the decision on her website, "[I]f there's one person society won't f*** with, it's a marathon runner. If there's one way to transcend oppression, it's to run a marathon in whatever way you want." She wanted her effort to make a feminist statement, and, as a bonus, she raised $6,000 for breast cancer research.[23]

The taboo against discussing menstruation made headlines during the 2016 Olympics when a swimmer, Fu Yuanhui, told reporters she didn't do as well as she'd hoped because she got her period that day. Menstruation is an issue for athletes because intense training can interrupt a cycle.[24] Some female athletes use birth control to regulate their cycles, too, which research suggests is safe with medical supervision.[25]

Policing Appearance

We live in an increasingly visual culture, with media that allow us to constantly assess and compare our bodies with others. It is no surprise, then, that the cosmetic surgery business in the United States hit $63 billion in 2022, exceeding the US weight-loss market's $58 billion in 2022.[26] Men and women feel the pressure, but women are judged more harshly. Women may be attracted to men with "dad bods," a normal, not-too-perfect physique, but there is no such thing as a "mom bod."[27] Women who've had children are encouraged to lose all evidence of their motherhood as quickly as possible.[28]

It is not socially acceptable to comment on a person's skin color or disability, but polite company will still comment on a person's weight. Many fashion and beauty companies make public claims about body positivity, but in the aggregate, messages from media continue to be mixed. Even when advertisers use "plus-size" models, they tend to be on the smaller side of plus, rarely a size 16 or higher. Plus-size models are sometimes encouraged to wear padding, so their body is curvy but their face remains thinner.[29]

Young women are especially vulnerable to these often unspoken but highly visible messages. Girls who use Instagram, for instance, are much more likely to hate their own bodies.[30] Even children's cartoons create false ideas about what women should look like. Artist Loryn Brantz uses her skills to show how cartoons so often misrepresent normal female bodies. The distortion is clear when she gives the figures of famous Disney princesses normal proportions.[31] Lizzo sings of body positivity and true liberation, but when she played James Madison's crystal flute onstage, outrage flooded social media with comments about her body and what she wore.[32]

This makes sense under the logic of women as decoration. If it's a woman's responsibility to be attractive, then she is not, under this expectation, doing her job if she's overweight. Jean Kilbourne, an advertising expert, argues that the food and diet industry has exploited women's insecurities for years, teaching them to essentially hate their own bodies. Her film *Killing us Softly* speaks to the incredible power of these advertisements over time. She notes that food is often equated with sex in ads, giving eating a moral dimension. "(I)f a woman comes back from a weekend these days and says she's been bad," she jokes, "we assume she broke her diet, not that she did something unusual sexually."[33]

HAIR

Hair is another target for body scrutiny. Historically, women were discouraged from wearing their hair short, and the bob was seen as an act of rebellion in the 1920s.[34] Men are also pressured to wear their hair in certain ways, and short hair is the rule for those who want to work in corporate suites or the military. Black women endure a particularly intense form of hair scrutiny because of social pressures to ascribe to standards of beauty associated with whiteness in order to appear professional. Black women often feel pressured to straighten their hair using hot irons or chemicals or to wear a wig. Chapter 10 describes the way Black women in broadcasting have historically had to change their hair, and only recently have some women successfully moved to natural or braided styles.[35] In his autobiography, Malcolm X decries hair straightening as a form of self-degradation; it plays a significant role in the movie based on his life.[36]

Hair discrimination is often in the news. In 2017, the US Army tried to ban dreadlocks and braids, even though for Black women, those styles would be neater and easier to maintain in the field. Minimum length requirements meant that Black women were pressured to chemically straighten their hair, even when deployed overseas. Wearing textured hair in a bun made it hard to wear certain helmets. The Army pulled back within a couple of months and went even further in 2021 to offer many more styling options for women with textured hair.[37] In 2018, a high school wrestler was forced to have his dreadlocks cut off before he could compete. The white referee who issued the ultimatum was subsequently suspended.[38]

Native American students have also endured forced haircuts by white educators. In 1920, a federal official ordered it to be done to all Native American children on reservations, and incidents still happen today.[39] Public outcry over hair discrimination has inspired some politicians to take action.[40] The CROWN Act, a law that would prohibit hair discrimination, has been passed in nineteen states and is under consideration by Congress. The proposal, supported by Dove Soap, would ban rules that deny people jobs because of hair texture or styles like braids, locs, twists, or Bantu knots.[41]

CLOTHING

Clothing controversies make headlines often. Girls in high school are frequently sent home for showing too much leg; revealing their shoulders, collarbones, or cleavage; or not wearing a bra. These dress codes are often justified as necessary to not distract boys in school, and some women are fighting in court against such rationalizations. Proms are another flashpoint for clothing regulation. In these very visual examples of the double bind, young women are sent home because they are expected to dress in a feminine way but not in a way that's too sexy. In other instances, girls have been

Profile: Lizzo, Musical Artist and Rapper (1988–)

Melissa Jefferson, known as the musical artist and rapper Lizzo, was born in Detroit and started singing as a child with her church choir. Growing up, she wanted to be an astronaut and enjoyed Sailor Moon anime. Her family moved to Houston when she was nine, where she eventually took up the flute in band class, and to this day, she considers herself a "band nerd." Lizzo's nickname was derived from Lisso, a name she adopted when performing with friends in a group she established called the Cornrow Clique.

She attended the University of Houston for two years, majoring in music, but abandoned her dream of becoming a professional flutist when academic and financial pressures became overwhelming. She struggled to establish herself in the music industry, at one point living out of her car while singing with a local band. Her luck changed when she moved to Minneapolis and performed on an album with Prince in 2014. Her third studio album, *Cuz I Love You*, brought her mainstream fame, and in 2019, she was nominated for eight Grammy Awards, including record of the year and song of the year for "Truth Hurts." Lizzo has used her celebrity to speak out about fat stigma, telling *Rolling Stone* in 2020, "I'm making music that hopefully makes other people feel good and helps me discover self-love. That message I want to go directly to Black women, big Black women, Black trans women. Period."

Lizzo.
Courtesy of Creative Commons, Raph_PH

Source: Latria Graham, "Why Lizzo's Eight Grammy Nominations Feel Different," *Undefeated*, November 22, 2019, https://theundefeated.com/features/lizzo-eight-grammy-nominations-hit-differently/; IMDb, "Lizzo," accessed November 26, 2021, http://www.imdb.com/name/nm6739779/bio; Brittany Spanos, "The Joy of Lizzo," *Rolling Stone*, January 22, 2020, https://www.rollingstone.com/music/music-features/lizzo-cover-story-interview-truth-hurts-grammys-937009/.

disciplined for not being feminine enough, as was the case for a Catholic school student who was sent home for wearing a pantsuit.[42] Consider how these cases reflect the way men and women are socially punished when they fail to meet stereotypical expectations of their gender.

Shoes can be a problem, too: Women are often expected to wear high heels, which can flatter legs that appeal to the male gaze while destroying women's feet. By contrast, men are usually not expected to harm their bodies to meet industry dress codes. In 2016, more than 150,000 women in Great Britain petitioned against high-heel requirements and won support from the government to wear flats to work.[43]

Intersectional Regulation

Chapter 8 describes the way police in New York subjected the patrons of the Stonewall Bar to genital checks to make sure they were wearing "appropriate" clothing for their sex.[44] Today, people who live outside the gender binary continue to face regulation associated with their genitals. Bathroom bills designed to force trans people to use facilities based on the sex assigned at their birth essentially deny their free access to public spaces. Such bills purport to protect people, women and children especially, from harm or intrusions on their privacy, though trans people are more likely to suffer violence in a public bathroom than cisgender people.[45] Some private schools have attempted to maintain the gender binary by requiring girls to wear skirts, but such rules have been deemed unconstitutional.[46]

In 2023, lawmakers in eight states made moves to regulate drag shows on grounds that they expose children to explicit sexuality.[47] Drag performers are not necessarily trans, and some feminists consider the exaggerated femininity in their performances to be problematic, if not misogynistic, but drag has been a form of entertainment for millennia.[48] Shakespeare's plays, for instance, often involve gender code switching, usually for the sake of comedy.[49] Many of the concerns about the bodies of queer and trans people seem rooted in patriarchal norms, which demand that there be clear differences between male and female. After all, a hierarchy cannot be enforced if the categories aren't distinct.

What about men's bodies? Considering the rules for uniforms, ties, or hair length, aren't men subjected to regulations, too? Yes, to a certain extent, they are. Men won't do well in finance careers if they don't wear a suit and tie, and they must wear uniforms in many professions, just as women do. The difference is that male bodies are treated as normal and don't need to be covered, hidden, or regulated to the extent that women's bodies are. What men *do* with their bodies, though, is subject to patriarchal expectations. Men are not supposed to complain about pain. They are expected to be able to give and take violence.[50] Reflecting the stereotype of men as the gender that takes action, they are also expected to risk their lives in service to the military or first-responder professions in ways that women are not.

Women's Economics

While the Equal Pay Act has reduced the wage gap between men and women, the difference between what men and women earn remains stubborn and significant. In 1963, when the law was signed, women earned 59 percent of what men did on average. In 2020, that average difference was up to 84 percent.[51] The gap is stubborn and remains in spite of women's increased educational achievements. While women in the United States graduate more often than men from high school and college and earn more PhDs, they still earn less than men overall. The number of women enrolled in high-paying STEM fields is increasing, but they remain outnumbered by men, and even in these fields, they earn less. As researchers from the Georgetown University Center on Education and the Workforce put it, "Even when they do everything 'right'—choose a high-paying field of study, pursue a high-paying major within that field, and get a job in a high-paying occupation—women still get paid less than their male peers."[52] The wage gap is significant because women also lose income when they are divorced or widowed. They are more likely than men to fall into poverty as they age, in part because their lifetime income is lower; they often have to take time out of the workforce to care for family members; and they tend to outlive their husbands.[53]

The earnings gap for women is not simply the result of employers paying women less, though even more than forty years after the Equal Pay Act, this remains part of the problem. In 2022, the US Equal Employment Opportunity Commission sued Walmart, accusing it of a pattern of discrimination against women and people of color.[54] In a class-action suit, women accused the big-box chain of paying women less, passing them over for promotion in spite of good evaluations, and repeatedly promoting less-qualified white men to management jobs.[55]

Discrimination might be subtle, the result of implicit bias in project assignments, raises, and salary negotiations. Women are not socialized to negotiate with confidence, harkening back to the cultish stereotype that strong women are mannish and vulgar. Even when women do use assertive negotiation skills, researchers have found a backlash effect, in which women are viewed as inappropriately aggressive and unlikeable, which hurts their bottom line.[56]

Because women often take off more time than men to have and raise children, their lifetime earnings tend to be less. In the United States, this translates to lower Social Security payments in their retirement, even though women might need that money more because they tend to live longer, so if they have any retirement savings, it has to stretch out longer.[57]

THE PRICE OF PARENTING

Motherhood is very expensive. Women take more time off than men after becoming a parent, and even before the COVID-19 pandemic, they often had to reduce their paid work hours in order to take care of their homes and families.[58] The career average earnings for childless women are more than double that of mothers.[59] More women than men had to leave their jobs during the COVID-19 pandemic in order to care for children, and women who worked in low-paying jobs were the hardest hit.[60] Even when the economy started to recover after the pandemic lockdowns, American women found themselves unable to return to the workforce.[61]

In the United States, the lack of affordable childcare prevents parents from being able to work. The US government spends far less to support childcare than other industrialized nations. Childcare is hard to find and expensive. One study reports that a third of American parents found it difficult to find childcare, and when they did find it, in twenty-eight states it is *more expensive than sending a child to college*. That same study argues that a lack of affordable childcare for American families drags the economy down by $57 billion a year in lost wages, productivity, and earnings. In other words, making it possible for women to work improves the economy overall.[62]

GENDER PENALTIES

The price of being female goes beyond the job. Women often pay more for products that have been gendered. The so-called pink tax means women pay more for their clothing, personal products, haircuts, and even dry cleaning, but blatant price discrimination like this has been banned in some places.[63] Some higher prices can be attributed to real differences. For instance, some women's haircuts are more detailed than men's (though this varies widely, of course). Dry cleaners have defended their price differences because women's blouses cannot be pressed as easily as a typical man's shirt. The sheer number of products women are expected to use on their bodies can also mean a larger bill at the drug store.

The pink tax affects car ownership, too. A study conducted by a car insurance company found that on average, women pay $7,800 more over the course of owning a car.[64] Women also are usually taxed when they purchase menstrual products—a necessity not unlike food or first-aid items, which are often tax free. (Texas, for instance, does not tax bandages or vitamins but does tax tampons.[65]) Class-action lawsuits have spurred some states to kill taxes on menstrual hygiene products, but the majority of states continue to classify tampons and pads as nonnecessities.[66]

NOT JUST MONEY

Working women are paid less and work more, especially if they have children. In 1989, Arlie Hochschild wrote *The Second Shift*, which describes the imbalance of household responsibilities for women who work *outside* the home. Her research found that women put in an additional month of work every year compared to their male spouses.[67] In the decades since, the needle has moved a little but not much.

Participants in a more recent survey of heterosexual male-female marriages reported that wives did more of the housework, child chores, bill paying, and household management.[68] A new term emerged to describe women's frustration with their role in household management, **mental load**, inspired in part by a story that went viral in 2017, *You Should Have Asked*.[69] Advice columns

You Should Have Asked. **A panel from a comic that went viral for its illustration of the way women tend to carry more than their share of day-to-day household management. The project became a book, *The Mental Load*, in 2018.**
Used with permission by Emma

and tweets by working parents lament the way schools continue to call moms about sick children, even when a father's name is the emergency contact; husbands rely on their wives to take care of birthday gifts for their side of the family; and couples frequently argue about whose job it is to decide what's for dinner. The emergence of a name for this problem, mental load, is another example of how language can and has shaped activism for gender rights.

Binaries and Stereotypes

News stories, like any narratives, need conflict to be interesting. Recall from chapter 4 that the cat-fight trope was often used in coverage of the second-wave feminist movement. That trope persists, along with the tried and true battle of the sexes that finds energy in questionable science. The demands of narrative affect how journalists frame stories, which means that gender issues are often covered to emphasize conflict instead of focusing on solutions.

MOMMY WARS

In her 2007 book *Mommy Wars*, Leslie Morgan Steiner describes a rivalry between women who worked outside the home and those who stayed home. No matter what choice they made, they often felt unhappy and judged.[70] Given that motherhood is imbued with so much importance, it's no surprise that people who have children will feel pressure to do it right. When stories are framed as mom versus mom, however, clickbait succeeds while the larger societal questions about how *all* parents can and should be supported are ignored. Stories about the mommy wars blame women for their troubles, often shaming those who work while representing stay-at-home parents in stereotypical ways. The mommy-wars frame, which echoes the cat-fight frame, tends to focus on white, middle-class women who usually have more choices about where, when, and how to work—another dimension less likely to make headlines.[71]

Motherhood is reified in modern culture, even though women are so harshly judged. It is spoken of in religious terms, and some politicians have claimed it to be so noble that even women who become pregnant by rape should consider the baby a blessing.[72] People who have birthed babies are imbued with almost magical powers, an instinct and superpower that comes with pregnancy. After giving birth, new mothers supposedly forget the pain because of their overwhelming love for a child. Scientific studies about motherhood and sex have historically interpreted data through stereotypical lenses. For example, women's pain is regarded with less concern by medical professionals. The pattern is worse for women of color.[73] More recent research suggests that a mother's instinct is a myth, which can be better explained by the overwhelming fast learning curve parents experience when caring for a newborn.[74]

Scientific efforts to show that men are innately more intelligent than women or that biology drives women to be monogamous often reflect the stereotypes of their time. As neuroscientist Lesley Rogers puts it, "It is common for the media and popular books to promote genetic/hormonal explanations of sex differences in behavior, often to the point of absurd oversimplification of biological processes."[75] Journalists also often oversimplify science and are prone to amplifying studies that match stereotypical worldviews. Popular culture is replete with such books as *Men Are from Mars, Women Are from Venus* and online articles about how women are more monogamous and men are more visual.[76] More recent science shows that earlier studies are biased—even those by Charles Darwin—and scientific studies that *support* stereotypical expectations were more likely to be approved for publication through peer review than those studies that counter stereotypes.[77]

COVERING THE SCIENCE OF SEX

In an interview with the Journalist's Resource, a website that helps reporters find and interpret research, science communication professor Dietram Scheufele offered five tips:

1. Understand how framing works.
2. Be mindful of how repetition of a frame in news can influence the way the audience understands the issue.
3. Consider that policy makers frame and counterframe issues.
4. Consider reporting on the larger body of academic research available instead of just one study.
5. Be aware of the way attacks on media can make the public less trusting of journalism.[78]

Similarly, political science professor Eric Merkley has found that journalists often do a poor job reporting on scientific consensus. He told the Journalist's Resource that reporters must avoid quoting individual researchers without explaining how their views compare with other scholars and that reporters should learn to look for reviews of *multiple* studies that can explain whether consensus exists or doesn't. Importantly, Merkley said journalists must avoid **false equivalence**, or giving equal weight to contrasting views when one side has largely been rejected by science. That is, Merkley encourages journalists to avoid giving attention to views that are contrary to **scientific consensus**, or the collective perspective of numerous scientists based on available evidence. It is important to not suggest that a certain percentage of scientists need to agree on something and to make sure to convey to the audience what scientific consensus is.[79] Journalists should also avoid suggesting that any study has proven something, as science usually is better able to declare something more or less likely to be true.[80]

For any individual study, reporters should always try to read it in full, not just the press release. They should examine the methods, including how many people participated in a survey or experiment. Statistics can be intimidating for reporters, so they need to ask for clarification when possible and to not rest an entire story on one number. Reporters should also ask who participated in any study. Were they all "WEIRD," as in "Western, educated, industrialized, rich and from democratic societies"? The vast majority of people studied in science are WEIRD, even though they are not the majority of the world's population.[81] Medical studies have neglected to include women, especially women of color, which has had an impact on treatment.[82]

Journalists need to learn to read the footnotes and citations: Who influenced the study? What were the differences between experimental conditions? When did the study take place? Perhaps most importantly, who *funded* the study? Corporations, political action groups, and think tanks often fund research that supports a particular viewpoint. Finally, any study that upholds stereotypes in a way that excuses discrimination or oppression demands extra scrutiny from reporters—*not* another battle-of-the-sexes clickbait headline.

Summary

Controversies over a woman's appearance make great headlines because they allow a news organization to present a story about policy while also talking about sex. A tut-tut report on the excesses of spring break in Florida can be accompanied by a photo of women in bikinis. A story about a young woman who wants to wear the same tank top as male students can still remind the audience of her sexuality. Journalists walk a fine line, therefore, when trying to cover these stories without exploiting stereotypes about women and female-identifying individuals. Word choice is crucial for journalists who wish to cover such controversies fairly without further objectifying the people involved. Race adds another variable to the regulation of bodies, as Black and Brown women are subjected to even more discipline, particularly when it comes to their hair, skin tone, facial features, even weight. Journalists must be aware of narrative demands that might highlight conflict frames instead of offering solutions. Science about race and gender needs to be assessed carefully by journalists, as studies have historically been influenced by stereotypes.

- **Reflection:** How should journalists approach body scrutiny and its connection to the stereotypical expectation that women exist to look good? Whose perspective is centered in these controversies?
- **Reflection:** How might the scrutiny of women's bodies affect their careers in journalism and media?
- **Media Critique:** Is there a way to write an interesting narrative without emphasizing binaries? How might journalists write about issues without framing them as mommy wars or a battle of the sexes?

CHAPTER 14

Gender and Sports Journalism

This chapter describes the experiences of women in sports journalism and explores the way news media have covered female athletes. Sports are traditionally a male space that has been hostile to women. In the United States, sports both contribute to and reflect the larger culture, including patriarchy and white supremacy. Whether they have wanted to play sports or cover sports as journalists, women have faced discrimination, unfair conditions, and even sexual abuse. Title IX, a federal antidiscrimination law, opened new opportunities for women, but stereotypes about how women should look and behave continue to impede their ability to compete and attract media coverage.

Key Concepts: Male Gaze, Misogynoir

Sports broadcaster Jamele Hill had worked for ESPN for more than ten years and was an anchor on *SportsCenter* when she ignited a social media firestorm with a tweet about the man who was president at the time: "Donald Trump is a white supremacist who has largely surrounded himself w/ other white supremacists." Hill, who is Black, quickly faced a firestorm from others on social media and the president himself. Trump's press secretary said the tweet was a "fire-able" offense.[1] ESPN issued a statement saying that Hill's comments "do not represent the position of ESPN. We have addressed this with Jemele and she recognizes her actions were inappropriate." Soon thereafter, Hill tweeted a clarification, though not an apology: "My comments on Twitter expressed my personal beliefs. My regret is that my comments and the public way I made them painted ESPN in an unfair light." This was not enough for Trump supporters or the president himself, who tweeted that ESPN and Hill should "Apologize for untruth!"[2] ESPN did not fire Hill over this incident, but within the year, the network bought out her contract. She now writes for the *Atlantic*.[3]

Hill's intersectional position as a Black woman made her an easy target for criticism from the public and other journalists. News about the incident framed her as an oddity in sports journalism because she is not white and not male. Some sports pundits suggested that she was racist and biased and needed to apologize for talking about politics.[4]

The backlash Hill experienced not only from President Trump and his supporters but also from other journalists illustrates the challenges—indeed, the hostility—women face when reporting on or playing sports. The incident also points to the relationship between sports and culture. Sports are ostensibly a place where nothing matters but the players and the game, but sports *coverage* often reflects social debates about race, gender, and politics.[5] Sports journalism, like journalism generally, often reflects color-blind racism that hides inequality behind a claim that sports are just a game.

Playing while Female

Athletes who identify as female face challenges on multiple fronts. Their very existence runs against the stereotypical expectation that women should be weak and submissive. Women (reminder: this book uses *woman* to describe any person who identifies as female) who compete and the women who write about sports are seen as invading a traditional male space. When they are good at what they do, they're on display, which draws attention to their sexuality, not their strengths and talents.

THE ATHLETIC DOUBLE BIND

In 1964, the editors of *Sports Illustrated* had a problem: Major league sports were between seasons in the winter, and there was little to publicize. The solution was typical for any marketing challenge: surround your product with beautiful women. And so, the *Swimsuit Edition* was born, though in its first iteration, it was only five pages long and accompanied by far less hoopla than today's publication. Originally a single issue devoted to women modeling swimwear, the *SI Swimsuit Edition* became a special edition in 1997 and eventually its own franchise, earning more than $1 billion over its history. It has come under fire for objectifying women but has capitalized on that controversy, and in recent years, the issue has featured female athletes, not just supermodels.[6] In 2023, Martha Stewart, at eighty-one, was featured on one of the issue's four covers that year, signifying an antiageist cultural statement.[7] The *SI Swimsuit Edition* illustrates how female athletes continue to be judged according to stereotypical expectations of beauty.

SEXY AND STRONG

Men and women today go to the same gyms, work out side by side, and wear athletic-style clothing even when they're not playing sports. Yet not all that long ago, an athletic woman was not considered to be sexy. As chapter 13 describes, women are subjected to bodily scrutiny nearly any place they can be seen. Women in sports are further challenged by the classic femininity-competence double bind (see chapter 5), which suggests that if they are strong, then they can't be feminine, but if they are pretty, then they must be bad athletes.

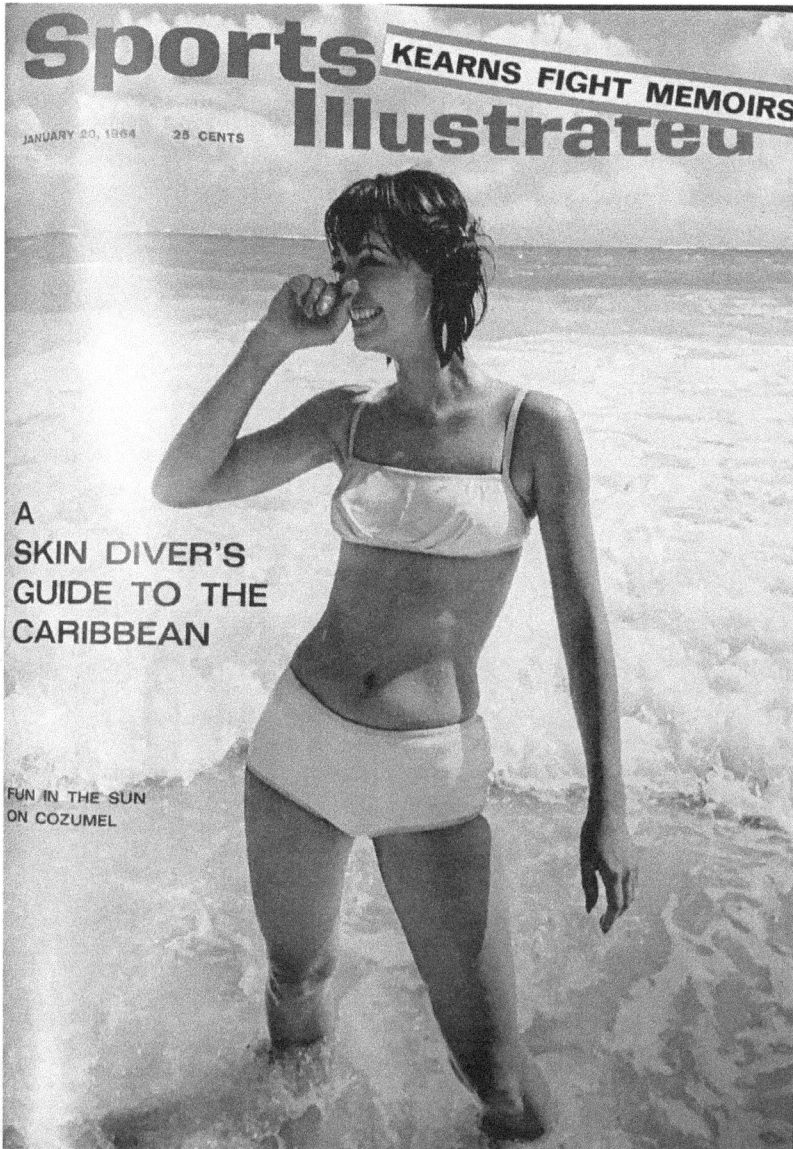

**The First *Sports Illustrated Swimsuit Edition*, January 20, 1964,
features a relatively tame cover.**
Courtesy of the Center for Sports Communication and Media at the University of Texas
   at Austin

   When women show off too much skin, they may face criticism, as well. That's
what happened to Brandi Chastain in 1999. After her winning goal in the Women's
World Cup, Chastain pulled off her jersey and knelt on the field in her sports bra,
crying out with joy. Her victory was overshadowed by critics who complained that
she was showing off her body (the *New York Daily News* called it her "burlesque
moment").[8] She was accused of being unladylike, flashing her abs, and trying to cash

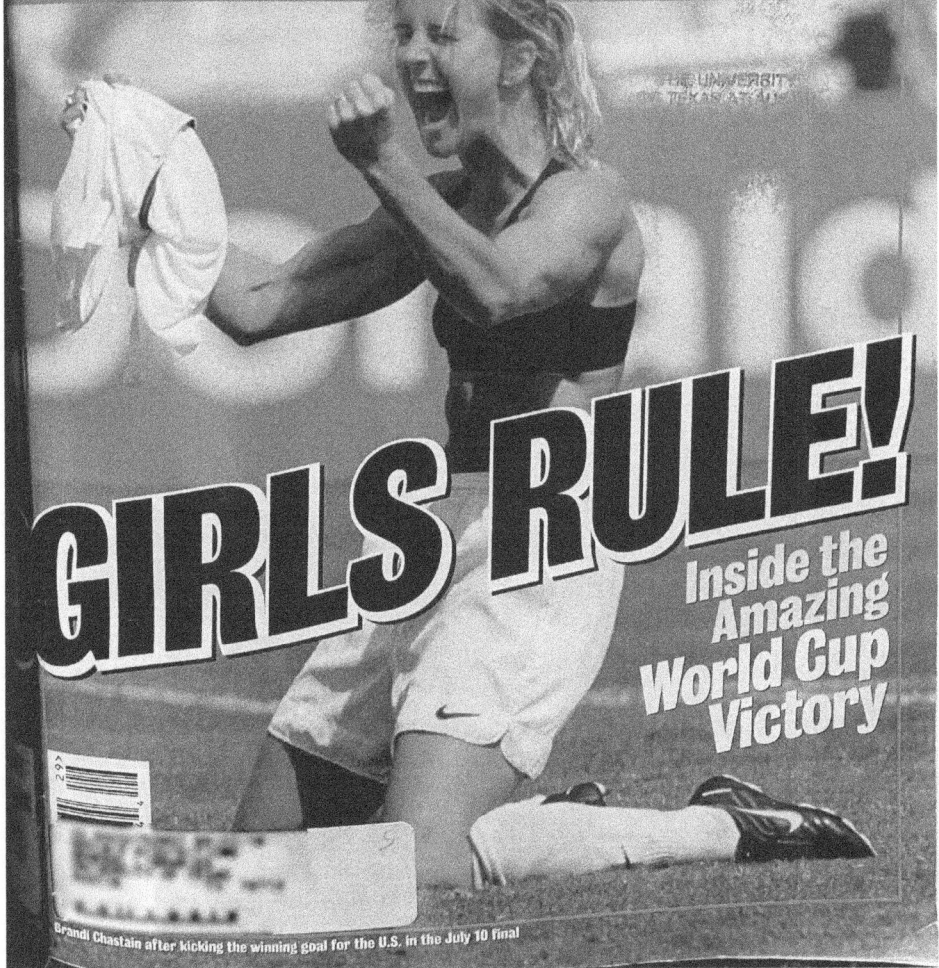

Brandi Chastain celebrates victory upon scoring the winning goal in the Women's World Cup in 1999. Note that *Newsweek* refers to the players as "girls" in the headline.

Fair use, courtesy of the collection of the University of Texas at Austin Libraries

in with sponsors.[9] All these criticisms could only be lobbed at a woman because after all, male athletes are not expected to be chaste, humble about their bodies, or too shy to take on commercial endorsements. This is sarcasm, of course. Men pull off their jerseys all the time in celebration, but their bodies, while they might be admired, have not been regulated as women's have.

THE MALE GAZE

Another concept that is helpful for thinking about how female athletes are presented in media is the **male gaze**, a term coined by feminist film theorist Laura Mulvey in 1975.[10] As described in chapter 4, a few years before Mulvey published an influential article where she labels the phenomenon, art critic John Berger had drawn attention to how depictions of women in art have long reflected a tradition of men viewing and watching women as objects.[11] Through cultural conditioning, men are taught to look at and automatically judge a woman's body, and women learn to put themselves on display for the sake of pleasing others—generally, men.

Because sports are traditionally considered a male territory, any woman who plays professional sports is subjected to this gaze, whether she wins or not. The expectation that female athletes exist to look good is reflected in dress codes old and new. Female tennis players were once required to wear skirts to play, but today they have the choice to wear shorts. In 2019, a year after Serena Williams was criticized for wearing a compression catsuit for medical reasons (even though a white woman had been allowed to wear leggings decades before), the women's tennis association changed the rules to allow leggings.[12] Objecting to the sexualization of their sport and arguing that their physical comfort matters, the 2021 German women's Olympic gymnastics team opted to wear ankle-length unitards instead of leotards with bare legs.[13] That same year, the Norwegian women's beach handball team was fined for insisting on wearing shorts instead of bikini bottoms in a European Federation competition. Within months, the federation backed off but not before the women's team made headlines complaining about the sexist requirement.[14] In these cases and others like them, the rules could not be said to ensure the athletes' comfort or competitive edge. These outfits please the eyes of heterosexual men (who are often the people making the rules) and play to the male gaze.

The hypersexualization of female athletes in sports coverage diminishes their accomplishments. In 2018, Norwegian soccer star Ada Hegerberg received the FIFA Women's Golden Ball (Ballon d'Or Féminin), a newly created award for the most valuable female player of professional football (American soccer). Before she could finish accepting the award, the presenter, French DJ Martin Solveig, asked Hegerberg whether she knew how to twerk.[15] Critics pointed out that Solveig's comment marred the significance of the award and was a blatant example of sexism within the sports world. More recently, the International Federation of Sport Climbing was compelled to apologize to a female competitor from Austria for livestream coverage that included a lingering camera closeup on her behind.[16]

THROWING LIKE A GIRL

Women have enjoyed competing in sports wherever they've been able, but throughout history, the opportunities have been limited. Women competed as hunters in ancient Greece and ran in outdoor races during the Middle Ages. During the turn of the last century, Victorian women were largely restricted from doing anything athletic for the sake of being ladylike and mistaken beliefs that anything strenuous was unhealthy for women. Of course, the concern for women's well-being was largely devoted to white women in the upper and middle classes, as other women were expected to put their muscles into menial labor.[17] During the battle for suffrage, women fought for the right to ride bicycles, which offered freedom of transportation, as well as the simple pleasure of physical movement outdoors. Riding a bike also requires less restrictive clothing, a material manifestation of what women were fighting for symbolically on the political stage.[18] In the 1920s and '30s, sports exploded as a form of modern entertainment, and institutions like the YMCA and YWCA formed to encourage healthy exercise. Many colleges established sports teams for men during this period. Still, opportunities for women to play were relatively scarce.

QUALIFIED LASSIES

In 1943, during the manpower shortage of World War II, chewing gum magnate Philip K. Wrigley wanted to keep ballparks like the one he owned in Chicago busy. He decided to invest in women's baseball and established the All-American Girls Professional Baseball League. The league was inspiration for the 1992 movie *A League of Their Own*.[19] Women who played ball for the real-life league were subjected to strict requirements for ladylike behavior. All-American Girls were required to take charm school lessons, wear lipstick at all times, and play in skirts. While there may be no crying in baseball (according to a famous line from the movie), there evidently was plenty of room in the league's handbook for other behavior associated with feminine stereotypes. The handbook included beauty advice to "assure all the niceties of toilette and personality. Especially 'after the game,' the All-American girl should take time to observe the necessary beauty ritual, to protect both her health and appearance."[20]

The league received positive coverage in the sports pages, but that coverage came with plenty of sexist stereotypes and a keen interest in what the women would wear. A story in the *Miami News* in 1943 includes not only the fact that the "girls" would wear three-quarter length flared skirts but also what the colors would be (pink, blue, yellow, or green).[21] The players are praised when they "hit the dirt hard" in skirts, and reports often stress how much their game was like "real baseball."[22] An announcement about the first game in Shreveport, Louisiana, comes with this headline: "Daring Dish of Baseball to Be Served Shreveport Fans in All-American Girls Game . . . Players Well Qualified to Put on Attractive Spectacle. 450,000 Saw Lassies Play in League Games in '45."[23] Note the way the headline includes hints that the male gaze would be satisfied, with words like *dish* and *attractive spectacle*.

After the war, the league dissolved, and while some women did not lose their taste for competition, social norms were decidedly opposed to women athletes, so opportunities to compete were scarce. The postwar Olympics opened some track and field events to women, but in America and Europe, fewer than 15 percent of women exercised or participated in sports on a regular basis. Even when physical education teachers encouraged women's sports, schools did not provide real support. Girls and women often had to raise their own money. They usually weren't allowed to travel, and they were often denied access to locker rooms, showers, and practice space. Female players were often mocked and stereotyped, and they sometimes played to empty stadiums.[24] Women's sports were drastically underfunded. In an example cited by an article in *Sports Illustrated* about the inequities of women's sports, a school district in Syracuse, New York, budgeted $90,000 for boys' sports but only $200 for girls in 1969.[25] Marge Snyder, who eventually went to work for the Women's Sports Foundation, recalls, "I played on my Illinois high school's first varsity tennis team from 1968 to 1970. We were 56–0 over my three years. We were permitted to compete as long as we made no efforts to publicize our accomplishments and personally paid for our uniforms and equipment."[26]

TITLE IX

Opportunities for women to play sports changed dramatically in 1972 with the arrival of Title IX. Spearheaded by congressional representative Patsy Mink of Hawaii, this federal law requires that educational opportunities be distributed evenly among the sexes in federally funded institutions. This applies to sexual safety on campus, access to computers, standardized tests, and so on, but it has also made a dramatic difference in terms of sports for women. Before Title IX, about 310,000 women played high school or college sports. Today, that number is more than three million.[27]

The debate over Title IX was, unsurprisingly, covered from the male perspective and framed using a win-loss binary. Communications scholar Julie Lane conducted a qualitative textual analysis of stories from national newspapers and found that the NCAA—which opposed extending Title IX to athletics—shaped much of the coverage. Lane's analysis finds that most of the reporting on the law framed it in terms of conflict between men and women, which "reinforced the notion that female athletes were trespassers in the American sport culture."[28] She notes that coverage focused on "revenue producing sports," such as football, and predicted that giving women equal opportunities in college sports would cause the entire system to collapse.[29] Clearly that hasn't happened, as the top five college sports conferences in the United States generate an estimated $4 billion a year.[30]

As with many of the debates about gender equity, the fears that men might be harmed by giving women rights did not materialize, though the notion that women are causing trouble continues to dominate the way Title IX's impact is framed in media. In 2020, female swimmers filed a lawsuit against the University of Iowa to prevent their program from being cancelled during the COVID-19 pandemic. The school had apparently been out of compliance in many ways for years by unfairly padding numbers for women's opportunities and by providing unequal resources.[31] Because the women filed a lawsuit to protect their rights, they were framed as demanding by the school's lawyer, echoing a theme that goes back to the earliest days of the gender rights movement.

THE BATTLE OF THE SEXES

Imagine the pressure on tennis star Billie Jean King in September 1973. She had agreed to play an exhibition match, a "Battle of the Sexes," with Bobby Riggs, a promoter and player who gleefully declared himself to be a chauvinist. He challenged her because she was, in his words, the "women's libber leader." King had won six Wimbledon championships. The match was highly publicized, and 30,000 people gathered in the Houston Astrodome to watch. Famed sports announcer Howard Cosell called the match. Riggs entered the arena with sexily dressed models. In keeping with the circus atmosphere and in a display of her sense of humor, King was also carried in—by male bodybuilders. She won the match in three straight sets.

It was much more than a tennis match, though, as it came to represent everything that second-wave feminism stood for: equality in access, rights, and pay. Rather than trash-talk Riggs after the match, King used the moment to call for diversity in sports. "I love tennis very much. I wanted it to change ever since I started this sport," she told reporters. "I thought it was just for the rich and just for the white. And ever since that day when I was 11 years old and I wasn't allowed in a photo because I wasn't wearing a tennis skirt, I knew then that I wanted to change the sport. And tonight, a lot of non-tennis people saw tennis for the first time. I don't even care what kind of match it was."[32]

PERENNIAL CHALLENGES

Despite the requirements of Title IX, inequities continue. In 2021, as the NCAA March Madness basketball tournament was about to start, a female player for the University of Oregon tweeted photos of the differences between the weight room that tournament organizers in San Antonio offered to male players and the one provided to the women. The contrast was striking. Her tweet went viral and sparked outcry over the inequality. Dick's Sporting Goods offered to donate equipment, and the NCAA took action to improve the facilities but not before athletes, fans, and sports journalists were reminded that female athletes remain, in many ways, second-class citizens.[33]

Women continue to push the envelope and try to compete wherever they wish, even on college football teams. Toni Harris became the first female skill position player to receive a college football scholarship in 2019 as a safety.[34] Previously the only women to be recruited were kickers.[35] There are more opportunities for women to play sports professionally, too. The LPGA, founded in 1950, continues to support women's professional golf. The WNBA started in 1997, and its games are often televised. The National Women's Soccer League was founded in 2012 and remains

Profile: Billie Jean King, Tennis Player (1943-)

Billie Jean King in action on the court in 1970.
Courtesy of the International Tennis Hall of Fame/Ed Fernberger

Billie Jean Moffitt was born into family of athletes in California. Her brother grew up to become a professional baseball player. Billie Jean's first sport was basketball, then softball, and she finally turned to tennis at the suggestion of her father. As a young player, she was not allowed to pose with a tournament team in 1955 because she was wearing shorts instead of the regulation skirt. The moment inspired her to push back against discrimination in sports and beyond. Billie Jean Moffitt became a professional player in 1959. She married a lawyer, Larry King, in 1965 and took his last name.

As a child, she once told her mother she would be the world's number one player, and in 1966, she was ranked number one in women's tennis. She would be ranked number one five more times and win twenty Wimbledon titles and thirty-nine Grand Slam titles. In 1972, she won Wimbledon, the US Open, and the French Open. She might be best known for her match against Bobbie Riggs, an exhibition heralded as the "Battle of the Sexes," in 1973, but that was hardly her only contribution to the cause for women's sports. That same year, she worked to establish the Women's Tennis Association and lobbied for equal prize money for women and men at the US Open. She continues to fight against all forms of discrimination in tennis and other sports. She divorced Larry King in 1987 and fell in love with a woman, Ilana Kloss, with whom she currently lives in New York City. In 2009, President Barack Obama awarded her America's highest civilian honor, the Medal of Freedom, for her work on behalf of women and LGBTQ+ people.

Source: Brendan Davis, "President Obama Honors Harvey Milk and Billie Jean King with Medal of Freedom," GLAAD, September 14, 2011, https://www.glaad.org/2009/08/13/president-obama-honors-harvey-milk-billie-jean-king-with-medal-of-freedom.

active, and the women's World Cup team has won four times.[36] The women's team had to fight for equal pay, however, and women in most professional sports are paid far less than men.[37]

Covering Women's Sports

Women's sports are underrepresented in the news. A study of thirty years' worth of TV sports coverage found that women's sports receive about the same amount of attention today as they did in the 1980s. Scholars also find that the play-by-play commentary for women's sports is "bland," whereas the commentary for men reflects excitement and praise with statements like "In command!" "On fire!" and "Unstoppable!"[38] A study of *Sports Illustrated* covers from 2000 to 2011 (excluding the *Swimsuit Editions*) found that women were on the cover less than 5 percent of the time.[39] Even when they are playing the same sport as men, such as track or swimming, women receive less coverage. Stories today may be less insulting or sexualized than in the past, but flagrant sexism hasn't gone away.[40] Researchers have seen some improvements with visual coverage, though. For example, a content analysis of the 2000 Olympics found that photos depicted female athletes in a realistic way and did not emphasize their sexuality.[41]

The dearth of women's coverage represents a frustrating circular logic. "No one goes to women's games, so why should we?" a male sports journalist once told sports critic Mariah Burton Nelson. When she suggested that covering women's sports might raise interest, his response was quick and emphatic: "Oh, we wouldn't want to do that!" he said "We're not social change agents. We're just here to report the news."[42]

The attitude that paltry coverage merely reflects a lack of interest in women's sports runs deep in sports journalism. Survey research by a team of journalism scholars found that more sports editors feel obligated to cover women's sports and hire more female journalists, but they still estimate audience interest to be low. While in the minority, some editors also still believe that women are naturally less athletic than men and less interested in sports.[43] When women's sports *are* covered, the patterns is usually "one and done": that is, a single story within a set of stories about men's teams, reflecting **tokenism**.[44] When media budgets get tight, women's sports coverage tends to be one of the first things to go. Media coverage of women's sports is scant, and the "big three" of men's sports (basketball, football, and baseball) receive more coverage even in their *off*-seasons than women's in-season sports. When women's sports *are* included in the pundit shows, coverage tends to be more respectful than it was years ago but is delivered with a sense of duty—or as one critic put it, in the same tone as parents say, "Eat your vegetables."[45]

How can we encourage more people, especially men, to watch more women's sports? Most people, male and female, seem to prefer watching men's sports, but it's not clear whether this is related to the games or the overwhelming media coverage of men's teams.[46] Experimental research suggests that men are more interested in watching women athletes if they appear to be feminine and compete in a traditional feminine sport, like gymnastics or volleyball.[47] Yet times might be changing. Another study found that boys who see sexy images of female athletes are likely to assess them in objectifying ways, but if they see representations of female athletes that emphasize their *performance*, the boys also made positive, sports-related statements about the players.[48] In other words, the cycle of "no interest, no coverage" can be broken with coverage that celebrates female athletes as strong, skillful competitors.

FEMALE SPORTS WRITERS

Just as it did with general news reporting and photojournalism, World War II opened opportunities for women in sports reporting. Mary Garber was working at a newspaper in North Carolina when the sports editor left to join the Navy in 1944. She took up the sports beat and throughout her career faced condescension from players and coaches and was barred from joining professional journalist organizations.[49] In one instance, even though she had proper credentials, she was turned away from the press box at a college game because she was a woman. Years later, during a radio interview, she recalled, "[W]hile I was talking with the sports information director, there was a little boy hopping up and down in the aisles in the press box, and he could sit there, but I couldn't." One of the keys to her success was her interest in covering stories outside the mainstream, such as the games at Black high schools and colleges during the time schools were segregated by race.[50]

Garber's difficulties in gaining access to the press box and locker rooms were typical for women in sports journalism. In 1977, Melissa Ludtke from *Sports Illustrated* was forced to stand in the hall outside the New York Yankees' locker room when they won the World Series, waiting for players to come outside. Locker room access matters after a game because that is when players talk to reporters and the emotion of the game is still in the air. The locker room was defended as a private male space, which makes sense until you consider that people carrying TV cameras could enter, making the room hardly private. Ludtke's editors supported her with a lawsuit against Major League Baseball, and she won the case on grounds that the team had violated her right to practice her profession. Her victory was limited, though. Male writers treated the case like a joke and questioned her journalistic abilities.[51] Also, the court order was only applicable to Yankee Stadium, so women continued to struggle for access to players and coaches. Women who fought for locker room access were accused of simply wanting to see men naked and of being groupies with press passes.

Women finally won the right to full access to Major League Baseball locker rooms in 1984. While reporting for the *Hartford Courant*, Claire Smith was physically pushed out of the San Diego Padres' locker room during a National League Championship series at Wrigley Field. The incident prompted the new league commissioner to order all MLB locker rooms open to female reporters. That didn't end the problems, though. Players harassed female writers by dropping their towels on purpose, tossing jock straps at them, and making lewd jokes. A player for the Detroit Tigers declared, "I don't talk to women when I'm naked unless they're on top of me or I'm on top of them."[52]

Today, women have won equal access to locker rooms and press boxes, but they continue to be harassed on the job by players and their own colleagues. Because they cover a beat that is stereotypically male, they are often accused of being too mannish

Profile: Claire Smith, Sports Journalist (1954–)

Claire Smith.
Courtesy of the Baseball Hall of Fame

Claire Smith is the first woman to cover baseball full time. She grew up in a suburb of Philadelphia and as a child loved writing so much that her parents gave her a typewriter. Her mother was a baseball fan, and Smith became one, too, with special appreciation for Jackie Robinson, the first Black man to play Major League Baseball for the Dodgers.

After graduating with a journalism degree from Temple University, she started as a sports reporter with the *Philadelphia Bulletin*. She moved to the *Hartford Courant* in Connecticut, and she was reporting on the National League Championship Series for that paper when she was forcibly pushed out of the San Diego Padres' locker room in 1984, even though she had credentials to be there. Shaken and embarrassed, she stood outside the door, determined to get the material she needed to write her story. Some of her male colleagues collected quotes for her. Years later, she recalled breaking down when player Steve Garvey came out of the locker room to help her and says his words that day stayed with her throughout her career: "You've got to pull yourself together. You've got a job to do." She said, "Sometimes you learn lessons of journalism from non-traditional sources."

Smith went on to cover sports at the *New York Times* and with ESPN. In 2017, she became the first woman to be inducted into the writers' wing of the Hall of Fame after she received the Baseball Writers Association of America's Career Excellence Award. In another meaningful moment, she received an award named for her childhood hero, the 2017 Robie Award for Lifetime Achievement by the Jackie Robinson Foundation. In 2021, she returned to Temple University to join the faculty there and codirect the Claire Smith Center for Sports Media.

Sources: Lauren Amour, "Exclusive Interview: The Pioneering Claire Smith, First Black Female Baseball Reporter," *Sports Illustrated*, March 24, 2022, https://www.si.com/mlb/phillies/news/exclusive-interview-philadelphia-phillies-claire-smith-first-black-female-mlb-reporter; Britni De La Cretaz, "The First Woman Is Inducted into the Writers' Wing of the Baseball Hall of Fame, and She Won't Be the Last," *Vogue*, August 1, 2017, https://www.vogue.com/article/claire-smith-baseball-hall-of-fame-women-sportswriters; Klein College of Media and Communication, "Claire Smith," Temple University, accessed February 25, 2023, https://klein.temple.edu/directory/claire-smith-tup35134; Ed Sherman, "Shut Out of the Locker Room with a Deadline Looming, Claire Smith Had a Job to Do," Poynter, July 27, 2017, https://www.poynter.org/business-work/2017/shut-out-of-the-locker-room-with-a-deadline-looming-claire-smith-had-a-job-to-do/; Visit Bucks County Pennsylvania, "Get to Know: Sports Journalist Claire Smith," accessed February 25, 2023, https://www.visitbuckscounty.com/about-bucks-county/famous-faces/get-to-know-sports-journalist-claire-smith/.

or are assumed to be lesbian. Focus-group research finds that they're also asked to walk a line between their identities as women and as journalists, defending their journalistic distance and objectivity by *avoiding* appearing to be too interested in women's teams.[53] Chapter 10 describes how women in broadcast news are assessed primarily according to their appearance, and it's no surprise that female sports broadcasters are similarly judged. An experiment found that male viewers spent more time assessing the bodies of female sportscasters than male sportscasters and considered the female sportscasters to be less credible.[54] Women continue to be plagued by rumors that they sleep with their sources and by sources and colleagues who flirt with them rather than share information. Female sportswriters say they continue to be passed over for promotions and the best assignments.[55]

The lack of women in sports departments contributes to the cycle of "no interest, no coverage." A report from the Institute for Diversity and Ethics in Sport gave the industry an *F* in 2018 for its diversity of gender hiring. This was the fifth *F* rating in a row for the industry.[56] As of 2017, one-third of the sports departments surveyed by the institute had no women at all; slightly more than one-third had one woman. As the researchers note, when there is only one token woman in a newsroom, they cannot have much of an impact on decision making.[57] Women represent about 12 percent of all sports writers, and even fewer women are sports *editors*.[58]

UNNECESSARY ROUGHNESS

Female sports journalists are especially vulnerable to online abuse. As described in chapter 12, the online abuse of female journalists has reached intolerable levels, and women on traditionally male beats receive some of the most hateful, violent comments. Women report that social media companies and sometimes their own newsrooms have done little to help; women are simply told to get a thicker skin. The difference, though, is that unlike their male colleagues, who might get nasty tweets about their skills as a writer, female sports writers are targeted with violent comments directed at their gender. One way to fight such stigmatizing language is to put it into full view. In 2016, a sports website did just that, producing a video titled *More than Mean*, in which male volunteers are asked to read comments out loud in the presence of the women who received them originally. Some of the men balk and don't want to continue. "I hope your boyfriend beats you," reads one. Another wrote, "One of the players should beat you to death with their hockey stick."[59] The video, which cost only $300 to produce, won a Peabody Award for its impact.[60]

SPORTS AND RAPE CULTURE

Women don't have to be athletes to run into trouble from toxic masculine institutions in the world of sports. The hypermasculine atmosphere, an emphasis on winning, and the general sense that women's lives are secondary to what men want have allowed abuse to fester behind closed doors. In 2016 and 2017, football players from Baylor

University in Texas were accused of multiple sexual assaults, including instances of gang rape. Baylor officials were accused of covering up assaults and fostering a culture that put young women at risk. The University's Title IX coordinator, Patti Crawford, resigned after alleging that Baylor did not allow her to do her job properly. An NCAA investigative committee cited Baylor leaders for "moral and ethical failings" and imposed fines and recruitment restrictions on the university. Two players were convicted of assault and sentenced to prison; a third was found not guilty.[61]

One of the largest sexual abuse scandals in sports history occurred at Michigan State University. In 2017, Larry Nassar was convicted of multiple counts of sexually assaulting female athletes sent to him for medical treatment. Michigan State lost a record-setting $4.5 million for its role in allegedly covering up the case, and the university's president resigned in wake of Nassar's conviction.[62] Investigative journalists with ESPN exposed the extent of Nasser's activities, with wrenching, impactful interviews from women who'd been sent to him for treatment. ESPN's documentary *Spartan Silence: Crisis at Michigan State* details how the abuse was able to continue in spite of complaints by athletes going back to the 1990s. It won a Peabody Award in 2019.[63] In 2022, a group of women sued the FBI, charging that the agency mishandled the investigation and let the abuse continue. Nassar is currently serving what is essentially a life sentence.[64]

Excerpt: "Nassar Surrounded by Adults Who Enabled His Predatory Behavior"

This excerpt is from one of the first stories about the Michigan State case, produced for a now cancelled ESPN program, Outside the Lines. *This story and others became part of the* Spartan Silence *documentary.*

Nassar, no older than 30 and putting the finishing touches on his medical degree, had called Jane's mother days before, explaining he was doing research about gymnasts' flexibility and wanted her daughter's help. On the day Jane was to participate, her mother was out of town, so a neighbor dropped her off, alone, at Nassar's one-bedroom apartment a few blocks from the Michigan State University campus. Once inside, Nassar had Jane do splits on his living room floor while she wore a gymnastics leotard. . . .

After Nassar said she should take a hot bath as part of the study's metrics, Jane got dressed in her leotard and did splits a second time. Then, she says, Nassar gave her what he called "her reward." On a training table crammed between the living room and kitchenette, he gave her a full-body massage. Once again, she was naked. The encounter didn't strike her as threatening; to the contrary, she recalls, she "felt special." Other girls from Great Lakes Gymnastics Club had been invited to Nassar's apartment, perhaps five to seven, she says, and to be asked was to become part of the chosen few.

Source: John Barr and Dan Murphy, "Nassar Surrounded by Adults Who Enabled His Predatory Behavior," ABC News, January 22, 2018, https://abcnews.go.com/Sports/nassar-surrounded-adults-enabled-predatory-behavior/story?id=52533983.

Intersectional Insults

Female athletes generally have been mocked, shamed, ignored, and hypersexualized. Athletes who are not white, straight, or cis face even more scrutiny, if not outright abuse. Gay men have fought hard to gain gradual acceptance on the field. The NFL's first active openly gay player, Carl Nassib, was re-signed to the Tampa Bay Buccaneers in 2022 after coming out on social media.[65] In his viral Instagram post, Nassib also announced a donation to the Trevor Project, a nonprofit dedicated to suicide prevention for LGBTQ+ youth.[66] The supportive media reception Nassib received for coming out strikes a stark contrast to the way another athlete came out in 1995. Diver Greg Louganis opened up to Barbara Walters in an interview about having been HIV positive during the 1988 Olympics. He won two gold medals during the competition but during one dive hit his head and bled into the water.[67] The incident resulted in discussion about how HIV is spread (and the way chlorine kills the virus that causes AIDS), and parents had to be reassured that it was safe for their children to swim.[68]

MISOGYNOIR

In addition to attacks on their femininity, Black female athletes face the weight of racism. Serena Williams has endured decades of racist attacks, ranging from a man in the stands of a California competition who yelled that he wished she could be lynched to comments from columnists about her muscularity and size.[69] A Fox columnist complained about what he called Serena Williams's "oversized backpack." He went on, "I am not fundamentally opposed to junk in the trunk, although my preference is a stuffed onion over an oozing pumpkin."[70] This combination of sexism and racism directed at Black women in popular culture is called **misogynoir**, a term coined in 2010 by feminist writer Moya Bailey.[71]

In 2007, a hugely popular radio show host, Don Imus, insulted the champion Rutgers women's basketball team by calling them "rough girls" and "nappy headed hos." He apologized, but he still lost his show, and his career never recovered. Imus died in Texas in 2019.[72] Brittney Griner, the professional basketball player who was jailed in Russia for ten months on an alleged drug offense, was characterized by President Trump as a "potentially spoiled" woman who went abroad "loaded up with drugs." His comments drew from multiple negative stereotypes about Black women. Griner had been caught with two bottles of hashish oil prescribed by her doctor. Upon her release from Russia, she returned to basketball in 2023 with the Phoenix Mercury.[73]

TRANS ATHLETES

Many Americans had not heard of trans issues nor considered the rights of trans people until they heard of Renée Richards in the 1970s. Richards was an ophthalmologist and professional tennis player who was born male, married, and fathered a child but suffered from depression and suicidal tendencies before being able to undergo gender reassignment surgery. She moved from New York to California and was playing tennis professionally when a local TV journalist outed her.[74] As a result, she was barred from playing in the women's US Open in 1976. She filed a lawsuit, won, and was cleared to play in 1977.[75] More recently, swimmer Lia Thomas, a trans woman, won the national championship in the 500 freestyle. Protesters gathered outside the facility, arguing that allowing Thomas to compete was a Title IX violation and an attack on women. Counterprotesters also picketed against transphobia.[76]

Much of the opposition to trans women in competition arises from questions about whether testosterone, the hormone responsible for male traits and aggressiveness, gives athletes an advantage. Regulators for international swimming and cycling have instituted rules about testosterone levels that effectively ban trans women from competing.[77] While she is not trans but intersex, Olympian middle-distance runner Caster Semenya has opted to run races outside her specialty instead of taking drugs to reduce her testosterone levels, as demanded by World Athletics, which regulates international track and field competition. Semenya was assigned female at birth and has been raised as a woman but has a genetic condition that gives her both male and female traits and levels of testosterone higher than average for most women.[78] The South African runner has undergone repeated invasive tests over time to prove she is a woman. When she was eighteen, she actually offered to show her vagina to officials to prove her femininity because she says taking the antitestosterone drugs make her sick. "It's like stabbing yourself every day," she said.[79]

Currently, state legislatures across the United States are proposing to regulate trans students' access to their school teams. One of the first laws banning trans athletes from competing was passed in Idaho on grounds that trans athletes who were male at birth have an unfair advantage and their participation might be unsafe for cisgender girls.[80] That law was blocked in court but not before other states, such as Texas, passed measures requiring students to play on a team according to the biological sex assigned to them on a birth certificate. The sponsor of the Texas bill argued that it protects women's rights in sports. Opponents argued that the bill only marginalizes trans students and does nothing to solve real problems facing women's sports, such as low funding, unequal pay, abuse, and harassment. At the time the Texas bill was passed, there had not been a single case of a trans student unfairly taking a cis girl's spot from a team or causing injury.[81]

Trans student controversies present an interesting case in rhetorical framing and stereotypes. Claiming that such bills protect women's rights invokes powerful ties to American values, such as liberty and freedom, but is also tied to deep-seated ideas about innate gendered differences. Advocates for trans athletes argue that hormones are just one factor in the biology of athletic achievement. They assert that testosterone exists in male *and* female bodies and is not necessarily an advantage, any more than being born tall, fast, or muscular.[82] Moreover, given that trans students endure harassment and abuse at such high rates that they drop out of school at disproportionate rates, supporters argue that allowing them to participate in sports improves their education.[83] As noted in chapter 8, media guides offer support for journalists seeking to cover trans issues with respect and care. After transgender weightlifter

Laurel Hubbard's participation in the 2021 Olympic Games in Tokyo, researchers interviewed sports reporters and found that some journalists made a concerted effort to educate themselves in order to cover the topic appropriately.[84]

Summary

Media are part of the way sports both create culture and reflect it. Sports are also traditionally male territory, so whether they are playing a game or covering it, women face significant barriers. They are a small minority in sports journalism and in coverage. While more women play professional sports than ever before, they are paid less than male professional athletes. Some writers and critics continue to use sexist and racist language when writing about female athletes. Female sports writers endure harassment from coworkers and the audience, especially online. Trans athletes face opposition and discrimination at every level of play. Only recently have schools and teams begun to address long-standing problems involving the sexual abuse of young athletes. The news, in short, is not good when it comes to women's sports and sports writing, except for this: More women than ever are able to enjoy athletic competition, which gives them healthier, happier lives. This will have to do until media equality is achieved.

- **Reflection:** How might stereotypes about female athletes affect the experiences of women who work as sports journalists?
- **Reflection:** Proposals to ban transgender women from school athletic competitions often rely on the belief that testosterone gives them an advantage. What other genetic traits, not rooted in gender, might give an athlete a competitive advantage?
- **Media Critique:** How well do media in your area cover local women's teams? How often are women on the front page of the sports section? What language is used to describe how they play?

CHAPTER 15

Gender, Journalism, and the Future

This chapter goes back to the beginning and looks to the future. As a reminder, this book emphasizes three themes: (1) Change occurs from the work of individuals, (2) language shapes social systems, and (3) the current structures of hierarchy and oppression involve multiple dimensions of human experience. Each chapter examines a facet of gender and the news, providing history as necessary to guide journalists and media professionals in presenting gender issues with fairness, accuracy, and integrity. This chapter pulls back for a global perspective on social justice and its relationship to the earth itself. How might the practices of journalism best adapt to an ever-evolving social system? What role do media play in supporting democracy and human rights?

Key Concepts: Centering, Democratic Voice, Ethic of Care

This book describes some of the dramatic ways society has changed over the past several centuries. Women and people of all races in the United States have the legal right to vote. Women are playing professional sports. Queer people can marry. Many people now recognize gender as a continuum and not a binary. At the same time, though, many things remain largely the same. News coverage continues to focus on division and controversy. Historic divisions continue to fester between white women and women of color and between people in economically privileged nations and the global South. Media continue to struggle with the best ways to cover science, especially the biology of gender, and often revert to stereotypical tropes. Individuals have worked for change around the world, yet women remain significantly disadvantaged.

Climate change is no longer a niche story for the science pages. It is fast becoming the most important story of our time. Rising temperatures around the world have the potential to damage coastal cities, interrupt the food supply, and worsen the spread of disease. The existential disaster it portends is already affecting women more than men, as women have far less income and are more likely to suffer the effects of floods, fires, and food shortages. Consider, for instance, that in some cultures, women and girls

Profile: Greta Thunberg, Climate Activist (2003–)

Greta Thunberg started working to save the climate as a teenager by skipping school on Fridays to protest outside the Swedish Parliament. Gradually more people joined her for these "Fridays for the Future" in Sweden and then in other countries, such as France, the United Kingdom, and the United States. She's been compared to Joan of Arc because of her age, gender, and ability to inspire. In only two years, she became the face of climate action, and in 2019, she addressed the United Nations with an emotional speech in which she scolded its members: "People are suffering. People are dying. Entire ecosystems are collapsing. We are in the beginning of a mass extinction, and all you can talk about is money and fairy tales of eternal economic growth. How dare you!" That speech and subsequent events and media appearances inspired *Time* magazine to name her 2019's person of the year.

She has become a target for social media trolls because of her youth, gender, and way of speaking. A Fox News commentator (who was immediately disavowed by the network) called her a "mentally ill Swedish child." In response to the *Time* magazine announcement, then president Donald Trump took to social media to call the decision "ridiculous" and suggested that Thunberg work on her "anger management problem." Thunberg has Asperger's syndrome, a condition on the autism spectrum in which a person may have high intelligence and be extremely focused on one thing. For Thunberg, that is the climate. She has shrugged off the criticism, noting that people attack her because they cannot deny the science of climate change, which portends dire consequences if global leaders do not take swift and significant action.

Greta Thunberg.
Courtesy of Creative Commons, European Parliament

Sources: Charlotte Alter, Suyin Haynes, and Justin Worland, "Greta Thunberg Is *Time*'s 2019 Person of the Year," *Time*, December 23, 2019, https://time.com/person-of-the-year-2019-greta-thunberg/; Allan Smith, "Trump Mocks Teen Climate Activist Greta Thunberg after She Wins *Time* Person of the Year," NBC News, December 12, 2019, https://www.nbcnews.com/politics/donald-trump/trump-mocks-greta-thunberg-after-she-wins-time-person-year-n1100531; David Wallace-Wells, "It's Greta's World but It's Still Burning. The Extraordinary Rise of a 16-Year-Old and Her Hail Mary Climate Movement," *New York Magazine*, September 17, 2019, https://nymag.com/intelligencer/2019/09/greta-thunberg-climate-change-movement.html; Karen Zraick, "Greta Thunberg, after Pointed U.N. Speech, Faces Attacks from the Right," *New York Times*, September 24, 2019, https://www.nytimes.com/2019/09/24/climate/greta-thunberg-un.html.

are more likely to have the responsibility to carry water to their homes. When a water system is interrupted by climate change, girls miss school to carry water, and women have less time to tend to their families. Women are the poorest people on the planet and therefore the most vulnerable to the impending calamity. Climate injustice and gender injustice overlap, as do their remedies.[1]

This book describes the impact gender has had on the people who cover the news, how news coverage has presented gendered issues, and how language can shape ideas about gender. Yet until now, this book has not touched on what may be the most important news story in history for all humans: climate change. Why is a topic that involves carbon emissions and the polar ice caps in a book about gender? First, because it affects all people, no matter their gender, but more specifically, because of the way the story has been covered in news. The language and framing of climate change is gendered, as is its potential impact.

Recall that one tenet of masculine hegemony is dominance over nature. Patriarchy encourages the exploitation of resources. Taking control of land, mining its elements, and hunting its animals are all activities associated with masculine behavior and can cause harm when unchecked. Consider how "Drill, baby, drill" took hold as a Republican slogan during the party's national convention in 2008.[2] The phrase harmonizes with the party's economic and cultural philosophies, which trust capitalism and celebrate the use of America's resources. The sexual double entendre is also hard to miss, again corresponding with traditionally masculine tropes. Sarah Palin, then a vice presidential candidate who embodied traditional patriarchal values as a beautiful frontier mother who knew how to use a gun, used the phrase on the campaign trail to the delight of her fans. Patriarchy is an essential dimension of contemporary conservatism, so the rejection of climate-change science is an understandable next step. Policy proposals to treat the earth with more care become associated with femininity.[3] Such masculine logic permeates nationalistic discourse, both in the United States and elsewhere in the world, for the way it draws on romanticized notions of male and female roles; zero-sum thinking; and the belief that only strong male leaders can protect national prestige from threats brought about by feminism, wokeness, or immigration.[4]

Beyond White Feminism

Human rights are integral to global politics, whether the focus is on race, income, orientation, gender, or any other dimension of identity. Just as various forms of oppression overlap and intersect, so do such global issues as education, voting rights, and economic stability. The strategies for these various battles are not one-size-fits-all, however, and they must be understood contextually. Consider, for instance, the case of Malala Yousafzai, who was shot in Afghanistan because of her advocacy on behalf of education for women and girls. She is the youngest person to be recognized with the Nobel Peace Prize.[5] In 2013, a year after her attack, she spoke to the United Nations on her birthday. As you read the excerpt from her speech, think back to the words of Mary Wollstonecraft in her *Vindication of the Rights of Women*, originally published in 1792.[6] Then and now, women are asking to be educated, to be considered full members of society, to be

Excerpt: Malala Yousafzai's Speech to the United Nations

Today I am focusing on women's rights and girls' education because they are suffering the most. There was a time when women activists asked men to stand up for their rights. But this time we will do it by ourselves. I am not telling men to step away from speaking for women's rights, but I am focusing on women to be independent and fight for themselves. So dear sisters and brothers, now it's time to speak up. So today, we call upon the world leaders to change their strategic policies in favor of peace and prosperity. . . .

We call upon all governments to ensure free, compulsory education all over the world for every child. We call upon all the governments to fight against terrorism and violence. To protect children from brutality and harm. We call upon the developed nations to support the expansion of education opportunities for girls in the developing world. We call upon all communities to be tolerant, to reject prejudice based on caste, creed, sect, color, religion or agenda to ensure freedom and equality for women so they can flourish. We cannot all succeed when half of us are held back. We call upon our sisters around the world to be brave, to embrace the strength within themselves and realize their full potential.

Source: Malala Yousafzai, "Malala Yousafzai: 'Our Books and Our Pens Are the Most Powerful Weapons,'" *Guardian*, July 12, 2013, https://www.theguardian.com/commentisfree/2013/jul/12/malala-yousafzai-united-nations-education-speech-text.

able to reach their full potential. Yousafzai's activism is also significant for how it puts the spotlight on the needs of women and girls beyond the West.

The feminism most familiar to people in America and Europe is, for the most part, white feminism associated the second wave. It is seen as somehow separate from racial civil rights and focuses on the interests of white, middle-class women in their careers and civic life. In this book, I apply intersectional feminism to my account of gender and media to draw attention to other forms of oppression, such as race, sexuality, and class. Even this, however, may not be a broad enough lens.

The interests of women in the industrialized West do not necessarily match those of women in other parts of the world. Feminism is at its worst when it attempts to speak for other women globally without actually listening to those women or considering their needs, interests, and lives.[7] This sort of tone-deaf feminism was blamed, in part, for the US failures in the war in Afghanistan. As civil rights lawyer Rafia Zakaria puts it, "[Y]ou cannot simultaneously bomb a country into the Stone Age and then also say you're going to empower and uplift women."[8]

When feminists focus on their own advancement in a capitalistic system or on foreign policy that keeps oil prices low, they are not considering the lives of women in other parts of the world. The white feminism described by Zakaria presumes to speak for other women instead of giving them a true voice, a chance to account for their own lives. Feminist philosophers have offered many alternatives to movements that empower some women at the expense of others, such as postcolonial, Indigenous, or global feminism.[9] These approaches reject the notion that women are the same, and they demand that all women be heard and considered. Such approaches require journalists to rethink how they go about producing the news. By pulling the lens of human rights way out, beyond the interests of the United States or the West, these alternative feminisms complicate our ideas about how to get to the truth.

Objectivity

What does it really mean to be objective? In 2021, a former *Washington Post* reporter sued the newspaper, alleging workplace discrimination after she disclosed that she was a sexual assault survivor. Editors allegedly changed her assignments on the grounds that she could not objectively cover the #MeToo movement or the controversy surrounding the confirmation hearings for Justice Brett Kavanaugh.[10] Her experience is familiar to many journalists whose objectivity has been questioned because of their identities. Conversely, journalists from marginalized groups have also experienced a discomfiting flip side to their newsroom identities, being assigned stories based on stereotypical expectations and tokenism.

Objectivity has not always been an expectation of journalists. The norm started in the late 1800s. Until then, newspapers were vociferously partisan; there was no question about whether a particular publication was Republican, Democratic, feminist, or abolitionist. Newspapers were expected to have a point of view. Some historians argue that technology fueled the shift to objectivity. The telegraph, for instance, enabled the establishment of the Associated Press, which used stories from many news organizations nationwide.[11] Technology was a factor in the development of a new way of news writing that helped to establish professional authority, with an inverted pyramid structure that gave the most important facts first and stuck with verifiable information and quotes.

Other scholars suggest that a desire to reach a mass audience may have influenced media executives to present the news objectively.[12] Why offend half of the potential readers? Journalism historian Michael Schudson, however, argues that the primary motivation for the objectivity norm reflected a desire by journalists to claim professional authority, to be seen as arbiters of truthful reality akin to modern science.[13] For American journalism, objectivity and professionalism are almost one and the same.

Yet objectivity has also challenged the role of marginalized people in the newsroom because it has been conflated with a white male perspective.[14] Women have been barred from covering gender issues because they might not be "objective" about their own rights. The same reasoning has been used to prevent people of color or queer people from covering stories about their own communities. Conversely, this has not prevented news organizations from assigning marginalized people from covering stories stereotypically attached to their demographic.

This diversity double bind may be one reason journalists of color have found newsrooms to be so unwelcoming, even when they were courted and hired for the very purpose of diversifying the workforce. As one research report notes, "The newsroom cultural impulse to retain traditional 'objectivity' may force minority journalists to choose between producing what they know reinforces stereotypes or to resist reproducing inaccurate or ethically inappropriate reporting at the risk of being perceived as biased."[15]

WHOSE OBJECTIVITY?

In 2021, Nikole Hannah-Jones, the MacArthur Genius Grant winner and *New York Times* journalist who conceived and produced the Pulitzer Prize–Winning *1619 Project*, was hired by her alma mater, the University of North Carolina, as an endowed professor funded by the Knight Foundation. Unusually, the university initially denied her tenure, normally automatic for a Knight Chair at UNC.[16] University trustees were reportedly influenced by the man for whom the UNC School of Journalism and Media is named, Walter E. Hussman, a major donor and former newspaper publisher, who had concerns about Hannah-Jones's reporting in the *1619 Project*. Some historians and many conservative commentators took issue with the project, as it suggests that the year slaves first arrived in the colonies could be considered America's "true founding" and for implying that a defense of slavery motivated all rebellious colonists in 1776.

The *New York Times* adjusted the phrasing for the online version of the material in both instances, but conservatives seized on these criticisms to cast Hannah-Jones herself as racist, un-American, and biased in her reporting.[17] After weeks of controversy, UNC eventually did offer her tenure, but by then, she decided to take a faculty position at Howard University, which, in combination with the hiring of author Ta-Nehisi Coates, attracted $25 million in grants from various foundations to establish a new Center for Journalism and Democracy.[18] Hussman did not back down from his critique, even after the university voted to grant Hannah-Jones tenure. In an email to NPR, he wrote, "I was especially concerned that the UNC Hussman School of Journalism and Media would become more closely associated with the 1619 Project than the school's core value of objectivity, impartiality, integrity, the pursuit of truth, and the separation of news and opinion."[19]

What sort of bias is Hussman concerned about, exactly? The Hannah-Jones case perfectly illustrates the way one perspective—that of straight, cisgender, white men—has been treated as truthful and objective, while other perspectives are considered biased. The *1619 Project* was an enormous undertaking, and the introductory section that was attacked by certain historians is an essay, not a straight news story. Some critics believe that criticizing white slaveowners imposes a presentist perspective on the past by interpreting history through today's morals.[20] Should the essay have included perspectives that defended slaveholders? This critique avoids the fact that millions of people opposed slavery during the time it was in place, including the four million individuals who were enslaved in the United States. More to the point, defending slavery denies the essential humanity of Black people, then and now.

Would anyone have questioned whether a white man with academic teaching experience, a multimillion dollar grant, and a Pulitzer Prize ought to receive tenure in a journalism department? Would concerns about Hannah-Jones's objectivity have been raised if she was a white man studying historic racism? The answer to this question lies is in the definition of *objectivity*. A colloquial definition of *journalistic objectivity* suggests that news should give all legitimate viewpoints a fair airing; focus on facts, not opinions; and be free of ideology. Yet as communication scholars point out, merely choosing what facts to include imposes a point of view. This book shows how framing imposes a particular view of the facts. Today's debate about objectivity reflects the role of perspective in news work and the way perspective has and is changing as newsrooms make room for new voices.

Historically, news in the United States has conveyed an ideology favored by those in power, one so widespread that it has appeared to be invisible. Part of this ideology is rooted in the Constitution and reflects the values of democracy and human rights, but this ideology has also reflected the interests of white, heteronormative patriarchy. As the chapters in this book describe, it has taken decades for news to shift its perspective regarding the rights of women, queer people, trans people, and people of color. Hussman's suggestion that the *1619 Project* was not objective seems not based on factual errors or problems with verification, as there were a few (not surprisingly for a project of this size) that the *New York Times* corrected. What is not objective, in this case, seems that the story is not told from the point of view Hussman is used to. If the straight, white, male perspective is objective, then everyone else's perspectives are biased. This accusation has plagued journalists who are female, queer, trans, and people of color—essentially anyone who is not a white, straight, cisgender male—because it casts doubt on their ability to cover stories associated with their identity objectively. These questions do not plague straight, white, male journalists because their perspective is **centered**. That is, their perspective on the world has been the accepted view, and all other views are somehow skewed.

If other peoples' perspectives are subjective, then what happens to one of journalism's core ideological principles? If nothing is objective, then are there no facts? If everything is subjective, then can anyone be believed? Even though these questions seem to complicate the ethics of journalism, if anything, they oversimplify the matter. Indeed, certain practices that seem to reflect objectivity can actually hide the truth, such as when two sides are always given equal weight even when one side is not based in fact, as happened in the early coverage of climate change.[21] In the case of Hannah-Jones, objectivity was defined by those who've been in power so long they cannot even conceive that their perspective is just as subjective as anyone else's.

Journalism's imperfect history with all-white, mostly male, heteronormative, and cisgender newsrooms means that it has not adequately dealt with the question of how perspective guides objectivity. Many journalists in the United States ascribe to a code of ethics from the Society of Professional Journalists and follow principles that reflect the importance of the Constitution's First Amendment to American democracy. In practice, objectivity is often reflected by a reporter's effort to include both sides. Both sides of what? Indeed, there may be far more than two perspectives about a single fact. Sides are perspectives; facts can be shown. Today, when many politicians and their supporters outright lie to the public, reporters have come to realize they cannot merely report what each side has said, and "both sides" or even "all sides" is not necessarily a useful approach.[22] Many journalists have scrambled to find ways to avoid stenographic both-sides-ism and present facts in the United States and beyond. A female journalist from Egypt put it this way to researchers: "Objectivity is a good word used in a bad way."[23]

Profile: Dori Maynard, Journalist and Educator (1958–2015)

Dori Maynard.
Published by arrangement with the Nieman Foundation of Journalism

Dori Maynard was a reporter, journalism speaker, and advocate for newsroom diversity. Her father, Robert C. Maynard, and stepmother, Nancy Hicks Maynard, were journalists in Oakland, California. They were among the cofounders of the Institute for Journalism Education in 1977 and became the first African Americans to own and operate a major metropolitan newspaper when they bought the *Oakland Tribune* in 1984. After her father's death, Dori joined what had been renamed the Robert C. Maynard Institute for Journalism Education in 1994.

Dori helped newsrooms across the country to adopt equitable newsroom practices, applying a framework her father developed called the Fault Lines framework for equitable newsroom practices. His framework introduced coverage "fault lines" of difference that journalists ought to consider as they cover the news: race, class, gender, generation, and geography. In recent years, sexual orientation was added as a sixth fault line.

Dori also argued that diverse newsrooms enable better coverage by ensuring that there are more people in the room who will have life experiences connected to these fault lines. In her words, "When we front load diversity, then we don't end up having to figure out and apologize, and our conversation isn't steered from what we wanted to talk about to: 'Why weren't women and people of color included?' I think my hope was that everyone's going to begin to see what's in it for them, and it's a better product." Dori died in 2015, but the institute continues to work toward building inclusive newsrooms by providing diversity training for newsrooms and professional development for journalists and media leaders.

Sources: Ava Macha, community engagement manager, Maynard Institute, personal communication with the author, February 17, 2023; Shorenstein Center on Media, Politics, and Public Policy, "Dori Maynard: Reflections on Technology and Diversity in the News Business," Harvard Kennedy School, February 25, 2015, https://shorensteincenter.org/dori-maynard-technology-news-diversity/. See also Maynard Institute, accessed May 18, 2023, https://mije.org/.

If *objectivity* can be used improperly, then what rules should there be? The answer is not easy, as ethics are not rules. They serve as a guide when the rules conflict or might not apply to a particular context. For instance, it is usually considered unethical to lie, but most of us lie every day, in small ways, often to save a person's feelings ("Your haircut looks fine!") or to spare others the truth about our horrible day. When it comes to ethical rules, one size rarely fits all. Because objectivity has become a problematic concept, some journalists choose to adhere to ethics of nonpartisanship, fairness, and transparency: that is, explaining the processes of fact finding and verification.

News organizations have struggled to find ways to point out a politician's lies because it is impossible when working with a public statement, to determine a person's *intent* to lie. Journalists eventually developed such phrases such as *demonstrably false* and *stated without evidence* to describe inaccuracies.[24] The objectivity debate is far from settled, as journalists and the people who depend on news consider how to best bring facts to light while honoring varied perspectives. What is clear is that unreflective practices that ignore the varied perspectives of journalism's stakeholders are no longer viable.

AN ETHIC OF CARE

If there is no single objective view, then is there no single morality? If there's no single morality, then can anyone do their own thing without worrying about ethics? Does this mean anything goes?

Feminist scholars have worked their way through this conundrum by proposing a morality that rests not on external rules but on our connections with others.[25] This is known as the ethic of care, which "reflects a cumulative knowledge of human relationships, evolves around a central insight, that self and other are interdependent."[26] That is, an ethic of care suggests that morality is not a matter of living one's life according to hard rules or predetermined principles. Instead, an ethic of care emphasizes the complexity of human connection and the way we are interrelated, shifting our focus from individual morality to mutual obligation.[27] An ethic of care replaces what feminist scholars describe as stone-engraved principles of patriarchal society that have often ignored half the world's population with an ethical system driven by "caring about and caring for" others.[28]

How might this ethic translate to the everyday practice of journalism? As a start, it compels journalists to cast a larger net for facts, quotes, and perspectives. Reporters would not write about women's rights without including the women affected. They would not write about crime in a neighborhood without spending time in that neighborhood, talking to the people who live there. Dori Maynard, who led a national organization devoted to newsroom diversity, argues that including people of color and their concerns in stories is not acquiescing to tokenism but a more accurate form of journalism that includes the entire community.[29] In a similar vein, a proposal by journalism scholar Meenakshi Gigi Durham for "strong objectivity" would compel journalists to consider and include their own identity standpoints and that of everyone they cover in their stories, embracing *multiple* perspectives instead of presuming a bird's-eye view.[30]

Some organizations are experimenting with new approaches to journalism. Solutions journalism, for example, goes beyond reporting on problems and explores how people are trying to fix them. Note that this does not mean solving a problem but shifting the reporting frame to provide useful context.[31] Another approach is solidarity journalism, which endeavors to include the perspective of people affected by an issue.[32] It is often surprising to know how often reporters rely only on police reports, for example, without tending to the individuals involved in an incident or only sourcing politicians for quotes without asking questions of the governed.

Perhaps most important for the pursuit of an objectivity that serves social justice is genuine inclusion. Journalists have played a role in *both* advancing equality *and* perpetuating inequality. Some of the most important improvements in gender representation have occurred as a result of individuals connecting with one another through media, whether with partisan newspapers in support of abolition in the 1800s or with alternative weeklies to advance LGBTQ+ rights. To print news is not enough; journalists work in a relationship with the audience.

Facts are objective, they are statements that can be *proven*, but this implies a relationship—a messenger proves the statement to another. Practices of verification that also consider varied perspectives can support such relationships. Recognizing the role of community in the pursuit of truth offers a way of establishing a useful form of objectivity. In other words, facts exist, but they are presented in language and understood in a communicative relationship. For democracy to thrive, all perspectives must be included in the conversation.

Voice and Visibility

What do people need in order to lead good lives? To answer that question, we need to first consider what a good life looks like. People who adhere to their faith consider living according to religious principles to be a good life. Cross-cultural psychological research suggests that a good, happy life is a matter of purpose and relationships.[33] While many participants in happiness surveys believe that material goods are not *essential* for happiness, a certain level of material security matters in our well-being.[34] Maslow's hierarchy of needs shows that it is hard to think about our higher purpose when we're hungry.[35] In the late 1800s, labor activists called for a balanced life as they fought for the eight-hour workday with the slogan "Eight hours for work, eight hours for rest, eight hours for what we will."[36] The *pursuit* of happiness is part of the opening lines of the Declaration of Independence, along with life and liberty, not happiness itself. Thomas Jefferson conceptualized the journey as the right.

More than two centuries later, an economist proposed a way to national well-being that goes beyond measurements of financial productivity, such as GDP (gross domestic product), which he called the "capabilities approach."[37] The capabilities approach suggests that our well-being depends on more than simple materiality; it depends on capabilities of self-determination. Can we pursue an education? Can we see a doctor? Can we control our immediate environment, such as deciding where to live, what furniture to buy, or with whom we want to live?

Philosopher Martha Nussbaum extends capabilities theory to feminism by considering women's capabilities around the world.[38] She argues that in order to live complete, good lives, women needed to have access to the literacy, education, and self-determination to participate in democracy. In this perspective, social well-being is more than a matter of finances; it is one of self-determination and autonomy. As climate change looms more menacingly, our need for things like clean air and water and a comfortable environment also take on more significance than traditional economic priorities.

Small wonder, then, that throughout history, even women who were economically secure still took the chance to fight for a right to be heard, the right to a voice. Democracy is intended as the government of self-determination, of having a voice, but for centuries, women, queer people, people of color, and people with disabilities were ignored. Having a voice is not just a matter of self-expression. A toddler can express an opinion about strained peas, but beyond spitting out the peas, they're not capable of self-determination. Their perspective on peas is not taken seriously. Similarly, democratic voices must also be more than expressing an opinion, even an informed opinion. Many of the four million people who were enslaved before the American Civil War had expressed opinions about their predicament, but their voices were still ignored by those in power.

Voice, therefore, entails expression and recognition. We must be heard, seen, and taken seriously. This book offers many examples of the way marginalized people have been ignored, mocked, trivialized, infantilized, or literally locked up for daring to speak their truth. As one scholar puts it, our civic voice needs to *valued*.[39] This is why activists have fought so hard for visibility, *as well as* voice. Marginalized people need to be recognized as fully human, capable individuals worthy of participation in civic life. With the AIDS quilt, white-dress suffrage marches, Pride parades, pussy hats, and slut walks, gender activists have used visual communication to gain literal visibility, in hope of metaphorical visibility. Simultaneously, they have endeavored to change the way they are *talked about* and therefore valued in society. Reclaiming words like *queer* and *bitch* is one strategy. The early suffrage movement's adaptation of the language of piety from the cult of true womanhood similarly changed the frame.

Journalism has long professed to give voice to the voiceless, but as this book shows, many voiceless individuals were long ignored. News organizations that do not reflect their entire audience cannot adequately serve democracy. Facts can be objective, but people always have perspective, so news is better when it includes multiple perspectives. This means not only covering stories about people who are not white, male, straight, and middle class but also including those people in the process of making news. Media no longer reflect the one-to-many model of mass communication. We are better connected in digital networks, and it is easier to use our voices and amplify the voices of others, if only we make the effort.

In Closing

In the preface to this book, I offered three thesis statements:

1. Change occurs from the work of individuals.
2. Language shapes social systems.
3. The current structures of hierarchy and oppression involve multiple dimensions of human experience.

The story of gender and news is one of an ongoing struggle for voice in all its dimensions. At the macrolevel, it is a story of groups of people fighting to be seen, heard, and listened to in order to have the self-determination necessary to live a good life. At the microlevel, it is a story of many individuals, often angry and inspired, who decided that they could no longer tolerate the status quo. No matter how valuable an idea might be, without human beings willing to show up and work for it, there is no change. By now, you've read the stories of the individuals who have worked, sometimes by risking their lives, for the sake of equality. People like Ida B. Wells, Jovita Idár, and Greta Thunberg have sacrificed what we would consider everyday lives in favor of changing society.

This book also offers explanations of the way language shapes social systems, demonstrating how changes in language can affect the way we think about things. Because you have been reading this textbook, it is likely that you are considering a job in media. I hope, therefore, that you have considered the power of language as you contemplate your own work. Words create the frames we use to think about the world around us. Whether by framing the battle for the Equal Rights Amendment as a cat fight or by reclaiming the slur of *queer*, we understand the world and each other through linguistic choices. The difference between *rape victim* and *rape survivor* is empowering. Calling a trans person by the name they use is a mark of respect. Covering queer rights without describing their very existence as a "lifestyle" places their lives on an equal footing with straight ones. Wondering whether something is stereotypical or unfair? Flipping the script usually provides an answer. Think about the profound impact it means to *"Say her name."* The words you choose now and the words you might choose in a media career will make a difference.

Finally, this book shows how the current structures of oppression reflect multiple dimensions of human experience beyond gender. Race, ethnicity, national origin, ability, and age are just some of the vectors that matter in the larger social system. I hope that this textbook shows that the journey toward human emancipation has not been a straight line. Intersectional rifts and divisions continue to complicate the effort. White feminism has dominated much of the conversation about women's rights, while the concerns of women of color, queer, trans, disabled, impoverished people and people living outside the United States have often been marginalized, if not ignored entirely. The struggle for human life, liberty, and the *dignity* essential for the pursuit of happiness is not over—and journalism has not always advanced the cause of equality. Unreflective versions of objectivity, coupled with the fact that journalists are human beings working in their own social contexts, have cultivated stereotypes, distortions, and outright bigotry in media.

It doesn't have to be that way. Each of us can decide how we want to contribute to civic life. Each of us, whether we are paid to work in news or simply participating in social media, has the power to choose our words. Each of us can decide what kind of world we want to live in and how we're going to build it.

- **Reflection:** Think about the culture you live in. How might that affect your ideas about what feminism is?
- **Reflection:** How has the internet changed the way people have or do not have a democratic voice?
- **Media Critique:** Based on what you've learned about framing, language, and news, what do you think is the best way journalists should practice objectivity? Should they hold onto the concept or change it?

Glossary

agentic (chapter 1). Able to take action, having the freedom to make decisions and do things.

Bechdel Test (chapter 13). A measure for checking sexism in media by asking whether the story has at least two female characters who talk to one another about something other than a man.

binary or binarism (chapter 1). All-or-nothing ways of approaching issues as either-or or win-lose instead of both-and.

cat-fight frame (chapter 4). A way of covering stories about women's issues that pit one group against another, such as stay-at-home moms versus career women.

centered, centering (chapter 15). The choice of perspective that is prioritized in media.

color-blind racism (chapter 6). The belief that individuals are to blame for their problems because the system is fair and that talking about racial politics is itself racist.

colorism (chapter 10). A form of racial bias within a nonwhite group that diminishes members of that group with darker skin.

confirmation bias (chapter 1). The human tendency to believe things that fit our preexisting beliefs.

consumer culture (chapter 10). A system in which branded products create social meaning.

counterpublic (chapter 2). A type of public sphere in which marginalized people directly engage in debate with the dominant society.

cult of true womanhood (chapter 2). A typology proposed by Judith Welter to describe the expectations of women as cultivated in nineteenth-century media.

double binds (chapter 5). Representations of women that place them in no-win situations, as when they cannot be considered smart if they're pretty, but if they're not smart, they cannot be taken seriously.

doxing (chapter 8). To publish a person's address or other personal information, usually online, often with an intent to harass or cause harm.

embodied, embodiment (chapter 11). Relating to the body and physicality.

enclave (chapter 2). A type of public sphere that offers safety and privacy for a marginalized group.

episodic framing (chapter 6). A news frame that emphasizes events (rather than ongoing issues).

ethic of care (chapter 15). A moral system that emphasizes the complexity of human connections over a singular set of rules for everyone.

false equivalence (chapter 13). Giving equal weight to contrasting views when one side has largely been rejected by science or easily is proven to be false or represents an extreme position.

framing (chapter 1). The process by which news presents reality, where journalists choose facts, words, images, or other elements to infer judgments or suggest solutions.

Gamergate (chapter 12). A controversy that at first accused a female gaming journalist of an unproven conflict of interest and then grew into an attack on numerous journalists and researchers with misogynistic harassment and threats of violence.

gender as social construction (chapter 1). The theory that gender is not related to innate characteristics but performed by human beings according to social expectations.

gender dysphoria (chapter 8). A condition when a person feels like their external body does not match their internal identity.

halo effect (chapter 5). The way positive attributes such as intelligence or virtue are ascribed to a person because they are physically attractive.

hegemonic masculinity (chapter 6). A social system that presents patriarchy as natural and normal.

hegemony (chapter 6). The combination of political domination and ideological leadership in a social system that hides oppressions or makes them seem natural.

heuristic (chapter 1). A shortcut in our thinking or a rule of thumb that lets us quickly make decisions.

ideology (chapter 1). A set of largely unspoken and assumed values about society.

incel (chapter 12). Originally, a person who is involuntarily celibate; now, a person who believes feminists are to blame for men's problems and what the FBI has labeled a violent extremist group.

infantilization (chapter 2). To treat or represent someone like a child.

intersectional, intersectionality (chapter 1). The overlapping of dimensions of oppression that benefit some people and intensify challenges for others, such as Black women, who are subjected to racism *and* sexism.

inverted pyramid style (chapter 3). A newswriting style that puts the most important facts first before providing details.

Kerner Commission (chapter 9). A group appointed in 1968 to investigate the causes of race riots in the United States; they put part of the blame on news coverage that ignored the interests of people of color.

male gaze (chapter 14). The way representations of women reflect a tradition of men looking at them and the effects it has on the way women present themselves.

marianismo (chapter 2). A cultural expectation that women emulate the Virgin Mary of Catholicism by living subservient, pure lives and are willing to endure suffering.

mass media (chapter 3). Industrialized media that communicate to large audiences.

media event (chapter 11). An event designed to attract media attention.

mental load (chapter 13). The cognitive effort necessary to manage a household and care for a family.

misandry (chapter 6). Denigration of or bias against men.

misogynoir (chapter 14). The combination of sexism and racism directed at Black women.

muckrakers (chapter 3). Investigative journalists who worked during the Progressive Era (the early 1900s) in the United States.

objectification (chapter 4). To be seen or visually represented as a *thing* for the pleasure of others, usually cis-, straight men.

outing (chapter 8). To publish information about a person's sexuality that they previously kept private.

patriarchy (chapter 1). A system built on the belief that men are superior to women and should hold power over women.

pornography (chapter 7). Sexually explicit material intended to incite sexual arousal.

protest paradigm (chapter 1). A news frame that presents protest as a disruptive problem and gives less attention to the conditions that inspire social unrest.

public sphere (chapter 2). A literal or metaphorical place where democratic citizens can discuss the issues of public importance.

qualitative textual analysis (chapter 2). A form of research that examines in detail the way an idea is presented and its various contexts.

quantitative content analysis (chapter 4). A form of research that counts and categorizes instances of words or images.

rape culture (chapter 7). A system of beliefs suggesting rape is inevitable and women must guard against it.

reclamation (chapter 8). Taking control of a word to eliminate the pain associated with it; to undo a slur by using it.

representation (chapter 11). The process of creating cultural meaning with language, images, and symbols.

revenge porn (chapter 7). Sexually explicit images created or shared without the depicted person's consent and published with the intent to harm or humiliate.

reversibility (chapter 5). Considering how a representation treats members of a group by replacing them with the other group (e.g., flipping genders).

Sapir-Whorf hypothesis (chapter 1). The principle of linguistic relativity that suggests that language evolves according to social needs but also shapes our thoughts.

satellite (public sphere) (chapter 2). A type of public sphere for marginalized people that is willfully separate and doesn't necessarily seek inclusion.

scientific consensus (chapter 13). The collective perspective of numerous scientists based on available evidence.

second wave (chapter 4). The feminist movement that started in the second half of the twentieth century and focused on rights at home, at work, and in civic life.

sexual harassment (chapter 9). Unwanted verbal or physical behavior that is sexual in nature.

stereotypes (chapter 1). Mental shortcuts about people that diminish their full humanity to a set of limited characteristics.

stigma (chapter 7). The characterization of something as shameful or embarrassing.

symbolic annihilation (chapter 13). Media representations that ignore, mock, or shame members of a group.

TERF (transexclusionary radical feminist) (chapter 8). A politically charged term for people who are hostile to the inclusion of trans women in the feminist movement.

thematic framing (chapter 6). Covering the context and issues of news in ways that explain the social forces that influence day-to-day events.

token, tokenism (chapter 3). Giving a member of a minority group a position more for the sake of appearance than actual inclusion; they are treated as a stand-in for the entire group.

toxic masculinity (chapter 6). A contested term that describes a set of beliefs about masculinity that causes harm to men and women.

visual activism (chapter 3). Gaining media attention with art or performative displays for a cause or idea.

voice (democratic voice) (chapter 15). Having a say in deliberation by being seen, recognized, and respected.

yellow journalism (chapter 3). A form of newspaper journalism from the early 1900s that emphasized sensationalism and scandal.

Notes

PREFACE

1. Associate Press, *The Associated Press Stylebook: 2022–2024*, 56th ed. (Basic Books, 2022); John Daniszewski, "AP Stylebook Updates Race-Related Terms," ACES: The Society for Editing, February 2, 2021, https://aceseditors.org/news/2021/ap-stylebook-updates-race-related-terms.

2. Quoctrung Bui, Sara Chodosh, Jessica Bennett, and John McWhorter, "Quiz: You Can't Say That! (Or Can You?)," *New York Times*, December 22, 2022, https://www.nytimes.com/interactive/2022/12/22/opinion/words-you-cant-use-anymore.html; Luis Noe-Bustamante, Lauren Mora, and Mark Hugo Lopez, "About One-in-Four U.S. Hispanics Have Heard of Latinx, but Just 3% Use It," Pew Research Center, August 11, 2020, https://www.pewresearch.org/hispanic/2020/08/11/about-one-in-four-u-s-hispanics-have-heard-of-latinx-but-just-3-use-it/.

3. Gregory Younging, *Elements of Indigenous Style: A Guide for Writing by and about Indigenous Peoples* (Brush Education, 2018).

CHAPTER 1

1. Nicholas Reimann, "*Washington Post* Fires Reporter Felicia Sonmez after Public Feud," *Forbes*, June 9, 2022, https://www.forbes.com/sites/nicholasreimann/2022/06/09/washington-post-fires-reporter-felicia-sonmez-after-public-feud/.

2. Lauren Lumpkin and Nick Anderson, "Nikole Hannah-Jones to Join Howard Faculty after UNC Tenure Controversy," *Washington Post*, July 6, 2021, https://www.washingtonpost.com/education/2021/07/06/howard-nikole-hannah-jones-tanehisi-coates/.

3. Alex Galbraith, "'Don't Say Gay' Law Is Not Forcing Orange County Teachers to Remove Photos of Same-Sex Partners," *Orlando Weekly*, July 1, 2022, https://www.orlandoweekly.com/news/dont-say-gay-law-is-not-forcing-orange-county-teachers-to-remove-photos-of-same-sex-partners-31934362.

4. Walter Lippmann, *Public Opinion* (Macmillan, 1922), 81.

5. "Confirmation Bias," in *Encyclopedia of Social Psychology*, ed. Roy Baumeister and Kathleen Vohs (Sage, 2007), 163–64, https://doi.org/10.4135/9781412956253.

6. John T. Jost and Mahzarin R. Banaji, "The Role of Stereotyping in System-Justification and the Production of False Consciousness," *British Journal of Social Psychology* 33, no. 1 (1994): 1–27, https://doi.org/10.1111/j.2044-8309.1994.tb01008.x.

7. Inge K. Broverman, Susan Raymond Vogel, Donald M. Broverman, Frank E. Clarkson, and Paul S. Rosenkrantz, "Sex-Role Stereotypes: A Current Appraisal," *Journal of Social Issues* 28, no. 2 (1972): 59–78, https://doi.org/10.1111/j.1540-4560.1972.tb00018.x.

8. Aaron C. Kay et al., "Panglossian Ideology in the Service of System Justification: How Complementary Stereotypes Help Us to Rationalize Inequality," in *Advances in Experimental Social Psychology*, vol. 39, ed. Mark P. Zanna (Academic Press, 2007), 305–58, https://doi.org/10.1016/S0065-2601(06)39006-5.

9. A. H. Eagly and V. J. Steffen, "Gender Stereotypes Stem from the Distribution of Women and Men into Social Roles," *Journal of Personality and Social Psychology* 46, no. 4 (1984): 735–54, https://doi.org/10.1037/0022-3514.46.4.735.

10. Peter Aaby, "Engels and Women," *Critique of Anthropology* 3, nos. 9–10 (January 1, 1978): 25–53, https://doi.org/10.1177/0308275X7800300902; Gerda Lerner, *The Creation of Patriarchy* (Oxford University Press, 1986).

11. Regina G. Lawrence and Melody Rose, *Hillary Clinton's Race for the White House: Gender Politics and the Media on the Campaign Trail* (Lynne Rienner, 2010).

12. Gwyneth Mellinger, *Chasing Newsroom Diversity: From Jim Crow to Affirmative Action* (University of Illinois Press, 2013).

13. Patricia Bradley, *Mass Media and the Shaping of American Feminism, 1963–1975* (University Press of Mississippi, 2003).

14. Kristina M. W. Mitchell and Jonathan Martin, "Gender Bias in Student Evaluations," *PS: Political Science and Politics* 51, no. 3 (July 2018): 648–52, https://doi.org/10.1017/S104909651800001X.

15. Jost and Banaji, "Role of Stereotyping."

16. Hannah-Hanh D. Nguyen and Ann Marie Ryan, "Does Stereotype Threat Affect Test Performance of Minorities and Women? A Meta-analysis of Experimental Evidence," *Journal of Applied Psychology* 93, no. 6 (2008): 1314–34, https://doi.org/10.1037/a0012702.

17. Brian A. Nosek et al., "Pervasiveness and Correlates of Implicit Attitudes and Stereotypes," *European Review of Social Psychology* 18, no. 1 (November 1, 2007): 36–88, https://doi.org/10.1080/10463280701489053.

18. Andrew M. Rivers et al., "On the Roles of Stereotype Activation and Application in Diminishing Implicit Bias," *Personality and Social Psychology Bulletin* 46, no. 3 (March 1, 2020): 349–64, https://doi.org/10.1177/0146167219853842.

19. Lippmann, *Public Opinion*, 91–92.

20. Candace West and Don H. Zimmerman, "Doing Gender," *Gender and Society* 1, no. 2 (June 1, 1987): 125–51, https://doi.org/10.1177/0891243287001002002.

21. Simone de Beauvoir and Sheila Malovany-Chevallier, *The Second Sex*, trans. H. M. Parshley, 1st American ed. (Vintage Books, 1974), 301.

22. "RuPaul Explains What 'We're All Born Naked and the Rest Is Drag' Means," interview by Oprah Winfrey, January 16, 2018, https://www.youtube.com/watch?v=9RPDSdRCDYs.

23. Sean P. O'Neill, "Sapir-Whorf Hypothesis," in *The International Encyclopedia of Language and Social Interaction*, ed. Karen Tracy (Wiley, 2015).

24. Dedre Gentner, *Language in Mind: Advances in the Study of Language and Thought* (MIT Press, 2003).

25. Amos Tversky and Daniel Kahneman, "The Framing of Decisions and the Psychology of Choice," *Science* 211, no. 30 (January 1981): 453–58.

26. Eran N. Ben-Porath, "Framing," in *Encyclopedia of Journalism*, vol. 2, ed. Christopher H. Sterling (Sage, 2009), 618–22; Robert M. Entman, "Framing: Toward Clarification of a Fractured Paradigm," *Journal of Communication* 43, no. 4 (1993): 51–58; Stephen D. Reese, "The Framing Project: A Bridging Model for Media Research Revisited," *Journal of Communication* 57, no. 1 (2007): 148–54.

27. Entman, "Framing," 52, italics in original.

28. Herbert Gans, *Deciding What's News: A Study of* CBS Evening News, NBC Nightly News, Newsweek *and* Time, 25th anniversary ed. (Pantheon Books, 1979).

29. J. M. Chan and C. C. Lee, "The Journalistic Paradigm on Civil Protests: A Case Study of Hong Kong," in *The News Media in National and International Conflict*, ed. A. Arno and W. Dissanayake (Westview Press, 1984), 183–202.

30. Guus Bartholomé, Sophie Lecheler, and Claes de Vreese, "Manufacturing Conflict? How Journalists Intervene in the Conflict Frame Building Process," *International Journal of Press/Politics* 20, no. 4 (October 1, 2015): 438–57, https://doi.org/10.1177/1940161215595514.

31. Brian Calfano, Jeffrey Layne Blevins, and Alexis Straka, "Bad Impressions: How Journalists as 'Storytellers' Diminish Public Confidence in Media," *Journal of Broadcasting and Electronic Media* 66, no. 1 (January 1, 2022): 176–99, https://doi.org/10.1080/08838151.2022.2036153.

32. Paul Colford, "'Illegal Immigrant' No More," *Definitive Source* (blog), April 2, 2013, https://blog.ap.org/announcements/illegal-immigrant-no-more.

33. Barbara Welter, "The Cult of True Womanhood: 1820–1860," *American Quarterly* 18, no. 2 (1966): 151–74, https://doi.org/10.2307/2711179.

34. Kimberlé Crenshaw, "Demarginalizing the Intersection of Race and Sex: A Black Feminist Critique of Antidiscrimination Doctrine, Feminist Theory and Antiracist Politics," *University of Chicago Legal Forum* 1989, no. 1 (1989): 139–67.

35. Crenshaw, "Demarginalizing the Intersection," 140.

36. Helen Rosner, "The Long American History of 'Missing White Woman Syndrome,'" *New Yorker*, October 8, 2021, https://www.newyorker.com/news/q-and-a/the-long-american-history-of-missing-white-woman-syndrome.

37. Sonia Rao, "R. Kelly Found Guilty on All Federal Charges in Sex Trafficking and Racketeering Trial," *Washington Post*, September 27, 2021, https://www.washingtonpost.com/arts-entertainment/2021/09/27/r-kelly-trial-guilty-verdict/.

38. Kimberlé Crenshaw, "How R. Kelly Got Away with It," *New York Times*, October 1, 2021, https://www.nytimes.com/2021/10/01/opinion/r-kelly-conviction.html.

39. Rachel Elizabeth Cargle, "When Feminism Is White Supremacy in Heels," *Harper's Bazaar*, August 16, 2018, https://www.harpersbazaar.com/culture/politics/a22717725/what-is-toxic-white-feminism/.

40. Julia R. Johnson, "Cisgender Privilege, Intersectionality, and the Criminalization of CeCe McDonald: Why Intercultural Communication Needs Transgender Studies," *Journal of International and Intercultural Communication* 6, no. 2 (May 1, 2013): 135–44, https://doi.org/10.1080/17513057.2013.776094; Tina Goethals, Elisabeth De Schauwer, and Geert Van Hove, "Weaving Intersectionality into Disability Studies Research: Inclusion, Reflexivity and Anti-Essentialism," *DiGeSt: Journal of Diversity and Gender Studies* 2, nos. 1–2 (2015): 75–94, https://doi.org/10.11116/jdivegendstud.2.1-2.0075.

CHAPTER 2

1. Vanessa Romo, "Malala Yousafzai, Nobel Laureate and Girls' Education Champion, Gets Married," NPR, November 9, 2021, https://www.npr.org/2021/11/09/1053939195/malala-married; Liam Stack, "Malala Yousafzai, Nobel Peace Prize Laureate, Starts at Oxford," *New York Times*, October 10, 2017, https://www.nytimes.com/2017/10/10/world/europe/malala-yousafzai-oxford.html.

2. Martha C. Nussbaum, *Women and Human Development: The Capabilities Approach* (Cambridge University Press, 2000).

3. Mary Wollstonecraft, *A Vindication of the Rights of Women and a Vindication of the Rights of Men* (Cosimo, 2008), 11.

4. Carlos Cortés, "Marianismo," in *Multicultural America: A Multimedia Encyclopedia* (Sage, 2013), 1408, https://doi.org/10.4135/9781452276274.

5. Cokie Roberts, *Founding Mothers* (Perennial, 2016).

6. Abigail Adams and John Adams, "'Remember the Ladies': Abigail Adams vs. John Adams," in *The Feminist Papers*, ed. Alice S. Rossi (Columbia University Press, 1973), 10.

7. Adams and Adams, 11.

8. Frances E. Dolan, "Battered Women, Petty Traitors, and the Legacy of Coverture," *Feminist Studies* 29, no. 2 (2003): 249–77.

9. Marylynn Salmon, *Women and the Law of Property in Early America* (UNC Press Books, 2016).

10. Carlos E. Castañeda, "The Beginning of Printing in America," *Hispanic American Historical Review* 20, no. 4 (November 1, 1940): 671–85, https://doi.org/10.1215/00182168-20.4.671.

11. Stephanie Kirk, *Sor Juana Inés de La Cruz and the Gender Politics of Knowledge in Colonial Mexico* (Routledge, 2016); Stephanie Merrim, "Sor Juana Inés de La Cruz: Mexican Poet and Scholar," Britannica, 1998, https://www.britannica.com/biography/Sor-Juana-Ines-de-la-Cruz.

12. Debra Michals, "Mary Church Terrell," National Women's History Museum, 2017, https://www.womenshistory.org/education-resources/biographies/mary-church-terrell.

13. Konstantin Dierks, "Goddard, Mary Katherine (1738–1816), Printer and Postmaster," *Oxford Dictionary of National Biography*, 2004, https://doi.org/10.1093/ref:odnb/74439.

14. John R. Vile, "John Peter Zenger," 2009, https://www.mtsu.edu/first-amendment/article/1235/john-peter-zenger.

15. Vincent Buranelli, "The Myth of Anna Zenger," *William and Mary Quarterly* 13, no. 2 (1956): 157–68, https://doi.org/10.2307/1920530.

16. Barbara Welter, "The Cult of True Womanhood: 1820–1860," *American Quarterly* 18, no. 2 (1966): 151–74, https://doi.org/10.2307/2711179.

17. Welter, "Cult of True Womanhood," 152.

18. Welter, "Cult of True Womanhood," 153.

19. Welter, "Cult of True Womanhood," 162.

20. Welter, "Cult of True Womanhood."

21. Amanda Fehlbaum, "Cult of Domesticity," in *Wiley-Blackwell Encyclopedia of Family Studies*, ed. Constance L. Shehan (Wiley, 2016).

22. J. Richardson, "Public Sphere," in *Key Concepts in Journalism Studies*, ed. Bob Franklin et al., (Sage UK, 2005).

23. Jurgen Habermas, *The Structural Transformation of the Public Sphere: An Inquiry into a Category of Bourgeois Society*, ed. F. Lawrence (Polity Press, 1989).

24. Zizi Papacharissi, "The Virtual Sphere: The Internet as a Public Sphere," *New Media and Society* 4, no. 1 (February 1, 2002): 9–27, https://doi.org/10.1177/14614440222226244.

25. Catherine R. Squires, "Rethinking the Black Public Sphere: An Alternative Vocabulary for Multiple Public Spheres," *Communication Theory* 12, no. 4 (2002): 446–68, https://doi.org/10.1111/j.1468-2885.2002.tb00278.x.

26. Christopher R. Matthews, "The Tyranny of the Male Preserve," *Gender and Society* 30, no. 2 (April 1, 2016): 312–33, https://doi.org/10.1177/0891243215620557.

27. Elizabeth J. Clapp, *A Notorious Woman: Anne Royall in Jacksonian America* (University of Virgina Press, 2016), https://muse.jhu.edu/book/44689.

28. Katie Gentile, "What about the Baby? The New Cult of Domesticity and Media Images of Pregnancy," *Studies in Gender and Sexuality* 12, no. 1 (January 12, 2011): 38–58, https://doi.org/10.1080/15240657.2011.536056; Pew Research Center, *America's Changing Religious Landscape* (Pew Research Center, May 12, 2015).

29. Rodney Stark and Roger Finke, "American Religion in 1776: A Statistical Portrait," *Sociology of Religion* 49, no. 1 (March 1, 1988): 39–51, https://doi.org/10.2307/3711102.

30. Holly Berkley Fletcher, *Gender and the American Temperance Movement of the Nineteenth Century*, Studies in American Popular History and Culture (Routledge, 2008), 8.

31. Cherise Kramarae and Ann Russo, *The Radical Women's Press of the 1850s* (Routledge, 2001), https://doi.org/10.4324/9780203708941.

32. Martha Watson, *A Voice of Their Own: The Woman Suffrage Press, 1840–1910* (University of Alabama Press., 1991).

33. Watson, *Voice of Their Own*.

34. Watson, *Voice of Their Own*, 32.

35. Sven Beckert, "Reconstructing the Empire of Cotton: A Global Story," in *Contested Democracy: Freedom, Race, and Power in American History*, ed. Manisha Sinha and Penny Von Eschen (Columbia University Press, 2007), 164–90, https://doi.org/10.7312/sinh14110-009.

36. Fehlbaum, "Cult of Domesticity."

37. Harriet Beecher Stowe Center, "*Uncle Tom's Cabin*: A Moral Battle Cry for Freedom," accessed July 19, 2021, https://www.harrietbeecherstowecenter.org/harriet-beecher-stowe/uncle-toms-cabin/; David S. Reynolds, *Mightier than the Sword: Uncle Tom's Cabin and the Battle for America* (W. W. Norton, 2011).

38. Harold Bloom, ed., *Harriet Beecher Stowe's* Uncle Tom's Cabin, Bloom's Notes (Chelsea House, 1996).

39. Bloom, *Harriet Beecher Stowe's*.

40. Bloom, *Harriet Beecher Stowe's*, 8.

41. Harriet Elizabeth Beecher Stowe, *Life and Letters of Harriet Beecher Stowe* (Houghton, Mifflin, 1897).

42. Sally McMillen, *Seneca Falls and the Origins of the Women's Rights Movement* (Oxford University Press, 2009).

43. Quoted in McMillen, *Seneca Falls*, 90.

44. Donna Batten, ed., "Women's Rights: Seneca Falls Declaration of Sentiments," in *Gale Encyclopedia of American Law*, 3rd ed., vol. 13 (Gale, 2011), 436–37.

45. Batten, "Women's Rights."

46. "Bolting among the Ladies," *Oneida Whig*, August 1, 1848.

47. Elizabeth Cady Stanton et al., *History of Woman Suffrage* (Fowler and Wells, 1881), 804, https://catalog.hathitrust.org/Record/001142954.

48. McMillen, *Seneca Falls*.

49. Lorraine Boissoneault, "Amelia Bloomer Didn't Mean to Start a Fashion Revolution, but Her Name Became Synonymous with Trousers," *Smithsonian Magazine*, May 24, 2018, https://www.smithsonianmag.com/history/amelia-bloomer-didnt-mean-start-fashion-revolution-her-name-became-synonymous-trousers-180969164/.

50. Cristina Devereaux Ramirez, *Occupying Our Space: The Mestiza Rhetorics of Mexican Women Journalists and Activists, 1875–1942* (University of Arizona Press, 2015), http://muse.jhu.edu/book/38303.

51. Jason H. Silverman, "Mary Ann Shadd and the Search for Equality," in *A Nation of Immigrants: Women, Workers, and Communities in Canadian History, 1840s–1960s*, ed. Franca Iacovetta, Paula Draper, and Robert Ventresca (University of Toronto Press, 2020), 101–14, https://doi.org/10.3138/9781442687271-008.

52. Megan Specia, "Overlooked No More: How Mary Ann Shadd Cary Shook Up the Abolitionist Movement," *New York Times*, June 7, 2018, https://www.nytimes.com/2018/06/06/obituaries/mary-ann-shadd-cary-abolitionist-overlooked.html.

53. Bob Ostertag, *People's Movements, People's Press: The Journalism of Social Justice Movements* (Beacon Press, 2007).

54. Reprinted in "The Need for Women's Publishing," *New Women's Times*, January 4–17, 1980, 2.

55. Allison Lange, "The 14th and 15th Amendments," History of U.S. Woman's Suffrage, 2015, http://www.crusadeforthevote.org/14-15-amendments.

56. Frederick Douglass, "We Welcome the 15th Amendment," in *The Speeches of Frederick Douglass: A Critical Edition*, ed. John R. McKivigan, Julie Husband, and Heather L. Kaufman (Yale University Press, 2018), 271.

CHAPTER 3

1. Joseph Turow, *Media Today*, vol. 2 (Houghton Mifflin, 2003).

2. Bob Ostertag, *People's Movements, People's Press: The Journalism of Social Justice Movements* (Beacon Press, 2007).

3. Quoted in Faye E. Dudden, *Fighting Chance: The Struggle over Woman Suffrage and Black Suffrage in Reconstruction America* (Oxford University Press, 2014), 3.

4. Ostertag, *People's Movements, People's Press*.

5. Ostertag, *People's Movements, People's Press*.

6. Linda Steiner, "Nineteenth Century Suffrage Journals: Inventing and Defending New Women," in *Front Pages, Front Lines: Media and the Fight for Women's Suffrage*, ed. Linda Steiner, Carolyn Kitch, and Brooke Kroeger (University of Illinois Press, 2020), 42–60.

7. Tadeusz Lewandowski, *Red Bird, Red Power: The Life and Legacy of Zitkala-Ša* (University of Oklahoma Press, 2016).

8. Rosalyn Terborg-Penn, *African American Women in the Struggle for the Vote, 1850–1920* (Indiana University Press, 1998).

9. Alison M. Parker, *Unceasing Militant: The Life of Mary Church Terrell* (UNC Press Books, 2020); Karen Fraser Wyche and Lisa Abern, "Mary McLeod Bethune: Voice of Change, Life of Service," in *Women of Vision: Their Psychology, Circumstances, and Success*, ed. Eileen Gavin, Aphrodite Clamar, and Mary Anne Siderits, Focus on Women Series (Springer, 2007), 95–109.

10. Eileen V. Wallis, "'Keeping Alive the Old Tradition': Spanish-Mexican Club Women in Southern California, 1880–1940," *Southern California Quarterly* (July 2009): 133–54.

11. Julie Greene, "Race, Immigration, Ethnicity," in *Companion to the Gilded Age and Progressive Era*, ed. Christopher McKnight Nichols and Nancy C. Unger, 1st ed. (Wiley and Sons, 2017), 137–48.

12. Rodger Streitmatter, *Mightier than the Sword: How the News Media Have Shaped American History* (Avalon, 1998).

13. Dustin Harp, *Desperately Seeking Women Readers: U.S. Newspapers and the Construction of a Female Readership* (Lexington Books, 2007); Streitmatter, *Mightier than the Sword*.

14. Streitmatter, *Mightier than the Sword*.

15. Nellie Bly, *The Complete Works of Nellie Bly* (CreateSpace, 2015).

16. Kim Todd, *Sensational: The Hidden History of America's "Girl Stunt Reporters"* (HarperCollins, 2021).

17. Catherine C. Mitchell, "Introducing Margaret Fuller," in *Margaret Fuller's New York Journalism: A Biographical Essay and Key Writings* (University of Tennessee Press, 1995), 3–13.

18. Marion Marzolf, "The Woman Journalist: Colonial Printer to City Desk," *Journalism History* 1, no. 4 (December 1, 1974): 100–146, https://doi.org/10.1080/00947679.1974.120 66749.

19. Bryan Denham, "Magazine Journalism in the Golden Age of Muckraking: Patent-Medicine Exposures before and after the Pure Food and Drug Act of 1906," *Journalism and Communication Monographs* 22, no. 2 (June 1, 2020): 100–159, https://doi.org/10.1177/ 1522637920914979.

20. Mark Thomas, "Ida M. Tarbell's Crusade against Standard Oil," Bill of Rights Institute, accessed December 31, 2022, https://billofrightsinstitute.org/essays/ida-m-tarbells-crusade -against-standard-oil; P. A. Treckel, "Lady Muckraker (Reporter Ida Tarbell and Her Investigation of John D. Rockefeller and the Standard Oil Company)," *American History* 36, no. 2 (2001): 38–44.

21. Margaret Fuller, "Dispatch 33: Rome under Siege," in *These Sad but Glorious Days: Dispatches from Europe, 1846–1850* (Yale University Press, 1991), 295–301.

22. James W. Carey, *Communication as Culture: Essays on Media and Society* (Unwin Hyman, 1989).

23. Horst Pottker, "News and Its Communicative Quality: The Inverted Pyramid—When and Why Did It Appear?" *Journalism Studies* 4, no. 4 (November 1, 2003): 501–11, https://doi .org/10.1080/1461670032000136596.

24. Michael Schudson, "The Objectivity Norm in American Journalism," *Journalism* 2, no. 2 (2001): 149–70.

25. Turow, *Media Today*.

26. Joseph Turow, "The Development of the Modern Advertising Industry," in *The Advertising Handbook*, ed. Jonathan Hardy, Iain Macrury, and Helen Powell (Routledge, 2018), 3–15.

27. Linda Ford, *Iron-Jawed Angels: The Suffrage Militancy of the National Woman's Party, 1912–1920* (University Press of America, 1991).

28. Harriot Stanton Blatch, *Challenging Years: The Memoirs of Harriot Stanton Blatch* (G. P. Putnam's Sons, 1940), 92.

29. Teri Finneman, "Covering a Countermovement on the Verge of Defeat: The Press and the 1917 Social Movement against Woman Suffrage," *American Journalism* 36, no. 1 (January 2, 2019): 124–43, https://doi.org/10.1080/08821127.2019.1572416.

30. L. O. Kleber, *The Suffrage Cook Book* (Echo Library, 2008). I use the word *suffragist* instead of *suffragette* because at the time *suffragette* was largely considered an insult. The term had been coined by an antifeminist columnist in Britain who wished to infantilize activists. See Alice Janigro, "Suffragists or Suffragettes?" *Suffrage 100MA* (blog), February 15, 2017, https:// suffrage100ma.org/resources/did-you-know/suffragists-or-suffragettes/.

31. Stephanie Hartle and Darcy White, *Visual Activism in the 21st Century: Art, Protest and Resistance in an Uncertain World* (Bloomsbury, 2022).

32. Todd Gitlin, *The Whole World Is Watching: Mass Media in the Making and Unmaking of the New Left* (University of California Press, 1980).

33. J. M. Chan and C. C. Lee, "The Journalistic Paradigm on Civil Protests: A Case Study of Hong Kong," in *The News Media in National and International Conflict*, ed. A. Arno and W. Dissanayake (Westview Press, 1984), 183–202.

34. D. M. McLeod and J. K. Hertog, "Social Control, Social Change and the Mass Media's Role in the Regulation of Protest Groups," in *Mass Media, Social Control and Social Change*, ed. D. Demers and K. Viswanath (Iowa State University Press, 1999), 305–30.

35. Christine Woodworth, "'Equal Rights by All Means!': Beatrice Forbes-Robertson's 1910 Suffrage Matinee and the Onstage Junction of the US and UK Franchise Movements," *Theatre History Studies* 37, no. 1 (2018): 209–24, https://doi.org/10.1353/ths.2018.0011.

36. Linda J. Lumsden, "Beauty and the Beasts: Significance of Press Coverage of the 1913 National Suffrage Parade," *Journalism and Mass Communication Quarterly* 77, no. 3 (September 1, 2000): 593–611, https://doi.org/10.1177/107769900007700309.

37. Kenneth Florey, *American Woman Suffrage Postcards: A Study and Catalog* (McFarland, 2016).

38. Florey, *American Woman Suffrage Postcards*.

39. Linda J. Lumsden, "Beauty and the Beasts: Significance of Press Coverage of the 1913 National Suffrage Parade," *Journalism and Mass Communication Quarterly* 77, no. 3 (September 1, 2000): 595, https://doi.org/10.1177/107769900007700309.

40. Lumsden, "Beauty and the Beasts."

41. Ford, *Iron-Jawed Angels*, 128.

42. Susan Ware, ed., *American Women's Suffrage: Voices from the Long Struggle for the Vote, 1776–1965*, Library of America no. 332 (Library of America, 2020), 527.

43. Tina Cassidy, *Mr. President, How Long Must We Wait? Alice Paul, Woodrow Wilson, and the Fight for the Right to Vote* (Simon and Schuster, 2020).

44. National Archives, "The Constitution: Amendments 11–27," November 4, 2015, https://www.archives.gov/founding-docs/amendments-11-27.

45. Ware, *American Women's Suffrage*.

46. Susan Cianci Salvatore and Neil Foley, "Civil Rights in America: Racial Voting Rights," in *Civil Rights in America: Racial Voting Rights* (National Historic Landmarks Program Cultural Resources, National Park Service, US Department of the Interior, 2009), 103–10.

47. Gabriela Cano, "Mexico: The Long Road to Women's Suffrage," in *The Palgrave Handbook of Women's Political Rights*, ed. Susan Fanceschet, Mona Lena Krook, and Netina Tan, Gender and Politics Series (Palgrave MacMillan, 2019), 115–27.

48. Nancy Janovicek and Melanee Thomas, "Canada: Uneven Paths to Suffrage and Women's Electoral Participation," in *The Palgrave Handbook of Women's Political Rights*, ed. Susan Fanceschet, Mona Lena Krook, and Netina Tan, Gender and Politics Series (Palgrave MacMillan, 2019), 169–84.

CHAPTER 4

1. Martha Weinman Lear, "The Second Feminist Wave," *New York Times*, March 10, 1968, https://www.nytimes.com/1968/03/10/archives/the-second-feminist-wave.html.

2. Benita Roth, *Separate Roads to Feminism: Black, Chicana, and White Feminist Movements in America's Second Wave* (Cambridge University Press, 2004).

3. Dorothy Sue Cobble, "Labor Feminists and President Kennedy's Commission on Women," in *No Permanent Waves: Recasting Histories of U.S. Feminism*, ed. Nancy Hewitt (Rutgers University Press, 2010), 144–67.

4. Lear, "Second Feminist Wave."

5. Jennifer A. Bennice and Patricia A. Resick, "Marital Rape: History, Research, and Practice," *Trauma, Violence, and Abuse* 4, no. 3 (July 1, 2003): 228–46, https://doi.org/10.1177/1524838003004003003.

6. Simone de Beauvoir, *The Second Sex*, trans. H. M. Parshley, 1st American ed (Vintage Books, 1974).

7. Judith Thurman, "Introduction to Simone de Beauvoir's 'The Second Sex,'" *New York Times*, May 28, 2010, https://www.nytimes.com/2010/05/30/books/excerpt-introduction-second-sex.html.

8. Betty Friedan, *The Feminine Mystique* (W. W. Norton, 2001).

9. Sherna Berger Gluck, *Rosie the Riveter Revisited: Women, the War, and Social Change* (Penguin Books USA, 1988).

10. Ramona R. Rush, Carol E. Oukrop, and Pamela J. Creedon, *Seeking Equity for Women in Journalism and Mass Communication Education: A 30-Year Update* (Taylor and Francis, 2013).

11. Naomi Rosenblum, *A History of Women Photographers* (Abbeville Press, 1994).

12. Dorothy Thompson, "Women and the Coming World," *Ladies Home Journal*, October 1943.

13. Thomas D. Snyder, *120 Years of American Education: A Statistical Portrait* (Washington D.C.: National Center for Education Statistics, 1993).

14. Karen Garner, "Global Feminism and Postwar Reconstruction: The World YWCA Visitation to Occupied Japan, 1947," *Journal of World History* 15, no. 2 (2004): 191–227.

15. Cobble, "Labor Feminists."

16. Cynthia E. Harrison, "A 'New Frontier' for Women: The Public Policy of the Kennedy Administration," *Journal of American History* 67, no. 3 (1980): 630–46, https://doi.org/10.2307/1889871.

17. Cobble, "Labor Feminists."

18. Maryann Barakso, *Governing NOW: Grassroots Activism in the National Organization for Women* (Cornell University Press, 2004); Donald Elisburg, "Equal Pay in the United States: The Development and Implementation of the Equal Pay Act of 1963," *Labor Law Journal* 29, no. 4 (April 1, 1978): 195–208.

19. Paulette Brown, "The Civil Rights Act of 1964," *Washington University Law Review* 92, no. 2 (2014): 527–52.

20. Carl M. Brauer, "Women Activists, Southern Conservatives, and the Prohibition of Sex Discrimination in Title VII of the 1964 Civil Rights Act," *Journal of Southern History* 49, no. 1 (1983): 37–56, https://doi.org/10.2307/2209305; Linda Napikoski, "How Women Became Part of the 1964 Civil Rights Act," ThoughtCo, February 4, 2020, https://thoughtco.com/women-and-the-civil-rights-act-3529477.

21. Brauer, "Women Activists, Southern Conservatives."

22. National Archives, "Civil Rights Act (1964)," October 5, 2021, https://www.archives.gov/milestone-documents/civil-rights-act.

23. Kate Millett, *Sexual Politics* (Doubleday, 1970).

24. Sheila Jeffreys, "Kate Millett's Sexual Politics: 40 Years On," *Women's Studies International Forum* 34, no. 1 (January 1, 2011): 76–84, https://doi.org/10.1016/j.wsif.2010.07.006.

25. Annie Anderson, "When the Mainstream Met the Second Wave: Media Representations of Women and Feminism in 1970s America" (honors thesis, Connecticut College, 2012), 68.

26. Bridget L. Murphy, "The Equal Rights Amendment Revisited," *Notre Dame Law Review* 94, no. 2 (2018): 937–57.

27. Proposing an Equal Rights Amendment to the Constitution, H.J. Res. 75, December 13, 1923.

28. Philippe R. Girard, "Equal Rights Amendment," in *Culture Wars in America: An Encyclopedia of Issues, Viewpoints, and Voices*, ed. Roger Chapman and James Ciment, 2nd ed., Credo Reference (Routledge, 2013).

29. Girard, "Equal Rights Amendment."

30. Donald T. Critchlow, *Phyllis Schlafly and Grassroots Conservatism: A Woman's Crusade* (Princeton University Press, 2008).

31. Amélie Ribieras, "'I Want to Thank My Husband Fred for Letting Me Come Here,' or Phyllis Schlafly's Opportunistic Defense of Gender Hierarchy," in *Male Supremacism in the United States* (Routledge, 2022).

32. Jeanne Dorin McDowell, "The True Story of 'Mrs. America,'" *Smithsonian Magazine*, April 15, 2020, https://www.smithsonianmag.com/history/true-story-mrs-america-180974675/.

33. Robert Barnes and Ann E. Marimow, "Supreme Court Ruling Leaves States Free to Outlaw Abortion," *Washington Post*, June 24, 2022, https://www.washingtonpost.com/politics/2022/06/24/supreme-court-ruling-abortion-dobbs/; Mary Ziegler, "Beyond Backlash: Legal History, Polarization, and *Roe v. Wade*," *Washington and Lee Law Review* 71, no. 2 (Spring 2014): 969–1024.

34. Lisa Baldez, Lee Epstein, and Andrew D. Martin, "Does the U.S. Constitution Need an Equal Rights Amendment?" *Journal of Legal Studies* 35, no. 1 (January 1, 2006): 243–83, https://doi.org/10.1086/498836.

35. Removing the Deadline for the Ratification of the Equal Rights Amendment, H.J. Res. 17, 117th Congress, March 23, 2021, https://www.congress.gov/bill/117th-congress/house-joint-resolution/17.

36. Timothy Williams, "Virginia Approves the E.R.A., Becoming the 38th State to Back It," *New York Times*, January 15, 2020, https://www.nytimes.com/2020/01/15/us/era-virginia-vote.html.

37. Gaye Tuchman, *Making News: A Study in the Construction of Reality* (Free Press, 1978).

38. Anne Marie Seward Barry, *Visual Intelligence: Perception, Image and Manipulation in Visual Communication* (State University of New York Press, 1997).

39. John Berger, *Ways of Seeing* (BBC and Penguin Books, 1972).

40. Amy Erdman Farrell, *Yours in Sisterhood:* Ms. Magazine *and the Promise of Popular Feminism* (University of North Carolina Press, 1998); *Killing Us Softly 4*, directed by Sut Jhally, written by Jean Kilbourne (2010).

41. Erving Goffman, *Gender Advertisements* (MacMillan, 1979).

42. Lucianne Goldberg and Jeannie Sakol, "Two Members of 'Pussycat League' Attack Women's Liberation," *Gazette*, October 30, 1971; Jeanne Lobmeyer, "'Purr' Is Putdown of Libbers," *Wichita Eagle*, November 14, 1971.

43. Bonnie J Dow, "Feminism, Miss America, and Media Mythology," *Rhetoric and Public Affairs* 6, no. 1 (2003): 127–49, https://doi.org/10.1353/rap.2003.0028.

44. Art Buchwald, "The Bra Burners," *New York Post*, September 12, 1968.

45. W. Joseph Campbell, *Getting It Wrong: Debunking the Greatest Myths in American Journalism* (University of California Press, 2017).

46. Laura Ashley and Beth Olson, "Constructing Reality: Print Media's Framing of the Women's Movement, 1966 to 1986," *Journalism and Mass Communication Quarterly* 75, no. 2 (June 1, 1998): 263–77, https://doi.org/10.1177/107769909807500203.

47. Anderson, "When the Mainstream Met."

48. "Who's Come a Long Way, Baby?" *Time*, August 31, 1970, https://content.time.com/time/subscriber/article/0,33009,876783-4,00.html.

49. Tuchman, *Making News*.

50. Susan Jeanne Douglas, *Where the Girls Are: Growing Up Female with the Mass Media* (Times Books, 1995).

51. Douglas, *Where the Girls Are*, 226.

52. Paul Wilkes, "Mother Superior to Women's Lib," *New York Times Magazine*, November 29, 1970: 140.

53. Douglas, *Where the Girls Are*, 230.

54. Roth, *Separate Roads to Feminism*, 3.

55. Quoted in Susan Brownmiller, "'Sisterhood Is Powerful,'" *New York Times*, March 15, 1970, https://www.nytimes.com/1970/03/15/archives/sisterhood-is-powerful-a-member-of -the-womens-liberation-movement.html.

56. Koa Beck, *White Feminism: From the Suffragettes to Influencers and Who They Leave Behind* (Atria Books, 2021).

57. Benita Roth, "Second Wave Black Feminism in the African Diaspora: News from New Scholarship," *Agenda* 17, no. 58 (2003): 46–58.

58. Frances M. Beal, "Double Jeopardy: To Be Black and Female," in *Sisterhood Is Powerful: An Anthology of Writings from the Women's Liberation Movement*, ed. Robin Morgan (Random House, 1970).

59. Roth, "Second Wave Black Feminism."

60. Daniel Geary, *Beyond Civil Rights: The Moynihan Report and Its Legacy* (University of Pennsylvania Press, 2015).

61. Ta-Nehisi Coates, "The Black Family in the Age of Mass Incarceration," *Atlantic*, September 14, 2015, https://www.theatlantic.com/magazine/archive/2015/10/the-black-family -in-the-age-of-mass-incarceration/403246/; Ben Spielberg, "Debunking the False Family Structure Narrative," HuffPost, March 20, 2015, https://www.huffpost.com/entry/debunking -the-false-famil_b_6907038.

62. Geary, *Beyond Civil Rights*; Roth, "Second Wave Black Feminism."

63. As noted in the introduction, I follow the Associated Press guidelines for terminology involving demographic groups. The members of this group used *Chicana* to describe themselves, and I follow their lead. See Associated Press, *Associated Press Stylebook: 2022–2024*, 56th ed. (Basic Books, 2022), https://www.apstylebook.com/ap_stylebook/race-related-coverage.

64. Maylei Blackwell, "Contested Histories: Las Hijas de Cuauhtémoc, Chicana Feminisms, and Print Culture in the Chicano Movement, 1968–1973," in *Chicana Feminisms: A Critical Reader*, ed. Gabriela F. Arredondo et al. (Duke University Press, 2003), 59–96.

65. Vicki L. Ruiz and Virginia Sanchez Korrol, eds., "Hijas de Cuauhtémoc (1971–1972)," in *Latinas in the United States: A Historical Encyclopedia*, vol. 2 (Indiana University Press, 2006), 326–27.

66. Maylei Blackwell, *¡Chicana Power! Contested Histories of Feminism in the Chicano Movement* (University of Texas Press, 2016).

67. Brownmiller, "'Sisterhood Is Powerful'"; Rachel Shteir, "Why We Can't Stop Talking about Betty Friedan," *New York Times*, February 4, 2021, https://www.nytimes .com/2021/02/03/us/betty-friedan-feminism-legacy.html.

68. Karla Jay, *Tales of the Lavender Menace*, in *The Stonewall Reader*, ed. New York Public Library (Penguin Books, 2019), 190–93.

69. Rosalyn Baxandall and Linda Gordon, "Second-Wave Feminism," in *A Companion to American Women's History*, ed. Nancy A. Hewitt, 1st ed., Blackwell Companions to American History (Blackwell, 2002); Stephanie Gilmore and Elizabeth Kaminski, "A Part and Apart: Lesbian and Straight Feminist Activists Negotiate Identity in a Second-Wave Organization," *Journal of the History of Sexuality* 16, no. 1 (2007): 95–113, https://doi.org/10.1353/sex.2007.0038.

70. Kennith Shonk, "Daughters of Bilitis," in *American Countercultures: An Encyclopedia of Nonconformists, Alternative Lifestyles, and Radical Ideas in U.S. History*, ed. Gina Misiroglu (Routledge, 2015), 196, https://doi.org/10.4324/9781315706580.

71. Heather Murray, "Free for All Lesbians: Lesbian Cultural Production and Consumption in the United States during the 1970s," *Journal of the History of Sexuality* 16, no. 2 (2007): 251–75.

72. Deborah L. Rhode, "Media Images, Feminist Issues," *Signs: Journal of Women in Culture and Society* 20, no. 3 (Spring 1995): 685.

73. Ian Buchanan, "Third Wave Feminism," in *A Dictionary of Critical Theory* (Oxford University Press, 2010).

74. Julia Jacobs, "Anita Hill's Testimony and Other Key Moments from the Clarence Thomas Hearings," *New York Times*, September 20, 2018, https://www.nytimes.com/2018/09/20/us/politics/anita-hill-testimony-clarence-thomas.html.

75. Roqayah Chamseddine, "Meet the Woman Who Coined the Term 'Third Wave Feminism,'" *Sydney Morning Herald*, March 2, 2018, https://www.smh.com.au/lifestyle/beauty/meet-the-woman-who-coined-the-term-third-wave-feminism-20180302-p4z2mw.html; Sarah Pruitt, "How Anita Hill's Testimony Made America Cringe—and Change," History, February 9, 2021, https://www.history.com/news/anita-hill-confirmation-hearings-impact.

76. Rebecca Walker, "Becoming the Third Wave," *Ms. Magazine*, January–February 1992.

77. Lynne E. Ford, "Third-Wave Feminism," in *Encyclopedia of Women and American Politics*, Facts on File Library of American History (Facts on File, 2007).

78. Arnaud Régnier-Loilier, Henri Leridon, and Fabrice Cahen, "Four Decades of Legalized Contraception in France: An Unfinished Revolution?" *Population Societies* 439, no. 10 (2007): 1–8.

79. National Women's Education Center, "History," accessed July 20, 2022, https://www.nwec.jp/en/about/information/history.html.

80. Sophia Powers, "Contextualising the Indian Women's Movement: Class, Representation and Collaboration," Tate, July 2021, https://www.tate.org.uk/research/in-focus/seven-lives-dream-sheba-chhachhi/contextualising-indian-womens-movement.

CHAPTER 5

1. Michael Baker and Nick Wilson, "New Zealand's Covid Strategy Was One of the World's Most Successful—What Can We Learn from It?" *Guardian*, April 5, 2022, https://www.theguardian.com/world/commentisfree/2022/apr/05/new-zealands-covid-strategy-was-one-of-the-worlds-most-successful-what-can-it-learn-from-it.

2. Amanda Taub, "Why Are Women-Led Nations Doing Better with Covid-19?" *New York Times*, updated August 13, 2020, https://www.nytimes.com/2020/05/15/world/coronavirus-women-leaders.html.

3. Carly Kempler and Barbara Benham, "As Cases Spread across U.S. Last Year, Pattern Emerged Suggesting Link between Governors' Party Affiliation and COVID-19 Case and Death Numbers," Johns Hopkins Bloomberg School of Public Health, March 10, 2021, https://www.jhsph.edu/news/news-releases/2021/as-cases-spread-across-us-last-year-pattern-emerged-suggesting-link-between-governors-party-affiliation-and-covid-19-case-and-death-numbers.html.

4. Sulzhan Bali et al., "Off the Back Burner: Diverse and Gender-Inclusive Decision-Making for COVID-19 Response and Recovery," *BMJ Global Health* 5, no. 5 (May 1, 2020): e002595, https://doi.org/10.1136/bmjgh-2020-002595; Devi Sridhar and Maimuna S. Majumder, "Modelling the Pandemic," *BMJ* 369 (April 21, 2020): m1567, https://doi.org/10.1136/bmj.m1567.

5. Rachel B. Vogelstein and Alexandra Bro, "Women's Power Index," Council on Foreign Relations, March 29, 2021, https://www.cfr.org/article/womens-power-index.

6. Center for American Women and Politics, "Women in Elective Office 2022," https://cawp.rutgers.edu/facts/current-numbers/women-elective-office-2022.

7. Center for American Women and Politics, "Women in Elective Office."

8. Gregory Krieg, "It's Official: Clinton Swamps Trump in Popular Vote," CNN, December 21, 2016, https://www.cnn.com/2016/12/21/politics/donald-trump-hillary-clinton -popular-vote-final-count/index.html.

9. Amy Chozick, "Hillary Clinton's Beijing Speech on Women Resonates 20 Years Later," *New York Times*, September 5, 2015, https://www.nytimes.com/politics/first-draft/2015/09/ 05/20-years-later-hillary-clintons-beijing-speech-on-women-resonates/.

10. Regina G. Lawrence and Melody Rose, *Hillary Clinton's Race for the White House: Gender Politics and the Media on the Campaign Trail* (Lynne Rienner, 2010).

11. Barbara Winslow, *Shirley Chisholm: Catalyst for Change* (Taylor and Francis, 2013).

12. Leonie Huddy and Nayda Terkildsen, "Gender Stereotypes and the Perception of Male and Female Candidates," *American Journal of Political Science* 37, no. 1 (1993): 119–47, https://doi.org/10.2307/2111526.

13. Daphne Joanna Van der Pas and Loes Aaldering, "Gender Differences in Political Media Coverage: A Meta-Analysis," *Journal of Communication* 70, no. 1 (February 1, 2020): 114–43, https://doi.org/10.1093/joc/jqz046; Kelly L. Winfrey and James M. Schnoebelen, "Running as a Woman (or Man): A Review of Research on Political Communicators and Gender Stereotypes," *Review of Communication Research* 7 (2019): 109–38.

14. Kathleen Hall Jamieson, *Beyond the Double Bind: Women and Leadership* (Oxford University Press, 1995).

15. Jamieson, *Beyond the Double Bind*.

16. Meagan Auer et al., "Invoking the Idealized Family to Assess Political Leadership and Legitimacy: News Coverage of Australian and Canadian Premiers," *Feminist Media Studies* 22, no. 2 (February 17, 2022): 338–53, https://doi.org/10.1080/14680777.2020.1790627.

17. Åsa Kroon Lundell and Mats Ekström, "The Complex Visual Gendering of Political Women in the Press," *Journalism Studies* 9, no. 6 (December 1, 2008): 891–910, https://doi .org/10.1080/14616700802227845; Charlotte Templin, "Hillary Clinton as Threat to Gender Norms: Cartoon Images of the First Lady," *Journal of Communication Inquiry* 23, no. 1 (January 1, 1999): 20–36, https://doi.org/10.1177/0196859999023001002.

18. Mary Angela Bock et al., "The Faces of Local TV News in America: Youth, Whiteness, and Gender Disparities in Station Publicity Photos," *Feminist Media Studies* 18, no. 3 (May 4, 2018): 440–57, https://doi.org/10.1080/14680777.2017.1415950.

19. Michelle Ruiz, "AOC'S Next Four Years," *Vanity Fair*, December 28, 2020, https:// www.vanityfair.com/news/2020/10/becoming-aoc-cover-story-2020.

20. Katie Glueck, "Ocasio-Cortez Says She Is a Sexual Assault Survivor," *New York Times*, February 2, 2021, https://www.nytimes.com/2021/02/01/nyregion/aoc-sexual-assault-abuse .html.

21. Liz Watts, "AP's First Female Reporters," *Journalism History* 39, no. 1 (April 1, 2013): 15–28, https://doi.org/10.1080/00947679.2013.12062897.

22. Ruby A. Black, interview, 1984, Ruby A. Black Papers, Manuscript Division, Library of Congress, 30.

23. Gil Klein, "NPC in History: Women's National Press Club Centennial," National Press Club, March 3, 2019, https://www.press.org/newsroom/npc-history-womens-national-press -club-centennial.

24. Maurine Beasley, "The Women's National Press Club: Case Study in Professional Aspirations," *Journalism History* 15, no. 4 (Winter 1988): 112–21; National Press Club, "History of the National Press Club," accessed May 18, 2022, https://www.press.org/npc-history-facts.

25. United Press International, "Bartender 'Welcomes' Women in National Press Club," *Santa Maria Times*, January 16, 1971.

26. Melanie McFarland, "'On the Trail' Spotlights CNN's Women Reporters and Prompts Examination of Campaign Coverage Bias," Salon, August 6, 2020, https://www.salon.com/2020/08/06/on-the-trail-review-hbo-max-cnn-2020-primaries/; Jessie Tu, "Top US News Networks Select Female Journalists to Lead White House Coverage," Women's Agenda, January 25, 2021, https://womensagenda.com.au/latest/top-us-news-networks-foregrounding-female-journalists-in-the-white-house/; Women's Media Center, *The Status of Women in the Media in 2017* (Women's Media Center, 2017).

27. Paul Lester, *Visual Communication: Images with Messages*, 5th ed. (Wadsworth Cengage Learning, 2010).

28. Chris Peters and Stuart Allan, "Weaponizing Memes: The Journalistic Mediation of Visual Politicization," *Digital Journalism* 10, no. 2 (February 7, 2022): 217–29, https://doi.org/10.1080/21670811.2021.1903958.

29. Lauren Alex O'Hagan, "Contesting Women's Right to Vote: Anti-Suffrage Postcards in Edwardian Britain," *Visual Culture in Britain* 21, no. 3 (September 1, 2020): 330–62, https://doi.org/10.1080/14714787.2020.1827971.

30. Templin, "Hillary Clinton as Threat."

31. Diana B. Carlin and Kelly L. Winfrey, "Have You Come a Long Way, Baby? Hillary Clinton, Sarah Palin, and Sexism in 2008 Campaign Coverage," *Communication Studies* 60, no. 4 (August 10, 2009): 326–43, https://doi.org/10.1080/10510970903109904; Jessica Ritchie, "Creating a Monster," *Feminist Media Studies* 13, no. 1 (February 1, 2013): 102–19, https://doi.org/10.1080/14680777.2011.647973.

32. Carlin and Winfrey, "Have You Come a Long Way."

33. Giorgia Aiello and Katy Parry, *Visual Communication: Understanding Images in Media Culture* (Sage, 2019).

34. Danny Hayes, Jennifer L. Lawless, and Gail Baitinger, "Who Cares What They Wear? Media, Gender, and the Influence of Candidate Appearance," *Social Science Quarterly* 95, no. 5 (2014): 1194–1212, https://doi.org/10.1111/ssqu.12113; Stewart J. H. McCann, "Height, Societal Threat, and the Victory Margin in Presidential Elections (1824–1992)," *Psychological Reports* 88, no. 3 (2001): 741–42, https://doi.org/10.2466/pr0.2001.88.3.741.

35. Alice H. Eagly et al., "What Is Beautiful Is Good, but . . . : A Meta-Analytic Review of Research on the Physical Attractiveness Stereotype," *Psychological Bulletin* 110, no. 1 (1991): 109–28, https://doi.org/10.1037/0033-2909.110.1.109.

36. Carl L. Palmer and Rolfe D. Peterson, "Halo Effects and the Attractiveness Premium in Perceptions of Political Expertise," *American Politics Research* 44, no. 2 (March 1, 2016): 353–82, https://doi.org/10.1177/1532673X15600517.

37. Carol K. Sigelman et al., "Gender, Physical Attractiveness, and Electability: An Experimental Investigation of Voter Biases," *Journal of Applied Social Psychology* 16, no. 3 (1986): 229–48, https://doi.org/10.1111/j.1559-1816.1986.tb01137.x.

38. Yiqin Alicia Shen and Yuichi Shoda, "How Candidates' Age and Gender Predict Voter Preference in a Hypothetical Election," *Psychological Science* 32, no. 6 (June 1, 2021): 934–43, https://doi.org/10.1177/0956797620977518.

39. Margaret Hunter, "The Persistent Problem of Colorism: Skin Tone, Status, and Inequality," *Sociology Compass* 1, no. 1 (2007): 237–54, https://doi.org/10.1111/j.1751-9020.2007.00006.x.

40. George Lakoff, *The All New Don't Think of an Elephant! Know Your Values and Frame the Debate* (Chelsea Green, 2014).

41. Thomas B. Edsall, "How You Feel about Gender Roles Can Tell Us How You'll Vote," *New York Times*, July 20, 2022, https://www.nytimes.com/2022/07/20/opinion/gender-gap-partisanship-politics.html.

42. Marion Löffler, Russell Luyt, and Kathleen Starck, "Political Masculinities and Populism," *NORMA: International Journal for Masculinity Studies* 15, no. 1 (January 2, 2020): 1–9, https://doi.org/10.1080/18902138.2020.1721154; Angela Smith and Michael Higgins, "Tough Guys and Little Rocket Men: @Realdonaldtrump's Twitter Feed and the Normalisation of Banal Masculinity," *Social Semiotics* 30, no. 4 (August 7, 2020): 547–62, https://doi .org/10.1080/10350330.2020.1763657.

43. Douglas Martin, "Yvonne Brill, a Pioneering Rocket Scientist, Dies at 88," *New York Times*, March 30, 2013, https://www.nytimes.com/2013/03/31/science/space/yvonne-brill -rocket-scientist-dies-at-88.html; Margaret Sullivan, "Gender Questions Arise in Obituary of Rocket Scientist and Her Beef Stroganoff," *Public Editor's Journal* (blog), April 1, 2013, https://publiceditor.blogs.nytimes.com/2013/04/01/gender-questions-arise-in-obituary-of -rocket-scientist-and-her-beef-stroganoff/.

44. Sullivan, "Gender Questions."

45. Carol Gilligan, "Moral Injury and the Ethic of Care: Reframing the Conversation about Differences," *Journal of Social Philosophy* 45, no. 1 (January 1, 2014): 89–106, https://doi.org/ 10.1111/josp.12050.

46. Meredith Conroy et al., "From Ferraro to Palin: Sexism in Coverage of Vice Presidential Candidates in Old and New Media," *Politics, Groups, and Identities* 3, no. 4 (October 2, 2015): 573–91, https://doi.org/10.1080/21565503.2015.1050412; Danny Hayes and Jennifer L. Lawless, "A Non-Gendered Lens? Media, Voters, and Female Candidates in Contemporary Congressional Elections," *Perspectives on Politics* 13, no. 1 (March 2015): 95–118, https://doi .org/10.1017/S1537592714003156; Linda Trimble et al., "Politicizing Bodies: Hegemonic Masculinity, Heteronormativity, and Racism in News Representations of Canadian Political Party Leadership Candidates," *Women's Studies in Communication* 38, no. 3 (July 3, 2015): 314–30, https://doi.org/10.1080/07491409.2015.1062836.

47. Rosalie Maggio, "Writing Guidelines," Women's Media Center, accessed July 21, 2022, https://womensmediacenter.com/unspinning-the-spin/new-writing-guidelines.

48. Associate Press, *The Associated Press Stylebook: 2022–2024*, 56th ed. (Basic Books, 2022).

49. Adam Johnson, "Copspeak: 7 Ways Journalists Use Police Jargon to Obscure the Truth," FAIR, July 11, 2016, https://fair.org/home/copspeak-7-ways-journalists-use-police -jargon-to-obscure-the-truth/.

CHAPTER 6

1. Philip Mansel, *Dressed to Rule: Royal and Court Costume from Louis XIV to Elizabeth II* (Yale University Press, 2005); Richard Wilkinson, *Louis XIV*, 2nd ed. (Routledge, 2017), https://doi.org/10.4324/9781315160795.

2. Jo Barraclough Paoletti, *Pink and Blue: Telling the Boys from the Girls in America* (Indiana University Press, 2012).

3. Samantha Allen, "Bigots Lose It over Target's Boy Toy Policy," *Daily Beast*, August 14, 2015, https://www.thedailybeast.com/articles/2015/08/14/bigots-lose-it-over-target-s-boy-toy-policy.

4. Jack Dutton, "Gender Reveal Parties Have Already Seen Four Deaths So Far This Year," *Newsweek*, April 1, 2021, https://www.newsweek.com/gender-reveal-parties-four-dead-1580477.

5. Antonia Noori Farzan, "A Border Patrol Agent Threw a Gender-Reveal Party. He Ended Up Starting a 47,000-Acre Wildfire," *Washington Post*, October 1, 2018, https://www.washington post.com/news/morning-mix/wp/2018/10/01/a-border-patrol-agent-threw-a-gender-reveal -party-he-ended-up-starting-a-47000-acre-wildfire/.

6. Jelle Versieren, "Hegemony," in *The Sage International Encyclopedia of Mass Media and Society*, ed. Debra L. Merskin, vol. 1 (Sage, 2020), 738.

7. Fabio de Nardis, "Gramsci, Antonio (1891–1937)," in *The Blackwell Encyclopedia of Sociology*, ed. George Ritzer and Chris Rojek (John Wiley and Sons, November 19, 2019).

8. R. W. Connell and James W. Messerschmidt, "Hegemonic Masculinity: Rethinking the Concept," *Gender and Society* 19, no. 6 (December 1, 2005): 832, https://doi.org/10.1177/0891243205278639.

9. Randolph M. Feezell, "Philosophy of Sport," *Teaching Philosophy* 15, no. 4 (November 1, 1992): 382–85, https://doi.org/10.5840/teachphil199215461; Vince Lombardi Jr., *What It Takes to Be Number #1: Vince Lombardi on Leadership* (McGraw-Hill, 2001).

10. Ryan Neville-Shepard and Meredith Neville-Shepard, "The Pornified Presidency: Hyper-Masculinity and the Pornographic Style in U.S. Political Rhetoric," *Feminist Media Studies* 21, no. 7 (June 27, 2020): 1–16, https://doi.org/10.1080/14680777.2020.1786429.

11. Arnaldo Testi, "The Gender of Reform Politics: Theodore Roosevelt and the Culture of Masculinity," *Journal of American History* 81, no. 4 (1995): 1509–33, https://doi.org/10.2307/2081647.

12. Doris Kearns Goodwin, *The Bully Pulpit: Theodore Roosevelt, William Howard Taft, and the Golden Age of Journalism* (Simon and Schuster, 2013); Mark Neuzil, "Hearst, Roosevelt, and the Muckrake Speech of 1906: A New Perspective," *Journalism and Mass Communication Quarterly* 73, no. 1 (March 1, 1996): 29–39, https://doi.org/10.1177/107769909607300104.

13. Goodwin, *Bully Pulpit*.

14. Stephen Ashton, "Theodore Roosevelt: A Letter to Boys on Manhood," *Trail Life* (blog), June 11, 2019, https://blog.traillifeusa.com/manhood-a-letter-to-boys-from-theodore-roosevelt.

15. Testi, "Gender of Reform Politics."

16. Nick Trujillo, "Hegemonic Masculinity on the Mound: Media Representations of Nolan Ryan and American Sports Culture," *Critical Studies in Mass Communication* 8, no. 3 (September 1, 1991): 290–308, https://doi.org/10.1080/15295039109366799.

17. Christine Agius, Annika Bergman Rosamond, and Catarina Kinnvall, "Populism, Ontological Insecurity and Gendered Nationalism: Masculinity, Climate Denial and Covid-19," *Politics, Religion and Ideology* 21, no. 4 (October 1, 2020): 432–50, https://doi.org/10.1080/21567689.2020.1851871; Anastasia Prokos and Irene Padavic, "'There Oughtta Be a Law against Bitches': Masculinity Lessons in Police Academy Training," *Gender, Work and Organization* 9, no. 4 (2002): 439–59, https://doi.org/10.1111/1468-0432.00168.

18. Martin Hultman, Anna Björk, and Tamya Viinikka, "The Far Right and Climate Change Denial: Denouncing Environmental Challenges via Anti-Establishment Rhetoric, Marketing of Doubts, Industrial/Breadwinner Masculinities Enactments and Ethno-Nationalism," in *The Far Right and the Environment* (Routledge, 2019).

19. Jackson Katz, *Macho Paradox: Why Some Men Hurt Women and How All Men Can Help* (Sourcebooks, 2006).

20. Levi Gahman, "Gun Rites: Hegemonic Masculinity and Neoliberal Ideology in Rural Kansas," *Gender, Place and Culture* 22, no. 9 (October 21, 2015): 1203–19, https://doi.org/10.1080/0966369X.2014.970137.

21. Meagan Flynn, "In Ad, Lawmaker Vows to Carry Her Glock around D.C. and on Hill," *Washington Post*, January 4, 2021, https://www.washingtonpost.com/local/legal-issues/boebert-capitol-guns/2021/01/04/a59f70f8-4e9d-11eb-83e3-322644d82356_story.html.

22. Lawrence A. Greenfield and Tracy L. Snell, *Women Offenders*, Bureau of Justice Statistics Special Report (US Department of Justice, October 3, 2000).

23. Greenfield and Snell, *Women Offenders*.

24. Shannon Catalano et al., *Female Victims of Violence* (US Department of Justice, October 23, 2009).

25. Shanto Iyengar, *Is Anyone Responsible? How Television Frames Political Issues* (University of Chicago Press, 1994).

26. Shanto Iyengar, "Framing Responsibility for Political Issues," *Annals of the American Academy of Political and Sociall Science*, no. 546 (July 1996): 59–70.

27. Kellie Cowan, "'Grabbed Me with His Nail': Gabby Petito Describes Utah Fight with Brian Laundrie in Newly-Released Bodycam," FOX 13 News, Tampa Bay, October 1, 2021, https://www.fox13news.com/news/grabbed-me-with-his-nail-utah-police-release-second-body cam-video-in-gabby-petito-case; Eduardo Medina, "Slain Woman Had Begged Apartment Complex to Change Locks, Lawsuit Claims," *New York Times*, November 26, 2021, https://www.nytimes.com/2021/11/26/us/nj-lawsuit-apartment-locks.html.

28. Alison Anderson, "Media, Politics and Climate Change: Towards a New Research Agenda," *Sociology Compass* 3, no. 2 (2009): 166–82, https://doi.org/10.1111/j.1751-9020.2008.00188.x.

29. Christina Maxouri, "A Timeline of 22-Year-Old Gabby Petito's Case," CNN, January 21, 2022, https://www.cnn.com/2021/09/16/us/gabby-petito-timeline-missing-case/index.html.

30. Scott Gleeson, "Report Finds Utah Police Made Mistakes in Meeting with Gabby Petito, Brian Laundrie," *USA Today*, January 13, 2022, https://www.usatoday.com/story/news/nation/2022/01/13/gabby-petito-report-police-errors-missing-details/9197558002/.

31. Helen Rosner, "The Long American History of 'Missing White Woman Syndrome,'" *New Yorker*, October 8, 2021, https://www.newyorker.com/news/q-and-a/the-long-american-history-of-missing-white-woman-syndrome.

32. Michael Tomasky, "Mitt Romney: A Candidate with a Serious Wimp Problem," *Newsweek*, July 29, 2012, https://www.newsweek.com/mitt-romney-candidate-serious-wimp-problem-65657.

33. Daniel Henninger, "Henninger: Mitt Romney's Summer Vacation; If That Jet-Ski Ride Was the Candidates' Call, His Campaign Is Headed for a Dukakis-like Catastrophe," *Wall Street Journal*, July 11, 2012.

34. Michael Tomasky, "A Mouse in the White House?" *Newsweek*, August 6, 2021.

35. Dana Milbank, "Why Tucker Carlson Wants Men to Aim Lasers at Their Private Parts," *Washington Post*, April 18, 2022, https://www.washingtonpost.com/opinions/2022/04/18/tucker-carlson-testicle-tanning-masculinity-wrong/.

36. Josh Hawley, *Manhood: The Masculine Virtues America Needs* (Regnery Publishing, 2023).

37. Michael S. Kimmel, "Men's Responses to Feminism at the Turn of the Century," *Gender and Society* 1, no. 3 (September 1, 1987): 261–83, https://doi.org/10.1177/08912438700 1003003.

38. Mariah Blake, "Mad Men: Inside the Men's Rights Movement—and the Army of Misogynists and Trolls It Spawned," *Mother Jones*, February 2015, https://www.motherjones.com/politics/2015/01/warren-farrell-mens-rights-movement-feminism-misogyny-trolls/.

39. Michael Schwalbe, "Mythopoetic Movement," in *International Encyclopedia of Men and Masculinities*, ed. Michael Flood et al. (Routledge, 2007), 450–53, https://doi.org/10.4324/9780203413067.

40. Robert Bly, *Iron John: A Book about Men* (Hachette Books, 2015).

41. Nellie Bowles, "Jordan Peterson, Custodian of the Patriarchy," *New York Times*, May 18, 2018, https://www.nytimes.com/2018/05/18/style/jordan-peterson-12-rules-for-life.html.

42. Nicole M. Fortin, Philip Oreopoulos, and Shelley Phipps, "Leaving Boys Behind: Gender Disparities in High Academic Achievement," *Journal of Human Resources* 50, no. 3 (July 1, 2015): 549–79, https://doi.org/10.3368/jhr.50.3.549.

43. Steven Mintz, "The Other Gender Gap," *Inside Higher Ed*, August 4, 2019, https://www.insidehighered.com/blogs/higher-ed-gamma/other-gender-gap.

44. Fortin, Oreopoulos, and Phipps, "Leaving Boys Behind"; Gary N. Marks, "Accounting for the Gender Gaps in Student Performance in Reading and Mathematics: Evidence from 31 Countries," *Oxford Review of Education* 34, no. 1 (February 1, 2008): 89–109, https://doi.org/10.1080/03054980701565279.

45. National Center for Education Statistics, "Table 219.70. Percentage of High School Dropouts among Persons 16 to 24 Years Old (Status Dropout Rate), by Sex and Race/Ethnicity: Selected Years, 1960 through 2016," Digest of Education Statistics, January 2021, https://nces.ed.gov/programs/digest/d17/tables/dt17_219.70.asp; Ortal Slobodin and Michael Davidovitch, "Gender Differences in Objective and Subjective Measures of ADHD among Clinic-Referred Children," *Frontiers in Human Neuroscience* 13 (2019), https://doi.org/10.3389/fnhum.2019.00441.

46. Michael Gurian, *The Minds of Boys: Saving Our Sons from Falling behind in School and Life*, 1st ed. (Jossey-Bass, 2005).

47. Hanna Rosin, *The End of Men: And the Rise of Women* (Penguin, 2012).

48. Risa Gelles-Watnick, "For Valentine's Day, 5 Facts about Single Americans," Pew Research Center, February 8, 2023, https://www.pewresearch.org/fact-tank/2023/02/08/for-valentines-day-5-facts-about-single-americans/.

49. Joe Burns and Paul Bracey, "Boys' Underachievement: Issues, Challenges and Possible Ways Forward," *Westminster Studies in Education* 24, no. 2 (January 2001): 155–66, https://doi.org/10.1080/0140672010240206.

50. Michael Kimmel, *Guyland* (HarperCollins, 2018).

51. US Census Bureau, "Male Nurses Becoming More Commonplace, Census Bureau Reports," February 25, 2013, https://www.census.gov/newsroom/archives/2013-pr/cb13-32.html.

52. Nicholas Eberstadt, *Men without Work: America's Invisible Crisis*, 1st ed. (Templeton Press, 2016); Ylan Q. Mui, "Why America's Men Aren't Working," *Washington Post*, June 20, 2016, https://www.washingtonpost.com/news/wonk/wp/2016/06/20/why-americas-men-arent-working/.

53. Carol Pinto Graham and Sergio Pinto, "Men without Work: A Global Well-Being and Ill-Being Comparison," IZA World of Labor, October 2, 2019, https://doi.org/10.15185/izawol.464.

54. Susan Scutti, "Males May Be More Likely to Become Addicted to Gaming, Say Researchers," CNN, November 28, 2018, https://www.cnn.com/2018/11/28/health/male-brain-internet-gaming-disorder/index.html.

55. Mark Aguiar et al., *Leisure Luxuries and the Labor Supply of Young Men* (National Bureau of Economic Research, July 3, 2017), https://doi.org/10.3386/w23552.

56. Danielle Paquette, "The Stunning Prevalence of Painkiller Use among Unemployed Men," *Washington Post*, September 7, 2017, https://www.washingtonpost.com/news/wonk/wp/2017/09/07/the-stunning-prevalence-of-painkiller-use-among-unemployed-men/.

57. Lukas Eggenberger et al., "Men's Psychotherapy Use, Male Role Norms, and Male-Typical Depression Symptoms: Examining 716 Men and Women Experiencing Psychological Distress," *Behavioral Sciences* 11, no. 6 (June 2021): 83, https://doi.org/10.3390/bs11060083.

58. Diane C. Denning et al., "Method Choice, Intent, and Gender in Completed Suicide," *Suicide and Life-Threatening Behavior* 30, no. 3 (Fall 2000): 282–88.

59. CDC, "From the CDC-Leading Causes of Death-Males All Races and Origins 2016," Centers for Disease Control and Prevention, September 27, 2019, https://www.cdc.gov/heal thequity/lcod/men/2016/all-races-origins/index.htm.

60. Jay Clarkson, "'Everyday Joe' versus 'Pissy, Bitchy, Queens': Gay Masculinity on StraightActing.Com," *Journal of Men's Studies* 14, no. 2 (March 1, 2007): 191–207, https://doi.org/10.3149/jms.1402.191.

61. Y. Joel Wong et al., "Asian American Male College Students' Perceptions of People's Stereotypes about Asian American Men," *Psychology of Men and Masculinity* 13, no. 1 (2012): 75–88, https://doi.org/10.1037/a0022800.

62. Megan Garber, "Annie Squall: Has the Famous Photog Blown Her Cover?" *Columbia Journalism Review*, March 28, 2008, https://www.cjr.org/behind_the_news/annie_squall.php.

63. Harold W. Neighbors et al., "Race, Ethnicity, and the Use of Services for Mental Disorders: Results from the National Survey of American Life," *Archives of General Psychiatry* 64, no. 4 (April 1, 2007): 485–94, https://doi.org/10.1001/archpsyc.64.4.485; Earlise Ward and Maigenete Mengesha, "Depression in African American Men: A Review of What We Know and Where We Need to Go from Here," *American Journal of Orthopsychiatry* 83, nos. 2–3 (2013): 386–97, https://doi.org/10.1111/ajop.12015.

64. Mary Angela Bock, *Seeing Justice: Witnessing, Crime and Punishment in Visual Media* (Oxford University Press, 2021); Allissa V. Richardson, "Bearing Witness while Black," *Digital Journalism* 5, no. 6 (July 3, 2017): 673–98, https://doi.org/10.1080/21670811.2016.1193818.

65. Bock, *Seeing Justice*; Amina Dunn, "As the U.S. Copes with Multiple Crises, Partisans Disagree Sharply on Severity of Problems Facing the Nation," Pew Research Center, July 14, 2020, https://www.pewresearch.org/fact-tank/2020/07/14/as-the-u-s-copes-with-multiple-crises-partisans-disagree-sharply-on-severity-of-problems-facing-the-nation/.

66. Eduardo Bonilla-Silva, *Racism without Racists: Color-Blind Racism and the Persistence of Racial Inequality in the United States* (Rowman and Littlefield, 2006).

67. Aasha M. Abdill, *Fathering from the Margins: An Intimate Examination of Black Fatherhood* (Columbia University Press, 2018); Ta-Nehisi Coates, "The Black Family in the Age of Mass Incarceration," *Atlantic*, September 14, 2015, https://www.theatlantic.com/magazine/archive/2015/10/the-black-family-in-the-age-of-mass-incarceration/403246/.

68. Coates, "Black Family."

69. Jo Jones and William D. Mosher, *Fathers' Involvement with Their Children: United States, 2006–2010*, National Health Statistics Report (US Department of Health and Human Services, Centers for Disease Control and Prevention, December 20, 2013).

70. bell hooks, *The Will to Change: Men, Masculinity, and Love* (Simon and Schuster, 2004), 32.

CHAPTER 7

1. Kathleen C. Basile et al., *The National Intimate Partner and Sexual Violence Survey: 2016/2017 Report on Sexual Violence* (National Center for Injury Prevention and Control Centers for Disease Control and Prevention, June 2022), https://stacks.cdc.gov/view/cdc/60893.

2. Basile et al., *National Intimate Partner.*

3. Donna St. George, "Teen Girls 'Engulfed' in Violence and Trauma, CDC Finds," *Washington Post*, February 14, 2023, https://www.washingtonpost.com/education/2023/02/13/teen-girls-violence-trauma-pandemic-cdc/.

4. Matthew Kimble et al., "Risk of Unwanted Sex for College Women: Evidence for a Red Zone," *Journal of American College Health* 57, no. 3 (November 1, 2008): 331–38, https://doi .org/10.3200/JACH.57.3.331-338.

5. David Cantor et al., *Report on the AAU Campus Climate Survey on Sexual Assault and Misconduct* (American Association of Universities, 2020).

6. Moriah Balinget and Nick Anderson, "Sweeping Title IX Changes Would Shield Trans Students, Abuse Survivors," *Washington Post*, June 23, 2022, https://www.washingtonpost .com/education/2022/06/23/title-ix-biden-trans-sexual-assault-college/.

7. Valerie J. Nelson, "Crusader for Increased Campus Security after Daughter's Murder," *Los Angeles Times*, January 12, 2008, https://www.latimes.com/archives/la-xpm-2008-jan-12 -me-clery12-story.html; RAINN, "Clery Act," accessed January 21, 2023, https://www.rainn .org/articles/clery-act.

8. Jeremy Bauer-Wolf, "Mattress Protest and Its Aftermath," *Inside Higher Ed*, July 24, 2017, https://www.insidehighered.com/news/2017/07/24/media-circus-surrounding-mattress -girl-case-changed-conversation-sexual-assault.

9. Cathy Young, "Columbia Student: I Didn't Rape Her," *Daily Beast*, February 3, 2015, https://www.thedailybeast.com/articles/2015/02/03/columbia-student-i-didn-t-rape-her.

10. Bauer-Wolf, "Mattress Protest."

11. Robin Field, "Rape Culture," in *Encyclopedia of Rape*, ed. Merrill D. Smith (Greenwood Press, 2004), 174–75.

12. Andrea Dworkin, *Our Blood: Prophecies and Discourses on Sexual Politics* (Harper and Row, 1976), 58.

13. Wilma King, "'Prematurely Knowing of Evil Things': The Sexual Abuse of African American Girls and Young Women in Slavery and Freedom," *Journal of African American History* 99, no. 3 (July 2014): 173–96, https://doi.org/10.5323/jafriamerhist.99.3.0173.

14. Susan Brownmiller, *Against Our Will: Men, Women and Rape* (Open Road Media, 2013).

15. Jennifer A. Bennice and Patricia A. Resick, "Marital Rape: History, Research, and Practice," *Trauma, Violence, and Abuse* 4, no. 3 (July 1, 2003): 228–46, https://doi.org/10.1177/ 1524838003004003003.

16. Pagan Kennedy, "There Are Many Man-Made Objects. The Rape Kit Is Not One of Them," *New York Times*, June 17, 2020, https://www.nytimes.com/interactive/2020/06/17/ opinion/rape-kit-history.html.

17. Charlie Huntington, Alan D. Berkowitz, and Lindsay M. Orchowski, "False Accusations of Sexual Assault: Prevalence, Misperceptions, and Implications for Prevention Work with Men and Boys," chap. 16 in *Engaging Boys and Men in Sexual Assault Prevention*, ed. Lindsay M. Orchowski and Alan D. Berkowitz (Academic Press, 2022), 379–99, https://doi.org/10.1016/ B978-0-12-819202-3.00005-5.

18. Kennedy, "Many Man-Made Objects."

19. Bryce Huffman, "Hundreds Convicted after Detroit Processes Thousands of Back-logged Rape Kits," BridgeDetroit, September 8, 2021, http://www.bridgedetroit.com/hundreds -convicted-after-detroit-processes-thousands-of-backlogged-rape-kits/.

20. Michelle Taylor, "Rape Kit Backlog Act Passes Senate 3 Months after Lapsing," *Forensic*, December 18, 2019, http://www.forensicmag.com/558960-Rape-Ki-Backlog-Act-Passes-Senate -3-Months-after-Lapsing/.

21. "Our Story," Joyful Heart Foundation, accessed September 1, 2022, https://www.joyful heartfoundation.org/about-us/our-story.

22. Tom Jackman, "Advocates Implore Congress to Reauthorize Funds for Backlogged DNA Rape Kits before Sept. 30 Expiration," *Washington Post*, September 7, 2019, https://www

.washingtonpost.com/crime-law/2019/09/07/advocates-implore-congress-reauthorize-funds-backlogged-dna-rape-kits-before-sept-expiration/.

23. Annette Gordon-Reed, *The Hemingses of Monticello: An American Family* (W. W. Norton, 2009).

24. Brenda Stevenson, "Founding Father's Folly?" *Washington Post*, June 15, 1997, https://www.washingtonpost.com/archive/entertainment/books/1997/06/15/founding-fathers-folly/0e0834c6-fb10-43c4-a29d-41e04a48dd78/.

25. Drew Gilpin Faust, "Clutching the Chains That Bind: Margaret Mitchell and *Gone with the Wind*," *Southern Cultures* 5, no. 1 (1999): 5–20, https://doi.org/10.1353/scu.1999.0032.

26. Nickie D. Phillips, *Beyond Blurred Lines: Rape Culture in Popular Media* (Rowman and Littlefield, 2016).

27. RAINN, "ABC's Most Popular TV Shows Tackle Sexual Violence, Feature RAINN's Hotline," Rape, Abuse, and Incest National Network, November 8, 2015, https://www.rainn.org/news/abcs-most-popular-tv-shows-tackle-sexual-violence-feature-rainn%E2%80%99s-hotline.

28. Jada Yuan, "'Orange Is the New Black' Is the Only TV Show That Understands Rape," *Vulture*, July 6, 2015, https://www.vulture.com/2015/07/orange-is-the-new-black-is-the-only-tv-show-that-understands-rape.html.

29. Matthew A. Baum, Dara Kay Cohen, and Yuri M. Zhukov, "Does Rape Culture Predict Rape? Evidence from U.S. Newspapers, 2000–2013," *Quarterly Journal of Political Science* 13, no. 3 (August 29, 2018): 263–89, https://doi.org/10.1561/100.00016124.

30. Geneva Overholser, "American Shame: The Stigma of Rape," *Des Moines Register*, July 11, 1990.

31. Nancy Ziegenmeyer and Larkin Warren, *Taking Back My Life* (HarperCollins, 1993).

32. Judy Mann, "Women's Empowerment Wins a Pulitzer Prize," *Washington Post*, April 12, 1991, https://www.washingtonpost.com/archive/local/1991/04/12/womens-empowerment-wins-a-pulitzer-prize/e0da6adb-dc09-4c8f-8cb7-26af03d01131/.

33. Sabrina Rubin Erderly, "A Rape on Campus," *Rolling Stone*, November 19, 2014.

34. Eriq Gardner, "*Rolling Stone* Settles Last Remaining Lawsuit over UVA Rape Story," *Hollywood Reporter*, December 21, 2017, https://www.hollywoodreporter.com/business/business-news/rolling-stone-settles-last-remaining-lawsuit-uva-rape-story-1069880/.

35. Sheila Coronel, Steve Coll, and Derek Kravitz, "*Rolling Stone* and UVA: The Columbia University Graduate School of Journalism Report," *Rolling Stone*, April 5, 2015, https://www.rollingstone.com/culture/culture-news/rolling-stone-and-uva-the-columbia-university-graduate-school-of-journalism-report-44930/#ixzz3WWvx3vYs.

36. Coronel, Coll, and Kravitz, "*Rolling Stone* and UVA."

37. *Jacobellis v. Ohio*, 378 U.S. 184 (1964), https://supreme.justia.com/cases/federal/us/378/184/.

38. Neil Malamuth, "Pornography," in *Encyclopedia of Social Psychology*, ed. Roy F. Baumeister and Kathleen D. Vohs, vol. 2 (Sage, 2007), 678–80.

39. Marie-Ève Daspe et al., "When Pornography Use Feels Out of Control: The Moderation Effect of Relationship and Sexual Satisfaction," *Journal of Sex and Marital Therapy* 44, no. 4 (May 19, 2018): 343–53, https://doi.org/10.1080/0092623X.2017.1405301.

40. Hans Maes, "Drawing the Line: Art versus Pornography," *Philosophy Compass* 6, no. 6 (2011): 385–97, https://doi.org/10.1111/j.1747-9991.2011.00403.x.

41. Robert Jensen, "Stories of a Rape Culture: Pornography as Propaganda," in *Big Porn Inc: Exposing the Harms of the Global Pornography Industry*, ed. Melinda Tankard Reist and Abigail Bray (Spinfex, 2011), 27.

42. Kathleen Ann Ruane, "Obscenity, Child Pornography, and Indecency: Brief Background and Recent Developments," chap. 3 in *The First Amendment: Select Issues*, ed. Rhonda L. Ferro (Nova Science, 2010), 65–71.

43. Andrea Dworkin, "Pornography Is a Civil Rights Issue for Women," *University of Michigan Journal of Law Reform 55* 21, nos. 1–2 (1988): 15.

44. Kristen L. Cole, "Pornography, Censorship, and Public Sex: Exploring Feminist and Queer Perspectives of (Public) Pornography through the Case of Pornotopia," *Porn Studies* 1, no. 3 (July 3, 2014): 227–41, https://doi.org/10.1080/23268743.2014.927708.

45. David L. Paletz, "Pornography, Politics, and the Press: The U.S. Attorney General's Commission on Pornography," *Journal of Communication* 38, no. 2 (1988): 122–36, https://doi.org/10.1111/j.1460-2466.1988.tb02052.x.

46. Alan M. Dershowitz, "Americans Don't Need Censorship Czar," *Albuquerque Journal*, January 29, 1986.

47. Paul J. Wright, Bryant Paul, and Debby Herbenick, "Preliminary Insights from a U.S. Probability Sample on Adolescents' Pornography Exposure, Media Psychology, and Sexual Aggression," *Journal of Health Communication* 26, no. 1 (January 2, 2021): 39–46, https://doi.org/10.1080/10810730.2021.1887980.

48. Ana J. Bridges and Patricia J. Morokoff, "Sexual Media Use and Relational Satisfaction in Heterosexual Couples," *Personal Relationships* 18, no. 4 (2011): 562–85, https://doi.org/10.1111/j.1475-6811.2010.01328.x.

49. Brad Stone, "An E-Commerce Empire, from Porn to Puppies," *New York Times*, May 18, 2008, https://www.nytimes.com/2008/05/18/technology/18gordo.html.

50. Shira Tarrant, *The Pornography Industry: What Everyone Needs to Know* (Oxford University Press, 2016).

51. Gillian Friedman, "Jobless, Selling Nudes Online and Still Struggling," *New York Times*, January 13, 2021, https://www.nytimes.com/2021/01/13/business/onlyfans-pandemic-users.html.

52. Tarrant, *Pornography Industry*.

53. Brian Y. Park et al., "Is Internet Pornography Causing Sexual Dysfunctions? A Review with Clinical Reports," *Behavioral Sciences* 6, no. 3 (September 2016): 17, https://doi.org/10.3390/bs6030017.

54. Park et al., "Internet Pornography."

55. Gail Dines, "The White Man's Burden: Gonzo Pornography and the Construction of Black Masculinity," *Yale Journal of Law and Feminism* 18, no. 1 (January 13, 2016), https://openyls.law.yale.edu/handle/20.500.13051/6940; Niki Fritz et al., "Worse than Objects: The Depiction of Black Women and Men and Their Sexual Relationship in Pornography," *Gender Issues* 38, no. 1 (March 1, 2021): 100–120, https://doi.org/10.1007/s12147-020-09255-2.

56. Deborah Willis and Carla Williams, *The Black Female Body: A Photographic History* (Temple University Press, 2002).

57. John R. Burger, *One-Handed Histories: The Eroto-Politics of Gay Male Video Pornography* (Routledge, 2020), https://doi.org/10.4324/9781315863733.

58. Shaka McGlotten, "Pornography: Gay and Lesbian," in *Encyclopedia of Gender in Media*, ed. Mary E. Kosut (Sage, 2012), 275–76.

59. Alvin Cooper et al., "Sexuality on the Internet: From Sexual Exploration to Pathological Expression," *Professional Psychology: Research and Practice* 30, no. 2 (1999): 154–64, https://doi.org/10.1037/0735-7028.30.2.154.

60. Rubén de Alarcón et al., "Online Porn Addiction: What We Know and What We Don't—A Systematic Review," *Journal of Clinical Medicine* 8, no. 1 (January 2019): 91, https://

doi.org/10.3390/jcm8010091; "Porn Addiction," *Psychology Today*, accessed August 14, 2022, https://www.psychologytoday.com/us/basics/porn-addiction.

61. Mark Regnerus, David Gordon, and Joseph Price, "Documenting Pornography Use in America: A Comparative Analysis of Methodological Approaches," *Journal of Sex Research* 53, no. 7 (September 1, 2016): 873–81, https://doi.org/10.1080/00224499.2015.1096886.

62. Jason S. Carroll et al., "The Porn Gap: Differences in Men's and Women's Pornography Patterns in Couple Relationships," *Journal of Couple and Relationship Therapy* 16, no. 2 (April 3, 2017): 146–63, https://doi.org/10.1080/15332691.2016.1238796; Daspe et al., "Pornography Use"; Franklin O. Poulsen, Dean M. Busby, and Adam M. Galovan, "Pornography Use: Who Uses It and How It Is Associated with Couple Outcomes," *Journal of Sex Research* 50, no. 1 (2013): 72–83, https://doi.org/10.1080/00224499.2011.648027.

63. Rebekah Wells, "The Trauma of Revenge Porn," *New York Times*, August 4, 2019, https://www.nytimes.com/2019/08/04/opinion/revenge-porn-privacy.html.

64. Amanda Levendowski, "Using Copyright to Combat Revenge Porn," *New York University Journal of Intellectual Property and Entertainment Law* 3, no. 2 (2014): 422–46.

65. Amanda Lenhart, Michele Ybarra, and Myeshia Price-Feeney, *Nonconsensual Image Sharing: One in 25 Americans Has Been a Victim of "Revenge Porn,"* Data Memo (Data and Society Research Institute, Center for Innovative Public Health Research, December 13, 2016).

66. Tessa Cole et al., "Freedom to Post or Invasion of Privacy? Analysis of U.S. Revenge Porn State Statutes," *Victims and Offenders* 15, no. 4 (May 18, 2020): 483–98, https://doi.org/10.1080/15564886.2020.1712567.

67. Chance Carter, "An Update on the Legal Landscape of Revenge Porn," National Association of Attorneys General, November 16, 2021, https://www.naag.org/attorney-general-journal/an-update-on-the-legal-landscape-of-revenge-porn/.

68. American Civil Liberties Union, *Is Sex Work Decriminalization the Answer? What the Research Tells Us* (American Civil Liberties Union, January 21, 2022), https://www.aclu.org/report/sex-work-decriminalization-answer-what-research-tells-us.

69. US Department of State, "About Human Trafficking," accessed September 9, 2022, https://www.state.gov/humantrafficking-about-human-trafficking/.

70. Gabrielle Moss, "The 3 Most Sensational and Sexist Spring Break News Stories—And What They Were Really About," Bustle, March 3, 2015, https://www.bustle.com/articles/67423-the-3-most-sensational-and-sexist-spring-break-news-stories-and-what-they-were-really.

71. Melissa Gira Grant, *Playing the Whore: The Work of Sex Work* (Verso Books, 2014).

72. Chelsea Reynolds, "'Craigslist Is Nothing More than an Internet Brothel': Sex Work and Sex Trafficking in U.S. Newspaper Coverage of Craigslist Sex Forums," *Journal of Sex Research* 58, no. 6 (July 24, 2021): 681–93, https://doi.org/10.1080/00224499.2020.1786662.

CHAPTER 8

1. Valerie Strauss, "Florida Law Limiting LGBTQ Discussions Takes Effect—and Rocks Schools," *Washington Post*, July 1, 2022, https://www.washingtonpost.com/education/2022/07/01/dont-say-gay-florida-law/.

2. Intersex Society of North America, "What Is Intersex?" accessed May 27, 2023, https://isna.org/faq/what_is_intersex/.

3. Associate Press, *The Associated Press Stylebook: 2022–2024*, 56th ed. (Basic Books, 2022).

4. "Schitt's Creek—The Wine Not the Label," 2016, https://www.youtube.com/watch?v=gdcmhvLaNUs.

5. Gilbert Herdt, *Same Sex, Different Cultures: Exploring Gay and Lesbian Lives* (Routledge, 2019), https://doi.org/10.4324/9780429497469.

6. Byrne Fone, *Homophobia: A History*, 1st ed. (Metropolitan Books, 2000).

7. Peter Tatchell, "Pratt and Smith—Last Men Hanged in England for Gay Sex," Peter Tatchell Foundation, February 26, 2019, https://www.petertatchellfoundation.org/pratt-smith-last-men-hanged-in-england-for-gay-sex/.

8. Hubert C. Kennedy, *Ulrichs: The Life and Works of Karl Heinrich Ulrichs, Pioneer of the Modern Gay Movement*, 1st US ed. (Alyson, 1988), 108.

9. Patrick Kelleher, "The First Public Coming Out Was Incredible—and So Was the Brave Man behind It," *PinkNews* (blog), October 11, 2021, https://www.thepinknews.com/2021/10/11/karl-heinrich-ulrichs-gay-coming-out/.

10. Michael J. Tyrkus, ed., *Gay and Lesbian Biography* (St. James Press, 1997); Kennedy, *Ulrichs*.

11. Tyrkus, *Gay and Lesbian Biography*.

12. Dominic Janes, "Oscar Wilde, Sodomy, and Mental Illness in Late Victorian England," *Journal of the History of Sexuality* 23, no. 1 (January 2014): 79–95, https://doi.org/10.7560/JHS23104.

13. *Lawrence v. Texas*, 539 U.S. 558 (2003).

14. Donald P. Haider-Markel, Mahalley D. Allen, and Morgen Johansen, "Understanding Variations in Media Coverage of U.S. Supreme Court Decisions: Comparing Media Outlets in Their Coverage of *Lawrence v. Texas*," *Harvard International Journal of Press/Politics* 11, no. 2 (April 1, 2006): 64–85, https://doi.org/10.1177/1081180X05286065.

15. Wesley J. Berg, "Court's Recent Decision Would Shock American Forefathers," *Record Searchlight*, July 29, 2003; Mitchell Sommers, "Santorum Makes a Valid Point on Sex," *Philadelphia Inquirer*, May 1, 2003.

16. Jim Kepner and Stephen O. Murray, "Henry Gerber (1895–1972): Grandfather of the American Gay Movement," in *Before Stonewall: Activists for Gay and Lesbian Rights in Historical Context*, ed. Vern L. Bullough (Routledge, 2013), 24–34, https://doi.org/10.4324/9781315801681.

17. James T. Sears, *Behind the Mask of the Mattachine: The Hal Call Chronicles and the Early Movement for Homosexual Emancipation* (Routledge, 2013).

18. Scott Simon, "Remembering a 1966 'Sip-In' for Gay Rights," NPR, June 28, 2008, https://www.npr.org/templates/story/story.php?storyId=91993823.

19. Polly Thistlethwaite, "Stonewall," in *Encyclopedia of Sex and Gender: Culture Society History*, ed. Fedwa Malti-Douglas (Thomson Gale, 2007).

20. Rodger Streitmatter, *From "Perverts" to "Fab Five": The Media's Changing Depiction of Gay Men and Lesbians* (Routledge, 2009).

21. Jack Drescher and Joseph P. Merlino, *American Psychiatry and Homosexuality: An Oral History* (Routledge, 2007).

22. Movement Advancement Project, "Conversion 'Therapy' Laws," accessed July 10, 2021, https://www.lgbtmap.org//equality-maps/conversion_therapy; Michael D. Shear, "Obama Calls for End to 'Conversion' Therapies for Gay and Transgender Youth," *New York Times*, April 8, 2015, https://www.nytimes.com/2015/04/09/us/politics/obama-to-call-for-end-to-conversion-therapies-for-gay-and-transgender-youth.html.

23. Human Rights Campaign, "The Equality Act," accessed September 25, 2022, https://www.hrc.org/resources/equality.

24. Editors of Encyclopaedia Britannica, "Don't Ask, Don't Tell: United States Policy," Britannica, January 9, 2023, https://www.britannica.com/event/Dont-Ask-Dont-Tell.

25. Human Rights Campaign, "Repeal of 'Don't Ask, Don't Tell,'" accessed February 1, 2023, https://www.hrc.org/our-work/stories/repeal-of-dont-ask-dont-tell.

26. Dan De Luce and Shannon Pettypiece, "Biden Admin Scraps Trump's Restrictions on Transgender Troops," NBC News, March 31, 2021, https://www.nbcnews.com/news/military/biden-admin-scraps-trump-s-restrictions-transgender-troops-n1262646.

27. Ryan K Pritchard, *Gay Pride: A Framing Analysis of Pictures from New York's Gay Pride Celebrations* (California State University, Sacramento, 2018).

28. Robert E. Goss, "Silencing Queers at the Upstairs Lounge: The Stonewall of New Orleans," *Southern Communication Journal* 74, no. 3 (July 28, 2009): 269–77, https://doi.org/10.1080/10417940903060948.

29. Lily Cummings, "Haunting Memories as N.O. Council Honors Victims of UpStairs Lounge Fire," 4WWL, June 6, 2022, https://www.wwltv.com/article/news/local/orleans/upstairs-lounge-fire-new-orleans-largest-mass-killing-of-gays-until-2016-new-orleans-council-apologizes/289-14225ff3-396b-4005-a221-1d4b4880c2ce.

30. Carlos A. Ball, *The First Amendment and LGBT Equality: A Contentious History*, The First Amendment and LGBT Equality (Harvard University Press, 2017), https://doi.org/10.4159/9780674977990.

31. Bob Ostertag, *People's Movements, People's Press: The Journalism of Social Justice Movements* (Beacon Press, 2007).

32. Katherine Sender, "Gay Readers, Consumers, and a Dominant Gay Habitus: 25 Years of the *Advocate* Magazine," *Journal of Communication* 51, no. 1 (March 1, 2001): 73–99, https://doi.org/10.1111/j.1460-2466.2001.tb02873.x; Rodger Streitmatter, "The *Advocate*: Setting the Standard for the Gay Liberation Press," *Journalism History* 19, no. 3 (October 1, 1993): 93–102, https://doi.org/10.1080/00947679.1993.12062367.

33. Tara Lynn Wagner, "After 52 Years, 'The Advocate' Remains Paper of Record for LGBTQ Community," Spectrum News, June 24, 2019, https://spectrumnews1.com/ca/la-west/news/2019/06/24/after-52-years—-the-advocate—remains-paper-of-record-for-lgbtq-community.

34. Joan W. Howarth, "Adventures in Heteronormativity: The Straight Line from Liberace to Lawrence Symposium: Pursuing Equal Justice in the West," *Nevada Law Journal* 5, no. 1 (2005 2004): 260–83.

35. Debora Hill, "Liberace," in *Gay and Lesbian Biography*, ed. Michael J. Tyrkus and Michael Bronski (St. James Press, 1977), 289–91.

36. Gabriel Rotello, "The Inning of Outing," *Advocate*, April 18, 1995; Robert Scheer, "Larry Gross and the Formation of the Gay Community," HuffPost, July 9, 2016, https://www.huffpost.com/entry/larry-gross-and-the-formation-of-the-gay-community_b_57805963e4b03288ddc67800.

37. Rotello, "Inning of Outing."

38. Michelangelo Signorile, *Queer in America: Sex, the Media, and the Closets of Power* (University of Wisconsin Press, 2003), 82.

39. David M. Douglas, "Doxing: A Conceptual Analysis," *Ethics and Information Technology* 18, no. 3 (September 1, 2016): 199–210, https://doi.org/10.1007/s10676-016-9406-0.

40. Monica Guzman, "Privacy and Reporting on Personal Lives," ONA Ethics, accessed February 2, 2023, https://ethics.journalists.org/topics/privacy-and-reporting-on-personal-lives/.

41. Cases of doxing and intimidation are covered in chapter 12.

42. Timothy E. Cook and David C. Colby, "The Mass-Mediated Epidemic: The Politics of AIDS on the Nightly Network News," in *AIDS: The Making of a Chronic Disease*, ed. Elizabeth Fee and Daniel M. Fox (University of California Press, 1992), 84–122.

43. William Grimes, "Randy Shilts, Author, Dies at 42; One of First to Write about AIDS," *New York Times*, February 18, 1994, https://www.nytimes.com/1994/02/18/obituaries/randy -shilts-author-dies-at-42-one-of-first-to-write-about-aids.html; Randy Shilts, *And the Band Played On: Politics, People, and the AIDS Epidemic*, 20th anniversary ed. (St. Martin's Griffin, 2007).

44. Dirk Johnson, "Ryan White Dies of AIDS at 18; His Struggle Helped Pierce Myths," *New York Times*, April 9, 1990, https://www.nytimes.com/1990/04/09/obituaries/ryan-white -dies-of-aids-at-18-his-struggle-helped-pierce-myths.html.

45. Paul M. Renfro, "This Teen's AIDS Diagnosis Changed History," *Teen Vogue*, December 6, 2021, https://www.teenvogue.com/story/ryan-white-teen-aids-narrative.

46. National AIDS Memorial, "History," accessed July 27, 2022, https://www.aidsmemorial .org/quilt-history.

47. Cassie Herbert, "Precarious Projects: The Performative Structure of Reclamation," *Language Sciences* 52 (November 2015): 131–38, https://doi.org/10.1016/j.langsci.2015.05.002.

48. Robin Brontsema, "A Queer Revolution: Reconceptualizing the Debate over Linguistic Reclamation," *Colorado Research in Linguistics* 17 (2004), https://doi.org/10.25810/dky3-zq57.

49. Ash Kreider, *Spectrum Media Guide 2021* (Spectrum Waterloo Region, March 2021), https://www.ourspectrum.com/wp-content/uploads/2021/06/Media-Style-Guide_horizontal .pdf.

50. Juliette Rocheleau, "A Former Slur Is Reclaimed, and Listeners Have Mixed Feelings," NPR, August 21, 2019, https://www.npr.org/sections/publiceditor/2019/08/21/ 752330316/a-former-slur-is-reclaimed-and-listeners-have-mixed-feelings.

51. "Remarks by the President in State of the Union Address: January 20, 2015," White House, Office of the Press Secretary, January 20, 2015, https://obamawhitehouse.archives.gov/ the-press-office/2015/01/20/remarks-president-state-union-address-january-20-2015.

52. Adam Liptak, "Supreme Court Ruling Makes Same-Sex Marriage a Right Nationwide," *New York Times*, June 26, 2015, https://www.nytimes.com/2015/06/27/us/supreme-court -same-sex-marriage.html.

53. Sender, "Gay Readers."

54. Tim Trull, "U.S. LGBT Consumer Travel Market Moves Mainstream," Lavidge, 2019, https://www.lavidge.com/industries/travel-and-hospitality/u-s-lgbt-consumer-travel-market -moves-mainstream.

55. Daya Czepanski, "Rainbow Washing Is a Thing, Here's Why It Needs to Stop," Urban List, February 4, 2022, https://www.theurbanlist.com/a-list/rainbow-washing.

56. Gay and Lesbian Alliance against Defamation, *GLAAD Media Reference Guide*, 11th ed., (GLAAD, 2022), https://www.glaad.org/reference.

57. Jennifer Vanasco, "Behind AP's New 'Husband, Wife' Guideline," *Columbia Journalism Review*, February 22, 2013, https://www.cjr.org/minority_reports/when_the_ap_appeared _to_be_lim.php.

58. Kristen Hare, "AP Style Change: Singular They Is Acceptable 'in Limited Cases,'" Poynter, March 24, 2017, https://www.poynter.org/reporting-editing/2017/ap-style-change -singular-they-is-acceptable-in-limited-cases/; Dennis Baron, "A Brief History of Singular 'They,'" *Oxford English Dictionary* (blog), September 4, 2018, https://public.oed.com/blog/ a-brief-history-of-singular-they/.

59. "Pronouns," in Associated Press, *The Associated Press Stylebook: 2022–2024*, 56th ed. (Basic Books, 2022), https://www.apstylebook.com/ap_stylebook/pronouns; italics added for emphasis.

60. "Frequently Asked Questions about Transgender People," National Center for Transgender Equality, January 26, 2015, https://transequality.org/issues/resources/frequently-asked-questions-about-transgender-people.

61. Gay and Lesbian Alliance against Defamation, *GLAAD Media Reference Guide*.

62. Buzz Bissinger, "Call Me Caitlyn," *Vanity Fair* (July 2015).

63. Jon Wertheim, "84-Year-Old Renée Richards Reflects on Breakthrough," *Sports Illustrated*, June 28, 2019, https://www.si.com/tennis/2019/06/28/renee-richards-gender-identity-politics-transgender-where-are-they-now.

64. Katie McDonough, "Laverne Cox Flawlessly Shuts Down Katie Couric's Invasive Questions about Transgender People," Salon, January 7, 2014, https://www.salon.com/2014/01/07/laverne_cox_artfully_shuts_down_katie_courics_invasive_questions_about_transgender_people/.

65. Samantha Allen, "'I Think I Made a Mistake': Katie Couric on Her Transgender Evolution," *Daily Beast*, February 5, 2017, https://www.thedailybeast.com/articles/2017/02/05/i-think-i-made-a-mistake-katie-couric-on-her-transgender-evolution.

66. Transrespect versus Transphobia Worldwide, "TMM Update TDoR 2021," November 11, 2021, https://transrespect.org/en/tmm-update-tdor-2021/.

67. S. E. James et al., *The Report of the 2015 U.S. Transgender Survey* (National Center for Transgender Equality, 2016).

68. Michelle M. Johns et al., "Transgender Identity and Experiences of Violence Victimization, Substance Use, Suicide Risk, and Sexual Risk Behaviors among High School Students: 19 States and Large Urban School Districts, 2017," *Morbidity and Mortality Weekly Report* 68 (2019), https://doi.org/10.15585/mmwr.mm6803a3.

69. National Center for Transgender Equality, *Failing to Protect and Serve: Police Department Policies towards Transgender People*" (National Center for Transgender Equality, May 7, 2019), https://transequality.org/sites/default/files/docs/resources/FTPS_FR_v3.pdf.

70. Kim Severson, "Christian Group Finds Gay Agenda in an Anti-Bullying Day," *New York Times*, October 14, 2012, https://www.nytimes.com/2012/10/15/us/seeing-a-homosexual-agenda-christian-group-protests-an-anti-bullying-program.html.

71. Erik Larson and Laurel Brubaker Calkins, "Top Texas Court Allows Child-Abuse Probes for Parents of Trans Kids," Bloomberg, May 13, 2022, https://www.bloomberg.com/news/articles/2022-05-13/top-texas-court-lifts-injunction-on-abbott-s-gender-care-rules.

72. Megan Russo, "Mismatched Gender Markers on State ID Cards," Regulatory Review, March 10, 2021, https://www.theregreview.org/2021/03/10/russo-mismatched-gender-markers-state-id-cards/.

73. Alex Barasch, "Sacred Bodies," Slate, June 20, 2018, https://slate.com/human-interest/2018/06/desistance-and-detransitioning-stories-value-cis-anxiety-over-trans-lives.html; Jesse Singal, "When Children Say They're Trans," *Atlantic*, June 18, 2018, https://www.theatlantic.com/magazine/archive/2018/07/when-a-child-says-shes-trans/561749/.

74. Sydney Bauer, "The *Atlantic* Tried to Artistically Show Gender Dysphoria on Its Cover. Instead It Damaged the Trust of Transgender Readers," Poynter, September 4, 2020, https://www.poynter.org/ethics-trust/2020/the-atlantic-tried-artistically-show-gender-dysphoria-cover-instead-damaged-trust-transgender-readers/.

75. Barasch, "Sacred Bodies."

76. Hare, "AP Style Change."

77. Nicole Schuman, "AP Style Updates: Diversity, Equity and Inclusion," PR News, August 18, 2021, https://prnewsonline.com/ap-style-diversity-equity-inclusion; the Associated Press, "Transgender Coverage Topical Guide," June 2, 2023, https://www.apstylebook.com/topicals/topicals-transgender-coverage-topical-guide-transgender-coverage-topical-guide.

78. Molly Roberts, "J. K. Rowling's Transphobia Shows It's Time to Put Down the Pen," *Washington Post*, June 9, 2020, https://www.washingtonpost.com/opinions/2020/06/09/jk -rowlings-transphobia-shows-its-time-put-down-pen/.

79. J. K. Rowling, "J. K. Rowling Writes about Her Reasons for Speaking out on Sex and Gender Issues," June 10, 2020, https://www.jkrowling.com/opinions/j-k-rowling-writes-about -her-reasons-for-speaking-out-on-sex-and-gender-issues/.

80. Jenny Gross, "Daniel Radcliffe Criticizes J. K. Rowling's Anti-Transgender Tweets," *New York Times*, June 7, 2020, https://www.nytimes.com/2020/06/07/arts/Jk-Rowling -controversy.html.

81. Colleen Newvine, "Style Tip of the Month," Associated Press Stylebook Online, June 13, 2023, https://discover.ap.org/webmail/62432/1152006009/8e0e875c2e9426c67ef9612b2 87de0e59899bd0560cf9b7e1fff699ff2f14487.

CHAPTER 9

1. Kirsten Eddy, Meera Selva, and Rasmus Kleis Nielsen, *Women and Leadership in the News Media 2022: Evidence from 12 Markets* (Reuters Institute for the Study of Journalism, March 2022).

2. Ramona R. Rush, Carol E. Oukrop, and Pamela J. Creedon, *Seeking Equity for Women in Journalism and Mass Communication Education: A 30-Year Update* (Taylor and Francis, 2013).

3. Adrienne LaFrance, "Nina Totenberg: What It Was Like to Be the Only Woman in the Newsroom," Only Woman in the Room, February 21, 2014, https://medium.com/ the-only-woman-in-the-room/nina-totenberg-what-it-was-like-to-be-the-only-woman-in-the -newsroom-19fadba096c4.

4. Sherwood Thompson, ed., "Tokenism," in *Encyclopedia of Diversity and Social Justice* (Rowman and Littlefield, 2014).

5. Stephanie A. Bluestein, "Agness Underwood's Historic Rise in an All-Male Newsroom: A Case Study," *Sage Open* 7, no. 2 (April 1, 2017): 2158244017710290, https://doi.org/ 10.1177/2158244017710290.

6. Dustin Harp, "Newspapers' Transition from Women's to Style Pages: What Were They Thinking?" *Journalism* 7, no. 2 (May 1, 2006): 197–216, https://doi.org/10.1177/ 1464884906062605.

7. Otto Kerner et al., *Report of the National Advisory Commission on Civil Disorders* (n.p., 1968), 211.

8. Gwyneth Mellinger, *Chasing Newsroom Diversity: From Jim Crow to Affirmative Action* (University of Illinois Press, 2013).

9. Mellinger, *Chasing Newsroom Diversity*, 44.

10. Sha-Shana N. L. Crichton, "The Incomplete Revolution: Women Journalists—50 Years after Title VII of the Civil Rights Act of 1964, We've Come a Long Way Baby, but Are We There Yet?" *Howard Law Journal* 58, no. 1 (2014): 49–112; Lynn Povich, *The Good Girls Revolt: How the Women of Newsweek Sued Their Bosses and Changed the Workplace* (Public-Affairs, 2012).

11. "35 Women Picket Gridiron Dinner," *New York Times*, March 14, 1971, https://www .nytimes.com/1971/03/14/archives/35-women-picket-gridiron-dinner-protest-club-policy -excluding-them.html.

12. "Newsmen's Dinner Opened to Women," *New York Times*, March 23, 1975, https://www.nytimes.com/1975/03/23/archives/newsmens-dinner-opened-to-women-guests-at-gridiron-include-fords.html.

13. Allan Cromley, "Women in the Bar? A Sobering Thought," *Daily Oklahoman*, January 16, 1971.

14. Women's Media Center, *The Status of Women in the U.S. Media 2021* (Women's Media Center, 2021).

15. Eddy, Selva, and Nielsen, *Women and Leadership*.

16. Ford N. Burkhart and Carol K. Sigelman, "Byline Bias? Effects of Gender on News Article Evaluations," *Journalism Quarterly* 67, no. 3 (September 1, 1990): 492–500, https://doi.org/10.1177/107769909006700303.

17. Cory L. Armstrong and Melinda J. McAdams, "Blogs of Information: How Gender Cues and Individual Motivations Influence Perceptions of Credibility," *Journal of Computer-Mediated Communication* 14, no. 3 (April 2009): 435–56, https://doi.org/10.1111/j.1083-6101.2009.01448.x; Trent Royce Boulter, "Following the Familiar: The Effects of Exposure and Gender on Follow Intent and Credibility of Journalists on Twitter" (PhD diss., University of Texas at Austin, 2017), https://doi.org/10.15781/T26T0HC48; Elena Klaas and Mark Boukes, "A Woman's Got to Write What a Woman's Got to Write: The Effect of Journalist's Gender on the Perceived Credibility of News Articles," *Feminist Media Studies* 22, no. 3 (April 3, 2022): 571–87, https://doi.org/10.1080/14680777.2020.1838596.

18. Klaas and Boukes, "Woman's Got to Write."

19. Dustin A. Hahn and R. Glenn Cummins, "Effects of Attractiveness, Gender, and Athlete–Reporter Congruence on Perceived Credibility of Sport Reporters," *International Journal of Sport Communication* 7, no. 1 (March 1, 2014): 34–47, https://doi.org/10.1123/IJSC.2013-0113.

20. Rupert Neate, "*New York Times* Boss Sued over Alleged Ageist, Racist and Sexist Hiring Practices," *Guardian*, April 28, 2016, http://www.theguardian.com/media/2016/apr/28/new-york-times-ceo-sued-discriminatory-hiring-practices.

21. Michael A. Deas, "New Media, Old Problem: Where's the Diversity?" Al Jazeera, accessed April 14, 2014, https://www.aljazeera.com/opinions/2014/4/14/new-media-old-problem-wheres-the-diversity.

22. Meredith D. Clark, *The ASNE Newsroom Diversity Survey* (American Association of Newspaper Editors, 2018).

23. US Census Bureau, "QuickFacts: United States," accessed September 17, 2022, https://www.census.gov/quickfacts/fact/table/US/PST045221.

24. Joshunda Sanders, *How Racism and Sexism Killed Traditional Media: Why the Future of Journalism Depends on Women and People of Color* (ABC-CLIO, 2015).

25. Kristin Grady Gilger and Julia Wallace, *There's No Crying in Newsrooms: What Women Have Learned about What It Takes to Lead* (Rowman and Littlefield, 2021), 77.

26. Monica Löfgren Nilsson, "'Thinkings' and 'Doings' of Gender: Gendering Processes in Swedish Television News Production," *Journalism Practice* 4, no. 1 (2010): 1–16, https://doi.org/10.1080/17512780903119693; Linda Steiner, "The 'Gender Matters' Debate in Journalism: Lessons from the Front," in *Journalism: Critical Issues*, ed. Stuart Allen (McGraw Hill Education, 2005), 42–53.

27. Richard Shafer, "What Minority Journalists Identify as Constraints to Full Newsroom Equality," *Howard Journal of Communications* 4, no. 3 (March 1, 1993): 195–208, https://doi.org/10.1080/10646179309359776.

28. Pamela Newkirk, *Within the Veil: Black Journalists, White Media* (NYU Press, 2000); Shafer, "What Minority Journalists Identify."

29. Mercedes Lynn de Uriarte, Cristina Bodinger-de Uriarte, and José Luis Benavides, *Diversity Disconnects: From Class Room to News Room* (Ford Foundation, 2003).

30. T. Franklin Waddell, "Who Thinks That Female Journalists Have Sex with Their Sources? Testing the Association between Sexist Beliefs, Journalist Mistrust, and the Perceived Realism of Fictional Female Journalists," *Journalism Studies* 22, no. 15 (June 10, 2021): 1–18, https://doi.org/10.1080/1461670X.2021.1938636.

31. Katharine Q. Seelye, "Laura Foreman, Reporter Whose Romance Became a Scandal, Dies at 76," *New York Times*, July 23, 2021, https://www.nytimes.com/2021/07/23/business/media/laura-foreman-dead.html.

32. Louise North, "'Just a Little Bit of Cheeky Ribaldry'?" *Feminist Media Studies* 7, no. 1 (March 1, 2007): 81–96, https://doi.org/10.1080/14680770601103738.

33. Heather McLaughlin, "Sexual Harassment," in *The Blackwell Encyclopedia of Sociology* (John Wiley, 2019), 1–2, https://doi.org/10.1002/9781405165518.wbeoss092.pub2.

34. Katherine Goldstein, "When Harassment Drives Women Out of Journalism," International Women's Media Foundation, accessed September 22, 2022, https://www.iwmf.org/2017/12/when-harassment-drives-women-out-of-journalism/.

35. Tarana Burke, "History and Inception," Me Too Movement, accessed September 29, 2022, https://metoomvmt.org/get-to-know-us/history-inception/.

36. Mary Pflum, "A Year Ago, Alyssa Milano Started a Conversation about #MeToo. These Women Replied," NBC News, October 15, 2018, https://www.nbcnews.com/news/us-news/year-ago-alyssa-milano-started-conversation-about-metoo-these-women-n920246.

37. Jodi Kantor and Megan Twohey, "Harvey Weinstein Paid Off Sexual Harassment Accusers for Decades," *New York Times*, October 5, 2017, https://www.nytimes.com/2017/10/05/us/harvey-weinstein-harassment-allegations.html.

38. Ethan Shanfeld, "Kevin Spacey Ordered to Pay $31 Million to 'House of Cards' Producer for Alleged Sexual Misconduct," *Variety*, August 4, 2022, https://variety.com/2022/tv/news/kevin-spacey-payment-house-of-cards-sexual-misconduct-allegations-1235333733/.

39. Adam B. Vary, "#MeToo Fallout beyond Weinstein: Kevin Spacey, R. Kelly and More," *Variety*, February 26, 2020, https://variety.com/gallery/metoo-fallout-kevin-spacey-r-kelly-les-moonves/.

40. Alix Langone, "#MeToo and Time's Up Founders Explain the Difference between the 2 Movements," *Time*, March 22, 2018, https://time.com/5189945/whats-the-difference-between-the-metoo-and-times-up-movements/.

41. Gilger and Wallace, *There's No Crying*.

42. Shaheen Pasha, "As a Woman in Media, Sexual Harassment Was the Norm. I Was Told to Keep It to Myself," World from PRX, October 20, 2017, https://theworld.org/stories/2017-10-20/female-journalist-sexual-harassment-was-norm-i-was-told-keep-it-myself.

43. Irene Khan, *#JournalistsToo: Women Journalists Speak Out* (Office of the High Commissioner for Human Rights, UNESCO, November 24, 2021), 12.

44. Gilger and Wallace, *There's No Crying*.

45. Khan, *#JournalistsToo*.

46. Katie Robertson, "Axel Springer Accused of Failing to Stop Sexual Harassment," *New York Times*, September 21, 2022, https://www.nytimes.com/2022/09/21/business/media/axel-springer-lawsuit.html.

47. Stephen Battaglio, "CBS Allegations Just the Latest in Long History of Sexual Harassment Claims in Network News," *Los Angeles Times*, July 31, 2018, https://www.latimes.com/business/hollywood/la-fi-ct-cbs-news-sexual-harassment-fallout-20180731-story.html.

48. Meg Heckman, Myojung Chung, and Jody Santos, "We Need to Teach Student Journalists about On-the-Job Harassment," Poynter, September 14, 2022, https://www.poynter.org/educators-students/2022/student-journalism-harassment-threats-intimidation-violence/.

49. Douglas Martin, "Leroy F. Aarons, 70, Founder of Gay Journalist Group, Dies," *New York Times*, November 30, 2004, https://www.nytimes.com/2004/11/30/obituaries/leroy-f-aarons-70-founder-of-gay-journalist-group-dies.html.

50. Martin, "Leroy F. Aarons."

51. Joseph P. Bernt and Marilyn S. Greenwald, "Differing Views of Senior Editors and Gay/Lesbian Journalists Regarding Newspaper Coverage of the Gay and Lesbian Community," *Newspaper Research Journal* 13, no. 4 (Fall 1992): 99–110.

52. Melody Kramer, "Comparing Parental Leave Policies in American Newsrooms," Poynter, April 18, 2017, https://www.poynter.org/reporting-editing/2017/comparing-parental-leave-policies-in-american-newsrooms/.

53. Louise North, "Still a 'Blokes Club': The Motherhood Dilemma in Journalism," *Journalism* 17, no. 3 (April 1, 2016): 320, https://doi.org/10.1177/1464884914560306.

54. Katherine Goldstein, "Where Are the Mothers?" Nieman Reports, July 26, 2017, https://niemanreports.org/articles/where-are-the-mothers/.

55. Katherine Goldstein, "What It's Like to Be a Breastfeeding Journalist," Nieman Reports, July 27, 2017, https://niemanreports.org/articles/what-its-like-to-be-a-breastfeeding-journalist/.

56. Eduardo Bonilla-Silva, *Racism without Racists: Color-Blind Racism and the Persistence of Racial Inequality in the United States* (Rowman and Littlefield, 2006).

57. Don Heider, *White News: Why Local News Programs Don't Cover People of Color* (Routledge, 2014); Cheryl D. Jenkins, "Newsroom Diversity and Representations of Race," in *Race and News: Critical Perspectives*, by Christopher P. Campbell et al. (Routledge, 2012), 22–42.

58. Steve Buttry, "Dori Maynard Helped Journalists View Diversity as a Matter of Accuracy," *Buttry Diary* (blog), February 25, 2015, https://stevebuttry.wordpress.com/2015/02/25/dori-maynard-helped-journalists-view-diversity-as-a-matter-of-accuracy/.

59. Cory L. Armstrong, "The Influence of Reporter Gender on Source Selection in Newspaper Stories," *Journalism and Mass Communication Quarterly* 81, no. 1 (March 1, 2004): 139–54, https://doi.org/10.1177/107769900408100110; Teresa Correa and Dustin Harp, "Women Matter in Newsrooms: How Power and Critical Mass Relate to the Coverage of the HPV Vaccine," *Journalism and Mass Communication Quarterly* 88, no. 2 (2011): 301–19, https://doi.org/10.1177/107769901108800205.

60. Brad Clark, "'Walking Up a Down-Escalator': The Interplay between Newsroom Norms and Media Coverage of Minority Groups," *InMedia: The French Journal of Media Studies*, no. 5 (September 17, 2014), https://doi.org/10.4000/inmedia.749; Katsuo A. Nishikawa et al., "Interviewing the Interviewers: Journalistic Norms and Racial Diversity in the Newsroom," *Howard Journal of Communications* 20, no. 3 (2009): 242–59, https://doi.org/10.1080/10646170903070175.

61. Robert M. Entman, "Representation and Reality in the Portrayal of Blacks on Network Television News," *Journalism and Mass Communication Quarterly* 71, no. 3 (1994): 509–20, https://doi.org/10.1177/107769909407100303; Heider, *White News*.

62. Jenkins, "Newsroom Diversity."

63. Sarach Macharia, ed., *Who Makes the News: 6th Global Media Monitoring Project* (GMMP, 2020), https://whomakesthenews.org/gmmp-2020-final-reports/.

64. Laura Hazard Owen, "The BBC's 50:50 Project Shows Equal Gender Representation in News Coverage Is Achievable—Even in Traditionally Male Areas," Nieman Lab, May 16, 2019, https://www.niemanlab.org/2019/05/the-bbcs-5050-project-shows-equal-gender-representation-in-news-coverage-is-achievable-even-in-traditionally-male-areas/.

65. Women Also Know Stuff, accessed September 22, 2022, https://www.womenalsoknow stuff.com/mission.

66. Women's Media Center, "WMC SheSource," accessed September 22, 2022, https://womensmediacenter.com/shesource/.

67. Eric Garcia McKinley and Lindsay Green-Barber, *KQED Analysis and Recommendations: Source Diversity* (Impact Architects, November 2020).

68. Danielle K. Brown and Rachel R. Mourão, "No Reckoning for the Right: How Political Ideology, Protest Tolerance and News Consumption Affect Support Black Lives Matter Protests," *Political Communication* 39, no. 6 (September 15, 2022): 1–18, https://doi.org/10.1080/10584609.2022.2121346.

69. Mary Angela Bock, *Seeing Justice: Witnessing, Crime and Punishment in Visual Media* (Oxford University Press, 2021); Robert M. Entman and Andrew Rojecki, eds., *The Black Image in the White Mind: Media and Race in America*, Studies in Communication, Media, and Public Opinion (University of Chicago Press, 2001); Nikki Usher, *News for the Rich, White, and Blue: How Place and Power Distort American Journalism* (Columbia University Press, 2021).

70. Meg Heckman, "Constructing the 'Gender Beat': U.S. Journalists Refocus the News in the Aftermath of #Metoo," *Journalism Practice* (November 15, 2021): 1–15, https://doi.org/10.1080/17512786.2021.1997151.

71. Benjamin Mullin, "The *New York Times* Is Launching Digital-First Teams to Cover Gender, Education and Climate Change," Poynter, August 26, 2016, https://www.poynter.org/tech-tools/2016/a-new-beat-structure-the-new-york-times-is-launching-gender-education-and-climate-change-teams-apart-from-the-newspaper/; "Subscribe to In Her Words: Where Women Rule the Headlines," *New York Times*, May 9, 2018, https://www.nytimes.com/2018/05/09/us/subscribe-in-her-words-newsletter.html.

72. *In Her Words, New York Times*, accessed February 5, 2023, https://www.nytimes.com/series/in-her-words; *Gender and Identity, Washington Post*, accessed February 5, 2023, https://www.washingtonpost.com/gender-identity.

73. Heckman, "Constructing the 'Gender Beat,'" 8.

CHAPTER 10

1. Margery W. Davies, *Woman's Place Is at the Typewriter: Office Work and Office Workers: 1870–1930* (Temple University Press, 1982).

2. Joseph Turow, *Media Today*, vol. 2 (Houghton Mifflin, 2003).

3. David T. Z. Mindich, *Just the Facts: How Objectivity Came to Define American Journalism* (New York University Press, 1998).

4. Donna Halper, *Invisible Stars: A Social History of Women in American Broadcasting* (Routledge, 2015).

5. Jim Wilson, "Radio Scouting," National Association for Amateur Radio, accessed August 25, 2022, http://www.arrl.org/radio-scouting.

6. National Association for Amateur Radio, "ARRL Now Offering New 'Radio and Wireless Technology' Patch Program for Girls Scouts," June 14, 2016, http://www.arrl.org/news/arrl-now-offering-new-radio-and-wireless-technology-patch-program-for-girl-scouts.

7. Michael Nelmes, "McKenzie, Florence Violet (1890–1982)," in *Australian Dictionary of Biography*, vol. 18 (National Centre of Biography, Australian National University, 2012), https://adb.anu.edu.au/biography/mckenzie-florence-violet-15485.

8. "The Feminine Wireless Amateur," *Electrical Experimenter*, October 1916.

9. Alison L. Eldridge and Suzanne C. Goodsell, "Betty Crocker: First Lady of Food," *Nutrition Today* 42, no. 7 (January/February 2007): 18–21.

10. Barbara W. Grossman, "Allen, Gracie (1895–1964), Actress and Comedienne," in *American National Biography* (Oxford University Press, 1999).

11. Quoted in Halper, *Invisible Stars*.

12. Tina Tallon, "A Century of 'Shrill': How Bias in Technology Has Hurt Women's Voices," *New Yorker*, September 3, 2019, https://www.newyorker.com/culture/cultural-comment/a-century-of-shrill-how-bias-in-technology-has-hurt-womens-voices.

13. John Schneider, "The Women Who Overcame Radio's Earliest Glass Ceilings," Radio World, August 1, 2020, https://www.radioworld.com/news-and-business/headlines/the-women-who-overcame-radios-earliest-glass-ceilings.

14. Matthew McAllister, "Consumer Culture," in *The Concise Encyclopedia of Communication*, ed. Wolfgang Donsbach (John Wiley, 2015).

15. Robert P. Snow, "Youth, Rock'n'roll, and Electronic Media," *Youth and Society* 18, no. 4 (1987): 326–43.

16. Archives of African American Music and Culture, "Golden Age of Black Radio—Part 4: Gender Equality and Civil Rights," Google Arts and Culture, accessed September 29, 2022, https://artsandculture.google.com/story/golden-age-of-black-radio-part-4-gender-equality-and-civil-rights/BAXhpUDz5MbzKw.

17. Teresa Paloma Acosta, "Spanish-Language Radio," Texas State Historical Association, July 27, 2016, https://www.tshaonline.org/handbook/entries/spanish-language-radio.

18. Marshall McLuhan, Eric McLuhan, and Frank Zingrone, *Essential McLuhan* (Routledge, 1997), 269.

19. Bob Papper, *2021 RTDNA/Newhouse School at Syracuse University Newsroom Survey* (RTDNA and Newhouse School at Syracuse University, 2021).

20. Katrina Ford, "Dickerson, Nancy," in *The Scribner Encyclopedia of American Lives, Thematic Series: The 1960s*, ed. William L. O'Neill and Kenneth T. Jackson, vol. 1 (Charles Scribner's Sons, 2003), 247–49.

21. Gail Shister, "Katie Couric Stands Alone," *Ledger*, April 8, 2006, https://www.theledger.com/story/news/2006/04/08/katie-couric-stands-alone/25830873007/.

22. Douglass K. Daniel, *Harry Reasoner: A Life in the News* (University of Texas Press, 2007); "Barbara Walters," in *Encyclopedia of World Biography*, vol. 16, 2nd ed. (Gale, 2004), 86–88.

23. Maya Yang and Patrick Wintour, "Iran Leader Shuns Christiane Amanpour Interview over Refusal to Wear Headscarf," *Guardian*, September 22, 2022, https://www.theguardian.com/world/2022/sep/22/christiane-amanpour-ebrahim-riasi-headscarf-interview-iran.

24. Paul Bond, "Former CBS News Reporter Lara Logan Recounts Gang Rape Ahead of New Series about Liberal Media Bias," *Newsweek*, April 13, 2020, https://www.newsweek.com/former-cbs-news-reporter-lara-logan-recounts-gang-rape-ahead-new-series-about-liberal-media-bias-1497219.

25. Kali Hays, "Lara Logan Lawsuit over NY Mag Story Tossed from Court," *Women's Wear Daily*, May 14, 2020, https://wwd.com/business-news/media/lara-logan-fox-news-cbs-lawsuit-new-york-magazine-benghazi-cbs-story-1203633819/; Kali Hays, "NY Mag Hit with $25M Lawsuit over Years-Old Lara Logan, CBS Story," *Women's Wear Daily*, December 17, 2019, https://wwd.com/feature/new-york-magazine-lara-logan-lawsuit-cbs-60-minutes-benghazi-story-1203402622/.

26. Jeremy W. Peters, "Lara Logan, Once a Star at CBS News, Is Now One for the Far Right," *New York Times*, May 22, 2022, https://www.nytimes.com/2022/05/22/business/media/lara-logan-cbs-news.html.

27. Kim Meltzer, *TV News Anchors and Journalistic Tradition: How Journalists Adapt to Technology* (Peter Lang, 2010).

28. Mary Angela Bock, "Smile More: A Subcultural Analysis of the Anchor-Consultant Relationship in Local Television News Operations" (master's thesis, Drake University, May 1986).

29. Meltzer, *TV News Anchors.*

30. Olivia Barker, "Carlson: Pants 'Not Allowed' on 'Fox and Friends,'" *USA Today*, September 20, 2013, https://www.usatoday.com/story/life/people/2013/09/20/gretchen-carlson-says-fox-and-friends-didnt-permit-pants/2844535/.

31. Sarah Ellison, "Fox Settles with Gretchen Carlson for $20 Million—and Is Expected to Offer an Unprecedented Apology," *Vanity Fair*, September 6, 2016, https://www.vanityfair.com/news/2016/09/fox-news-settles-with-gretchen-carlson-for-20-million.

32. Bock, "Smile More"; Erika Engstrom and Anhony J. Ferri, "From Barriers to Challenges: Career Perceptions of Women TV News Anchors," *Journalism and Mass Communication Quarterly* 75, no. 4 (December 1, 1998): 789–802, https://doi.org/10.1177/107769909807500412.

33. Christine Craft, *Too Old, Too Ugly, and Not Deferential to Men* (Prima, 1988).

34. Libby Copeland, "Sleeveless," Slate, April 29, 2013, https://slate.com/human-interest/2013/04/female-tv-newscasters-and-the-sleeveless-sheath-dress.html.

35. Mary Angela Bock, *Video Journalism: Beyond the One Man Band* (Peter Lang, 2012).

36. Bock, "Smile More."

37. Jack Shafer, "TV's Aryan Sisterhood," Slate, February 21, 2006, http://www.slate.com/articles/news_and_politics/press_box/2006/02/tvs_aryan_sisterhood.html.

38. Mary Angela Bock et al., "The Faces of Local TV News in America: Youth, Whiteness, and Gender Disparities in Station Publicity Photos," *Feminist Media Studies* 18, no. 3 (May 4, 2018): 440–57, https://doi.org/10.1080/14680777.2017.1415950.

39. Bock et al., "Faces of Local TV News."

40. Jessica Alas, "Nowhere to Hide: TV Journalists Face the Pressure of Cosmetic Procedures," Beyond Bylines, November 4, 2015, https://mediablog.prnewswire.com/2015/11/04/cosmetic-surgery-trends/.

41. Bob Papper and Karen Henderson, *The RTDNA/Newhouse School at Syracuse University Survey* (Syracuse University, 2022).

42. Asian American Journalists Association, *The AAJA Broadcast Snapshot Project: Underrepresentation of AAPIs on Local TV News* (Asian American Journalists Association, May 4, 2022).

43. Suzanne S. LaPierre, "Hispanic Representation Lags in Media," Digital Content Next, October 18, 2022, https://digitalcontentnext.org/blog/2022/10/18/the-growth-of-hispanic-representation-lags-in-media/.

44. Amudalat Ajasa, "These Black Women Are Changing TV Weather, a Field Long Dominated by White Men," *Washington Post*, February 3, 2023, https://www.washingtonpost.com/weather/2023/02/03/black-women-meteorologists-tv-weather/; Kimberley Wilson, "These Black Women Are Making Moves at Major News Networks," *Essence*, February 7, 2022, https://www.essence.com/entertainment/black-women-making-moves-major-news-networks/#1021752.

45. Whitney Harris, "Changing Our Roots: How Having Black Hair Shapes Student Perspectives on Pursuing Careers in Broadcast Journalism," *Electronic News* 16, no. 2 (February 1, 2022), http://journals.sagepub.com/doi/full/10.1177/19312431221075342.

46. Amaris Castillo, "For Black Women Journalists, Wearing #NaturalHairOnAir Is a Point of Pride and Resistance," Poynter, February 22, 2022, https://www.poynter.org/business-work/2022/black-women-journalists-natural-hair-naturalhaironair/.

47. Bock et al., "Faces of Local TV News."

48. Margaret Hunter, "The Persistent Problem of Colorism: Skin Tone, Status, and Inequality," *Sociology Compass* 1, no. 1 (2007): 237–54, https://doi.org/10.1111/j.1751-9020.2007.00006.x.

49. Ramya M. Vijaya, "The New Economics of Colorism in the Skin Whitening Industry: Case of India and Nigeria," in *Race in the Marketplace: Crossing Critical Boundaries*, ed. Guillaume D. Johnson et al. (Springer International, 2019), 227–44, https://doi .org/10.1007/978-3-030-11711-5_14.

50. A. J. Katz, "Rachel Maddow, Anderson Cooper Lead the *Advocate*'s List of 50 Most Influential LGBTs in Media," *AdWeek*, August 19, 2017, https://adweek.it/39AkJCt.

51. John Moore, "Denver TV Host Eden Lane Opens Up about Her Life and Challenges," *Denver Post*, October 18, 2012, https://www.denverpost.com/2012/10/18/denver-tv-host-eden -lane-opens-up-about-her-life-and-challenges/.

52. Ed Leibowitz, "Becoming Zoey Tur," *Los Angeles Magazine*, December 22, 2014, https://www.lamag.com/longform/becoming-zoey-tur/.

53. Papper and Henderson, *RTDNA/Newhouse School*.

54. Robert J. Richardson, "Local TV Newsroom Diversity: Race and Gender of Newscasters and Their Managers," *Journal of Broadcasting and Electronic Media* 66, no. 5 (September 14, 2022): 823–42, https://doi.org/10.1080/08838151.2022.2121834.

CHAPTER 11

1. Robert Hariman and John Louis Lucaites, *No Caption Needed: Iconic Photographs, Public Culture, and Liberal Democracy* (University of Chicago Press, 2007).

2. Lennard Davis, "*Migrant Mother*: Dorothea Lange and the Truth of Photography," Los Angeles Review of Books, March 4, 2020, https://www.larevewofbooks.org/article/migrant -mother-dorothea-lange-truth-photography/.

3. Naomi Rosenblum, *A History of Women Photographers* (Abbeville Press, 1994).

4. Michael L. Carlebach, *American Photojournalism Comes of Age* (Smithsonian Institution, 1997).

5. "America's Left Bank: Jessie Tarbox Beals's Greenwich Village Photographs," *Missouri Review* 45, no. 1 (2022): 41–49, https://doi.org/10.1353/mis.2022.0012.

6. Eileen Chanin, "Soldiers and Suffragettes: The Photography of Christina Broom (Review)," *Modernism/Modernity* 23, no. 1 (2016): 243–48, https://doi.org/10.1353/mod.2016 .0023.

7. Frances Benjamin Johnston et al., *A Talent for Detail: The Photographs of Miss Frances Benjamin Johnston, 1889–1910* (Harmony Books, 1974), https://catalog.hathitrust.org/ Record/008703629.

8. Rosenblum, *History of Women Photographers*.

9. Cecil Carnes, *Jimmy Hare, News Photographer; Half a Century with a Camera* (Macmillan, 1940); Historic Camera, "James 'Jimmy' Hare, Photographer at Historic Camera," accessed September 30, 2022, https://historiccamera.com/cgi-bin/librarium2/pm.cgi ?action=app_display&app=datasheet&app_id=3744&.

10. Richard Whelan, *This Is War! Robert Capa at Work* (International Center of Photography, 2007).

11. Christopher T Assaf and Mary Angela Bock, "The Robert Capa Myth: Hegemonic Masculinity in Photojournalism's Professional Indoctrination," *Communication, Culture and Critique* 15, no. 1 (March 1, 2022): 84–101, https://doi.org/10.1093/ccc/tcab049.

12. Marc Aronson and Marina Budhos, *Eyes of the World: Robert Capa, Gerda Taro, and the Invention of Modern Photojournalism* (Henry Holt, 2017).

13. Rosenblum, *History of Women Photographers.*

14. Vicki Goldberg, *Margaret Bourke-White: A Biography* (Harper and Row, 1986), 291.

15. Anne-Marie Beckmann and Felicity Korn, *Women War Photographers: From Lee Miller to Anja Niedringhaus* (Prestel, 2019).

16. Rosenblum, *History of Women Photographers,* 188.

17. National Press Photographers Association, "Historic Documents," January 27, 2017, https://nppa.org/historic-documents.

18. Carolyn Lee, "The First Female Photographers Brought a New Vision to the *New York Times,*" *New York Times,* March 29, 2019, https://www.nytimes.com/2019/03/29/nyregion/first-female-photographers-new-york-times.html.

19. Rosenblum, *History of Women Photographers.*

20. Beckmann and Korn, *Women War Photographers.*

21. Nina Strochlic, "Inside the Daring Life of a Female War Photographer," *National Geographic,* August 17, 2018, https://www.nationalgeographic.com/culture/article/world-photography-day-dickey-chapelle-female-war-photographer-combat-vietnam.

22. Jack T. Paxton, "Dickey Chapelle: 'What's a Woman Doing Here? . . . Indeed!'" *Leatherneck* 98, no. 11 (November 2015): 28–32.

23. College Raptor, "Photojournalism," accessed October 1, 2022, https://www.collegeraptor.com/Majors/Details/9.0404/Level/Bachelors-degree/State/All/Photojournalism/.

24. Daniella Zalcman, "Yes, We Can Reach Gender Parity in Photojournalism," Nieman Reports, September 30, 2019, https://niemanreports.org/articles/yes-we-can-reach-gender-parity-in-photojournalism/.

25. Adrian Hadland, David Campbell, and Paul Lambert, *The State of News Photography: The Lives and Livelihoods of Photojournalists in the Digital Age* (Reuters Institute for the Study of Journalism in Association with World Press Photo, September 2015), https://reutersinstitute.politics.ox.ac.uk/sites/default/files/research/files/The%2520State%2520of%2520News%2520Photography.pdf.

26. National Press Photographers Association, "Code of Ethics," accessed May 17, 2023, http://www.nppa.org/resources/code-ethics.

27. Verónica Sanchis Bencomo, "About," Foto-Feminas.com, October 14, 2014, https://foto-feminas.com/about/.

28. Katie Eastman, "Attendees Enriched by Women in Visual Journalism Conference WIVJ," National Press Photographers Association, October 25, 2018, https://nppa.org/magazine/attendees-enriched-women-visual-journalism-conference-wivj; Zalcman, "Yes, We Can."

29. Wilson Lowrey, "Word People vs. Picture People: Normative Differences and Strategies for Control over Work among Newsroom Subgroups," *Mass Communication and Society* 5, no. 4 (2002): 411–32.

30. Saumava Mitra, Brenda L. Witherspoon, and Sara Creta, "Invisible in This Visual World? Work and Working Conditions of Female Photographers in the Global South," *Journalism Studies* 23, no. 2 (January 25, 2022): 149–66, https://doi.org/10.1080/1461670X.2021.2007163.

31. Lori King, "Precautions, Concerns Shared in First NPPA Town Hall Webinar on Working in the Coronavirus Era," National Press Photographers Association, March 27, 2020, https://nppa.org/news/precautions-concerns-shared-first-nppa-town-hall-webinar-working-coronavirus-era.

32. Tony Webster, "Minneapolis Settles Lawsuit with Linda Tirado, Journalist Blinded in One Eye during May 2020 Unrest," Minnesota Reformer, May 26, 2022, https://minnesota

reformer.com/2022/05/26/minneapolis-settles-lawsuit-with-linda-tirado-journalist-blinded-in
-one-eye-during-may-2020-unrest/.

33. Adrian Hadland and Camilla Barnett, *The State of News Photography 2018: Photojour-nalists' Attitudes toward Work Practices, Technology and Life in the Digital Age* (World Press Photo Foundation, 2018).

34. Caylie M. Silveira, "Behind the Lens: How Women Photojournalists' Experiences Are Impacted by Gendered Double Standards and Emotion Management on the Sidelines of the National Football League" (master's thesis, West Virginia University, 2021), https://www .proquest.com/docview/2553748930/abstract/CF942AAF7B5743CEPQ/1.

35. Kyser Lough, "Patriarchal Pits: The Gendered Experiences of Female Concert Photog-raphers," *Journal of Gender Studies* 29, no. 7 (October 2, 2020): 820–31, https://doi.org/10 .1080/09589236.2020.1821178.

36. Rachel Somerstein, "'She's Just Another Pretty Face': Sexual Harassment of Female Photographers," *Feminist Media Studies* (October 25, 2021): 11, https://doi.org/10.1080/146 80777.2021.1984274.

37. Harriet Sim, "The Disturbing List of Sexual Assault and Harassment Allegations against Terry Richardson," *Marie Claire*, October 25, 2017, https://www.marieclaire.com.au/ terry-richardson-every-sexual-harassment-and-assault-allegation.

38. Vanessa Friedman and Elizabeth Paton, "Terry Richardson Is Just the Tip of the Ice-berg," *New York Times*, October 27, 2017, https://www.nytimes.com/2017/10/27/style/terry -richardson-sexual-harassment-fashion-photographers.html.

39. Kristen Chick, "Photojournalists under David Furst Felt 'Set up to Fail,'" *Columbia Journalism Review*, July 6, 2021, https://www.cjr.org/special_report/david-furst-departure-p hoto-editor-new-york-times.php/; Erik Wemple, "Awards Buoyed Former *New York Times* Editor Who Mistreated Freelance Photographers," *Washington Post*, July 9, 2021, https://www .washingtonpost.com/opinions/2021/07/09/awards-buoyed-former-new-york-times-editor -who-mistreated-freelance-photographers/.

40. Stuart Hall, ed., *Representation: Cultural Representations and Signifying Practices* (Sage, 1997).

41. Paul Martin Lester and Susan Dente Ross, eds., *Images That Injure: Pictorial Stereotypes in the Media*, vol. 2 (Praeger, 2003).

42. Daniel Boorstin, *The Image: A Guide to Pseudo Events in America* (Harper and Row, 1961).

43. Danielle Kathleen Kilgo, "Black, White, and Blue: Media and Audience Frames from Visual News Coverage of Police Use of Force and Unrest" (PhD diss., University of Texas at Austin, August 2017), https://doi.org/10.15781/T2PZ5231G; Danielle K. Kilgo and Rachel R. Mourão, "Protest Coverage Matters: How Media Framing and Visual Communication Affects Support for Black Civil Rights Protests," *Mass Communication and Society* 24, no. 4 (February 4, 2021): 576–96, https://doi.org/10.1080/15205436.2021.1884724.

44. Cara A Finnegan, "Social Engineering, Visual Politics, and the New Deal: FSA Photog-raphy in 'Survey Graphic,'" *Rhetoric and Public Affairs* 3, no. 3 (2000): 333–62.

45. Rosenblum, *History of Women Photographers*.

46. National Press Photographers Association, "Code of Ethics."

47. Annette Young, "The 51%—A Different Perspective: Women in Photog-raphy," France 24, September 2, 2021, https://www.france24.com/en/tv-shows/the-51/ 20210902-a-different-perspective-women-in-photography.

48. Donna DeCesare, *Unsettled: Children in a World of Gangs/Desasosiego: Los Niños En Un Mundo de Las Pandillas* (University of Texas Press, 2013).

49. Danielle Villasana, *A Light Inside* (FotoEvidence, 2018). See also Danielle Villasana, A Light Inside, accessed May 17, 2023, https://www.daniellevillasana.com/projects/a-light-inside.

50. Beckmann and Korn, *Women War Photographers*.

CHAPTER 12

1. Margaret Sullivan, "Online Harassment of Female Journalists Is Real, and It's Increasingly Hard to Endure," *Washington Post*, March 14, 2021, https://www.washingtonpost.com/lifestyle/media/online-harassment-female-journalists/2021/03/13/ed24b0aa-82aa-11eb-ac37-4383f7709abe_story.html.

2. Julie Posetti et al., *Online Violence against Women Journalists* (United Nations Educational, Scientific, and Cultural Organization, 2020).

3. Nathan L. Ensmenger, William Aspray Jr., and Thomas J. Misa, *The Computer Boys Take Over: Computers, Programmers, and the Politics of Technical Expertise* (MIT Press, 2010).

4. J. Fuegi and J. Francis, "Lovelace and Babbage and the Creation of the 1843 'Notes,'" *IEEE Annals of the History of Computing* 25, no. 4 (October 2003): 16–26, https://doi.org/10.1109/MAHC.2003.1253887.

5. B. J. Copeland, "Alan Turing: British Mathematician and Logician," Britannica, February 7, 2023, https://www.britannica.com/biography/Alan-Turing; Caroline Davies, "Enigma Codebreaker Alan Turing Receives Royal Pardon," *Guardian*, December 24, 2013, https://www.theguardian.com/science/2013/dec/24/enigma-codebreaker-alan-turing-royal-pardon.

6. Lois Mandel, "The Computer Girls," *Cosmopolitan*, April 1967.

7. Simon Worrall, "The Secret History of the Women Who Got Us beyond the Moon," *National Geographic*, May 8, 2016, https://www.nationalgeographic.com/culture/article/160508-rocket-girls-women-moon-mars-nathalia-holt-space-ngbooktalk.

8. Nathan Ensmenger, "Making Programming Masculine," in *Gender Codes: Why Women Are Leaving Computing*, ed. Thomas J. Misa (Wiley, 2010), 115–41, https://doi.org/10.1002/9780470619926.

9. Sarah K. White, "Women in Tech Statistics: The Hard Truths of an Uphill Battle," CIO, March 13, 2023, https://www.cio.com/article/201905/women-in-tech-statistics-the-hard-truths-of-an-uphill-battle.html.

10. Arianna Johnson, "Meet the Women CEOs of the 2022 Cloud 100 List," *Forbes*, August 9, 2022, https://www.forbes.com/sites/ariannajohnson/2022/08/09/meet-the-women-ceos-of-the-2022-cloud-100-list/.

11. Catherine Adams, "Female Technology Journalists Report Abuse Is Still the Name of the Game," *Guardian*, October 11, 2015, https://www.theguardian.com/media/2015/oct/11/female-technology-journalists-abuse-zoe-quinn.

12. Entertainment Software Association, "U.S. Consumer Video Game Spending Totaled $60.4 Billion in 2021," Cision: PR Newswire, January 18, 2022, https://www.prnewswire.com/news-releases/us-consumer-video-game-spending-totaled-60-4-billion-in-2021--301462631.html.

13. Andrew Perrin, "5 Facts about Americans and Video Games," Pew Research Center, September 17, 2018, https://www.pewresearch.org/fact-tank/2018/09/17/5-facts-about-americans-and-video-games/.

14. Brittne Nelson Kakulla, "Who Is the 50+ Gamer? Gaming Attitudes and Habits of Adults Ages 50-Plus," AARP, December 2019, https://doi.org/10.26419/res.00328.001.

15. Adrienne Shaw, *Gaming at the Edge: Sexuality and Gender at the Margins of Gamer Culture* (University of Minnesota Press, 2015).

16. Perrin, "5 Facts about Americans."

17. Michael M. Kasumovic and Jeffrey H. Kuznekoff, "Insights into Sexism: Male Status and Performance Moderates Female-Directed Hostile and Amicable Behaviour," *PLOS ONE* 10, no. 7 (July 15, 2015): e0131613, https://doi.org/10.1371/journal.pone.0131613.

18. PickFu and Utopia Analytics, "Online Gaming in 2021: A New Survey of Gamers Shows Toxicity, Misogyny, and a Lack of Effective Moderation Risks Becoming Normalized," Cision: PR Newswire, November 11, 2021, https://www.prnewswire.com/news-releases/online-gaming-in-2021-a-new-survey-of-gamers-shows-toxicity-misogyny-and-a-lack-of-effective-moderation-risks-becoming-normalized-301421391.html.

19. Berrin Beasley and Tracy Collins Standley, "Shirts vs. Skins: Clothing as an Indicator of Gender Role Stereotyping in Video Games," *Mass Communication and Society* 5, no. 3 (August 1, 2002): 279–93, https://doi.org/10.1207/S15327825MCS0503_3.

20. Adrienne Shaw and Elizaveta Friesem, "Where Is the Queerness in Games? Types of Lesbian, Gay, Bisexual, Transgender, and Queer Content in Digital Games," *International Journal of Communication* 10 (July 27, 2016): 3877–89.

21. Caitlin Dewey, "The Only Guide to Gamergate You Will Ever Need to Read," *Washington Post*, October 14, 2014, https://www.washingtonpost.com/news/the-intersect/wp/2014/10/14/the-only-guide-to-gamergate-you-will-ever-need-to-read/.

22. Milo Yiannapolis, "Feminist Bullies Tearing the Video Game Industry Apart," Breitbart, September 1, 2014, https://www.breitbart.com/europe/2014/09/01/lying-greedy-promiscuous-feminist-bullies-are-tearing-the-video-game-industry-apart/.

23. Alex Hern, "Feminist Games Critic Cancels Talk after Terror Threat," *Guardian*, October 15, 2014, https://www.theguardian.com/technology/2014/oct/15/anita-sarkeesian-feminist-games-critic-cancels-talk.

24. Anita Sarkeesian, *Feminist Frequency 2021 Annual Report* (Feminist Frequency, 2021).

25. Callum Borchers, "The Bernie Bros Are Out in Full Force Harassing Female Reporters," *Washington Post*, November 25, 2021, https://www.washingtonpost.com/news/the-fix/wp/2016/06/07/the-bernie-bros-are-out-in-full-force-harassing-female-reporters/; Caitlin Ring Carlson and Haley Witt, "Online Harassment of U.S. Women Journalists and Its Impact on Press Freedom," *First Monday* 25, no. 11 (November 2, 2020), https://doi.org/10.5210/fm.v25i11.11071.

26. Annina Claesson, "'I Really Wanted Them to Have My Back, but They Didn't': Structural Barriers to Addressing Gendered Online Violence against Journalists," *Digital Journalism* (August 16, 2022): 1–20, https://doi.org/10.1080/21670811.2022.2110509.

27. Gina Masullo Chen et al., "'You Really Have to Have a Thick Skin': A Cross-Cultural Perspective on How Online Harassment Influences Female Journalists," *Journalism* 21, no. 7 (July 1, 2020): 877–95, https://doi.org/10.1177/1464884918768500.

28. Claesson, "'I Really Wanted."

29. Posetti et al., *Online Violence.*

30. Carlson and Witt, "Online Harassment."

31. Chen et al., "'Have to Have Thick Skin.'"

32. Laure Delisle et al., "Troll Patrol Findings: Using Crowdsourcing, Data Science, and Machine Learning to Measure Violence and Abuse against Women on Twitter," Amnesty International, December 19, 2018, https://decoders.amnesty.org/projects/troll-patrol/findings#what_did_we_find_container.

33. Chen et al., "'Have to Have Thick Skin.'"

34. Ela Stapley, *A Guide to Protecting Newsrooms and Journalists against Online Violence* (International Women's Media Foundation, September 2022), https://www.iwmf.org/newsroom-policy-guide/.

35. Lucy Westcott, "'The Threats Follow Us Home': Survey Details Risks for Female Journalists in U.S., Canada," Committee to Protect Journalists, September 4, 2019, https://cpj .org/2019/09/canada-usa-female-journalist-safety-online-harassment-survey/.

36. Center for Countering Digital Hate, *Hidden Hate: How Instagram Fails to Act on 9 in 10 Reports of Misogyny in DMs* (Center for Countering Digital Hate, April 6, 2022).

37. Lene Bech Sillesen, "The Invaluable Service of TrollBusters," *Columbia Journalism Review*, July 6, 2015, https://www.cjr.org/analysis/the_invaluable_service_of_trollbuster.php; TrollBusters, "About: TrollBusters: Offering Pest Control for Journalists," accessed May 17, 2023, https://yoursosteam.wordpress.com/about/.

38. Committee to Protect Journalists, "Online Harassment Archives," accessed September 22, 2022, https://cpj.org/tags/onlineharassment/.

39. Stapley, *Guide to Protecting Newsrooms*.

40. Julian Dibbell, "A Rape in Cyberspace: How an Evil Clown, a Haitian Trickster Spirit, Two Wizards, and a Cast of Dozens Turned a Database into a Society," *Village Voice*, December 23, 1993.

41. Nicholas Negroponte, *Being Digital* (Knopf Doubleday, 2015).

42. Lisa Nakamura, *Cybertypes: Race, Ethnicity, and Identity on the Internet* (Taylor and Francis, 2002).

43. Yu-Jen Chou, Shao-Kang Lo, and Ching-I. Teng, "Reasons for Avatar Gender Swapping by Online Game Players: A Qualitative Interview-Based Study," *International Journal of E-Business Research* 10, no. 4 (October 1, 2014): 1–17, https://doi.org/10.4018/ijebr .2014100101.

44. Jonathan Griffin, "Incels: Inside a Dark World of Online Hate," BBC News, August 13, 2021, https://www.bbc.com/news/blogs-trending-44053828.

45. Bruce Hoffman, Jacob Ware, and Ezra Shapiro, "Assessing the Threat of Incel Violence," *Studies in Conflict and Terrorism* 43, no. 7 (July 2, 2020): 565–87, https://doi.org/10.1080/1 057610X.2020.1751459; US Secret Service, "Secret Service's Latest Research Highlights Mass Violence Motived by Misogyny," March 15, 2022, https://www.secretservice.gov/newsroom/ releases/2022/03/secret-services-latest-research-highlights-mass-violence-motived-misogyny.

46. Staff of the US Secret Service National Threat Assessment Center (NTAC), *Hot Yoga Tallahassee: A Case Study of Misogynistic Extremism* (Department of Homeland Security, United States Secret Service, National Threat Assessment Center, March 2022), https://www .documentcloud.org/documents/21417518-secret-service-2018-yoga-class-shooting-case-study.

47. Caitlin Gibson, "'Do You Have White Teenage Sons? Listen Up.' How White Supremacists Are Recruiting Boys Online," *Washington Post*, September 17, 2019, https:// www.washingtonpost.com/lifestyle/on-parenting/do-you-have-white-teenage-sons-listen-up -how-white-supremacists-are-recruiting-boys-online/2019/09/17/f081e806-d3d5-11e9-9343 -40db57cf6abd_story.html.

48. M. T. G. Martinez, "El Vuelo de Las Colibríes. Defensa Personal Como Praxis Política Feminista En La Abya Yala," *Millcayac-Revista Digital de Ciencias Sociales* 7, no. 12 (2020): 141–52.

49. Meredith D. Clark, "To Tweet Our Own Cause: A Mixed-Methods Study of the Online Phenomenon 'Black Twitter'" (PhD diss., University of North Carolina at Chapel Hill, 2014), https://search.proquest.com/docview/1648168732/abstract/94FEC6267BAB499BPQ/1.

50. Clark, "Tweet Our Own Cause."

51. Philip Drost, "Changes at Twitter May Put Activists and Protesters at Risk, Say Experts," CBC, November 17, 2022, https://www.cbc.ca/radio/thecurrent/twitter-elon-musk-activism-1.6654034.

CHAPTER 13

1. Vivian Yee and Farnaz Fassihi, "'They Have Nothing to Lose': Why Young Iranians Are Rising Up Once Again," *New York Times*, September 24, 2022, https://www.nytimes.com/2022/09/24/world/middleeast/iran-protests-raisi-khamenei-hijab.html.

2. Constant Méheut and Monique Jaques, "The Female Soccer Players Challenging France's Hijab Ban," *New York Times*, April 18, 2022, https://www.nytimes.com/2022/04/18/sports/soccer/france-hijab-ban-soccer.html.

3. John Berger, *Ways of Seeing* (BBC and Penguin Books, 1972), 47.

4. George Gerbner and Larry Gross, "Living with Television: The Violence Profile," *Journal of Communication* 26, no. 2 (June 1, 1976): 172–94, https://doi.org/10.1111/j.1460-2466.1976.tb01397.x.

5. G. Tuchman, A. Kaplan Daniels, and J. Benet, *Hearth and Home: Images of Women in the Mass Media* (Oxford University Press, 1978).

6. Michael Ray Fitzgerald, "Television Portrayals of Native Americans: From Tonto to Uncle Ray (1949–2006)," *Left Curve*, no. 31 (2007): 129–38, 144; Shaun Hittle, "Sourcing-Level Symbolic Annihilation and Newspaper Coverage of Homelessness" (master's thesis, University of Kansas, 2011), http://search.proquest.com/docview/963541484/abstract; Alfred P. Kielwasser and Michelle A. Wolf, "Mainstream Television, Adolescent Homosexuality, and Significant Silence," *Critical Studies in Mass Communication* 9, no. 4 (December 1, 1992): 350–73, https://doi.org/10.1080/15295039209366839.

7. Merriam-Webster, "Bechdel Test," accessed September 30, 2022, https://www.merriam-webster.com/dictionary/Bechdel%20Test; Lois Neville, "What Is the Bechdel Test?" *Backstage*, September 17, 2022, https://www.backstage.com/magazine/article/what-is-the-bechdel-test-75534/.

8. Hannah Hartig, "About Six-in-Ten Americans Say Abortion Should Be Legal in All or Most Cases," Pew Research Center, June 13, 2022, https://www.pewresearch.org/fact-tank/2022/06/13/about-six-in-ten-americans-say-abortion-should-be-legal-in-all-or-most-cases-2/.

9. Marsha L. Vanderford, "Vilification and Social Movements: A Case Study of Pro-Life and Pro-Choice Rhetoric," *Quarterly Journal of Speech* 75, no. 2 (May 1, 1989): 166–82, https://doi.org/10.1080/00335638909383870.

10. Robert Barnes and Ann E. Marimow, "Supreme Court Ruling Leaves States Free to Outlaw Abortion," *Washington Post*, June 24, 2022, https://www.washingtonpost.com/politics/2022/06/24/supreme-court-ruling-abortion-dobbs/.

11. Celeste Huang-Menders, "The Fight to Protect Contraceptive Rights after *Dobbs*," Women's Media Center, August 4, 2022, https://womensmediacenter.com/fbomb/the-fight-to-protect-contraceptive-rights-after-dobbs.

12. D. J. Taylor et al., "Demographic Characteristics in Adult Paternity for First Births to Adolescents under 15 Years of Age," *Journal of Adolescent Health: Official Publication of the Society for Adolescent Medicine* 24, no. 4 (April 1999): 251–58, https://doi.org/10.1016/s1054-139x(98)00122-0.

13. Caroline K. Kaltefleiter, "Sixteen and Pregnant: Media Mommy Tracking and Hollywood's Exploitation of Teen Pregnancy," in *Hollywood's Exploited: Public Pedagogy, Corporate*

Movies, and Cultural Crisis, ed. Benjamin Frymer et al., Education, Politics, and Public Life (Palgrave Macmillan, 2010), 171–88, https://doi.org/10.1057/9780230117426_11.

14. Office of Population Affairs, "Trends in Teen Pregnancy and Childbearing," US Health and Human Services, accessed October 2, 2022, https://opa.hhs.gov/adolescent-health/reproductive-health-and-teen-pregnancy/trends-teen-pregnancy-and-childbearing.

15. Tanya R. Berry et al., "Women's Perceptions of Heart Disease and Breast Cancer and the Association with Media Representations of the Diseases," *Journal of Public Health* 38, no. 4 (December 2, 2016): e496–503, https://doi.org/10.1093/pubmed/fdv177.

16. Mary Angela Bock, Paromita Pain, and JhuCin Jhang, "Covering Nipples: News Discourse and the Framing of Breastfeeding," *Feminist Media Studies* 19, no. 1 (January 2, 2019): 53–69, https://doi.org/10.1080/14680777.2017.1313754.

17. Phillip Rucker, "Trump Says Fox's Megyn Kelly Had 'Blood Coming Out of Her Wherever,'" *Washington Post*, August 8, 2015, https://www.washingtonpost.com/news/post-politics/wp/2015/08/07/trump-says-foxs-megyn-kelly-had-blood-coming-out-of-her-wherever/.

18. Period Project, "We Advocate," accessed September 25, 2022, https://periodproject.org/pages/we-advocate.

19. Megan Specia, "Tackling 'Period Poverty,' Scotland Is 1st Nation to Make Sanitary Products Free," *New York Times*, November 24, 2020, https://www.nytimes.com/2020/11/24/world/europe/scotland-free-period-products.html.

20. Li Cohen, "Scotland Becomes 1st Country to Make Free Period Products the Law," CBS News, November 25, 2020, https://www.cbsnews.com/news/free-period-product-scotland/.

21. Thais Alves and Emily Spears, "The Period Project: The Fight for Menstrual Equity in Prisons," *Ms. Magazine*, February 24, 2022, https://msmagazine.com/2022/02/24/period-project-menstrual-equity-women-prisons/.

22. Jacqueline Gaybor, "Everyday (Online) Body Politics of Menstruation," *Feminist Media Studies* 22, no. 4 (2022): 898–913.

23. Adam Withnall, "Woman Explains Why She Ran the London Marathon on Her Period without a Tampon," *Independent*, August 10, 2015, https://www.independent.co.uk/life-style/health-and-families/kiran-gandhi-woman-runs-london-marathon-without-tampon-to-fight-the-stigma-of-a-woman-s-period-10447363.html.

24. Tom Phillips, "'It's Because I Had My Period': Swimmer Fu Yuanhui Praised for Breaking Taboo," *Guardian*, August 16, 2016, https://www.theguardian.com/sport/2016/aug/16/chinese-swimmer-fu-yuanhui-praised-for-breaking-periods-taboo.

25. "Birth Control: How to Skip Your Monthly Period," Mayo Clinic, accessed September 30, 2022, https://www.mayoclinic.org/healthy-lifestyle/birth-control/in-depth/womens-health/art-20044044.

26. Grand View Research, "Cosmetic Surgery and Procedure Market Size, Share and Trends Analysis Report by Type (Invasive, Non-invasive), Region (North America, Asia Pacific, Middle East and Africa, Latin America, Europe), and Segment Forecasts, 2022–2030," accessed October 2, 2022, https://www.grandviewresearch.com/industry-analysis/cosmetic-surgery-procedure-market; Research and Markets, "Overview of the $58 Billion U.S. Weight Loss Market 2022," GlobeNewswire, March 23, 2022, https://www.globenewswire.com/en/news-release/2022/03/23/2408315/28124/en/Overview-of-the-58-Billion-U-S-Weight-Loss-Market-2022.html.

27. Barbara Ellen, "Sorry, Gym Bunnies, but Men with Dad Bods Just Make Better Fathers," *Guardian*, September 5, 2020, https://www.theguardian.com/commentisfree/2020/sep/05/sorry-gym-bunnies-but-men-with-dad-bods-make-better-fathers-every-time.

28. Emma Bedor and Atsushi Tajima, "No Fat Moms! Celebrity Mothers' Weight-Loss Narratives in *People* Magazine," *Journal of Magazine Media* 13, no. 2 (August 2012), https://doi.org/10.1353/jmm.2012.0001.

29. Amanda M. Czerniawski, "Beauty beyond a Size 16," *Contexts* 15, no. 2 (May 1, 2016): 70–73, https://doi.org/10.1177/1536504216648157; Amanda M. Czerniawski, "Size Matters (in Modeling)," in *The Routledge Companion to Beauty Politics*, ed. Maxine Leeds Craig (Routledge, 2021).

30. Billy Perrigo, "Instagram's Body Image Problem May Be Unfixable, Experts Say," *Time*, September 16, 2021, https://time.com/6098771/instagram-body-image-teen-girls/.

31. Cavan Sleczkowski, "Disney Princesses with Realistic Waistlines Look Fabulous," HuffPost, October 30, 2014, https://www.huffpost.com/entry/disney-princess-real-waistline_n_6076634.

32. "Lizzo Plays 200-Year-Old Flute Owned by Former US President," BBC News, accessed September 28, 2022, https://www.bbc.com/news/entertainment-arts-63058818.

33. *Killing Us Softly 4: Advertising's Image of Women*, directed by Sut Jhally (Media Education Foundation, 2010).

34. Sara Idacavage, "Fashion History Lesson: The Bob Haircut, Feminism's Ultimate Style Statement," Fashionista, April 11, 2017, https://fashionista.com/2017/04/bob-short-haircut-hairstyle-history.

35. Amaris Castillo, "For Black Women Journalists, Wearing #NaturalHairOnAir Is a Point of Pride and Resistance," Poynter, February 22, 2022, https://www.poynter.org/business-work/2022/black-women-journalists-natural-hair-naturalhaironair/.

36. Malcolm X, *The Autobiography of Malcolm X* (Random House Publishing Group, 2015).

37. Christopher Mele, "Army Lifts Ban on Dreadlocks, and Black Servicewomen Rejoice," *New York Times*, February 10, 2017, https://www.nytimes.com/2017/02/10/us/army-ban-on-dreadlocks-black-servicewomen.html; Baze Mpinja, "The New Battle Braids of the U.S. Military," *Allure*, June 1, 2022, https://www.allure.com/story/black-hairstyles-updated-military-guidelines.

38. Darryl C. Murphy, "N.J. Ref Suspended for 2 Years over Forced Haircut of Wrestler with Dreadlocks," WHYY, September 18, 2019, https://whyy.org/articles/n-j-ref-suspended-for-2-years-over-forced-haircut-of-wrestler-with-dreadlocks/.

39. Rebecca Onion, "The Infamous Government Order Mandating Forced Haircuts for Native Americans," Slate, August 20, 2013, https://slate.com/human-interest/2013/08/haircut-order-commissioner-jones-letter-demanding-that-supervisors-force-native-americans-to-cut-their-hair.html; Cat Schuknecht, "School District Apologizes for Teacher Who Allegedly Cut Native American Child's Hair," NPR, December 6, 2018, https://www.npr.org/2018/12/06/673837893/school-district-apologizes-for-teacher-who-allegedly-cut-native-american-childs-.

40. Russell Contreras, "States Face Pressure to Ban Race-Based Hairstyle Prejudice," AP News, April 20, 2021, https://apnews.com/article/us-news-ap-top-news-wa-state-wire-ca-state-wire-new-mexico-7d614665ca6e2920c2970206d9194115.

41. Official CROWN Act, "About," accessed September 30, 2022, https://www.thecrownact.com/about.

42. Stephanie Petit, "High School Girl Kicked Out of Prom for Wearing Suit," *People*, May 23, 2016, https://people.com/health/high-school-girl-kicked-out-of-prom-for-wearing-suit/.

43. Dan Bilefsky, "Sent Home for Not Wearing Heels, She Ignited a British Rebellion," *New York Times*, January 25, 2017, https://www.nytimes.com/2017/01/25/world/europe/high-heels-british-inquiry-dress-codes-women.html.

44. Polly Thistlethwaite, "Stonewall," in *Encyclopedia of Sex and Gender*, ed. Fedwa Malti-Douglas (Thomson Gale, 2007).

45. Leland G. Spencer, "Bathroom Bills, Memes, and a Biopolitics of Trans Disposability," *Western Journal of Communication* 83, no. 5 (October 20, 2019): 542–59, https://doi.org/10.1 080/10570314.2019.1615635.

46. María Luisa Paúl and Anne Branigin, "A School Made Girls Wear Skirts. A Court Ruled It Unconstitutional.," *Washington Post*, June 15, 2022, https://www.washingtonpost.com/ nation/2022/06/15/north-carolina-dress-code-skirts/.

47. Juan Perez Jr., "Republican States Are Fuming—and Legislating—over Drag Performances," Politico, February 5, 2023, https://www.politico.com/news/2023/02/05/drag-show -bans-gop-statehouses-00081193.

48. Sadie E. Hale and Tomás Ojeda, "Acceptable Femininity? Gay Male Misogyny and the Policing of Queer Femininities," *European Journal of Women's Studies* 25, no. 3 (March 28, 2018): 310–24.

49. Roger Baker, Peter Burton, and Richard Smith, *Drag: A History of Female Impersonation in the Performing Arts* (NYU Press, 1994).

50. Mark Greene, "Dominance-Based Man Box Culture and White Supremacy," in *The Routledge Companion to Masculinity in American Literature and Culture*, ed. Lydia R. Cooper (Routledge, 2022).

51. Amanda Barroso and Anna Brown, "Gender Pay Gap in U.S. Held Steady in 2020," Pew Research Center, May 25, 2021, https://www.pewresearch.org/fact-tank/2021/05/25/ gender-pay-gap-facts/; Janet Napolitano, "Women Earn More College Degrees and Men Still Earn More Money," *Forbes*, 2018, https://www.forbes.com/sites/janetnapolitano/2018/09/04/ women-earn-more-college-degrees-and-men-still-earn-more-money/.

52. Anthony P. Carnevale, Nicole Smith, and Artem Gulish, *Women Can't Win: Despite Making Educational Gains and Pursuing High-Wage Majors, Women Still Earn Less than Men* (Georgetown University Center on Education and the Workforce, 2018), 4, https://cew .georgetown.edu/cew-reports/genderwagegap/.

53. US Government Accountability Office, *Retirement Security: Women Still Face Challenges* (US Government Accountability Office, July 2012).

54. Edward Segal, "Walmart Is Sued for Gender and Race Discrimination by EEOC," *Forbes*, February 11, 2022, https://www.forbes.com/sites/edwardsegal/2022/02/11/walmart-is -sued-for-gender-and-race-discrimination-by-eeoc/.

55. Chavie Lieber, "Walmart Just Got Hit with a Major Gender Discrimination Lawsuit," Vox, February 15, 2019, https://www.vox.com/the-goods/2019/2/15/18223752/walmart -gender-discrimination-class-action-lawsuit-2019.

56. Jennifer E. Dannals et al., "The Dynamics of Gender and Alternatives in Negotiation," *Journal of Applied Psychology* 106, no. 11 (2021): 1655–72, https://doi.org/10.1037/ apl0000867.

57. Maurie Backman, "Why Do Women Get Less Money from Social Security than Men?" Motley Fool, July 23, 2019, https://www.fool.com/retirement/2019/07/23/why-do-women -get-less-money-from-social-security-t.aspx.

58. Barroso and Brown, "Gender Pay Gap."

59. Matthew S. Rutledge, Alice Zulkarnain, and Sara Ellen King, "How Much Does Social Security Offset the Motherhood Penalty?" (paper no. 21-11, Center for Retirement Research, Boston College, July 2021), https://crr.bc.edu/briefs/how-much-does-social-security-offset-the -motherhood-penalty/.

60. Nicole Bateman and Martha Ross, "Why Has COVID-19 Been Especially Harmful for Working Women?" Brookings, October 14, 2020, https://www.brookings.edu/essay/why-has -covid-19-been-especially-harmful-for-working-women/.

61. Michael Sainato, "'I Don't Have a Choice': Childcare Cost Preventing US Women from Returning to Work," *Guardian*, November 5, 2021, https://www.theguardian.com/us-news/2021/nov/05/childcare-us-women-workforce.

62. Sandra Bishop-Josef et al., *Want to Grow the Economy? Fix the Child Care Crisis* (Ready Nation, January 2019).

63. Maggie Angst, "Goodbye 'Pink Tax': California Prohibits Charging Premiums for Women's Products," *Sacramento Bee*, September 29, 2022, https://www.sacbee.com/news/politics-government/article266437031.html.

64. Gabrielle Olya, "Women Pay $8K More than Men during Length of Car Ownership—Let's Change That," GOBankingRates, March 7, 2022, https://www.gobankingrates.com/money/financial-planning/women-pay-8k-more-than-men-during-length-of-car-ownership-lets-change-that/.

65. Glenn Hegar, Texas Comptroller of Public Accounts, "Sales Tax Exemptions for Healthcare Items: Over-the-Counter Drugs, Medicines, First Aid Supplies and Supplements," May 2020, https://comptroller.texas.gov/taxes/publications/94-155.php.

66. Roxanne Bland, "Taking Down the Tampon Tax," *Forbes*, March 25, 2021, https://www.forbes.com/sites/taxnotes/2021/03/25/taking-down-the-tampon-tax/.

67. Arlie Hochschild and Anne Machung, *The Second Shift: Working Families and the Revolution at Home* (Penguin, 1989).

68. Barroso and Brown, "Gender Pay Gap."

69. Steinem, "If Men Could Menstruate," *Ms. Magazine*, October 1978.

70. Leslie Morgan Steiner, ed., *Mommy Wars: Stay-at-Home and Career Moms Face Off on Their Choices, Their Lives, Their Families*, reprint ed. (Random House Trade Paperbacks, 2007).

71. Toni Schindler Zimmerman et al., "Deconstructing the 'Mommy Wars': The Battle over the Best Mom," *Journal of Feminist Family Therapy* 20, no. 3 (August 27, 2008): 203–19, https://doi.org/10.1080/08952830802264524.

72. Adam Clark Estes, "Republican Senate Candidate Says Rape Pregnancies Are a 'Gift from God,'" *Atlantic*, October 24, 2012, https://www.theatlantic.com/politics/archive/2012/10/republican-senate-candidate-says-rape-pregnancies-are-gift-god/322172/.

73. Lindsey Bever, "Women's Pain Often Is Dismissed by Doctors," *Washington Post*, December 13, 2022, https://www.washingtonpost.com/wellness/interactive/2022/women-pain-gender-bias-doctors/.

74. Chelsea Conaboy, "Maternal Instinct Is a Myth That Men Created," *New York Times*, August 26, 2022, https://www.nytimes.com/2022/08/26/opinion/sunday/maternal-instinct-myth.html.

75. Lesley J. Rogers, "Sexing the Brain: The Science and Pseudoscience of Sex Differences," *Kaohsiung Journal of Medical Sciences* 26, no. S6t (June 1, 2010): 55–56, https://doi.org/10.1016/S1607-551X(10)70051-6.

76. John Gray, *Men Are from Mars, Women Are from Venus: The Classic Guide to Understanding the Opposite Sex* (Zondervan, 2009).

77. Jerry Bergman, *The Darwin Effect: It's Influence on Nazism, Eugenics, Racism, Communism, Capitalism and Sexism* (New Leaf, 2014); Sean P. David et al., "Potential Reporting Bias in Neuroimaging Studies of Sex Differences," *Scientific Reports* 8, no. 1 (April 17, 2018): 6082, https://doi.org/10.1038/s41598-018-23976-1.

78. Chloe Reichel, "Research-Based Tips for Reporting on Science Research," Journalist's Resource, November 22, 2019, https://journalistsresource.org/home/research-communicating-science-dietram-scheufele/.

79. Denise-Marie Ordway, "Covering Scientific Consensus: What to Avoid and How to Get It Right," Journalist's Resource, November 23, 2021, https://journalistsresource.org/media/scientific-consensus-news-tips/.

80. Ordway, "Covering Scientific Consensus."

81. Joseph Henrich, Steven J. Heine, and Ara Norenzayan, "The Weirdest People in the World?" *Behavioral and Brain Sciences* 33, no. 2–3 (June 2010): 61–83, https://doi.org/10.1017/S0140525X0999152X.

82. Esteban G. Burchard et al., "Moving toward True Inclusion of Racial/Ethnic Minorities in Federally Funded Studies: A Key Step for Achieving Respiratory Health Equality in the United States," *American Journal of Respiratory and Critical Care Medicine* 191, no. 5 (March 1, 2015): 514–21, https://doi.org/10.1164/rccm.201410-1944PP; Moon S. Chen et al., "Twenty Years Post-NIH Revitalization Act: Enhancing Minority Participation in Clinical Trials (EMPaCT): Laying the Groundwork for Improving Minority Clinical Trial Accrual," *Cancer* 120, no. S7 (March 18, 2014): 1091–96, https://doi.org/10.1002/cncr.28575;Sam S. Oh et al., "Diversity in Clinical and Biomedical Research: A Promise Yet to Be Fulfilled," *PLOS Medicine* 12, no. 12 (December 15, 2015): e1001918, https://doi.org/10.1371/journal.pmed.1001918.

CHAPTER 14

1. David Nakamura, "White House: ESPN's Jemele Hill Should Be Fired for Calling Trump a 'White Supremacist,'" *Washington Post*, September 13, 2017, https://www.washingtonpost.com/news/post-politics/wp/2017/09/13/white-house-espns-jemele-hill-should-be-fired-for-calling-trump-a-white-supremacist/.

2. German Lopez, "Donald Trump's War with ESPN and Jemele Hill, Explained," Vox, September 15, 2017, https://www.vox.com/identities/2017/9/15/16313800/trump-jemele-hill-espn-white-supremacist.

3. Jacob Bogage, "Jemele Hill Stands by Calling President Trump a White Supremacist: 'I Thought I Was Saying Water Is Wet,'" *Washington Post*, December 26, 2018, https://www.washingtonpost.com/sports/2018/12/26/jemele-hill-stands-by-calling-president-trump-white-supremacist-i-thought-i-was-saying-water-is-wet/.

4. Ever J. Figueroa, "'If I Tweeted Like That, It's Entirely Possible I'd Get Fired': Sports Journalists Discourse of Jemele Hill versus Donald Trump," *Feminist Media Studies* (2023), http://doi.org./10.1080/14680777.2023.2229045.

5. Michael L. Butterworth, "The Athlete as Citizen: Judgement and Rhetorical Invention in Sport," *Sport in Society* 17, no. 7 (August 9, 2014): 867–83, https://doi.org/10.1080/17430437.2013.806033; Michael L. Butterworth, *Baseball and Rhetorics of Purity: The National Pastime and American Identity during the War on Terror* (University of Alabama Press, 2010).

6. Charlene Weaving, "Examining 50 Years of 'Beautiful' in *Sports Illustrated Swimsuit Issue*," *Journal of the Philosophy of Sport* 43, no. 3 (September 1, 2016): 380–93, https://doi.org/10.1080/00948705.2016.1208534.

7. Ruth Ferla, "At 81, Martha Stewart Is the *Sports Illustrated Swimsuit Issue* Cover Star," *New York Times*, May 15, 2023, https://www.nytimes.com/2023/05/15/style/martha-stewart-sports-illustrated-cover.html.

8. Mitch Abramson, "1999 World Cup Champion Brandi Chastain Gets Things off Her Chest," *New York Daily News*, August 22, 2009, https://www.nydailynews.com/sports/more-sports/1999-world-cup-champion-brandi-chastain-chest-article-1.398009.

9. Barry Glendenning, "Women's World Cup Game-Changing Moments No. 4: Brandi Chastain in 1999," *Guardian*, June 20, 2019, https://www.theguardian.com/football/2019/

jun/20/womens-world-cup-game-changing-moments-no4-brandi-chastain-1999;   Richard Sandomir, "Sports Business: Was Sports Bra Celebration Spontaneous?" *New York Times*, July 18, 1999, https://www.nytimes.com/1999/07/18/sports/sports-business-was-sports-bra-celebration-spontaneous.html; George Vecsey, "Sports of the Times: Will Women Enjoy a League of Their Own?" *New York Times*, July 12, 1999, https://www.nytimes.com/1999/07/12/sports/sports-of-the-times-will-women-enjoy-a-league-of-their-own.html.

10. Laura Mulvey, "Visual Pleasure and Narrative Cinema," *Screen* 16, no. 3 (1975).

11. John Berger, *Ways of Seeing* (BBC and Penguin Books, 1972).

12. Saba Aziz, "WTA 'Modernises' Tennis Dress Code after Catsuit Ban," Al Jazeera, February 20, 2019, https://www.aljazeera.com/features/2019/2/20/after-catsuit-controversy-womens-tennis-modernises-dress-code.

13. Sanya Mansoor, "'It's about Creating Equity.' The Significance of German Gymnasts' Full-Length Bodysuits at the Tokyo Olympics," *Time*, July 25, 2021, https://time.com/6083431/german-gymnasts-unitard-olympics/.

14. Jenny Gross, "Handball Federation Ends Bikini Bottom Requirement for Women," *New York Times*, November 1, 2021, https://www.nytimes.com/2021/11/01/sports/women-beach-handball-bikini.html.

15. Ed Aarons, "Ada Hegerberg: First Women's Ballon d'Or Marred as Winner Is Asked to Twerk," *Guardian*, December 4, 2018, https://www.theguardian.com/football/2018/dec/03/ballon-dor-ada-hegerberg-twerk-luka-modric.

16. Sasha DiGiulian, "Media Outlets, Stop Sexualizing Women in Sports," *Outside*, October 18, 2021, https://www.outsideonline.com/outdoor-adventure/climbing/women-sports-media-johanna-farber/.

17. Jaime Schultz, *Women's Sports: What Everyone Needs to Know* (Oxford University Press, 2018).

18. Haley Shapley, "Sports Played a Surprising Role in Women's Suffrage," *Teen Vogue*, August 18, 2020, https://www.teenvogue.com/story/womens-suffrage-sports-history.

19. Katharina Bonzel, "A League of Their Own: The Impossibility of the Female Sports Hero," *Screening the Past* 37 (2013), http://www.screeningthepast.com/issue-37-first-release/a-league-of-their-own-the-impossibility-of-the-female-sports-hero/.

20. All-American Girls Professional Baseball League, "Charm School," accessed March 27, 2022, https://www.aagpbl.org/history/charm-school.

21. "Wrigley Puts $100,000 into Girls Softball," *Miami News*, May 2, 1943.

22. "Baseball in Skirts Ventures into Hudson Field Tonight," *Journal Herald*, May 12, 1950; "Daring Dish of Baseball to Be Served Shreveport Fans," *Shreveport Times*, May 8, 1946.

23. "Daring Dish of Baseball."

24. Manisha Aggarwal-Schifellite, "What It Was Like to Be a Female Athlete before Title IX," *Harvard Gazette*, November 19, 2020, https://news.harvard.edu/gazette/story/2020/11/what-it-was-like-to-be-a-female-athlete-before-title-ix/; Olivia B. Waxman, "She Exposed the Discrimination in College Sports before Title IX. Now She's a Women's History Month Honoree," *Time*, March 1, 2018, https://time.com/5175812/title-ix-sports-womens-history/.

25. Bil Gilbert and Nancy Williamson, "Sport Is Unfair to Women," *Sports Illustrated*, May 28, 1973.

26. Barbara Winslow, *The Impact of Title IX* (Gilder Lehrman Institute of American History, September 24, 2016).

27. Maria Cramer, "How Women's Sports Teams Got Their Start," *New York Times*, April 28, 2022, https://www.nytimes.com/2022/04/28/sports/title-ix-anniversary-womens-sports.html.

28. Julie B. Lane, "Women Are a Problem: Title IX Narratives in the *New York Times* and the *Washington Post*, 1974–1975," *Communication and Sport* 6, no. 1 (2018): 36, https://doi .org/10.1177/2167479516685578.

29. Lane, "Women Are a Problem," 36.

30. Rey Mashayekhi, "The Financial Fallout of a Canceled College Football Season," *Fortune*, August 10, 2020, https://fortune.com/2020/08/10/college-football-cancelled-2020-ncaa -financial-impact-revenue-schools-big-ten-sec-acc-big-12-pac-12/.

31. Ryan Foley, "Bias Suit Seeks to Block Iowa from Cutting Women's Swim Team," *Washington Post*, September 25, 2020, https://www.washingtonpost.com/sports/bias-suit-seeks-to-block-iowa-from-cutting-womens-swim-team/2020/09/25/79d2c732-ff50-11ea-b0e4-350e4e60cc91_story.html.

32. Jacey Fortin, "The 'Hustler' vs. the Feminist Champion: Inside the 'Battle of the Sexes,'" *New York Times*, September 30, 2017, https://www.nytimes.com/2017/09/29/movies/battle -of-sexes.html; Joe Garner and Bob Costas, *And the Crowd Goes Wild: Relive the Most Celebrated Sporting Events Ever Broadcast* (Sourcebooks, 2002).

33. Georgia Slater, "Dick's Sporting Goods Sends Workout Equipment to NCAA Women's Teams after Weight Room Controversy," *People*, March 22, 2021, https://people.com/sports/ dicks-sporting-goods-sends-workout-equipment-ncaa-womens-teams/.

34. Steve Almasy, "Toni Harris Gets a College Football Scholarship to Play Defense on Men's Team," CNN, March 1, 2019, https://www.cnn.com/2019/02/28/sport/missouri -female-football-player-scholarship-spt-trnd.

35. Will Levith, "Will Becca Longo Become the First Woman Drafted into the NFL?" InsideHook, June 15, 2017, https://www.insidehook.com/article/sports/will-becca-longo-nfls -first-female-player.

36. Andrew Keh, "U.S. Wins World Cup and Becomes a Champion for Its Time," *New York Times*, July 7, 2019, https://www.nytimes.com/2019/07/07/sports/soccer/us-wins-world -cup-and-becomes-a-champion-for-its-time.html.

37. Peter Keating, "Analysis: What Equal Pay in Women's Sports Really Means," ESPN, May 14, 2020, https://www.espn.com/espnw/article/28971949/analysis-equal-pay-sports -really-means-fight-goes-us-women-soccer.

38. Cheryl Cooky et al., "One and Done: The Long Eclipse of Women's Televised Sports, 1989–2019," *Communication and Sport* 9, no. 3 (June 1, 2021): 347–71, https://doi .org/10.1177/21674795211003524.

39. Jonetta D. Weber and Robert M. Carini, "Where Are the Female Athletes in *Sports Illustrated*? A Content Analysis of Covers (2000–2011)," *International Review for the Sociology of Sport* 48, no. 2 (April 1, 2013): 196–203, https://doi.org/10.1177/1012690211434230.

40. Michael A. Messner, Margaret Carlisle Duncan, and Cheryl Cooky, "Silence, Sports Bras, and Wrestling Porn: Women in Televised Sports News and Highlights Shows," *Journal of Sport and Social Issues* 27, no. 1 (February 1, 2003): 38–51, https://doi.org/ 10.1177/0193732502239583.

41. Marie Hardin et al., "Olympic Photo Coverage Fair to Female Athletes," *Newspaper Research Journal* 23, nos. 2–3 (March 22, 2002), 64–79.

42. Mariah Burton Nelson, *The Stronger Women Get, the More Men Love Football: Sexism and the American Culture of Sports* (Avon Books, 1995), 221.

43. Pamela C. Laucella et al., "Diversifying the Sports Department and Covering Women's Sports: A Survey of Sports Editors," *Journalism and Mass Communication Quarterly* 94, no. 3 (September 1, 2017): 772–92, https://doi.org/10.1177/1077699016654443.

44. Cooky et al., "One and Done."

45. Cooky et al., "One and Done"; Sarah Scire, "Most TV Completely Ignores Women's Sports, a 30-Year Study Finds," Nieman Lab, March 24, 2021, https://www.niemanlab.org/2021/03/most-tv-completely-ignores-womens-sports-a-30-year-study-finds/.

46. Menelaos Apostolou, Nicholas Frantzides, and Andromahi Pavlidou, "Men Competing, Men Watching: Exploring Watching-Pattern Contingencies in Sports," *International Journal of Sport Communication* 7, no. 4 (December 2014): 462–76; Qingru Xu and Andrew C. Billings, "Feelings of Pleasure, Arousal, and Dominance: Men and Women's Responses to Athletic Images in Different Types of Sports," *Journal of Gender Studies* 31, no. 7 (October 3, 2022): 796–811, https://doi.org/10.1080/09589236.2020.1867831.

47. Amy Jones and Jennifer Greer, "You Don't Look like an Athlete: The Effects of Feminine Appearance on Audience Perceptions of Female Athletes and Women's Sports," *Journal of Sport Behavior* 34, no. 4 (2011): 358–77.

48. Elizabeth A. Daniels and Heidi Wartena, "Athlete or Sex Symbol: What Boys Think of Media Representations of Female Athletes," *Sex Roles* 65, no. 7 (October 1, 2011): 566–79, https://doi.org/10.1007/s11199-011-9959-7.

49. Association for Women in Sports Media, "Mary Garber Pioneer Award," accessed February 14, 2023, http://awsmonline.org/mary-garber-pioneer-award.

50. Association for Women in Sports Media, "Mary Garber Pioneer Award."

51. Joanne Lannin, *Who Let Them In? Pathbreaking Women in Sports Journalism* (Rowman and Littlefield, 2022).

52. Paola Boivin, "43 Years after Melissa Ludtke, Female Sports Journalists Face the Same Treatment," Global Sport Matters, March 12, 2021, https://globalsportmatters.com/culture/2021/03/12/43-years-after-melissa-ludtke-female-sports-journalists-face-the-same-treatment/.

53. Marie Hardin and Stacie Shain, "'Feeling Much Smaller than You Know You Are': The Fragmented Professional Identity of Female Sports Journalists," *Critical Studies in Media Communication* 23, no. 4 (October 1, 2006): 322–38, https://doi.org/10.1080/07393180600933147.

54. R. Glenn Cummins, Monica Ortiz, and Andrea Rankine, "'Elevator Eyes' in Sports Broadcasting: Visual Objectification of Male and Female Sports Reporters," *Communication and Sport* 7, no. 6 (October 21, 2018), http://journals.sagepub.com/doi/full/10.1177/2167479518806168.

55. Tracy Everbach, "'I Realized It Was about Them . . . Not Me': Women Sports Journalists and Harassment," in *Mediating Misogyny: Gender, Technology, and Harassment*, ed. Jacqueline Ryan Vickery and Tracy Everbach (Springer International, 2018), 131–49, https://doi.org/10.1007/978-3-319-72917-6_7; Hardin and Shain, "'Feeling Much Smaller.'"

56. Richard Lapchick, *The 2018 Associated Press Sports Editors Racial and Gender Report Card* (The Institute for Diversity and Ethics in Sport, May 2, 2018).

57. Laucella et al., "Diversifying the Sports Department."

58. Lapchick, *2018 Associated Press Sports Editors.*

59. Katie Mettler, "The Disgustingly Obscene 'Everyday' Harassment of Sports Media Women: A Lesson for Men," *Washington Post*, accessed October 2, 2022, https://www.washingtonpost.com/news/morning-mix/wp/2016/04/28/morethanmean-a-graphic-lesson-for-men-in-the-everyday-harassment-of-women-in-sports-media/.

60. Richard Deitsch, "Behind the Peabody-Winning #MoreThanMean Video," *Sports Illustrated*, May 7, 2017, https://www.si.com/media/2017/05/07/peabody-awards-more-than-mean-sarah-spain-julie-dicaro.

61. Rachel Axon, "Ex-Baylor Title IX Officer Criticizes School's Sex Assault Response," *USA Today*, November 2, 2016, https://www.usatoday.com/story/sports/ncaaf/big12/2016/11/02/patty-crawford-former-baylor-title-ix-officer-sexual-assault-response-football/

93212234/; Camila Domonoske, "New Lawsuit Alleges Baylor Players Gang-Raped Women as 'Bonding Experience,'" NPR, May 17, 2017, https://www.npr.org/sections/thetwo-way/2017/05/17/528804172/new-lawsuit-alleges-baylor-players-gang-raped-women-as-bonding-experience; Kate McGee, "NCAA Declines to Punish Baylor over Handling of Sexual Assault Allegations but Criticizes University for 'Moral and Ethical Failings,'" *Texas Tribune*, August 11, 2021, https://www.texastribune.org/2021/08/11/baylor-sexual-misconduct-investigation-ncaa/; Matthew Watkins, "Lawsuit Alleges Even More Rapes by Baylor Football Players," *Texas Tribune*, January 28, 2017, https://www.texastribune.org/2017/01/27/lawsuit-alleges-even-more-rapes-baylor-football-pl/.

62. Christine Hauser, "13 Nassar Abuse Victims Seek $10 Million Each from F.B.I.," *New York Times*, April 21, 2022, https://www.nytimes.com/2022/04/21/sports/larry-nassar-usa-gymnastics-fbi.html.

63. Molly Mita, "ESPN Nets Prestigious Peabody Award for Coverage of Michigan State Gymnastics Stories," ESPN Front Row, April 23, 2019, https://www.espnfrontrow.com/2019/04/espn-nets-prestigious-peabody-award-for-coverage-of-michigan-state-gymnastics-stories/.

64. Hauser, "13 Nassar Abuse Victims"; Laurel Wamsley, "Nassar Gets Up to 175 Years in Prison; Michigan State President Resigns," NPR, January 24, 2018, https://www.npr.org/sections/thetwo-way/2018/01/24/580304914/larry-nassar-sentenced-to-up-to-175-years-in-prison-by-michigan-judge.

65. Associated Press, "Carl Nassib, the First Openly Gay Active NFL Player, Signs with Buccaneers," Sportsnet, August 17, 2022, https://www.sportsnet.ca/nfl/carl-nassib-the-first-openly-gay-active-nfl-player-signs-with-buccaneers/.

66. Ken Belson, "Raiders' Carl Nassib Announces He's Gay, an N.F.L. First," *New York Times*, June 21, 2021, https://www.nytimes.com/2021/06/21/sports/football/carl-nassib-gay-nfl.html.

67. Amanda Onion, "How Greg Louganis' Olympic Diving Accident Forced a Conversation about AIDS," History, June 10, 2021, https://www.history.com/news/greg-louganis-diving-accident-aids.

68. Bettina Boxall and Frank Wiliams, "Louganis Disclosure Greeted with Sadness," *Los Angeles Times*, February 24, 1995.

69. Jenée Desmond-Harris, "Despite Decades of Racist and Sexist Attacks, Serena Williams Keeps Winning," Vox, January 28, 2017, https://www.vox.com/2017/1/28/14424624/serena-williams-wins-australian-open-venus-record-racist-sexist-attacks.

70. Jenée Desmond-Harris, "Serena Williams Is Constantly the Target of Disgusting Racist and Sexist Attacks," Vox, March 11, 2015, https://www.vox.com/2015/3/11/8189679/serena-williams-indian-wells-racism.

71. Eliza Anyangwe, "Misogynoir: Where Racism and Sexism Meet," *Guardian*, October 5, 2015, https://www.theguardian.com/lifeandstyle/2015/oct/05/what-is-misogynoir.

72. Michael J. de la Merced, "Citadel Broadcasting Files for Bankruptcy," *New York Times*, December 21, 2009, https://www.nytimes.com/2009/12/21/business/media/21citadel.html; Robert D. McFadden, "Don Imus, Radio Host Who Pushed Boundaries, Dies at 79," *New York Times*, December 27, 2019, https://www.nytimes.com/2019/12/27/arts/don-imus-dead.html.

73. Jonathan Abrams, "Brittney Griner Will Return to W.N.B.A.," *New York Times*, February 19, 2023, https://www.nytimes.com/2023/02/18/sports/basketball/brittney-griner-phoenix-mercury.html; Dave Zirin, "By Attacking Brittney Griner, Trump Signals to His Base: 'I'm Still Racist,'" *Nation*, August 2, 2022, https://www.thenation.com/article/politics/brittney-griner-trump-racism/.

74. Kelefa Sanneh, "Tucker Carlson's Fighting Words," *New Yorker*, April 3, 2017, https://www.newyorker.com/magazine/2017/04/10/tucker-carlsons-fighting-words.

75. Renée Richards, *No Way Renée: The Second Half of My Notorious Life* (Simon and Schuster, 2007).

76. Katie Barnes, "Thomas First Transgender Athlete to Win D-I Title," ESPN, March 17, 2022, https://www.espn.com/college-sports/story/_/id/33529775/amid-protests-pennsylvania-swimmer-lia-thomas-becomes-first-known-transgender-athlete-win-division-national-championship.

77. FINA, *Policy on Men's and Women's Competition* (FINA, n.d.), https://www.documentcloud.org/documents/22063914-fina-policy-on-mens-and-womens-competition.

78. Sean Ingle, "Caster Semenya Out of World 5,000 m as Coe Signals Tougher Female Sport Rules," *Guardian*, July 21, 2022, https://www.theguardian.com/sport/2022/jul/21/caster-semenya-out-of-world-5000m-as-coe-signals-tougher-female-sport-rules.

79. Reuters, "Caster Semenya Offered to Show Officials Her Vagina to Prove She Is Female," *Guardian*, May 24, 2022, https://www.theguardian.com/sport/2022/may/24/caster-semenya-800m-world-athletics-hbo-interview.

80. American Civil Liberties Union, "The Coordinated Attack on Trans Student Athletes," February 26, 2021, https://www.aclu.org/news/lgbtq-rights/the-coordinated-attack-on-trans-student-athletes/; Candice Hare, "Idaho Transgender Athlete Legislation, the Blueprint for the Nation," KMVT11, April 6, 2021, https://www.kmvt.com/2021/04/07/idaho-transgender-athlete-legislation-the-blueprint-for-the-nation/.

81. Chuck Lindell, "Texas Senate, Moving with Haste, Passes Transgender Sports Bill," *Austin American-Statesman*, updated October 16, 2021, https://www.statesman.com/story/news/2021/10/15/texas-state-senate-approves-transgender-sports-bill-student-athletes/8476389002/.

82. Maggie Mertens, "Separating Sports by Sex Doesn't Make Sense," *Atlantic*, September 17, 2022, https://www.theatlantic.com/culture/archive/2022/09/sports-gender-sex-segregation-coed/671460/.

83. Chase Strangio and Gabriel Arkles, "Four Myths about Trans Athletes, Debunked," American Civil Liberties Union, April 30, 2020, https://www.aclu.org/news/lgbtq-rights/four-myths-about-trans-athletes-debunked/.

84. Holly Thorpe, et al., "Journalists on a Journey: Towards Responsible Media on Transgender Participation in Sport," *Journalism Studies* (May 3, 2023): 1–19, https://doi.org/10.1080/1461670X.2023.2206920.

CHAPTER 15

1. Adrian Parr, "The Gender-Climate-Injustice Nexus," in *The Oxford Handbook of Feminist Philosophy*, ed. Kim Q. Hall and Ásta (Oxford University Press, 2021), https://doi.org/10.1093/oxfordhb/9780190628925.013.39.

2. Kate Sheppard, "'Drill, Baby, Drill?' Blame Michael Steele," *Mother Jones*, May 5, 2010, https://www.motherjones.com/politics/2010/05/drill-baby-drill-blame-michael-steele/.

3. Christine Agius, Annika Bergman Rosamond, and Catarina Kinnvall, "Populism, Ontological Insecurity and Gendered Nationalism: Masculinity, Climate Denial and Covid-19," *Politics, Religion and Ideology* 21, no. 4 (October 1, 2020): 432–50, https://doi.org/10.1080/21567689.2020.1851871.

4. Agius, Rosamond, and Kinnvall, "Populism, Ontological Insecurity," 449.

5. Elian Peltier, "Malala Yousafzai Graduates from Oxford University," *New York Times*, June 19, 2020, https://www.nytimes.com/2020/06/19/world/europe/malala-oxford-graduation.html.

6. Mary Wollstonecraft, *A Vindication of the Rights of Women and a Vindication of the Rights of Men* (Cosimo, 2008).

7. Rafia Zakaria, *Against White Feminism: Notes on Disruption* (W. W. Norton, 2021).

8. Anne Strainchamps, "How Afghanistan Became America's 'First Feminist War,'" Wisconsin Public Radio, October 1, 2021, https://www.wpr.org/how-afghanistan-became-americas-first-feminist-war.

9. Elena Ruíz, "Postcolonial and Decolonial Theories," in *The Oxford Handbook of Feminist Philosophy*, ed. Kim Q. Hall and Ásta (Oxford University Press, 2021), https://doi.org/10.1093/oxfordhb/9780190628925.013.45.

10. Dominick Mastrangelo, "Reporter Suing *Washington Post* for Discrimination after Coming Forward about Sexual Assault," *Hill*, July 22, 2021, https://thehill.com/homenews/media/564356-reporter-suing-washington-post-for-discrimination-after-coming-forward-about.

11. Donald L. Shaw, "News Bias and the Telegraph: A Study of Historical Change," *Journalism Quarterly* 44, no. 1 (March 1, 1967): 3–31, https://doi.org/10.1177/107769906704400101.

12. Bob Ostertag, *People's Movements, People's Press: The Journalism of Social Justice Movements* (Beacon Press, 2007).

13. Michael Schudson, "The Objectivity Norm in American Journalism," *Journalism* 2, no. 2 (2001): 149–70.

14. Mercedes Lynn de Uriarte, Cristina Bodinger-de Uriarte, and José Luis Benavides, *Diversity Disconnects: From Class Room to News Room* (Ford Foundation, 2003).

15. de Uriarte, Bodinger-de Uriarte, and Benavides, *Diversity Disconnects*, 75.

16. Joe Killian, "Knight Foundation Urges UNC-Chapel Hill Trustees to Approve Tenure for Acclaimed Journalist," Pulse, May 21, 2021, http://pulse.ncpolicywatch.org/2021/05/21/knight-foundation-urges-unc-chapel-hill-trustees-to-approve-tenure-for-acclaimed-journalist/.

17. Jake Silverstein, "On Recent Criticism of *1619 Project*," *New York Times*, October 16, 2020, https://www.nytimes.com/2020/10/16/magazine/criticism-1619-project.html; Jake Silverstein, "An Update to the *1619 Project*," *New York Times*, March 11, 2020, https://www.nytimes.com/2020/03/11/magazine/an-update-to-the-1619-project.html.

18. Joe Killian, "Nikole Hannah-Jones Declines UNC Tenure Offer, Heads to Howard University," NC Policy Watch, July 6, 2021, https://ncpolicywatch.com/2021/07/06/nikole-hannah-jones-declines-unc-tenure-offer-heads-to-howard-university/.

19. David Folkenflik, "After Contentious Debate, UNC Grants Tenure to Nikole Hannah-Jones," NPR, June 30, 2021, https://www.npr.org/2021/06/30/1011880598/after-contentious-debate-unc-grants-tenure-to-nikole-hannah-jones.

20. James H. Sweet, "Is History History? Identity Politics and Teleologies of the Present," *Perspectives on History* 60, no. 6 (September 2022), https://www.historians.org/publications-and-directories/perspectives-on-history/september-2022/is-history-history-identity-politics-and-teleologies-of-the-present.

21. Sissel McCarthy, "Q: What's Wrong with Bothsidesism?" News Literacy Matters, October 21, 2022, https://newsliteracymatters.com/2022/10/21/%ef%bf%bcq-whats-wrong-with-bothsidesism/.

22. McCarthy, "What's Wrong with Bothsidesism?"

23. Sahar Khamis and Rasha El-Ibiary, "Egyptian Women Journalists' Feminist Voices in a Shifting Digitalized Journalistic Field," *Digital Journalism* 10, no. 7 (August 9, 2022): 1245, https://doi.org/10.1080/21670811.2022.2039738.

24. Derek Thompson, "Trump's Lies Are a Virus, and News Organizations Are the Host," *Atlantic*, November 19, 2018, https://www.theatlantic.com/ideas/archive/2018/11/should -media-repeat-trumps-lies/576148/.

25. Margaret A. McLaren, *Feminism, Foucault, and Embodied Subjectivity*, SUNY Series in Contemporary Continental Philosophy (State University of New York Press, 2002).

26. Carol Gilligan, *In a Different Voice: Psychological Theory and Women's Development* (Harvard University Press, 1993), 74.

27. McLaren, *Feminism, Foucault*.

28. Joan C. Tronto, "Women and Caring: What Can Feminists Learn about Morality from Caring?" in *Gender/Body/Knowledge: Feminist Reconstructions of Being and Knowing*, ed. Alison M. Jaggar and Susan Bordo (Rutgers University Press, 1989), 224–55.

29. Steve Buttry, "Dori Maynard Helped Journalists View Diversity as a Matter of Accuracy," *Buttry Diary* (blog), February 25, 2015, https://stevebuttry.wordpress.com/2015/02/25/dori-maynard-helped-journalists-view-diversity-as-a-matter-of-accuracy/.

30. Meenakshi Gigi Durham, "On the Relevance of Standpoint Epistemology to the Practice of Journalism: The Case for 'Strong Objectivity,'" *Communication Theory* 8, no. 2 (May 1, 1998): 117–40, https://doi.org/10.1111/j.1468-2885.1998.tb00213.x.

31. Solutions Journalism Network, accessed September 10, 2022, https://www.solutions journalism.org/.

32. Anita Varma, "Evoking Empathy or Enacting Solidarity with Marginalized Communities? A Case Study of Journalistic Humanizing Techniques in the San Francisco Homeless Project," *Journalism Studies* 21, no. 12 (September 9, 2020): 1705–23, https://doi.org/10.108 0/1461670X.2020.1789495.

33. Michael Argyle, *The Psychology of Happiness* (Routledge, 2013).

34. Samuel S. Franklin, *The Psychology of Happiness: A Good Human Life* (Cambridge University Press, 2010).

35. A. H. Maslow, "A Theory of Human Motivation," *Psychological Review* 50 (1943): 370–96.

36. Roy Rosenzweig, *Eight Hours for What We Will: Workers and Leisure in an Industrial City, 1870–1920* (Cambridge University Press, 1985).

37. Thomas L. Jacobson, "Amartya Sen's Capabilities Approach and Communication for Development and Social Change," *Journal of Communication* 66, no. 5 (October 6, 2016): 789–810, https://doi.org/10.1111/jcom.12252; Amartya Sen, "Human Rights and Capabilities," *Journal of Human Development* 6, no. 2 (July 1, 2005): 151–66, https://doi.org/10.1080/14649880500120491.

38. Martha C. Nussbaum, "Education and Democratic Citizenship: Capabilities and Quality Education," *Journal of Human Development* 7, no. 3 (November 1, 2006): 385–95, https://doi.org/10.1080/14649880600815974; Martha C. Nussbaum, *Women and Human Development: The Capabilities Approach* (Cambridge University Press, 2000).

39. Nick Couldry, *Why Voice Matters: Culture and Politics after Neoliberalism* (Sage, 2010).

Index

About the Author

Mary Angela Bock is an associate professor in the Moody College of Communication at the University of Texas at Austin. She is a former journalist turned academic with an interest in the sociology of photographic practice, the rhetorical relationship between words and images, and digital media. She is particularly concerned with matters of truth and authenticity in the process of image production and the relationship between media practices and social justice.

Her previous career was spent primarily in local television news, first as a TV reporter for KCCI-TV in Des Moines, Iowa, then as an assignment editor and field producer in Philadelphia's WPVI-TV. She has also worked short stints as a newspaper reporter, a radio journalist, and public relations writer.

Her work can be found in such publications as the *Journal of Communication*, *Visual Communication Quarterly*, and *Journalism and Mass Communication Quarterly*. Her latest book, *Seeing Justice: Witnessing, Crime, and Punishment* (2021), theorizes the relationship between media and the state in the production of visual representations of crime, the courts, and justice. *Seeing Justice* won the Diane S. Hope Book of the Year Award from the National Communication Association's Visual Communication Division. Bock also coauthored *Visual Communication Theory and Research* (2014) with Shahira Fahmy and Wayne Wanta. Her 2012 book *Video Journalism: Beyond the One-Man Band* examines the relationship between solo multimedia practice and news narratives.

Bock has two daughters who are proud feminists. She lives in Austin with her husband, David Schneider, and their two cats, who frequently claim to always be on the edge of starvation in spite of regular feedings.

www.ingramcontent.com/pod-product-compliance
Lightning Source LLC
Chambersburg PA
CBHW080550270326
41929CB00019B/3247